WALTHER VON LOEWENICH is the author of numerous books, including the classic *Luther's Theology of the Cross*. He is professor emeritus of church history at the University of Erlangen.

LAWRENCE W. DENEF is executive director for parish life of the Evangelical Lutheran Church in Canada.

Martin Luther
The Man and His Work

Martin Luther
The Man and His Work

**Walther
von
Loewenich**

Translated by Lawrence W. Denef

AUGSBURG Publishing House • Minneapolis

MARTIN LUTHER: THE MAN AND HIS WORK

First published 1982 by Paul List Verlag under the title *Martin Luther: Der Mann und das Werk*.

Copyright © 1982 Paul List Verlag, Munich. English translation copyright © 1986 Augsburg Publishing House, Minneapolis.

Scripture quotations unless otherwise noted are from the Revised Standard Version of the Bible, copyright 1946, 1952, and 1971 by the Division of Christian Education of the National Council of Churches.

Quotations from *Luther's Works*, American Edition, volumes 6, 13, 14, 25, 26, 27, 28, and 29, copyright © 1970, 1956, 1958, 1972, 1963, 1964, 1973, and 1968 Concordia Publishing House, are used by permission of Concordia Publishing House.

Quotations from *Luther's Works*, American Edition, volumes 31-55, copyright © 1957, 1958, 1972, 1960, 1960, 1959, 1961, 1971, 1970, 1958, 1966, 1969, 1968, 1966, 1962, 1967, 1971, 1963, 1972, 1975, 1959, 1974, 1965, 1967 Fortress Press, are used by permission of Fortress Press.

Quotations from *The Book of Concord*, copyright © 1959 Fortress Press, are used by permission of Fortress Press.

Library of Congress Cataloging-in-Publication Data

Loewenich, Walther von, 1903–
    MARTIN LUTHER: THE MAN AND HIS WORK.

    Translation of: Martin Luther: der Mann und das Werk.
    Bibliography: p.
    Includes index.
    1. Luther, Martin, 1483–1546. 2. Reformation—
Germany—Biography. I. Title.
BR325.L6213   1986   284.1'092'4 [B]   83-70513
ISBN 0-8066-2019-6

Manufactured in the U.S.A.   APH 10-4296

1   2   3   4   5   6   7   8   9   0   1   2   3   4   5   6   7   8   9

Contents

PART THREE: THE CONTINUATION OF
THE REFORMATION

Translator's Preface

With this volume, Walther von Loewenich brings a comprehensive, theological approach to the study of Luther's life and work. More than 1500 quotations from Luther's writings enable the reformer to speak for himself and come to life for us today.

Wherever possible, Luther quotations are cited from the American Edition of Luther's Works (AE), published by Concordia Publishing House and Fortress Press. Unless otherwise noted, I have furnished my own translation (from the author's German) of those passages not found in the American Edition.

LAWRENCE W. DENEF

Preface

The 1983 Luther anniversary reminds us of an endangered inheritance. Interest in Luther has largely dwindled. Even evangelical theologians display a painful lack of knowledge about Luther. This book was written with the conviction that it is rewarding to study Luther seriously. It is directed not only to theologians, but also to every inquiring mind. All of the Latin quotations have been translated. Complete documentation of primary sources was necessary and has been provided in the footnotes; these will prove helpful to those who wish to do further exploration. The more than 1500 quotations are from the Weimar Edition of Luther's works. Genuine understanding of Luther cannot be achieved without serious engagement. Those who approach Luther — the man and his work — will be captivated by his dynamism. Separation in time does not divide persons when their lives touch. Luther has a message for the church and the world today.

March 1982   WALTHER VON LOEWENICH

PATHS TO LUTHER

A Controversial Figure

Luther has always been a sign that is spoken against, a historical figure who remains controversial up to our own day. As such he shares a common destiny with many great figures. Yet there is a sense in which Luther also towers above their ranks. In his case the pros and cons involved have, as their particular focus, issues of ultimate concern. Behind them lies the question about the Christian understanding of truth, a question that confronts each generation anew and will always remain controversial. Previous conflicts subside; new ones arise. Even in an age characterized by historical relativism, religious indifference, and theological toleration, opinions concerning Luther—the man and his work—will vary.

It was with his early exegetical lectures on the Psalms, Romans, Galatians, and Hebrews that Luther, as a young professor, won his first followers. They sensed the opening of a new door; they recognized that theology was being carried on in a new way, and they joined him. In the "springtime of the Reformation," the years 1517 to 1521, Luther became the most popular figure of his time, a celebrated hero of the German nation. It was as such that he stood before the nation and the emperor at Worms. But the opposition had already sprung to life. The Dominicans defended their fellow friar, Tetzel, against the Augustinian monk, Luther. Albert of Mainz reported the situation to Rome and canonical proceedings were initiated. The hearing before Cajetan was, at best, unproductive. The disputation with Eck revealed irreconcilable differences.

After the publication of the papal bull threatening Luther with excommunication, he broke with Rome. Following Worms he lived
under the imperial ban. The ensuing polemic degenerated rapidly
into crude and offensive attacks and counterattacks. The *Corpus
Christianum* fell apart into opposing confessions.

Among the Lutheran theologians, Luther became a Father of the
church. It is as such that he appears in the last of the Lutheran
Confessions, the Formula of Concord of 1577, which is concerned
with the reunification of the Philippists—followers of Melanchthon—
and the Orthodox Lutherans, or so-called Gnesio-Lutherans. The
Orthodox Lutherans rejoiced in the restorer of "pure doctrine," and
interpreted Rev. 14:6, the passage about the angel with an eternal
gospel, as pointing to the reformer. According to the official Catholic position, on the other hand, Luther was an apostate who had
destroyed the unity of the church, the Antichrist, or at the very
least an ignorant or spiritually ill man. Only recently has a fundamental change occurred. The Catholic church historian Adolf
Herte has demonstrated that until the threshold of our times Catholic portrayals of Luther remained under the influence of the spiteful
characterization of his contemporary Johannes Cochläus, and that
the few exceptions to this that can be reported were almost always
placed on the index of forbidden books.[1]

The orthodox image of Luther came under fire during the Enlightenment, when Luther was seen as the champion of religious
freedom who released us from the yoke of ecclesiastical authority
and tradition. It was in this sense that Lessing carried on his dispute with head pastor Goeze of Hamburg.[2] For Lessing, Luther
was a "great, misunderstood man." Nor did the controversy about
Luther cease with the 19th century. Luther fell prey to the slogans
of hero worship and of German nationalism and became the very
personification of "the German." Of course there were numerous
adverse reactions, among them the French depiction of Luther.[3]
Luther was caught up in the warfare between nations, and so
finally it happened that a grotesque line was drawn from Luther
to Hitler. Several statements were made at the beginning of the
so-called Third Reich that were intended positively; they soon
proved to be a passing aberration. More worrisome were the accusations against Luther that these statements had provoked. It
was thought that one could detect certain Germanic traits in Luther

that found their final, distorted expression in Hitler. No one less than Karl Barth occasionally formulated his questions in this manner.[4] Others in and outside of Germany picked up this theme and used it as propaganda. We have to thank the English Luther scholar Gordon Rupp for setting the facts straight.[5] It is no wonder that in contemporary theological circles there are so many, often conflicting, interpretations of Luther. Nevertheless it is not Luther's significance that is being questioned; the problem is one of interpretation.

Today the controversy revolves around Luther's approach to public life. At the heart of the debate lies Luther's position regarding the Peasants' War. Here the accusations become monumental. Luther, it is said, failed completely to uphold the right of social revolution and became a puppet of the princes, an assertion usually supported by referring to a study of the Peasants' War by Frederick Engels published in 1850. An essay titled *Thomas Münzer als Theologe der Revolution* [6] by Ernst Bloch has also had a strong impact on many. Luther research within the German Democratic Republic is, with few exceptions, colored by a communistic view of history.[7] However, many theologians in the West—chiefly the younger ones—have also been influenced by Marxism. For them Luther was the great traitor to the cause of the people and Thomas Müntzer the true prophet of the Germans.

In its most blatant form, this evaluation appears in a play by Dieter Forte [8] titled *Martin Luther und Thomas Münzer oder Die Einführung der Buchhaltung* (Martin Luther and Thomas Müntzer: An Introduction to Accounting).[9] Money, it is said, was at the heart of the Reformation and was also Luther's primary interest. The vast capitalistic endeavors of a Jakob Fugger govern the course of history. Luther was in the employment of this capitalism and at the same time subservient to the princes. Thomas Müntzer is the only person in this play who is portrayed positively. The drama concludes with a blasphemous liturgy to "holy capital," followed immediately and intentionally by Luther's song of faith, "A Mighty Fortress."

Apparently Forte's play has enjoyed tremendous success, for which the vigorous promotion of the public media deserves much credit. Still, it has obviously addressed a prevalent spirit of the times. In many circles people are more than willing to pass judgment on Luther. While contemporary Catholic theology, at least in Germany, is making the most of Luther's heritage, evangelical theologians are exhibiting an astonishing reserve about the reformer. Of course this has had an effect on congregational life. Though Forte's play consists largely of direct quotations, it is still "manipulated history." [10] Despite the assurance of the author that "the texts are by and large original texts" and that "the figures and the facts are correct," the work is a completely controlled, propagandistic distortion of history. The observation that Luther could not have been a "democrat" in the modern sense may be true, but it also provides many West Germans with an all-too-easy excuse for not getting involved. Gustav Heinemann is a significant representative of this position.

The relationship of Thomas Mann to Christianity, to the Reformation, and to Luther has undergone numerous changes.[11] The good-natured lampooning of outmoded expressions in the meaning of the First Article of Luther's *Small Catechism* by old Buddenbrooks [a character in one of Thomas Mann's books] is well-known. However, Mann's remarks about Luther in a 1949 speech (usually cited in theological journalism as "The Stockholm Address") raised a great furor. This speech, titled "The Three Powers," is about Luther, Goethe, and Bismarck. In it we hear the following comments concerning Luther:

> The first of these men, Martin Luther, the reformer who demolished the confessional unity of the continent, appeared in the 16th century. He was a resolute man of destiny; an intense, rough-hewn, but deeply spiritual and intensely personal expression of German nature; an individual, at the same time boorish and tender, full of power and restlessness, characterized by the native drive of a common peasant; theologian and monk, but an impossible monk, practical yet sensual, revolutionary yet reactionary; a throwback to the Middle Ages, insensitive to the humanism of the Renaissance; in constant bouts with the devil, overwhelmed by superstitious beliefs in demons, spiritually beclouded yet remarkably open to life thanks to his love for wine, women, and song; a man who was an argumentative proclaimer of "evangelical freedom"; a quarrelsome man of great hatreds, ready from the depths of his heart to spill blood; a militant advocate of individualism, his immediate relationship with God and spiritual subjectivity pitted against the objective orders and regulations of the church, and at the same time an advocate of obedience before divinely ordained

authorities who encouraged them to stab, beat, and strangle rebellious peasants; a complete stranger to the humanism of his day,
even in its German form, yet all the more emotionally immersed
in German mysticism; an obstinate proponent of orthodoxy who left
the church only to establish a counterchurch with its own dogma, its
own priestly scholasticism, and its own forms of denunciation; not
merely anti-Roman, but anti-European; furiously nationalistic and
anti-Semitic; deeply musical, and as such the molder of the German language—his translation of the Bible, a literary accomplishment of the first order, spread among the people in thousands of
copies by the newly developed printing press, was the result of his
musical gifts as well as of his loving ear for the inner tones of
mysticism; it created the language of German literature and so
provided a literary unity for a land torn asunder by political and
religious strife. That which came after him and from him—the
dreadful bloodshed of religious conflicts, St. Bartholomew's Day
massacre, the Thirty Years War, the depopulation of Germany
and the regression of its culture by three times as many years—
all this the great, bullnecked, barbarian of God would willingly
have shouldered himself: "Here I stand, I can do nothing else." [12]

One certainly cannot blame the theological reviewers for being
disturbed by these remarks made by one of the leading figures of
German literature and European intellectual life. We will refrain
here from correcting his individual statements. Those who know
anything at all about Luther will immediately recognize that this
speech is filled with extreme exaggerations. In view of the authority
that Thomas Mann possessed in the cultured world, it is most regret-
table that the negative impressions amassed here about Luther were
circulated, and quite naturally well received, by those who prided
themselves on their modern spirit. Yet in this process the juxtaposition of ideas was easily overlooked. Throughout Mann's speech,
negative remarks were at least partially balanced by positive statements. One has the impression that Thomas Mann was so caught
up in his great power with words [13] that he said more than he
could assume full responsibility for. This fits the statement in a
letter addressed to the Herder community in Weimar dated
March 1950 [14] in which Mann defended himself against the accusation that he had slandered Luther. "It was a hastily sketched characterization. No irreverence was intended, either for the great man
or for the truth. If I felt no reverence for Luther I would have to
be as stupid as my critics, who know of nothing better than to

seek opportunities for indignation." The critics certainly did not deserve such a rebuke, and the words smack of self-justification. Nevertheless, they help us understand Thomas Mann the way he– at least belatedly–wished to be understood. In the remainder of his life Mann vacillated between admiration and aversion in his portrayal of Luther.

But is this really so astonishing? Even those who love and respect Luther are confronted by the puzzles he poses. He was a man of intense contrasts.[15] On the one hand he had an extremely sensitive disposition. We can recognize it in the moving words of his hymn, "From Heav'n Above to Earth I Come," in the charming letters to his son Hans from the Coburg Castle, or in the consoling message sent to his adversary Tetzel as he lay on his deathbed. But the same Luther could easily work himself into a rage and feel particulary productive in the process. In crudeness his virtuosity far surpassed that of his crude contemporaries, a characteristic that can actually be repugnant to us today. His use of toilet language can be extremely tiring.

Luther had a childlike disposition; he could rejoice in all things good and beautiful, in a single flower or in a blossoming cherry tree, yet he was a typical representative of his very "masculine" century. By nature he was timid, yet he stood as a champion before the emperor and the nation at Worms. He could be exceptionally charitable and understanding when dealing with questions in the realm of Christian freedom, as in his stance concerning images. On the other hand his ability to display dogmatic intolerance and lack of appreciation for other viewpoints is offensive to us. He could, for example, flatly state that a Zwingli or an Erasmus was not a Christian. He often advised that evil spirits be allowed to destroy each other, yet he still encouraged the authorities to expel his colleague Karlstadt from the territory.

Personally he was exceptionally modest and humble, refusing to let anyone use his "unholy name." He respected Melanchthon's unique gifts without envy, and considered him far superior to himself. Nevertheless, he had a strong sense of self-awareness based on the conviction that he had the Lord Jesus on his side—he alone, and not his opponents. Therefore he confidently and fearlessly called himself a prophet whom God had sent to Christendom.

Proud of his peasant heritage, the reformer was endowed with the sober realism of a man of the people. When matters in Witten-berg threatened to get out of hand, he recognized the precarious nature of the situation and bridled the overly zealous rush toward reform. The same thoughtful realism was evident in his assessment of the circumstances surrounding the Imperial Diet of Augsburg in 1530 and in the religious debates of the 40s. Yet one cannot overlook a certain naive idealism that characterized at least the young Luther. In the beginning he generally assumed that every-one thought and felt as he did, that they were just as troubled as he was by the question of the salvation of the soul, and that once they saw the light, they would—like him—joyfully accept the good news of the gospel. Only gradually did he come to realize that for many of his followers—though not all—the Reformation involved very earthly problems. This recognition increasingly led to bitter-ness, a bitterness that eventually erupted in his unjust condemna-tion of the "rabble" as asses that needed to be beaten. His opinion about a wise or upright prince as "a mighty rare bird" should be understood in the same way. At the outset he maintained that Jews could be pardoned for not becoming Christians, since they had never been offered the pure gospel. But later, when it became obvious that the Reformation had not moved them to change their views, Luther's initial anticipation turned to a rage that indicated the depth of his disappointment.

Luther was one of those few troubled Christians who loom large in the history of the church. Unlike most of the church's heroes, he was never free of doubts concerning the promises of God and the salvation of his soul. Throughout his life he wrestled with the devil, who wanted to rob him of God's grace. More than any of the others, he experienced the anguish of God's hiddenness. Yet it was the same Luther who asserted in his refutation to Erasmus that the Holy Spirit is not a skeptic; a Christian must state things confidently and put down any doubts that arise as inspirations of the devil.

Luther's candid opinions concerning individual books of the Bible are well-known. He considered James to be a "straw epistle"; Esther, he said, ought best be dropped from the canon; and he characterized the law of Moses as a Jewish *Sachsenspiegel* [a medieval law book written by the Saxon Eike von Repkow]. For Luther it was the spirit of Scripture and not the letter that counted.

Yet at the Marburg Colloquy he adamantly maintained the literal wording of the text, underscoring the "is" of the words of institution three times. If Christ were to order him to eat manure, he would do it. If the story of Jonah in the belly of the great fish were not recorded in the Bible, he would consider it a fairy tale. Spiritual freedom and literal conformity stood side by side in Luther.

We take pleasure in Luther's rich humor, and detect his hidden melancholy. As a pastoral counselor he could give his troubled brothers very practical advice: Eat, drink, joke, and flee loneliness! Yet he remained convinced that Christ was the sole consolation for the world. As the head of a household he appeared almost middle-class. He was one who longed for the judgment day, yet he was occupied day and night with the destiny of the church. With his work of reform he pointed to the future, yet at the same time he was deeply anchored in the past.

Indeed, Luther was not a book that could be read easily; he was a human being with his contradictions. It is no wonder that he is so controversial. To see Luther from only one perspective is to do him an injustice. The concern to achieve an objective judgment must not decrease, but those who only observe Luther from a cool distance will never be able to grasp the richness of his being. No matter how we approach him, many puzzles will remain. How could it be otherwise? Life cannot be captured in stereotypes. The person of Luther belongs to history, but whoever approaches him is touched by life.

2

On the Eve
of the Reformation

The word *reformation* originally meant the return to an earlier and better condition and norm. Since the publication of Leopold von Ranke's *Deutsche Geschichte im Zeitalter der Reformation* in 1839, the word has been adopted in its present sense. Ranke recognized the uniquely religious character of the Reformation, yet at the same time described its extensive influence on national and political affairs. In this connection we ought not lose sight of the fact that the Reformation is more than a German phenomenon; indeed it cannot be understood at all apart from the development of European history as a whole. The international policies of Charles V had a significant influence on the history of the Reformation.

The decisive factor for the origin of the Reformation, however, was and remains Luther's encounter with the gospel and his reforming activities. Despite its continuity, the progress of history cannot be understood without taking into account the irrational impact of creativity. Luther's Reformation was not only a product of the time, even though the time was ripe for it. A sense of urgency, a longing for something new—for change—pervaded every area of life during the decades preceding the Reformation.

The political situation at the conclusion of the medieval period was characterized by two factors: the formation of the nation-states of France, England, and Spain, with their centralization of power in the hands of the royalty, and the emergence of territorial states in Italy and Germany. The most significant political constellation came into being through the establishment of a link between Spain and the House of Hapsburg. By means of the marriage of Maximilian, the "last of the knights," to Mary of Burgundy, a daughter of Charles the Bold, in 1477, the Hapsburgs obtained that wealthy and culturally prominent kingdom; through the marriage of Maximilian's son Philip the Handsome to Joanna "the Mad" in 1496, the whole of Spain was acquired. Upon being elected German emperor in 1519, Charles V united this enormous inheritance under his rule. When one recognizes that these lands included the newly discovered territories of America, his motto *"Plus ultra"* (that is, the expansion of his possessions beyond the pillars of Hercules) becomes understandable; so does his proud boast that the sun never set on his empire.

It is little wonder that this emperor considered the Lutheran Reformation but a provincial matter; it did not fit into his universal political concept. His chief rival in Europe was Francis I of France (1515-1547); the main object of their contention was Italy. In addition there was the continuous threat of the Turks, who in 1529, under Suleiman (the Magnificent), advanced to Vienna and established themselves in Hungary. It is against the backdrop of this world political situation that the history of the Reformation must be seen. The papal states were one of many Italian territories, each engaged in its own political affairs. The papacy sought accord sometimes with France, at other times with Spain. Through its constant conflict with the Hapsburgs, the curia indirectly helped foster the Reformation.

The attempt to centralize authority within the German empire met with little success. The real life of the nation took place in the territories. It was within them that central government was organized, the line of succession guaranteed, and financial and legal matters established. Through the Reformation the territorial system was noticeably consolidated and became the political base for growing confessionalism. The new church order in the evangelical territories could attach itself to the regional church structure of the late Middle Ages. Through agreements called *concordats* the rights of territorial rulers to participate in the regulation of ecclesiastical matters was established. The underlying principle is expressed in the proverb: *"Dux Cliviae est papa in terris suis"*—"The prince of Cleve is pope in his own land." The churches were adequately provided for.

In the late Middle Ages the princes took particular pride in founding their own territorial universities. In rapid succession the universities of Greifswald (1456), Ingolstadt (1472), Tübingen (1477), Mainz (1477), Wittenberg (1502), and Frankfurt on the Oder (1506) were established. Visitations were carried out, the governing bodies were centralized, the church was included in the tax structures, and life within the monasteries underwent reform. Even the politics of indulgences was controlled by the princes, who wanted to keep their subjects' money within their own territories. For example, Frederick the Wise resisted the sale of indulgences in electoral Saxony by Tetzel for the benefit of the prince Albert of Mainz.

Processions and special services of thanksgiving and mourning were introduced. Similar efforts were undertaken in the affairs of the municipal churches. Here the princes fought against the economic privileges of the clergy and opposed the intrusion of bishops and monastic orders. Tasks previously carried out by the church, such as caring for the poor, were increasingly assumed by the municipalities themselves. Tendencies appeared that later became characteristic of the Reformation. At the same time cities and towns became the centers for the early beginnings of capitalism, most significantly represented by the Fuggers of Augsburg.

There was, however, no lack of fighting between the various levels of society; often the underprivileged sympathized with the peasants. The peasant class was generally scoffed at and oppressed, more through its lack of rights than through economic distress. Even before the Reformation, this had resulted in peasant uprisings. The lesser nobility also experienced troubled times. Knighthood, which had assumed an important role during the imperial campaigns of the high Middle Ages, lost its status. With their outmoded weapons, the knights were no longer a match for the newly developing artillery and were replaced by mercenary armies. Those knights who were unable to marry into the monied aristocracy of the municipalities or obtain court appointments sank to the level of robber barons.

On the eve of the Reformation, ecclesiastical and religious life presented a colorful panorama. The papacy, having successfully resisted conciliar attempts at reform, succumbed to complete secularism. In the bull *Execrabilis* of 1460 Pope Pius II condemned the appeal to a general council as heresy and an offense against authority. In the bull *Pastor aeternus* of 1516 Leo X labeled episcopacy as heresy. (As opposed to papism, *episcopacy* is the theory that the church rests on the community of bishops rather than on the office of pope.) That was one year before the posting of the 95 Theses.

As a patron of the arts and sciences the papacy of the 15th and early 16th centuries can, without a doubt, be credited with much. As a religious institution, however, it had reached its lowest ebb, comparable only to its condition in the 9th century.

Pope Sixtus IV (1471-1484) encouraged nepotism and was an accessory in the attempted assassination of Lorenzo de Medici. Innocent VIII (1484-1492) did not hesitate in granting his illegitimate children public recognition. The Borgia Pope Alexander VI (1492-1503), a notorious poisoner and an opponent of Savonarola, wanted to make the papal states into an inheritable principality for his descendants. Julius II (1503-1513) was a distinguished statesman and a valiant soldier, but also violent and subject to sensual excesses. Bramante, Michelangelo, and Raphael were engaged in his service. He authorized the beginning of construction on St. Peter's Basilica and founded the Vatican museum. Leo X (1513-1521), the son of the Medici Lorenzo the Magnificent, unabashedly embraced nepotism. He was a good-natured epicure and extravagant spender who was as interested in culture as he was in vulgar amusements or in the hunt. Raphael worked for him on the *Stanzas*.

Pope Leo X did not have the slightest insight into or sympathy for the Reformation. In political matters he had a lucky touch, and in 1517 he was able to conclude the Fifth Lateran Council. On the eve of the Reformation the papacy appeared to be secure. The only contemporary complaints we are aware of concerned the shameless management of funds by the curia, the keeping of mistresses, and the prostitution that was so prevalent in Rome. The following anecdote was commonly related: A Jew came to Rome and converted to Christianity. When asked why, he is said to have replied, "If Christianity can exist despite the conditions in Rome, then it must be of God."

Nevertheless the Reformation did not grow out of the criticism of Rome; rather, it emerged from what Luther recognized and experienced in his study of the Bible.[1]

The bishops came from the nobility and were secular rulers. Most often others represented them in spiritual matters. The innumerable endowments made for masses and sacred rites were managed by "Mass priests," who formed a sort of spiritual proletariat. The regular income of the bishops included franchise monies related to the widespread practice of clerical concubinage. The curates in the cities were the most learned; they became the chief bearers of the Reformation. The sermons of the beggar monks were indeed loved by the people; in general, however, monasticism was scorned and often became an object of ridicule. Numerous reforms attempted to correct the worst offenses in the monasteries. Andreas Proles (d. 1463) was active among the Augustinian Friars of Germany; he was followed by Johannes von Staupitz, the head of the order during Luther's time. In the Netherlands the Brethren of the Common Life came together in 1380 as a pious, monastic-like community. They concerned themselves primarily with teaching, and in Magdeburg Martin Luther was one of their students.

Despite many questionable manifestations of piety, the late Middle Ages were not simply a time of religious decline. Such a one-sided picture, painted by the critique of the Reformation and humanism, has been refuted by Catholic research. To the contrary, the period was intensively and extensively religious. In fact, it was precisely the religious fervor of the times that allowed the Reformation to capture the imagination of an entire nation. Throughout history the Catholic church has been a noteworthy educator of peoples; that was true also during the Middle Ages. The church had recognized the value of outward forms, stable orders, and pious practices. To be sure, the corresponding results were often quite shallow, but genuine spiritual life was hidden beneath the surface. The spirit of Christianity can be felt in all of the manifestations of medieval culture.

Shining at the heart of religious devotion was the celebration of the holy Mass. In this celebration Christ was present. Gathered around this center were the seven sacraments and a wealth of sacramental acts that met the needs of ordinary people. Veneration of saints and relics was just as popular. The inner unrest, characteristic of the medieval or late Gothic period, was shown by the rapid increase and growing diversity of religious practices. Worship services were conducted with great splendor. The fulfillment of obligations toward the saints and the dead gave rise to a vast number of religious rites: prayers to Mary and the saints, masses for departed souls, anniversary masses (that is, requiem masses said annually on the day of death), and extended wakes that required watchers to relieve one another at the bier for several days. Masses for the dead involving 20 to 30 priests were not unusual. Often they took place without listeners, as pious works in and of themselves. In the collegiate Church of All Saints in Wittenberg 8,881 masses were said by 64 priests in one year. In Cologne more than 1000 masses were said daily in 11 collegiate churches, 22 cloisters, 19 parish churches, and 100 chapels.

Within the rich realm of church music, counterpoint was developed to its greatest perfection. The singing of hymns in the language of the people flourished; even Luther conceded, "Under the papacy we sang marvelous hymns." Sermons were far more numerous than earlier in the Middle Ages; many were folksy and unpolished. Catechisms for the instruction of adults and children evolved from questions that were prepared for those who confessed their faith. Religious plays often went on for days; they were church-sponsored folk festivals, and at times they degenerated into burlesque.

Support for religious causes was organized and promoted by spiritual brotherhoods. In 1520 there were 21 of these brotherhoods in Wittenberg, about 80 in Cologne, and more than 100 in Hamburg. Members committed themselves to saying a certain number of prayers, which then entitled them to be included in masses, rosary meditations, and other religious acts. These brotherhoods were therefore a sort of religious insurance association, which explains why many lay persons joined several at the same time. The deeds of charity engaged in by these brotherhoods, though indirectly supported by religious egotism, are just as worthy of recognition as are the pious endowments of ecclesiastical art made possible by the increased emphasis on works righteousness. Begging thrived; by giving alms one acquired treasure in heaven.[2]

The popular nature of late medieval piety found particular expression in the growing veneration of saints. Without a doubt this was paganism; the old gods frequently lived on in the saints. On the other hand the saints were usually historical or legendary figures of some stature. The veneration of saints had two advantages: it was, so to speak, piety on a small scale, prepackaged for everyday religion, and it kept alive the memory of that great "cloud of witnesses," the communion with those already in heaven. Admittedly it was also infused with a strong strain of religious eudaemonism.

At the pinnacle of all the saints stood Mary the mother of God. To be sure, she was not entitled to worship but to "extraordinary veneration." Yet in reality she was adored as a goddess. Even Christ was eclipsed by her. The more he was portrayed as a stern judge, the more one sought the advocacy of "our beloved lady." Mary satisfied the human longing to adore that which is eternally feminine. Mary became all in all: the esteemed lady of knightly chivalry, the incarnation of everything that represented feminine dignity in the German mind: virgin, mother, queen. Legends arose around her person; through form and color, in music and in verse she was veiled in mystery. Since the 14th century the Ave Maria had risen to her whenever the faithful prayed the rosary. In cloisters and monasteries Saturdays were dedicated to her, even as Sundays had been dedicated to Christ. The festivals of Mary were strung out through the church year like pearls on a string. She had a motherly heart for every situation, from the fairest to the most painful. Under the protective shelter of her robe the faithful could feel secure.

The Franciscans, in distinction from the Dominicans, emphasized the *immaculata conceptio,* the "immaculate conception." Pope Sixtus IV recognized this teaching in 1476,[3] but in 1483 he forbade the prevalent denunciation of other positions.[4] It was not until December 8, 1854, that the teaching of the immaculate conception was finally given official status as church dogma by Pius IX.[5] In 1472 the Loreto legend arose, according to which, sometime between the years 1291 and 1295, angels had carried the "holy house" of Mary in two stages from Nazareth to Loreto, near Ancona. Loreto subsequently developed into one of the most beloved pilgrimage shrines in Europe and was regularly showered with gifts.

There were relatively few saints canonized during the early Middle Ages. In the Gothic period, however, saints became legion, despite the fact that the pope had reserved the right of canonization to himself.[6] The required proof of miracles was easily supplied, and the shrines at which the respective saints were venerated thrived. At times pilgrimages almost seemed to be like epidemics. One journeyed to Rome, to St. Jago di Compostella, to the Shrine of the Holy Blood in Wilsnack (near Havelsberg on the Elbe), to the Shrine of the Beautiful Mary in Regensburg, to Mary of Einsiedeln, to Altötting, and to the holy rock in Trier. There were national saints like Bernard of Siena, Joan of Arc, and John of Nepomuk in Prague.

The association of individual saints with different social classes and stations in life was typical of the late Middle Ages. Anthony protected swine, Gallus geese, Apollonia healed toothaches, Blase cured sore throats, Lawrence rheumatism, and Sebastian and Roch warded off pestilence. The miners called on St. Anne, who had become an especially helpful and popular saint after 1450, riders appealed to St. George, and pilgrims to St. James.

The veneration of relics was vigorously promoted. A copious supply of them had been provided by the Crusades. The seamless robe of Christ was displayed in Trier, the diapers of the Christ child in Aachen, the bodies of the three kings in Cologne. Rome was unsurpassed in this regard, with its catacombs and celebrated holy staircase. By revering the relics in the castle church of Wittenberg one could earn almost two million years of indulgence, and in Halle almost 40 million years. The Nuremberg patrician Nikolaus Muffel had the ambition of possessing a relic for each day of the year. He managed to obtain 308 objects before he was hanged; in his enthusiasm he had misappropriated municipal funds.

The world of the late Middle Ages was also governed by devils who haunted everything. It was rumored that the devil had once been seen even in the church; but his husky voice immediately gave him away. The devil could also engage in sexual intercourse with women; one called the devil's children "changelings" or *incubi* and *succubi*. Fear of witches was a terrible aberration of the time, despite the fact that it had originally been opposed by the church. After Thomas Aquinas there were those who sought to justify it theologically. In a bull of Dec. 3, 1484, Pope Innocent VIII affirmed the relationship between heresy and magic and admonished the Inquisition to eradicate the abomination of witchcraft in the "secular realm."[7] Heinrich Institoris and Jakob Sprenger, both Dominicans and professors of theology, were the authors of the notorious "Witch-Hammer," the *Malleus maleficarum*. And so the saints and the sacred rites of the church were needed more than ever.

The religious ferment of the period was also expressed outside the official life of the church. After the triumph of the papacy at the end of the 12th century, the church was accompanied by heresy as if by its own shadow. Despite every form of persecution, the Waldensians could not be stamped out. The territorial church of Bohemia existed in schism with Rome. It sought connections with the Waldensians, and in 1522 entered into relationship with Luther.

Dissatisfaction with the mismanagement of church affairs gave rise to apocalyptic expectations. The differences between the existing church and the true church were too glaring. The last day could no longer be far off. There were many reported appearances of the Antichrist or his forerunners. (The common people also spoke of *"der Endchrist"* [the end-time Christ]). Old Joachimite thoughts reappeared.[8] Dark prophecies of violent changes and floods frightened the people. The most gripping artistic expressions of this mood are the woodcuts depicting scenes from the book of Revelation by Albrecht Dürer. Hans Böhm, the "piper of Niklashausen," preached a return to nature while sitting "naked in a tavern." Others withdrew into solitude and sought their salvation in lay mysticism.[9]

Religious unrest was indeed a sign of the times, but was not sufficient to trigger the Reformation. Even the so-called forerunners of the Reformation—Peter Waldo, John Wycliffe, John Hus, and Girolamo Savonarola—who sit at Luther's feet as part of the famous Luther memorial at Worms, were unable to do more than criticize ecclesiastical mismanagement and strive for reform. In their thinking they remained prisoners of medieval Catholicism.

A few decades ago one could still hear that what the Reformation was to religion, the Renaissance was to the arts and humanism was to the sciences. This oversimplification hardly needs to be refuted today. The Renaissance, seen in its totality, was more a counterpole to the Reformation, and humanism was characterized by both its affirmation and opposition. But on the other hand one dare not overrate the differences, for there were points of convergence and even synthesis. Dürer, for example, was unquestionably influenced both by the Reformation and by the Renaissance. And Melanchthon was as much a humanist as he was a Christian reformer.

According to Jakob Burckhardt, it was during the Renaissance that a new discovery of human beings took place, primarily as a result of the growing sense of autonomy experienced throughout the Western world. Autonomy means self-determination. People do not find the law by which their lives are governed outside themselves, but within themselves. Medieval persons were bound to an external law; they obeyed authorities. They thought heteronomously, not autonomously. A truth was proven by appealing to the proper authorities. Individuals were obligated to follow the rules of the particular guild and class to which they belonged. Statues of the medieval period lean on pillars or are sheltered by altar niches; those of the Renaissance, like those of antiquity, stand freely in space and can be viewed from all sides.

Throughout the Middle Ages, heteronomy reigned supreme in the sciences, in the arts, in societal life, and in religion. With the coming of the Renaissance it was replaced by autonomy. Genius freed itself from the guild. Science became critical. In 1440 Lorenzo Valla exposed the *Donation of Constantine* as a forgery; he questioned the genuineness of *Dionysius the Areopagite;* indeed he even questioned the authenticity of the apostolic literature. "*Ad fontes*," (Back to the sources!) is the critical scientific principle of humanism. The art of the high Renaissance was no longer primarily in the service of piety, but of beauty, even when for all practical purposes it was still commissioned by the church. Art itself became a religion. Life was understood as a work of art. According to Niccolo Machiavelli (1469-1527), politics had but one goal: to strengthen the power of the state.

Consequently the ideal of autonomy exerted a strong, this-worldly influence; it also influenced morality. A superior understanding of the arts was apparently able to tolerate unbridled immorality. Jakob Burckhardt provided sufficient examples of this in his classic work on the art of the Italian Renaissance. Certainly this was not universal; there were also deeply religious artists such as Michelangelo, and in the Florentine Academy platonic metaphysics found a protective seedbed.

In what ways did the Reformation and the Renaissance parallel each other? The various historical relationships are too numerous to be described here. Basically we can say the following: the Reformation shared the Renaissance rejection of medieval heteronomy, at least in religious matters. Luther refused to acknowledge any earthly authority as unconditionally binding. His *Freedom of a Christian* signaled the end of medieval heteronomy. Yet this freedom differed completely from the autonomy of the Renaissance or from modern autonomy. It remained bound to God and to the Word of God in Holy Scripture. This God was not the god of one's own sentiment, but the Lord. The Reformation affirmed *theonomy* rather than autonomy. God was the law of life. This may sound like heteronomy. However, it would be heteronomous only if God were understood simply as a reality over against human beings, and if obedience to God were bound to earthly authorities. Yet God addressed us through our consciences; no earthly authority was able to intervene between God and the conscience. Luther's biblical faith was not submission to an outer authority; rather, it was the experience and inner conquest of one's heart and conscience. Therefore the Reformation took a spiritual stance that put it "between the times." [10]

These general insights provide, as we have already said, only a basic understanding, for which the high Renaissance serves as a useful historical model. When we look at specific detail the situation is much less clear. One can still find many heteronomous elements in the Reformation; on the other hand, one can also detect trends that point toward modern autonomy and secularization. Conversely it is also true (and why should it not be?) that the Renaissance knew of a right relationship to God. The same was true for German humanism.

In the aftermath of the fall of Constantinople in 1453, many Greek scholars fled to Italy. The most valuable treasure they brought with them was their language. Many eagerly endeavored to acquire it. Marsilio Ficino (1433-1499) translated Plato from the original and gave lectures on Paul. Pico della Mirandola (1463-1494) also recognized a relationship between Paul and Plato. In Padua, Aristotelianism was preserved and promulgated. In France, Jakob Faber Stapulensis (1455-1536) was the most significant humanist. He employed various sources to develop a Christian humanism, and his biblical commentaries made a lasting impression

on Luther. In England, as well, humanism exhibited strong religious features. John Colet delivered lectures on the Pauline letters. Thomas More (1478-1535) was fascinated by Plato and Paul.
John Fisher in Cambridge (1459-1535) affirmed a stoic understanding of the *lex Christi* (law of Christ). In Spain the University of
Alcalá (Complutum) became the center of humanism. It was there
in 1517 that the important Polyglot Bible originated. German humanism was greatly fertilized by the visit of Italian humanists
during the councils of the 15th century. We need but note the
delightful little novel *Plautus im Nonnenkloster* by Conrad Ferdinand Meyer! Enea Sylvio Piccolomini, who later became Pope
Pius II (1458-1464), spent 23 years in Germany. Academically the
contribution of humanists such as Willibald Pirckheimer (1470-
1532) in Nuremberg and Konrad Peutinger (1465-1547) in Augsburg was more significant than that of wandering poets and rhetori-
cians like Konrad Celtes (1459-1508). The development of educational theory was undertaken by Rudolf Agricola (1442-1485). The
schools in Deventer and Schlettstadt became famous. Basel emerged
as a center of humanism and of printing. Humanism was already a
public force in Germany when the two preeminent stars appeared:
Reuchlin and Erasmus.

Johannes Reuchlin (1455-1522), the great-uncle of Melanchthon
who assumed the Greek name Capnio, came from Pforzheim. He
was the first Greek scholar in Germany and the first Hebrew
scholar of the Renaissance. Among his chief works was a Hebrew
grammar. His interests also included numerology and neopytha-
gorean philosophy. He drew much public attention through his
conflict with the baptized Jew Pfefferkorn, who in 1509 had obtained an imperial mandate for the confiscation of Jewish literature.
Reuchlin opposed him. The Cologne faculty then instituted legal
proceedings against Reuchlin and so provoked the mockery of the
Letters of Obscure Men (1514 and 1517), grotesque satires on the
questionable ethics and lack of education in university circles.
Hutten also participated in the writing of these letters. Reuchlin
was initially declared innocent in 1514, but in 1520 was condemned
to silence in the wake of heightened tension between the Lutherans
and Rome. Nonetheless, public opinion remained on his side. Reuchlin did not join the Reformation.

The most significant of the humanists was Desiderius Erasmus of

Rotterdam (1469-1536).[11] He attended schools in Deventer and Herzogenbusch, where the *Devotio moderna* was practiced—the same new, simple piety favored by the Brethren of the Common Life. Pressured by his guardian (Erasmus was the illegitimate son of a priest), he entered the cloister Steyn near Gouda in 1488, where he was extremely unhappy. After managing to get out in 1492, he became secretary to the bishop of Cambrai. During a period of study in Paris he engaged in a critical analysis of scholasticism. Called to England by John Colet, he immersed himself in Cicero, Socrates, and Paul.

With the *Enchiridion militis christiani* (Handbook of the Militant Christian) of 1502, Erasmus became famous. In this booklet he advocated a stoically Christian form of lay spirituality and encouraged serious Bible study. The book received considerable attention during the Reformation. In 1505 he issued the *Annotationes* of Lorenzo Valla (a commentary on the New Testament) and called for a return to the original texts. The most significant service that Erasmus provided the Reformation was the publication in 1516 of a Greek New Testament that included variant readings from the Vulgate along with annotated footnotes. In the introduction, *"Methodus perveniendi ad veram theologiam,"* he described the method one must use in order to achieve a true theology through a study of the Bible.

Luther used the Greek New Testament of Erasmus soon after it appeared for his lectures on Romans, and again at the Wartburg as the basis for his German translation of the Bible. The religious sincerity of Erasmus cannot be denied. He wanted a reform of the church that would abolish outward ceremonies and return to the simple Christianity which, in his opinion, Jesus had taught. But he did not have what it required to become a reformer. He was not a prophet, but rather a scholar who had the weaknesses of a scholar. Filled with a strong sense of vanity, his intellect outstripped his character. He did not have the religious depth of Luther. Yet through his philological works he provided effective tools for the Reformation, although he increasingly distanced himself from it. Because of his criticism of external religious forms he appeared to be an ally of the Reformation, yet he himself neither could nor would seek a radical change of the Catholic system. Both Zwingli and Melanchthon received their initial inspiration from

Erasmus and were, to that extent, his students. This shows that despite all the obvious differences, there was still an inner connection between humanism and the Reformation. Both recognized a unity expressed not only in their mutual criticism of church conditions, but above all in the slogan, "Back to the sources!" and the related appreciation of the ancient languages. The Reformation also played a role in strengthening the self-esteem of the growing middle class.

This brief and necessarily sketchy description of the decades just preceding the Reformation will have to be sufficient to provide some insight into the new impulses for change that were surfacing everywhere. For the Reformation itself, however, we are indebted to the efforts of the man whom we call—for very good reasons—"the reformer."[12]

The Development
of the Reformer

Childhood and Youth

Martin Luther came from German peasant stock. [1] Despite the contempt under which peasants in those days suffered, he readily declared: "I am a peasant's son. My father, my grandfather, and my great grandfather were all true peasants." [2] His ancestors, he informs us, came from the countryside around Möhra, one hour north of Salzungen, the ancient border area between Thuringia and Franconia. As Luther rode from Eisenach to Rennsteig in May 1521, he was struck by the spread of the name Luther throughout the region.[3] When in 1540 Luther maintained that he was not a Thuringian but a Saxon, this was most likely nothing more than a momentary expression of irritation.[4] The family line cannot be traced back any farther than to his grandparents.

To conclude from portraits of the times that Luther was of Slavic extraction is sheer conjecture. The Weimar altarpiece that has led to this assumption was not painted until nine years after Luther's death, by Lucas Cranach the Younger. The authenticity of the death mask in the Marienbibliothek in Halle is questionable.[5] The Luther portraits by Cranach the Elder leave one with the impression that they were not able to capture the genius of the reformer. It would be better to refrain from drawing wide-ranging conclusions from them. The name Luther is most likely derived from the Old High German name *Lothar*. Nothing is known of any Slavic settlements in the region of Möhra. Whatever the case, this question does not deserve the attention it was once accorded in previous Luther controversies (or by Thomas Mann in *The Magic Mountain*). Luther bore the imprint of the German character. His famous remark (written in Latin!), "I am born for my Germans, whom I want to serve," [6] is quoted frequently for good reason.

Martin Luther was born in Eisleben shortly before midnight on November 10, 1483, as the oldest (perhaps also the second) son of his parents. The house in which he was born stood on the Langen Gasse, known today as *Lutherstrasse*. It was largely destroyed by fire in 1689. It is uncertain whether 1483 was actually the year of Luther's birth.[7] At any rate Luther disagreed with Melanchthon about it, who claimed that Luther's mother had spoken to him of a later year. The day, however, is definite, for on the morning following his birth Luther was baptized and given the first name of the saint of that day, St. Martin of Tours.

Luther's childhood proceeded much more normally than the Luther legends already circulating during his lifetime would have us believe. Otto Scheel was able to refute most of the stories in his thoroughgoing study. Luther's father, Hans Luther, came from Möhra. *His* father, Heine Luder (as he wrote the name), ran a farm. Since it was the custom of the time that the youngest son inherited the land, Hans Luther had to seek another occupation; he became a miner in the nearby earldom of Mansfeld. He moved first to the town of Eisleben, and in the spring of 1484 to Mansfeld, which lay in the heart of the mining district. At first he did not have an easy time of it, particularly since he eventually had four sons and four daughters to support. All the same, in 1491 he was able to lease a small smelting furnace, and by 1508 or 1509 he was part owner of eight mine shafts and three foundries. Therefore, while he never became a wealthy man, he nevertheless attained easier and more comfortable circumstances.

Luther's mother Margarethe was formerly thought to have been born a Ziegler; more recent research, however, holds that her maiden name was Lindemann, and that *her* mother was born a Ziegler. [8] Presumably she came from middle-class Frankish stock. The polemicists of the 16th century, of course, were better informed about Luther's parents. Some claimed Martin was a changeling and his mother was a whore and bathmaid. [9] Others wanted to make him a Hussite: born in Bohemia, educated in Prague, and instructed in the writings of Wycliffe.[10]

That Luther's parents were terribly poor is one of the exaggerations of the Luther legends. It finds its source in one of Luther's
later comments: "In his youth my father was a poor miner. My
mother carried all her wood home on her back. It was in this way
that they brought us up, enduring hardships the world today
would no longer put up with." [11] Early in his career (1491)
Hans Luther was elected to be one of the "Four Men," four
leading citizens whose task it was to represent the interests of the
community before the town council. Such a position implies a
certain sense of rapport with his fellow citizens as well as relative
economic independence. In addition, the fact that Luther's mother
—as a thrifty and hardworking housekeeper—carried her own fire-
wood from the forest is not a sign of poverty. In his reflection on
those early days Luther was simply expressing his respect for his
parents and at the same time pointing out that in the past people
were more efficient and unassuming. We know that in Eisenach
Luther sang from door to door with the boys' choir, playing the
role of alms collector; perhaps he had already done so in Mansfeld. [12] But it was not unusual for the sons of wealthy families, or
even of patricians, to sing in these choirs. It was considered whole-
some for young people to experience what it meant to have to beg
for daily bread. At any rate, thrift was insisted on in the Luther
household. Luther's parental home was certainly not "cultured";
he grew up in middle-class circumstances, among people who still
clung to the habits and customs of their peasant heritage.

Luther was brought up strictly, in accordance with the times.
Later he was fond of comparing the harshness of medieval education with the sternness of the law before it knew anything of the
gospel. "One shouldn't whip children too hard. My father once
whipped me so severely that I ran away from him, and he was
worried that he might not win me back again." [13] Among other
things this comment tells us that Luther's father was not a raving
tyrant. The same can be said of his mother. "My parents kept me
under very strict discipline, even to the point of making me timid.
For the sake of a mere nut my mother beat me until the blood
flowed. By such strict discipline they finally forced me into the
monastery [?]; though they meant it heartily well, I was only made
timid by it. They weren't able to properly distinguish temperaments and punishments. One must punish in such a way that

the rod is accompanied by the apple. It's a bad thing if children and pupils lose their spirit on account of their parents and teachers." [14]

Despite the harshness of his upbringing, Luther was grateful toward his parents. "If I could enter my father's house again," he said in 1532, "I would see things quite differently than I did then. The best thing I received of all my father's possessions was that he educated me." [15] In the foreword to a book by Urbanus Rhegius, Luther told of a little song his mother used to sing:

> If people don't like you and me,
> The fault's with us, it's plain to see.[16]

The circumstances in which his mother sang this song are not known. It need not be seen as a sign of rejection or bitterness; the words also convey a sense of thoughtful humor. Melanchthon and Spalatin spoke highly of her.

What about the assertion that Luther's father was a drunkard? In this connection a comment from a 1540 table talk is usually quoted. In it Luther accused his sister's son Hans Polner of being a drunkard and reprimanded him for supplying Luther's opponents with something to gossip about by his violent anger. His father, he said, was different. He enjoyed a good drink but remained pleasant and gentle; he joked, laughed, and sang.[17] Men such as Luther's father occasionally enjoyed a generous amount of wine. But one cannot conclude from this that they were excessive drinkers. Hans Luther enjoyed wine as a good gift of God; nothing more is implied. If he had been a drunkard he would never have been able to accomplish what he did for his family, nor attain the respect of the community. Incidentally, the accusation of drunkenness has also been leveled against the reformer himself in the light of some of his remarks about drinking; but the sheer quantity of his accomplishments is enough to unmask it as a mere insinuation.

In 1958 Erik H. Erikson, one of America's most distinguished psychoanalysts, wrote a book in which he analyzed Luther's relationship to his parents. [18] He attempted to trace the theological and religious development of young Luther back to conflict with his father and the breakdown of his mother.[19] Erikson assumed that the sensitive youngster was brought up too strictly by his parents, who failed to recognize his true "genius" and so were unable to apply appropriate corrective measures.

It may be true that Martin was easily intimidated by adults and always expected the worst from them. One could quote his remarks concerning an event from his childhood suggesting that we tremble and flee even from Christ who wishes only to give us every good. "This also happened to me as a boy in my homeland when we sang in order to gather sausages. A townsman jokingly cried out, 'What are you boys up to? May this or that evil overtake you!' At the same time he ran toward us with two sausages. With my companion I took to my feet and ran away from the man who was offering his gift. This is precisely what happens to us in our relation to God." [20]

Apart from these somber recollections of childhood, Luther also expressed thoughts of gratitude. His father took great pains to win him back. Both parents were "good at heart." Certainly it was not the harsh discipline of his parents that drove Luther into the monastery. Nor can we be certain that it was the "identity crisis" of youth, when for the first time he discovered and asserted himself, which led Luther to enter the monastery, or whether his decision to become a monk was merely accompanied by this crisis. The sources provide no basis for making such an assumption. Luther's father was strict, but he concerned himself with the development of his son, not merely out of personal ambition, but also out of paternal concern; and he was willing to sacrifice to make this possible. [21]

That Luther's relationship to his mother was characterized by an Oedipus complex cannot be substantiated. Luther's mother once complained that she would be in perfect health if she had never had a child. [22] But one can hardly conclude from this remark that her husband was unwilling to curb his sexual appetite. In those days many women would have complained about the abundance of children and the work associated with them. Moreover, it is impossible to demonstrate that this assumed condition generated feelings of hatred toward his father within young Martin. The attempt to derive Luther's image of God from the alleged image he is said to have had of his father goes too far. Luther's crisis as a young man was in essence a religious crisis. Luther's reaction to the news of his father's death while he was at the Coburg shows how deeply he respected and loved his father. His letters of June 5, 1530, to Wenceslas Link [23] and to Melanchthon [24] are moving expressions of his devotion. Even if we take into account that one sees things differently in retrospect, it is still remarkable that Luther spoke of the "sweet companionship" of his father. His letter to his dying mother written on May 20, 1531, is filled with the tender love of a son and the faithful concern of a pastor. [25]

Martin may have suffered occasionally under the severity of his upbringing. Individual instances obviously made a particular impression; but this apparently did not seriously affect his love of and trust in his parents. "My father was angry with me for an hour, but what harm is there in that? He also had some 10 years of trouble and work with me." [26] Does this sound like a father complex from which the religious development of young Luther can supposedly be explained? Did God appear to him in the monastery as an angry father because he had incurred the wrath of his earthly father by deciding to become a monk? Erikson began his book with the sentence, "The literature on Luther, and by Luther, is stupendous in volume. Yet it gives us few statements about his childhood and youth." Every psychological interpretation of Luther's early days, no matter how notable, suffers under this difficulty.

The piety of the Luther home appears to have been little different from the usual. Hans Luther was not an enlightened critic of the church. In the year 1497 he, together with other citizens, tried to obtain an episcopal indulgence for the parish church of St. George. Clerics were welcomed into his home. It was primarily for personal reasons that he opposed Luther's entrance into the monastery; he had greater things in mind for his son. This explains why he invoked the Fourth Commandment. [27] When Luther added that his father looked down on monks, his comment must be taken with a grain of salt. Most people, even the most faithful lay members of the church, had very little respect for monks.

Luther's father does not appear to have been overly religious. During a serious illness, when he was pressed by clergy to make a special contribution to the church, he refused, saying, "I have many children and I want to leave it to them; they need it more." [28] He did, however, have his thoughts about life. Once he told Martin that he believed there were many more people in the world than sheaves of grain in the fields.[29] And on one occasion, when he lay near death, he rejected any mention of his good works, confessing that he would rely solely on the merits of Christ.[30] Luther took this to be evidence that even under the papacy people knew about the forgiveness of sins. This attitude appears repeatedly in the late medieval death registries and has nothing to do with any critique of pre-Reformation religious practices. On his deathbed Luther's father was asked by the pastor what he believed. He responded by confessing the faith of his son.[31]

Luther's home was not free of the superstitions of the time. Luther's father was once called to the deathbed of a Mansfeld miner who showed him his back and said, "That's how the devil beat me in the shaft." Luther tells us that this event so disturbed his father that he almost died.[32] According to a remark made by Luther in 1539, the devil was especially active in mines. There, far more vividly than above ground, he deceived and vexed miners to such an extent that they imagined they saw silver where there was none.[33] The reformer still believed in changelings and monsters. His mother thought that one of their neighbors was a witch who cursed children so that they cried to death. When a preacher grabbed her, even he was poisoned and died. The witch had cursed soil from his footprints and thrown it into water; without that soil he could not be cured.[34] In his larger commentary on Galatians Luther reported that one of his brothers was poisoned in his knee by the devil and died as a result.[35] Water was considered a favorite habitat of the devil. Luther never doubted that his illnesses were attacks of the devil: "I believe that my illnesses aren't natural but are pure sorcery."[36]

All his life Luther clung to the intense belief in devils and demons that had been instilled in him as a child; in this regard he remained a medieval man.[37] But the believing person was never completely at the mercy of this world full of devils and evil spirits. The church provided an entire arsenal of defenses. Chief among them were the saints, and St. Anne was the most important saint for miners. On days on which one had seen the image of St. Christopher, one was protected from an evil death. There were 14 auxiliary saints who were ready to help in particular distresses or dangers. The sacraments provided a solid wall of defense against the wiles of the devil. Relics, holy candles, consecrated herbs, and many other helps could also be counted on. The reformer was never emancipated from the onslaughts of the devil; but he replaced the ritual means of protection provided by the church with Christ, the righteous man who fought on his behalf.

Luther did not gladly recall his school days in Mansfeld. Education basically consisted of beatings and thrashings. He referred to the school as a prison and a hell.[38] "Today, schools are not what they once were, a hell and purgatory in which we were tormented with *casualibus* and *temporalibus,* and yet learned less than nothing despite all the flogging, trembling, anguish, and misery." [39] "Some teachers are as cruel as hangmen. I was once beaten fifteen times before noon, without any fault of mine, because I was expected to decline and conjugate although I had not yet been taught this." [40] But the school at Mansfeld does not really appear to have been all that bad. The students learned Latin — not humanistic Latin, but medieval Latin—as well as church hymns. During class sessions it was forbidden to speak German. Violations of this rule were recorded by a fellow student, and at the end of the week students were punished for them with blows.[41] In his letter of 1524 encouraging town council members to establish schools, Luther gave medieval schools high praise: "When I was a lad they had this maxim in school: 'It is just as bad to neglect a pupil as to despoil a virgin.' " [42] The most significant parts of the catechism were also memorized.

Shortly before Easter of 1497, Luther's father decided to send his son, along with a friend, to the city of Magdeburg. There the Brethren of the Common Life taught at a school that was widely known. We have no evidence that Martin was particularly impressed by this school. However, he was deeply impressed by Prince Wilhelm of Anholt, who walked through the streets as a Franciscan friar, carrying his beggar's sack. The poor man had so castigated himself that he resembled death itself. "Those who saw him just shook their heads at his devotion and felt ashamed of their own standing." [43] At Eastertime in 1498 Martin was brought back to Mansfeld; we do not know why. In any case, his father remembered that he had a number of relatives in Eisenach. He sent his son to stay with the sexton or sacristan of St. Nicholas, Konrad Hutter, who was so poor, however, that he was unable to offer the boy lodging. As a result Martin had to live in the parish school, which was not uncommon in those times. Quite naturally he also had to participate in the boys' choir that made the rounds and collected alms. While doing this, a "matron" of the church is said to have taken notice of his voice. But even Johannes Mathesius, the earliest of the Luther biographers, was unable to tell us the name of this "matron." More than likely she was the wife of Heinrich Schalbe, whose son Martin was required to look after.[44] He earned his meals by doing this. Nevertheless, Luther's doctor, Matthäus Ratzeberger, maintained that he found "lodging and food" at the home of Kunz Cotta, whose wife Ursula was born a Schalbe. Perhaps we can assume that Martin lived with the Cottas and took his meals at the Schalbes.

For the first time, Martin entered a lively religious circle and a cultured milieu. The Schalbes were known as the most devout family in Eisenach. They had made sizable contributions to the small Franciscan monastery at the foot of the Wartburg. In that cloister lived Johann Braun, the priest and fatherly friend of Luther.

Later Luther invited Braun to the celebration of his first Mass, and on that occasion he referred to the "Schalbe Foundation" to which he owed so much. He had not dared to invite the other prominent men themselves, but asked Braun to assure them of his gratitude.[45] Undoubtedly the Eisenach community had some influence on Luther's decision to enter the monastery. Johann Braun and the Schalbe and Cotta families were also fond of music and fostered its expression. The young Luther received this stimulation with great eagerness. Contempt for worldly affairs was alien to this setting. Luther learned to know a more congenial family life, and it obviously made an impression. "My landlady during the time I attended school in Eisenach [Ursula Cotta] was right when she told me as I went to school, 'There is nothing sweeter on earth than the love of a woman, when it is shared.'"[46] The context reveals that she was referring to marital love between husband and wife. The years in Eisenach were the happiest years of Luther's youth. Much later, in 1530, he still called Eisenach his "beloved city."[47] It was there that the timid boy became a cheerful young man.

4

Erfurt

Luther attended school in Eisenach for three years. During that time he reached the age of 18. And then what awaited him? His father had great plans. As a lawyer his son would achieve honor and wealth. His father gladly sacrificed in order to see this happen. It was not easy; he still had seven other children to care for. Nevertheless he had in the meantime accumulated sufficient assets to provide an education for his son.

Two universities presented themselves as possibilities—Leipzig, which was closer, and Erfurt, which was more progressive. Father Luther preferred the latter; he did not want to economize in the wrong place.

At that time Erfurt ranked among the three or four largest cities in Germany. It lay at a major crossroads and its economy was booming. Erfurt had tried unsuccessfully to become a free imperial city. Ecclesiastically it was part of the archbishopric of Mainz. Politically it was subject to the umbrella rule of the Wettiners, to whom it pledged military allegiance. As a result the city was drawn into the rivalries between these two territorial rulers.

The majestic Erfurt cathedral was located near the equally impressive *Severistift*. The new cathedral organ, installed in 1483, was one of the most famous in Germany and could compete with the organ of St. Peter's in Rome. No less than 12 monastic orders defined the life of the church. Relics were in abundance. It is little wonder that Erfurt proudly called itself "little Rome."

Students in the late Middle Ages knew nothing of what later became famous as "academic freedom." When Luther was enrolled at the end of April 1501, he had already arranged for a room in Georg's student house next to Lemann's Bridge (a place with a good reputation, in spite of the fact that students had nicknamed it "the Beer Pocket"). Life in the house was regulated almost monastically. Rules were strict. One had to be up at 4:00 A.M. and in bed by 8:00 P.M. The clothing consisted of a sort of uniform, and the food was prescribed.

Students were not allowed to study what they wished, but rather had to complete a detailed syllabus, at the end of which was the master's examination. Anything except the required lectures could be attended only with special permission; but there was little time left over anyway. The reading program was strictly supervised.

Naturally certain devotional periods were also prescribed. The life of the residents was subjected completely to the supervision of the rector and the master of the house. Students in those days did not feel they were under unbearable constraints; they had never lived in any other way. Apparently, serious offenses seldom occurred. Contact with questionable women was strictly forbidden, even outside the house.

Nevertheless, gayety had its rightful place. Luther was accepted by his fellow students as a sociable and lively companion. Many student customs were rather crude. After entering the university each student was subjected to "deposition," a form of initiation in which the *"Beane"* was dressed in a degrading costume and decorated with horns and long asses' ears. These in turn were torn off during insulting ceremonies that culminated in a sort of "baptism" by dousing with water or wine. While this custom seems strange to us, Luther was not offended by it. In fact, later he also participated in the ritual, for he believed the "dethronement" taught one to be humble. The student ceremony was a symbol of life: "You'll be subjected to hazing all your life." [1]

At that time, before one decided to study theology, law, or medicine, one was required to be in the faculty of arts.[2] The faculty of arts cannot be equated with the later faculty of philosophy. It provided rather a form of preparatory studies from which each student was required to graduate before entering a specific field. It was called the faculty of arts because one had to study the "liberal" or "free" arts. They consisted of the *Trivium* (grammar, dialectic, and rhetoric) and the *Quadrivium* (arithmetic, astronomy, geometry, and music). This pattern dates back to late antiquity.

Dialectic, that is, logic, formed the core of the *Trivium;* the *Quadrivium* concentrated on mathematics. The study of music did not concern itself with the practical matters of performance, but with a numerical theory of intervals, rhythms, and meters. Normally one studied in the faculty of arts for four years.

Luther studied diligently and completed his final examination on time. He had already finished the *Trivium* and the baccalaureate exam by the fall of 1502. From there he busied himself with the natural, metaphysical, and ethical writings of Aristotle and studied the subjects of the *Quadrivium*.

On January 7, 1505—the earliest date possible—he completed his master's examination in second position among 17 graduates. Later the reformer fondly recalled the academic celebration. "What magnificence there was at the graduation of the masters, with the torches that were carried before them! I don't believe any earthly celebration could equal it. Great splendor was also displayed at the doctoral graduation; one rode all around the city on horseback. That is all gone now. I wish it were still so celebrated today." [3] Luther's father gratefully acknowledged the fact that his son was a diligent student, and, once he had earned his master's, his father no longer addressed him with the familiar *du*, but rather with the respectful *Ihr*.

Later in life Luther judged the worth of his student years very harshly. Yet he did acknowledge one thing: at the university he had learned method and logic. These served him well in the regular disputations that he regarded highly throughout his life. In his student days his circle of friends considered him to be a musician and a well-informed philosopher. [4]

The faculty of arts in Erfurt professed the *Via Moderna*, the philosophy of Occam (1285-1349). Luther held firmly to this philosophy: "I belong to the Occamist party," he declared in 1520, at a time when he had long since given up Occamist theology. [5] In 1532 Luther still called Occam his teacher and identified him as "the greatest dialectician." [6] He also held his own teachers in high regard, above all Jakob Truttvetter of Eisenach and Bartholomäus

Arnoldi of Usingen. His later critique of Occamism was not related to its methodology, logic, or interpretation of Aristotle, but rather its theological content.

The reformer also remained firm with regard to Occam's theory of knowledge, at least so long as he was really interested in such questions. All knowledge is the result of sensory perception. An individual thing is perceived (the *res singularis*). Universal ideas or concepts, the knowledge of which was so important to the platonists, function only as *termini,* as concepts in the judgment (if they even have reality in the mind). Therefore logical judgment presupposes sensory perception. This eliminates the intuitive foundation necessary for attaining knowledge of God. Taken in its strictest sense, this also excludes abstract knowledge of God.

Not all the nominalists, however, drew this radical conclusion (e.g., Gabriel Biel). Within fixed limits, a rational foundation was still secured for theology. But for the most part, statements about God became logically incomprehensible. As rationality and reason became less significant, all the more weight was placed on authority. The authority was Holy Scripture, as interpreted by the church and by dogma.

In his later theology Luther did not waver from Occamistic principles. For him the question of reason and faith had been channeled in a particular direction. Of course he held only the Holy Scriptures to be authoritative, not the teachings of the church. Yet the opposition between natural reason and the authority of God's Word remained. For the Thomists there was no conflict between reason and faith; faith simply completed that which reason lacked. The Occamist Luther pitted faith against reason, insofar as reason was not enlightened by God's Spirit.

However, one certainly receives the impression that Luther did not proceed primarily on the basis of epistemological considerations. His mistrust of *ratio in divinis,* of the ability of reason in divine matters, arose much more out of *maiestas materiae,* the religious impression of God's incomprehensibility. *Maiestas materiae* leaps the boundaries of rational thought. The theology of the cross is an *offense* to reason, not merely epistemological skepticism.

Occamism provided only a secondary function in Luther's development. One might ask whether Luther would have become a reformer if he had gone through a Thomist school in his youth.

Even then he would probably have experienced the inner turmoil that finally found its release in the discovery of the gospel. Throughout his time as an Augustinian monk in the monastery, Luther experienced not only Occamistic influences, but also learned to know the Augustinian tradition of his order. We do not know whether he also read the *Summa* of Thomas at that time. *The Table Talk* gives us no information concerning this. His encounter with Cajetan, the most famous Thomist of the time, was in any case fruitless, and the wide-ranging Thomistic arguments of Erasmus for the freedom of the will made no impression on Luther. Even if, as a student of theology, Luther had himself become acquainted with the Thomistic tradition, he would have learned an Occamistic interpretation.

Today there is a remarkable tendency in Catholic theology possibly to narrow the differences between Luther and Thomas on the doctrine of grace.[7] The neo-Thomism of the 19th century had very different thoughts on this subject. The only place where a reading of the *Summa* of Thomas is evident is in Luther's lectures on Isaiah of 1527-1530.[8] But it seemed to Luther that the writing of the *Summa* was a wasted effort. He did not indicate a date for this reading.

During his studies in the faculty of arts, Luther occupied himself continuously with the works of Aristotle. " 'I once read the writings of Aristotle diligently,' Dr. Luther said, 'and since he observes the method precisely he should be esteemed.' " "Among Aristotle's best books are those dealing with physics, metaphysics, and the soul, and I am sure that I fully understand those." [9] It is well-known that Luther later sharply criticized Aristotle.[10] Above all he criticized Aristotle's *Ethics*, and he placed Cicero far above him.[11] But he also found something to object to in the *Metaphysics:* "In Book 12 of the *Metaphysics* he stated, 'The highest Being observes itself; if it were to look beyond itself, it would see the poverty of the world.' In this passage he implicitly denies God." [12] Aristotle "doesn't believe that God cares about human affairs, or if he believes it, he thinks that God governs the world the way a sleepy maidservant rocks a child in a cradle." [13] Luther referred to Erasmus's God, also, as Aristotle's God "who drowses," who effects neither the salvation nor the damnation of human beings.[14]

Luther's teachers at Erfurt did not follow Aristotle blindly. They attempted to accommodate him to the doctrines of the church. In various facets of the natural sciences they believed they had exceeded him. At that time Luther had already adopted the view that astrology—in contrast to astronomy and mathematics—had no substance: [15] ". . . astrology is not a science because it has no principles and proofs. On the contrary, astrologers judge everything by the outcome and by individual cases and say, 'This happened once and twice, and therefore it will always happen so.' They base their judgment on the results that suit them and prudently don't talk about those that don't suit." [16] It is known that Melanchthon was a follower of astrology. Luther's critique can no doubt still be traced to Truttvetter's lectures on natural philosophy. Luther held fast to the basic principles of Aristotelian physics.

Luther did not limit himself to the prescribed studies. He also enjoyed becoming absorbed in the classical "poets," perhaps stimulated by the references of Truttvetter and Usingen. He read Ovid, Virgil, Plautus, and perhaps Horace and Juvenal. The writings of Plautus and Virgil were the only books he took with him into the monastery,[17] a sign of how much he had learned to enjoy these authors. Yet he did not become a humanist. To be sure, his friends at the time included Johann Jäger of Dornheim (called Crotus Rubeanus), who later belonged to the circle of poets in Erfurt around canon Konrad Mut (Mutianus) of Gotha. In a letter from Bologna on October 16, 1519, he reminded Luther of their close friendship with one another in Erfurt while devoting themselves to the noble arts.[18] At the time they may both have lived in Georg's house. However, Luther certainly did not belong to the circle of poets around Mutianus, for it developed after he had already entered the monastery. In later years Luther still enjoyed reading the Latin classics.

We know next to nothing about Luther's inner life during this period. We have already noted that he got along well with his house colleagues. He also appears to have traveled frequently to Mansfeld—a three-day journey. On one of these trips he jabbed himself in the thigh with his sword and severed his femoral artery. The profuse bleeding could not be stopped. Fearing death, he cried out, "Mary, help!" A surgeon was found to bind up the wound, but during the night it broke open again. Once more he called on the Blessed Virgin. In a table talk Luther said, "I would have died

with my trust in Mary." [19] During the weeks that followed, when
he had to remain in bed, he taught himself to play the lute, without
the benefit of a teacher. Crotus Rubeanus, also, referred to Luther
as a musician.[20]

One ought not attach too much significance to the story so often
repeated by Protestant polemicists, of how at the age of 20 Luther
discovered a Bible in the university library. Afterward Luther maintained that he had never before seen an entire Bible. Opening it,
he had read about Hannah, the mother of Samuel. Unfortunately
he had to stop because the bell for lectures had sounded. Until
then he had not known that there were other Gospels and Epistles
than those that were read in the pericopes. Shortly afterward he
purchased a postil that contained more gospel selections than
were usually read during the church year.[21] The Bible was a precious book, chained to a table in the library in order to prevent it
from being stolen. This is where the legend of the "chained Bible"
comes from. It is no wonder that Bibles were seldom found under
private ownership; they were far too scarce and expensive, and for
the most part also unintelligible to the laity. The Bible did not
play a role either in the activity of the schools or in the educational
preparation of the faculty of arts. It is therefore quite possible that
Luther was 20 when he first had a Bible in his hands. That it
awakened his lively interest is evident; but we ought not conclude
that he must already have been moved by the inner affliction that
later came to him in the monastery. The decisive hour in his life
had not yet come.

Entrance into the Monastery

On January 7, 1505, Luther received his master's degree from the faculty of arts. Of course this was merely a prerequisite for further achievements. Luther was required to lecture in the faculty of arts for two more years. This time could be used for study in one of the three higher faculties. Medicine was out of the question; at that time Erfurt was completely unknown for it. Theology did not fit his father's plans. That left law. As a lawyer, Hans Luther's gifted son could rightly expect a successful career. Luther's father even had a wealthy bride in mind for him. And he had already purchased his son a *corpus juris*, a set of legal textbooks. Luther began his lectures as a master of arts on April 24; his legal studies began on May 20.

Martin was probably in Mansfeld during the time between his inaugural lecture as master of arts at the beginning of February and the beginning of his new responsibilities. There is no way of knowing for certain what was on his mind while he was there. It is conceivable that he reflected on his vocational future. Without a doubt his father's wishes were decisive; he did not consider questioning them. All the same, perhaps he was privately uncomfortable, wondering whether his father's plans were right for him.

In any case we do know that on June 20, shortly after beginning his study of law, he returned to Mansfeld and remained there for about a week. We do not know why. The claim that at that time he was continually despondent cannot be substantiated. Of course one can point to the statement in one of his table talks, "When I was a young master in Erfurt I was quite unhappy." [1] Several similar remarks, however, suggest that he was most likely referring to the time immediately after his entrance into the monastery. It is impossible to be absolutely certain.

To his friends, at least according to Mathesius, Luther appeared to be "a lively and jovial young companion." [2] But Mathesius is not a completely reliable witness. In the table talk just quoted we are also told that at that time of *Anfechtung*** Luther devoted himself to intensive biblical studies in the Erfurt library, and that these gave rise to his first suspicions about the errors of the papacy. He then said to himself, "Should I alone be wise?" This is reminiscent of so many similar passages that one cannot trust the historicity of this table talk.

Around June 30 Luther set out from Mansfeld to Erfurt. On July 2 he was only a few hours from Erfurt when, near the town of Stotternheim, a terrifying thunderstorm overtook him. A bolt of lightning struck next to him, and air pressure threw him to the ground. In deathly panic he cried out, "St. Anne, help me! I will become a monk!"

This famous story raises two questions: (1) Was the vow a chance occurrence, or was there inner preparation for it? (2) Was the vow binding? Did Luther affirm it inwardly, or was he merely externally bound to it?

(1) It was not accidental that Luther turned to St. Anne; she was the patron saint of miners, and in Luther's parental home she was often called upon when emergencies arose. We have already faced the difficult question of whether Luther's vow was preceded by inner preparation. Already as a student Luther had struggled to find a gracious God. A sermon of 1534 indicates that it was such thoughts that led him "to monkdom." [3] But in this case "monkdom" certainly refers to the rigorous practices of monasticism rather than entrance into the monastery. Moreover, we have this sermon only

---

* Translator's note: The term *Anfechtung* (plural = *Anfechtungen*) occurs repeatedly in Luther studies and cannot adequately be translated by means of one English word. While the conventional definition is "temptation," with Luther it refers much more to a severe torment of the inner spirit and conscience. Since the German term is familiar to English-speaking students of Luther, I have let it stand.

in a later, printed edition edited by Cruciger, a student of Luther's. According to Melanchthon and Mathesius, the sudden death of a dear friend in 1505 disturbed Luther so deeply that he considered entering monastic life. Luther himself says nothing of this. We have already mentioned table talk no. 3593 in connection with Luther's visit to Mansfeld. In another place Luther maintained that, "I regretted my vow, and many tried to dissuade me from keeping it."[4] His friends considered it hasty and catastrophic. Not until 1519 did Crotus Rubeanus compare the bolt of lightning near Erfurt with Paul's experience on the Damascus road.[5]

We cannot help but assume that Luther had previously entertained the thought of entering the monastery. Otherwise his vow to become a monk in a moment of anxiety would hardly make sense. Up to that point he had felt bound to carrying out his father's wishes.

In his treatise on monastic vows of 1521 Luther included a dedication to his father. There he wrote that his father had doubted whether he, as a 22-year-old youth, would be able to abstain from sexual involvements, and so had already thought of a rich bride for him. But "I did not become a monk of my own free will and desire, still less to gain any gratification of the flesh, but . . . I was walled in by the terror and the agony of sudden death and forced by necessity to take the vow."[6] That sounds as though he had sworn the oath of Stotternheim in the anguish of the moment rather than having been drawn into it by some inner desire; on the other hand, the affirmation that he did not become a monk for his "stomach's sake" seems to indicate that there were indeed more serious grounds. It is also possible that the memories of Eisenach exerted more of an influence on him than he himself was aware of. One can marshal sufficient arguments to support either position. However, it seems unlikely that Luther would have vowed to enter the monastery at this moment of intense inner distress if he had not been thinking about doing so for some time. Yet Luther's most severe *Anfechtung* was still to come in the monastery.

(2) Was the vow binding? Luther could have requested the pope to release him from it, but that would have been a long and involved process. Of course from the outset Luther's vow had to be sworn in full consciousness and with a clear mind in order to be considered binding. On September 9, 1521, Luther wrote Me-

lanchthon a long and carefully thought-out letter on the monastic
vow in which he said his present view was that anyone who made
such a vow in order to achieve salvation made it in an ungodly
way. "I am uncertain with what kind of an attitude I took my vow.
I was more overpowered than drawn. God wanted it this way. I am
afraid that I, too, may have taken my vow in an impious and sacri-
legious way." [7]

Luther spoke of being caught up in a *raptus* ("rapture"), which
one could interpret as being "involuntary." But obviously Luther
himself did not understand it that way. He allowed 14 days to
pass before he appeared at the gates of the monastery. Several
of his friends tried to dissuade him, saying that he was not under
obligation. Luther did not accept their opinions; he felt bound.
"God wanted it so," he wrote to Melanchthon. From our vantage
point we have no choice but to agree with his judgment. Luther's
entrance into the monastery was neither an accident of fate nor
a tragedy, but an act of divine leadership. If one assumes that the
young master of arts was attracted to the monastic ideal, it also
follows that he would have wished to practice it. Only a monk
who had personally experienced the most rigorous form of medieval piety was called on to surmount that piety from within.

In a table talk of July 16, 1539, Luther told how he took leave
of his friends. [8] God had graciously accepted his vow.

> I regretted the vow I had made and many advised against keep-
> ing it. But I insisted, and on the day before Alexius [July 16] I
> invited my best friends for a farewell so that they might accom-
> pany me to the cloister the next day. When they attempted to re-
> strain me, I said, "Today you see me, but never again." Then with
> tears in their eyes they went along. . . . I never thought I would
> leave the monastery. I had died completely to the world.

He had not told his parents of his decision beforehand. [9] His father
was beside himself with anger. "When I bècame a monk my father
was furious and foolish. He wrote me a contemptuous letter, addressing me as '*du*,' after having called me '*Ihr*' before, and completely withdrew his parental favor." [10] One can understand Luther's father; he saw himself cheated of all his wishes and plans,
and he believed his financial sacrifices had been in vain. The letter
did not arrive until after the 17th of July. Therefore Luther had

taken the responsibility for his decision fully and completely on himself.

As far as we know, this is the first time he acted independently of his father and asserted his own "identity." The courage to take this step was drawn from the situation itself. He placed the vow and his allegiance to God above allegiance to his earthly father. We know that it was not easy for him. An often-quoted conversation with his father at the time of his first Mass shows that this problem still occupied his mind. But his conscience forced him to take this step.

The identity crisis Luther experienced during this break with his father is commonly illustrated by a story that Cochläus, an opponent of Luther, preserved in his *Kommentaren über die Taten und Schriften Luthers*.[11] Reiter and, above all, Erikson have dealt with this.[12] According to the story, Luther was once sitting in the choir during the Mass when the Gospel was read about the expulsion of the demons from the man who was deaf and dumb.[13] Luther is said to have broken down and shouted, "It's not me! It's not me!" In that Gospel it is the father who brings the son with the dumb spirit to Jesus. In addition to Cochläus, Dungersheim and Oldecop (both opponents of Luther) also reported this story. There is a strong possibility that this is legendary material, and Erikson admitted this possibility. The three versions given by these authorities differ from one another, but even if they agreed on the historical details, interpretation of the event would be problematic. Some have seen it as an epileptic seizure; Erikson related the "fit in the choir" to Luther's identity crisis. The three original reporters had neither epilepsy nor a father complex in mind, but saw Luther's outburst as a sign of demon possession. To draw the wide-reaching conclusions from this story that Erikson does appears risky.

Friends attempted to persuade Luther's father that he ought willingly to sacrifice his dearest and best to God, but to no avail.[14] Only after two of Luther's brothers had died and the rumor had spread to Mansfeld that Martin had contracted the plague that was rampant in Erfurt did his father relent—yet even then with a reluctant heart. Evidently Luther had not yet been received into the order. That did not occur until September; acceptance into a monastic order was not granted immediately. The petitioner was first allowed time for conscientious self-examination; in addition he was observed by the brothers and the prior to see whether he was suited for life in the order. Hans Luther's reluctant consent would have arrived prior to Luther's reception into the order at the beginning of September.

In addition to the Augustinian choir monastery there were at that time no less than six other cloisters for men in Erfurt: Benedictine, Carthusian, Dominican, Franciscan, Servite, and the "Black Cloister" of the Augustinian Friars. After the vow made on July 2 Luther's first task was to decide which of these cloisters he wished to enter. Though he never mentioned the reasons for his final choice, we can guess what they were. The Augustinian Friars placed particular emphasis on the ascetic ideal; the "severity" of the order would have attracted Luther, since it was his earnest conviction that self-denial was the best possible path to evangelical perfection. Moreover, academic pursuits were highly esteemed in the Black Cloister. Within its walls one could devote oneself to a general course of studies which at the same time allowed for attendance at the university. In other words, Luther selected a monastery that had high academic standards, in addition to being a fraternity of St. Anne, the saint to whom Luther had pledged his vow.

Luther's solemn reception as a novitiate took place at the beginning of September 1505, about six weeks after his entrance into the monastery. Beforehand he had to make a general confession to the prior. At the beginning of the ceremony Luther's hair was clipped; the tonsure came at the conclusion of the celebration. Luther was required to prostrate himself on the floor before the prior. To the question, "What do you desire?" he replied, "God's grace and your mercy." Then he was asked about his personal relationships, whether he was married, whether he was a free man, and if he was afflicted with any disease. The harsh nature of monastic life was vividly described. Luther declared himself ready to bear all of the privations demanded of him. This promise was followed by a probationary period of one year within the community of brothers. While the cantor intoned the hymn, "Great Father Augustine," Luther was stripped of his worldly clothing and given a monk's habit.

Inside the cloister Augustinian Friars dressed entirely in white, wearing a long-sleeved, white woolen shirt that reached to the ankles, a white scapular (a strip of cloth draped across the shoulders and hanging over the breast and back, reaching to the feet), and a broad white cowl with shoulder coverings. For all official occasions, for preaching, and for street use, a black cowl was worn over the white habit (a black robe with a black hood and black shoulder coverings). Almost all of the white habit was then covered. The tonsure was severe: only a ring of hair no wider than the breadth of two fingers was allowed. Luther obtained a new habit in Nuremberg in 1518 while he was on his way to meet Cajetan in Augsburg; it was not until October 9, 1524, that he finally discarded it.

The change of clothing was intended to symbolize the putting off of the old person and the putting on of a new person. It was followed by still more hymns and prayers. Luther had to lie down on the floor in prayer in the form of a cross before the high altar. After that he was led to the assembly and received the kiss of peace from all present. His monastic name became Augustinus, but evidently it was soon forgotten.[15] The service was concluded with the admonition, "Not he who begins, but he who endures to the end, will be saved." With that began a novitiate that lasted a year. Only after this probationary period would there be final reception through the so-called profession, by which an everlasting vow was made. As a novitiate Luther was also given his own cell. It was noticeably plain, about three meters deep and two meters wide, unheated, and with only one window. The furnishings consisted of a table, a chair, a candlestick, and a storage cabinet. There were no featherbeds, only a straw sack with wool blankets. No decoration was allowed. The door could not be locked from the inside, in order that the cell might be checked regularly, even at night, from the outside. The scapular was not to be removed at night. Talking was forbidden in the cell; even prayers had to be said silently.

The Augustinian Friars were a mendicant order, but the Erfurt cloister was prosperous enough not to have to depend on begging. The voting monks of the first class, the "fathers," were those advanced men who concerned themselves with academic and religious exercises. The simple tasks were the concern of the friars. Of course part of a novitiate's initiation into the practice of monastic humility included the completion of menial tasks. He not only had to keep his own cell clean, but—according to Mathesius—the latrine as well.[16] Certainly he was also sent through the streets with his beggar's sack.

Mathesius and Ratzeberger (who later was Luther's physician and left us a number of notations about Luther's life) mention the abuse that was meted out with particular enthusiasm to Luther as a university-trained master.[17] "Look at the sack on your neck! It's begging, not studying, that supports the monasteries." [18] Only through the advocacy of one of his former professors was Luther supposedly freed of such harassment. This is certainly polemical exaggeration. The novice Luther certainly would not have taken such minor irritations seriously; they were part and parcel of what it meant to acquire the proper monastic mentality. It was also necessary for him to become a monk in his outward manner. Everything was prescribed in minute detail: when and before whom to bow, when to prostrate oneself. He was required to walk along with bent neck and downcast eyes. He was never allowed to eat or drink outside of the appointed times, or to take bread and water without the prescribed prayers. He had to suppress all laughter, and most of the time only a painstaking form of sign language was allowed. Of course the master of the novices, particularly, was concerned with the spiritual development of those in his charge. Confession and Bible study were, according to the rules of the order, the most important means of formation.

The first book Luther received was presumably a copy of the Latin Bible, bound in red leather. He became so familiar with the text that he could quickly locate any passage.[19] At least once each week he was required to make confession. Confession and Bible study led Luther to the self-analysis and reflection that gave rise to his *Anfechtung*. It was the novice master who determined the extent of mortification, not individual inclination. Luther soon became accustomed to the meager diet, and even in later years he did not complain about it. Much worse was the cold; one could escape it only by going to the heated communal hall.

Luther fulfilled his novitiate duties to the complete satisfaction of his superiors. At the conclusion of one year from the time of his reception, the community unanimously agreed to let the novice Augustinus make his profession. This took place in September 1506. Once more Luther had the opportunity to leave the order. He made a conclusive decision to live the life of a monk. The ritual followed a precisely prescribed order. Luther put off the unconsecrated clothing of the novitiate and put on the consecrated garments of profession. The rule of the order was placed in the novice's hands. He vowed everlasting obedience to this rule. "If you keep this rule," said the prior, "I promise you eternal life." [20] The profession was followed by a solemn procession into the high chancel, where the final step was completed. Luther received the kiss of peace and was given his place in the choir.

Shortly after his profession Luther was informed that he had been selected to become a priest. In preparation for his celebration of the Mass he had to study the massive explanation of the canon of the Mass by the Tübingen professor Gabriel Biel. Biel, who died in 1495, was the last outstanding representative of Occamism, and Luther's theology was strongly influenced by him. It is said that Luther could quote the explanation of the canon of the Mass almost verbatim.[21] His ordination to the priesthood took place in the Erfurt Cathedral on April 4, 1507. With that Luther received the right to celebrate the Mass. His first Mass took place in the cloister church on May 2, 1507. At the suggestion of his superiors, Luther invited his father—who, surprisingly, accepted the invitation and rode into Erfurt with a cavalcade of 20 companions (most likely to impress the monks).

As Luther stood before the altar he was overtaken by fear. The liturgy of the Mass was a complicated ritual in which not one word could be omitted and no incorrect gestures could be made. Later Luther made it known that he almost died of fright when he said his first Mass.[22] During the offertory he would rather have left the altar, but the prior prevented him.[23] Upon reaching the high point of the service, the moment of consecration, he was suddenly filled with terror before the majesty of God, whom he, as priest, was making present.[24] Through transubstantiation Christ was actually on the altar, and, for Luther, Christ was God himself.

After the ceremony a banquet was held in the refectory, and the guests were invited to take part. Luther's father had donated a generous sum toward the celebration, and Martin concluded from this that his father had finally reconciled himself to his entrance into the monastery. He therefore assured him that he had been called by a heavenly voice. To this his father replied soberly—and perhaps even superstitiously—"Let us hope it was not a ghost!" This objection disconcerted Luther, and he vigorously refuted it to the point where he was even indignant. His father responded by saying, "Have you never heard that one is to obey one's parents?" Luther observed in 1521 that he had hardly ever heard such a statement from anyone. Those words continued to haunt him. At the time he had admittedly dismissed them rather self-righteously as human words, but in the depths of his being he could not avoid their impact.[25]

So the discord between father and son continued, and we can assume that the situation weighed heavily on Luther over the years, up until 1521. But there is no valid reason for concluding that Luther's attacks of *Anfechtung* in the monastery were the result of an uncontrollable father complex. Luther entered the cloister to achieve eternal salvation.[26] He did not doubt the inner necessity of that step. That is why even the explosive conversation with his father after his first Mass was unable to deter him, despite the deep impression his father's objections made on him. At the time he believed that he had to put obedience to God before the wishes of his father. Even in his letter of dedication of 1521 Luther did not affirm his father's position. The fact that Luther now felt free from his vow did not mean that his father had at last prevailed; Luther's view of vows was an insight that had been awakened in him by God.[27] "My conscience has been freed, and that is the most complete liberation. Therefore I am still a monk and yet not a monk . . . [God], who has taken me out of the monastery, has an authority over me that is greater than yours." [28] His father should acknowledge that that which he had at first thought was bad had turned out to be good. "Thus I hope that he has taken from you one son in order that he may begin to help the sons of many others through me. You ought not only to endure this willingly, but you ought to rejoice with exceeding joy—and this I am sure is what you will do." [29] In 1521 Luther did not submit once again to the will of his father; rather, he placed both his will and that of his father under the will of God.

After his first Mass, Luther had to devote himself intensively to the study of theology, along with the general studies required by the monastery. His principal teacher was Father Johann Nathin, a devotee and student of Gabriel Biel, to whom we have already referred. In addition to Biel's *Collectorium*, Nathin conducted extensive lectures on the *Sentences* of Peter Lombard (d. 1160), which had been the starting point for dogmatic theology for hundreds of years.

That Luther was forbidden to read the Bible is a legend of Mathesius. To the contrary, during this period Luther was quite busy with the Scriptures. As his primary critical tools he used the *glossa ordinaria,* the most important medieval handbook of biblical interpretation, and the biblical commentary of Nicolas of Lyra (d. 1340), who used the literal rather than the allegorical method of interpretation.[30] We also know the other books Luther worked through during the months from May 1507 to October 1508. He obviously took his studies seriously, and with thoroughness and pleasure he became knowledgeable concerning Occamists. The accusation of the Catholic church historian Denifle, that Luther was ignorant of scholastic theology, is not valid. His religious order respected his knowledge and soon selected him to be a teacher.

6

Between Erfurt, Wittenberg, and Rome

In the fall of 1508, when he was in the middle of his theological studies at Erfurt, Luther was suddenly transferred to the Augustinian monastery in Wittenberg, where he was to assume responsibility for lecturing on moral philosophy in the faculty of arts. The University of Wittenberg had been founded in 1502 by the Elector Frederick the Wise. At the beginning it was hardly able to compete with Erfurt and Leipzig, but that changed with the progression of the Reformation.

The city was wretched. In 1532 Luther still said, "The Wittenbergers are on the border of civilization; if they advance just one small step further, they will be deep in barbarism." [1] He could not understand why the elector had established a university there. [2] Even in 1539 Luther insisted Wittenberg would never become a real city. [3] Luther regarded the people as inhospitable drunkards without commitments or decency. By 1545 he had grown so weary of the place that after a journey he did not want to return. Christoph Scheurl of Nuremberg, the rector of the new high school, reprimanded the Wittenbergers for their gluttony and drunkenness. Even harsher words were used by Cochläus, Luther's ardent opponent, who hoped thereby to discredit the Reformation. The first rector of the university, the doctor of medicine Martin Polich of Mellerstadt, who had previously taught at Leipzig, called Wittenberg a "knacker's carcass." [4]

Elector Frederick, however, had good financial reasons for establishing a university there. A monastery connected with the castle church could support 12 of the 22 professors at no cost to the electoral prince. Three additional teaching positions were filled by the Franciscans and the Augustinian Friars, leaving only seven professors for the elector himself to support. Johann von Staupitz, who at that time was general of the Augustinian Friars in Saxony, also favored this undertaking, since it increased the prestige of his community.

According to the statutes, two professorships were to be filled by the Augustinians: the chair of Bible in the theological faculty and the chair for moral theology in the faculty of arts. Since 1502 the biblical chair had been occupied by Staupitz, but he was so burdened by his official duties that he could barely keep up with his teaching tasks. In addition, he had been named dean of the theological faculty for the 1508-1509 winter semester. Whether or not it was Staupitz who had brought Luther to Wittenberg is uncertain. It is at least likely that Luther was known to him from a brief meeting in Erfurt. However it is also possible that Jakob Truttvetter, a member of the Wittenberg faculty since 1507, had drawn attention to Luther.

Luther did not actually assume the chair of moral philosophy— he was only asked to fulfill its responsibilities. There was no lack of work. He was required to lecture four hours each day on the *Nicomachean Ethics* of Aristotle, beginning at 2:00 P.M., as well as supervise the student disputations three times a week; in addition he had his own studies in theology to pursue, requiring him to attend lectures and participate in scheduled debates. After he received the degree of bachelor of Bible in March 1509 he was also required to lecture regularly on individual chapters of the Bible.

Luther found little pleasure in lecturing on moral philosophy. On March 17, 1509, he wrote to Johann Brown, the vicar of the monastery in Eisenach, that from the very beginning he would gladly have exchanged philosophy for theology, if it were a theology "that searches out the nut from the shell, the kernel from the grain, and the marrow from the bones."[5] In the fall of 1509 he completed his theological studies and became a *Sententiar*—one who bore the task of interpreting the *Sentences* of Peter Lombard. But in October 1509, even before he was able to deliver his first lecture in Wittenberg, he was called back to Erfurt — just as suddenly and unexpectedly as he had been transferred to Wittenberg the previous year. It may well be that the director of Luther's studies, Johann Nathin, wanted him back in Erfurt because of his own work load. Against the will of the faculty, Nathin had succeeded in having the Wittenberg *Sententiarius* recognized in Erfurt, and he arranged for his first lecture to be delivered there.

Luther expounded Lombard's *Sentences* three or four times a week in the lecture hall of the monastery until October 1510. We have a copy of Luther's lecture notes, as well as a volume of Augustine's writings that he was studying at the time. The numerous marginal comments reveal how carefully Luther worked through that book.[6] On the inside front cover of Lombard's *Sentences* Luther extolled the fact that Lombard took his direction less from philosophy than from the "shining lights of the church," above all Augustine, who "cannot be praised too highly."[7] In 1538 he still respected Lombard and referred to him as "a very diligent man with a superior mind." Yet he did not apply his full strength to the Holy Scriptures; that is why his book fell into error through "many useless questions."[8]

At that time Luther read Lombard—as he did Augustine—with the eyes of an Occamist. We cannot assume that his comments on Rom. 9:16 underscoring the primacy of grace above human will reflect an early Reformation theology. None of the marginal notes in the writings of Augustine are expressly anti-Pelagian, in spite of the importance Luther later attached to this issue. In 1538 he maintained that it was the Pelagians who first "awakened Augustine and made him a man."[9] It is interesting that Luther made a number of critical literary observations. The work *On the Recognition of the True Life* could not be considered genuine, on stylistic grounds,[10] and *De spiritu et anima* merely contained the thoughts of Augustine; it was no more written by him than the apocryphal Wisdom of Solomon was written by Solomon.[11] It is worth noting that during this period Luther also began to learn Hebrew; he used the textbook written by Reuchlin. At first he made very little progress, particularly since at that time he still accepted the Vulgate (the Latin translation of the Bible) as the authentic text. Not until 1515 did he begin to doubt its authority.

While Luther was diligently engaged in studies within the solitude of the monastery, the city of Erfurt experienced its "year of madness." In January 1510 the old town council was deposed by craftsmen and journeymen who rebelled against oppressive taxation and mismanagement. During the conflict that ensued, the main building of the university was burned down, taking the library with it. One of the most prominent men on the old council was executed by those who had seized power. Luther condemned the uprising at the time as well as later.[12]

Another significant event in Luther's life occurred in 1510: his journey to Rome.[13] This came about in connection with a dispute within the order. In June 1503 Egidio Canisio of Viterbo had assumed leadership of the order, and he committed himself enthusiastically to its long-sought reform. The advocates of more lax practices—the Conventualists—resisted him. The reformed communities —the Observants—opposed union with the Conventualists for fear they would lose their special privileges and practices. The reform of the entire order made little progress, and the resulting standoff led to conflict in the Saxon communities.

Egidio had appointed Johann von Staupitz, the vicar-general of the reformed German communities (who were Observants), to serve at the same time as the provincial of the order in Saxony. In that role he was to unite the unreformed monasteries in the province of Saxony with the reformed German communities. Twenty-two of the 29 reformed communities declared themselves in favor of this union; seven were opposed, including Nuremberg and Erfurt. They decided on an appeal to Rome.

Luther was assigned as the *socius itinerarius,* or traveling companion, of a Nuremberg priest, because the rules of the order prohibited him from traveling alone. The two men were to represent to Rome the cause of the seven opposition monasteries, with the Nuremberg father (whose name we do not know) serving as spokesman. They failed to convince the general of the order, who remained in favor of the union. Then Staupitz himself became more conciliatory. Though not willing to give up his provincial rule over the Saxon communities, he was ready to listen to proposals that might lead to peace. The majority of the Erfurt cloister did not support him.

Luther and his friend Johann Lang were in favor of Staupitz's plea for peace. As a result Lang was expelled from the community and ended up going to Wittenberg. The fact that in the late fall of 1511 Luther also spent time in Wittenberg may have been because he too left Erfurt during the unrest. Perhaps Staupitz himself had arranged his transfer to Wittenberg. In May of 1512 Staupitz finally dropped the union plan. Peace was restored, and within a few years both Luther and Lang were reconciled with Erfurt. Luther's transfer to Wittenberg can be regarded as providential; in 1512 he succeeded Staupitz as professor of Bible.

Now let us return to Luther's journey to Rome. The two brothers traveled the entire way by foot, as the rules of the order required. They left Nuremberg before the middle of November 1510 and most likely entered Rome by the end of the year or early in 1511. The interim stops are not all known to us. They crossed the Alps by way of the seven-step route to Milan. The weather was poor. In Bologna there was deep snow on January 2. In Rome it rained almost incessantly. Overnight accommodations were no problem; everywhere monasteries of their order stood at their disposal. The return trip, begun sometime in January or early February 1511, led over the snow-covered Brenner Pass to Innsbruck, from there to Augsburg, and then to Nuremberg, where they arrived in March. Luther stayed there before finally returning to Erfurt sometime in April.

Later in life he freely shared his impressions of the journey.[14] He judged the lands through which he passed with the eyes of a peasant. Productivity was the measure, and Switzerland fared poorly.[15] He also had something to say about the people. The Italians were unpleasant. He did not understand their language well enough, and therefore didn't trust them;[16] but they did have skilled tailors.[17] In Florence he admired the hospital and the foundling home.[18] Works of art were not mentioned, nor did he have much to say about the scenery. His greatest interest was in religious practices. In Milan he was unable to celebrate Mass because they used the Ambrosian liturgy.[19] In Augsburg he visited the "miracle girl" Anna Lammenit, who had allegedly lived 10 years while being sustained only by the communion host. She was later exposed as a fraud.[20]

At his first glimpse of Rome Luther prostrated himself and exclaimed: "Hail, holy Rome! Holy indeed, drenched with the blood of the holy martyrs."[21] The two brothers stayed at the Augustinian monastery of Santa Maria del Popolo, immediately to the left of the Porta del Popolo. Whether Luther took notice of the wonderful frescoes of Pinturicchio in the adjoining church is not known; he did seek out a Madonna supposedly painted by St. Luke.[22]

Since it took Egidio about four weeks to announce his final position, Luther had ample opportunity to become familiar with the *Mirabilia urbis Romae*, a popular guide for pilgrims that listed all of the sacred shrines. Luther did not look at Rome through the eyes of a modern tourist, but with the intention of fully experiencing the city's treasures of grace. He set out on an exhausting pilgrimage that included the seven principal churches of the city, ending with Communion at St. Peter's. Of course he also visited the catacombs, where so many martyrs were buried. "When I made by pilgrimage to Rome, I was such a fanatical saint that I dashed through all the churches and crypts, believing all the stinking forgeries of those places. I ran through about a dozen Masses in Rome and was almost prostrated by the thought that my mother and father were still alive, because I should gladly have redeemed them from purgatory with my Masses and other excellent works and prayers. . . . But it was too crowded, and I could not get in; so I ate a smoked herring instead." [23]

Luther did not see Julius II, the reigning pope; he and his court had been away from the eternal city for several months. The magnificence of the cardinals' palaces disturbed Luther,[24] and his judgment of the Roman priests was predictably negative. "I was not in Rome very long, but I celebrated many Masses there and also saw many Masses; it horrifies me to think of it. I overheard the officials at mealtime laughing and boasting about how some Masses were done, saying over bread and wine, 'Bread you are, and bread you will remain,' and then holding up the bread and wine [at the elevation]. Now I was a young and truly pious monk, and I was shocked by such words. Indeed I was disgusted that they could celebrate the Mass so flippantly, as if they were performing some kind of trick. Before I had even gotten to the Gospel [to its reading in the Mass], the priest beside me had already concluded a Mass and shouted at me: '*Passa, Passa* — enough now, finish it off.' " [25] "We were simply laughed at because we were such pious monks. A Christian was taken to be nothing but a fool.

I know priests' who said six or seven masses while I said only one. They took money for them and I didn't." [26]

Luther found but one admirable exception, the church of Santa Maria dell' Anima: "The German church, which is the best, has a German pastor." [27] At the time Luther was not skeptical of the shrines and relics. Nor did he discover any significant Reformation insights in Rome, despite the testimony of his son Paul, who claimed he heard his father speak of such insights. [28] But Paul was only 11 at the time, and it was not until 38 years later in Augsburg, on August 7, 1582, that he wrote of his father telling how, "as he set out to perform his *preces graduales* [graduated prayers] on the Lateran steps, the saying of the prophet Habakkuk, which Paul quoted in Rom. 1:17, occurred to him, namely, 'the just shall live by faith,' whereupon he ceased praying. And as he returned to Wittenberg, it was this very epistle of Paul that he claimed as his most firm foundation." [29] It is quite apparent that we are dealing with a flawed memory, for this story does not at all agree with Luther's own statements about his stay in Rome.

To be sure, in 1545 Luther did express himself in a sermon in such a way as to raise questions: "In order to release my grandfather from purgatory, I climbed the stairs of Pilate [*Santa Scala*], praying a *Paternoster* on each step, for it was the prevailing belief that whoever prayed in this way could free a soul [from purgatory]. But when I arrived at the top, I thought, 'Who knows whether it is true? Such a prayer is worth nothing.'" [30] The legend Paul Luther repeats may well have arisen from similar expressions of Luther that are no longer available to us. Still, even the sermon illustration dare not be pushed too far; we do not usually hear skeptical comments about holy things from Luther.

Much that Luther later said about the corruption of Rome did not have its source in his own recollections, but came from his reading and general rumors. Of course his own experiences were of great value to him in later years. "I wouldn't take one thousand florins for not having seen Rome because I wouldn't have been able to believe such things if I had been told by somebody without having seen them for myself." [31] He may have been offended by much, but at the time nothing could shake his faithfulness to the church. Even the following judgment should be seen as a product of later reflection: "Whoever came to Rome with money received the forgiveness of sins. Like a fool, I carried onions to Rome and brought back garlic." [32]

The journey to Rome was ambivalent as far as Luther's development was concerned. The negative impressions took root only later. What Luther learned from the dispute within his order is far more significant. Unlike most of his Erfurt brothers, he realized that obedience was more important than maintaining one's personal position, and that peace was worth more than justifying oneself by relying on outward observance. The most significant thing to come out of these years was Luther's transfer to Wittenberg, a move precipitated by his disagreement with his Erfurt colleagues.

The Struggle to Find
a Gracious God

Luther entered the monastery in an effort to achieve salvation through perfection. In the midst of terrible *Anfechtung*,* he must have recognized that this path would not lead to his goal. We do not know exactly when this *Anfechtung* began. During his novitiate he still appeared to be completely at peace and self-assured.[1] While conducting his first Mass he was overwhelmed by the majesty of God, but in the subsequent conversation with his father he seemed to have totally regained his composure. Since he expected to experience the grace of God and attain the certainty of salvation by becoming a monk, his quest for a gracious God must certainly have begun earlier.

Luther took his life as a monk very seriously. "I was a devout monk and wanted to force God to justify me because of my works and the severity of my life." [2] "I was a good monk, and kept the rule of my order so strictly that I may say that if ever a monk got to heaven by his monkery, I would have gotten there as well. All my brothers in the monastery who knew me will bear me out. If I had kept on any longer, I would have killed myself with vigils, prayers, readings, and other works." [3] He did more than what the rule required of him. Often for periods of up to three days he did not take a drop of water or a piece of bread. [4] The vow of chastity provided no difficulty. "When I was a monk I did not feel much

* See translator's note on p. 54.

desire. I had nocturnal pollutions in response to bodily necessity. I didn't even look at the women when they made their confession, for I didn't wish to recognize the faces of those whose confessions I heard. In Erfurt I heard the confession of no woman, in Wittenberg of only three women." [5] Nevertheless he was unable to find inner peace. "I was very pious in the monastery, yet I was sad because I thought God was not gracious to me." [6]

We ought not think of Luther as just another overly zealous monk — a figure familiar to monastic spiritual directors, and one for whom established exercises could have been prescribed. Luther's struggle for a gracious God had deeper roots. As a monk he had been trained in disciplined self-analysis, and he practiced it more radically than most of those who preceded and followed him. He broke through the usual illusions that distort the perception of self and of God. [7]

The rule of the Augustinian order required two things: absolute love of God and one's neighbor, and perfect humility. Luther was forced to admit to himself that he was unable to fulfill this dual demand. In the process he discovered that self-centeredness is the motivating drive of the human heart. He called this drive *concupiscentia,* but did not limit it to sensual lust (libido), as the term had been used previously. Instead, he understood it in a more comprehensive sense, equating it with human egocentricity *per se.* Human beings are self-willed and seek to have their own way in all things, even in "good works," indeed, even (and often especially) in religion. Human nature "sets itself in the place of all other things, even in the place of God, and seeks only those things which are its own and not the things of God. Therefore it is its own first and greatest idol." "Scripture . . . describes man as so turned in on himself *[incurvatus in se]* that he uses not only physical but even spiritual goods for his own purposes and in all things seeks only himself." [8] Luther recognized the motif of egocentricity as a hidden motive in the aspirations of late medieval piety, but projected into the life to come.

Not until the advent of modern psychoanalysis have we been offered a comparably deep view of the human spirit. Of course the modern view is that self-centeredness is a natural human phenomenon, and some even call it "self-realization." This view, however, fails to take into account the fact that true self-realization occurs only when one subjects oneself to the law of self-negation, dying in order to become. Those who cling desperately to themselves remain curved inward, and so are unable to grow and develop. True self-realization is accomplished only by those who dedicate themselves to the welfare of others and to that supreme will that governs all of life.

For Luther, self-centeredness was original sin *per se*, the sin against the First Commandment. Human beings thereby desire to make themselves into God. This attempt to grasp equality with God is the source of all the world's misery; it turns life into a torment. It robs individual persons as well as humanity of peace. But is this self-centeredness tainted by guilt? One simple experience is enough to point out that being confronted by the self-centeredness of others is not something "natural," but rather immoral. We undermine our own dignity as human beings when we dismiss our egoism simply as a biological fact. We are not simply the products of heredity and environment. To talk delinquents out of their guilt feelings is to divest them of the last bit of self-respect they have.

Self-centeredness is apparent not only in actions that are universally recognized as "immoral"; according to Reformation theology it also plays a role in so-called "good works." "Even in the best life, nothing we do counts." Of course it is preposterous to make such an assertion as a *moral* judgment. With Goethe we can say, "Surely one can make some progress." Certainly our deeds are not in vain if we assess them according to worldly standards. Luther's statement is valid only if we measure what we do according to an absolute. As a moral judgment his words are an exaggeration; yet they are a theological judgment. For Luther, the absolute standard was the command of God. For him God was not a peripheral thought, a "working hypothesis" or idea, not an "ultimate Being" or supreme mystery, but rather the greatest living reality of personal character.

We have already heard his criticism of Aristotle's "sleeping God." Luther's God was the personal God of the Bible, not the abstract God of metaphysics. Only when we recognize this will we understand his struggle for a gracious God. Only a person—not an idea or the "ground of Being" (Tillich)—can be angry or forgiving. Admittedly at this point it is difficult for us to follow Luther completely. The anthropomorphic elements in his portrayal of God as well as in the God of the Scriptures are all too prominent. We can only consider them as pointers to a reality that lies "behind" them. It has become clear to us that all of our statements about God will always be inadequate and approximate.

That which we now understand as metaphorical or figurative language, Luther took literally. If his struggle for a gracious God is to mean something to us today, it must first be translated into less figurative language. That is not easy, and it will not be convincing if we merely act as if we, also, have experienced Luther's struggle for a gracious God. Perhaps part of the problem is the fact that for centuries we have known the answer that was given to Luther. We have become accustomed to avoiding the fires of *Anfechtung* because we want to enter paradise together with Luther. It is a misunderstanding of Luther, as well as a questionable consequence of his reforming discovery, that grace has become cheap to us. Even our hymnal provides occasionally shocking examples of this. It is all too easy for us to say the words that God's wrath has been atoned for by the suffering of Christ.

What sort of reality should we visualize for God's wrath? We can only begin with our own experiences and then compare them with what the Bible says about God's wrath. We know, for example, that those who sow to their own "flesh" will from the flesh reap corruption,[9] or that righteousness exalts a nation, but sin is a reproach to any people.[10] We know that as long as we are unwilling to assume the responsibility for our own wrongdoing, we will never achieve inner peace. We know that no problem is ever truly solved through injustice. We know that the unbroken chain of guilt and retaliation can only be severed by forgiveness. We know that wealth does not guarantee happiness. In all of these and in similar instances we experience something of what the Bible calls "God's wrath." We cannot confine this reality to the realm of human emotions, as merely the expression of pent-up feelings — although we experience it daily. It was this reality that Luther encountered in his monastic struggles, but of course with a severity that only few experience.

Of course the late medieval church had an answer to the question, How do I find a gracious God? By means of its sacraments it dispensed the grace of God. But recalling his Baptism did not help

Luther. "I was a monk for 15 years, and yet I was never able to trust my baptism." [11] The blessed reception of the Eucharist was dependent on the remorse of the recipient. But Luther was never certain his remorse was sufficient, or whether he had indeed confessed everything, even though he confessed frequently — often daily. "I made a practice of confessing and reciting all my sins, but always with prior contrition; I went to confession frequently, and I performed the assigned penances faithfully. Nevertheless, my conscience could never achieve certainty but was always in doubt and said, 'You have not done this correctly. You were not contrite enough. You omitted this in your confession.' " [12] "When another sin came to my mind I would run back to the priest, so that once he said to me, 'God has commanded us to place our hope in his mercy. Go in peace!' " [13] So Luther never experienced the feeling of peace the sacraments were said to bestow. "I prepared myself for Mass and prayer with great reverence; but even when I was most devout, I still proceeded to the altar as a doubter, and as a doubter I returned." [14]

The church also encouraged good works. But Luther saw egoism at work in them. Monasticism was regarded as an especially good work. After his initiation into the order he was addressed as if he were an innocent child who had just emerged from Baptism. Indeed he would gladly have taken pride in his "monk's baptism," but "no sooner did one little *Anfechtung* of death or sin appear, than I collapsed and found neither Baptism nor monasticism of any help. On such occasions I was the most miserable person on earth. My days and nights were so filled with weeping and doubt that no one could put up with me. Bathed and baptized in my monkery, I had reason to sweat, for I did not know Christ other than as a severe judge from whom I desperately wished to flee but from whom I was never able to escape." [15]

For a time Luther resorted to mysticism, though not the German mysticism with which he later became acquainted and learned to value for its experiential theology. "The speculative learning of the theologians is altogether worthless. I have read Bonaventure [1221-1274] on this, and he almost drove me mad because I desired to experience the union of God with my soul. . . . Likewise, the mystical theology of Dionysius [16] is nothing but trumpery." [17] Mysticism teaches that God lives in the innermost depth of the soul; one need but renounce the world and enter deeply enough into one's self in order to find God. Luther was unable to verify this supposition. Whenever he peered into the depths of his being, it was his own egoism, not God, that he found.

As an Occamist Luther had learned that when a person does what he is capable of doing, God will not deny him grace—a fairly reasonable view, and one that is reminiscent of the closing scene of Goethe's *Faust* (Part Two). But Luther could never find peace in this way. He saw works in it as well. "We were taught to do sufficient good work to earn the forgiveness of sins." [18] In thesis 13 of the Heidelberg Disputation of 1518 Luther asserted: "Free will, after the fall, exists in name only, and as long as it does what it is able to do, it commits a mortal sin." [19] In thesis 16 he strengthened his position: "The person who believes that he can obtain grace by doing what is in him adds sin to sin so that he becomes doubly guilty." [20] Individual acts of divine love *(actus eliciti)* are not sufficient, because they do not involve one's entire will.[21] The human self is a whole; therefore the essence of sin cannot be comprehended in individual acts; it resides in the person. It is for this reason that Luther's theology often speaks of "personal sin."

At that time even the Bible could not help Luther. He read it as "law" rather than as "gospel." When he heard that God was righteous, he was shaken to the very depths of his being.[22] Christ appeared to him to be the dreadful Judge of the world, who sat on a rainbow with a sword in his mouth — the way he was depicted in the cemetery at Wittenberg. "I was often terrified before the name of Jesus. When I saw his figure on the cross, it seemed as if I had been struck by lightning. When his name was spoken I would rather have heard the devil mentioned, for I thought that I would have to do good works until by them Christ had been made my gracious friend." [23]

Of course medieval piety also knew about the mercy of God and salvation through Christ. Jesus was not only the Judge, he was also the Savior. Luther could not have been unaware of that. But he could not acknowledge it, because he was completely caught up in thoughts of works righteousness. He could see only the demands of God — sharpened and intensified through Jesus — and the promise of grace could not free him as long as he still had to satisfy those demands.

Luther was thrust into new *Anfechtung* as he read Augustine and bumped into the doctrine of predestination. According to this teaching, God in his incomprehensible will has already selected persons either for damnation or for salvation—without considering their works. This robbed Luther of his last hope. He could no longer understand such a God; indeed, he actually began to hate God. As a result he was driven to the conclusion that he was numbered among the rejected rather than among the chosen. In his treatise against Erasmus he admitted, ". . . it gives the greatest possible offense to common sense or natural reason that God by his own sheer will should abandon, harden, and damn men as if he enjoyed the sins and the vast, eternal torments of his wretched creatures. . . . And who would not be offended? I myself was offended more than once, and brought to the very depth and abyss of despair, so that I wished I had never been created a man." [24] "When I dwell on these thoughts [about predestination], I forget everything else about God and Christ, and entertain the conclusion that God is a villain. In thinking about predestination we forget God; our *laudate* [praise] ceases and our *blasphemate* [blasphemy] begins." [25] In this 1532 reflection he recalled his own experience. He described it in even more moving fashion in his *Explanations of the Ninety-Five Theses* (1518): "I myself 'knew a man' [2 Cor. 12:2] who claimed that he had often suffered these torments, in fact over a very brief period of time. Yet they were so great and so much like hell that no tongue could adequately express them, no pen could describe them, and one who had not himself experienced them could not believe them. And so great were they that, if they had been sustained or had lasted for half an hour, even for one tenth of an hour, he would have perished completely and all of his bones would have been reduced to ashes. At such a time God seems terribly angry, and with him the whole creation. At such a time there is no flight, no comfort, within or without, but all things accuse. . . . In this moment . . . the soul cannot believe that it can ever be redeemed. . . . All that remains is the stark-naked desire for help and a terrible groaning, but it does not know where to turn for help. In this instance the person is stretched out with Christ so that all his bones may be counted, and every corner of the soul is filled with the greatest bitterness, dread, trembling, and sorrow in such a manner that all these last forever." [26]

Catholic biographers have not been the only ones to occupy themselves with the question of whether or not Luther's monastic struggles were pathological in nature. His religious struggles far surpassed those experienced by most people. Relatively few have wrestled with the demands of God with such intensity or engaged in self-analysis and critique so radically. But is it valid to judge a person's condition pathological merely because the measure of his or her mental and emotional experience is greater than usual? That would merely add credence to the saying, "Genius is madness." It may not be compatible with current theological vocabulary, but it *is* possible to describe Luther as a religious genius. We ought not imagine that Luther lived with unceasing *Anfechtung*—that would have been impossible for anyone to endure. Yet despite his robust nature, Luther was spiritually very sensitive. But sensitivity is not the same as illness. An ill man would not have been able to accomplish the work Luther did.

Another question is whether Luther exaggerated the emphasis medieval piety placed on individual works. That "Luther wrestled within himself against a Catholicism that was not truly catholic" is a widely-known thesis proposed by Joseph Lortz.[27] There is some validity to this, in that Occamism represented just one direction within the universal Catholic system; moreover, neither Augustinianism nor Thomism ascribed the theological significance to human works attributed to them during the late Middle Ages. Nevertheless, neither the Augustinian nor the Thomistic doctrines of grace radically excluded works righteousness. We are unable to say whether Luther might have avoided his *Anfechtung* if he had been trained in the Thomistic tradition.

We do know that in later years Luther was not satisfied with the rejection of works righteousness by Thomism or Augustinianism. Despite his emphasis on grace, Thomas was never able to relinquish the concept of merit, and so found it impossible to completely exclude works righteousness. Augustine was criticized by Luther for not having expressed himself clearly enough concerning the imputation of righteousness. To be sure, he came much closer to St. Paul than did the scholastics,[28] but still not close enough. "At first I devoured, not merely read, Augustine. But when the door was opened for me in Paul, so that I understood what justification by faith is, it was all over with Augustine."[29]

These factors make it impossible for us to subscribe completely to the thesis of Lortz. Luther not only wrestled within himself against a distorted form of Catholicism, he distanced himself from Catholicism *per se*. It was not a misunderstanding of Catholicism he attacked, even when many of his statements missed the mark. Only by calling Christendom back from a religion of works righteousness to a religion of grace could Luther fulfill his providentially appointed task. As it turned out, by pursuing this task he also served Catholicism by strengthening Augustinian elements, which in turn continued to spur new Catholic reforms.

Luther did not remain without pastoral counsel during his *Anfechtung*. Later he felt gratitude for those who had helped him. "Sometimes my confessor said to me. . . . 'God is not angry with you, but you are angry with God.' This was magnificently said, although it was before the light of the gospel." [30] On another occasion a brother comforted him with a single word: "God himself has commanded us to hope. Our salvation is faith in God. Why shouldn't we trust in God, who bids and commands us to hope?" [31] The word of a fellow Augustinian also made an impression on him: "Anyone who reflects on predestination without taking Christ into account, from his cradle on, will of necessity fall into despair." [32]

Luther's most significant encouragement came from Johann von Staupitz (1469-1524).[33] The son of an aristocratic Saxon family, he had been the prior of the Augustinian order in Tübingen, and in 1503 became dean of the theological faculty at the newly established University of Wittenberg. Staupitz was a Thomist as well as an adherent of mysticism, the *devotio moderna* exemplified by Thomas a Kempis. His position in the Observantism dispute has already been mentioned. It is in connection with this struggle that he first became aware of Luther. Luther's call to Wittenberg also seems to be traceable to him. Staupitz decisively determined Luther's course.

Presumably it was in September 1511 that the famous conversation concerning Luther's future took place under the pear tree in the cloister garden. Staupitz more or less pressed Luther into getting his doctor of theology degree. When Luther gave several reasons that were opposed to it and said he would die doing it, Staupitz told him that God could also use the counsel of doctors in heaven.[34] With monastic obedience, Luther submitted.[35] On October 19, 1512, Luther received the doctorate of theology and succeeded Staupitz as professor of Bible. Almost in the same month he began his lectures. Later in life, when he became overburdened with responsibilities, he repeatedly took refuge in the fact that he himself had not insisted on becoming a doctor; he had been called by others.

Staupitz also became Luther's pastoral confidant and counselor. It was to him that Luther regularly made his confessions, "not about women but about really serious sins. He said, 'I don't understand you'. . . . Afterward when I went to another confessor I had the same experience. . . . Then I thought, 'Nobody has this temptation except you,' and I became as dead as a corpse." Eventually Staupitz became aware of Luther's deep sorrow. Yet he was of the opinion that the *Anfechtung* served a useful purpose. Without it Luther, the proud academician, could easily become arrogant.[36] Once Luther wrote to Staupitz, "Oh my sin, my sin, my sin!" Staupitz emphatically rebuked him: "You haven't actually committed any real sins at all." He would have to do something really serious to call it a sin, such as murder his parents, blaspheme in public, scorn God, commit adultery, or the like. He ought not come before Christ with such "hobby horses and pet sins." [37]

Clearly, Staupitz considered Luther's *Anfechtung* to be the self-inflicted emotional despair of an overly zealous person. Nevertheless, he was able to provide real help. His words about true penance left a lasting impression. In a letter to Staupitz accompanying the *Explanations,* Luther gratefully recalled having heard him say, like a voice from heaven, "that *poenitentia* is genuine only if it begins with love for justice and for God and that what they [the scholastics] consider to be the final stage and completion is in reality the very beginning of *poenitentia.*" [38] "Your word pierced me like the sharp arrow of the Mighty." He compared it with the texts of Holy Scripture and found it to be confirmed. Where once the word *penance* was the most "bitter" word in all Scripture, it now sounded "sweeter or more pleasant" than any other.[39] But Luther went on and learned more about this, especially when Melanchthon made clear to him the original meaning of the Greek word that had been translated as *penance.*[40] The turning point, however, had come by means of Staupitz's remark.

Staupitz also helped Luther in his *Anfechtung* concerning predestination. "If you wish to debate predestination, begin with the wounds of Christ; then your debate over predestination will suddenly cease." [41] "Predestination is to be sought and found in the wounds of Christ—nowhere else." [42] Another unforgettable word for Luther was, "One must keep one's eyes fixed on that man who is called Christ." [43] At times Luther went too far in his thankfulness for the advice: "Staupitz is the one who started the teaching [of the gospel in our time]." [44] "I got the whole thing from Dr. Staupitz; he helped me to it." [45] Actually Staupitz never completely overcame the teaching of works, though he placed much more emphasis on grace. Nor did he join the Reformation; it was not possible for him to break with the old church.

On August 28, 1520, Staupitz resigned his office as vicar-general of the Augustinian order and went to Salzburg, where he became the abbot of the Benedictine Abbey of St. Peter. In a judgment of November 1523 he explicitly referred to Luther's followers as heretics. In a letter dated September 17, 1523, Luther affirmed his thankfulness, but also his regret that Staupitz had placed himself under the jurisdiction of Cardinal Archbishop Matthew Lang of Salzburg, an outspoken opponent of the Reformation.[46] In the end Staupitz—this honorable representative of the old faith, and moreover a Thomist—could not help Luther. From this point of view, as well, it appears that Lortz's thesis is in need of refinement.

8

Rediscovery of the Gospel

Luther found no release from his struggle to find a gracious God as long as he believed that he had to achieve this through his own effort. The Bible did not help him move any farther because he did not recognize the difference between law and gospel.[1] Even in the New Testament he read about the demands and the righteousness of God. Romans 1:17 states, "For in it [the gospel] the righteousness of God is revealed." Luther read even these words as requiring something, since he had already become convinced that grace could not be earned. In the 1545 preface to the first volume of his Latin works, Luther reflected on the beginnings of the Reformation and reported how he came to a new understanding of the phrase, "the righteousness of God."[2] He wrote:

> Meanwhile, I had already during that year returned to interpret the Psalter anew. I had confidence in the fact that I was more skillful, after I had lectured in the university on St. Paul's epistles to the Romans, to the Galatians, and the one to the Hebrews. I had indeed been captivated with an extraordinary ardor for understanding Paul in the Epistle to the Romans. But up till then it was not the cold blood about the heart, but a single word in Chapter 1 [:17], "In it the righteousness of God is revealed," that had stood in my way. For I hated that word "righteousness of God," which, according to the use and custom of all the teachers, I had been taught to understand philosophically regarding the formal or active righteousness, as they called it, with which God is righteous and punishes the unrighteous sinner.

Though I lived as a monk without reproach, I felt that I was a sinner before God with an extremely disturbed conscience. I could not believe that he was placated by my satisfaction. I did not love, yes, I hated the righteous God who punishes sinners, and secretly, if not blasphemously, certainly murmuring greatly, I was angry with God, and said, "As if, indeed, it is not enough, that miserable sinners, eternally lost through original sin, are crushed by every kind of calamity by the law of the decalogue, without having God add pain to pain by the gospel and also by the gospel threatening us with his righteousness and wrath!" Thus I raged with a fierce and troubled conscience. Nevertheless, I beat importunately upon Paul at that place, most ardently desiring to know what St. Paul wanted.

At last, by the mercy of God, meditating day and night, I gave heed to the context of the words, namely, "In it the righteousness of God is revealed, as it is written, 'He who through faith is righteous shall live.'" There I began to understand that the righteousness of God is that by which the righteous lives by a gift of God, namely by faith. And this is the meaning: the right-eousness of God is revealed by the gospel, namely, the passive righteousness with which merciful God justifies us by faith, as it is written, "He who through faith is righteous shall live." Here I felt that I was altogether born again and had entered paradise it-self through open gates. There a totally other face of the entire Scripture showed itself to me. Thereupon I ran through the Scrip-tures from memory. I also found in other terms an analogy, as, the work of God, that is, what God does in us, the power of God, with which he makes us strong, the wisdom of God, with which he makes us wise, the strength of God, the salvation of God, the glory of God.

And I extolled my sweetest word with a love as great as the hatred with which I had before hated the word "righteousness of God." Thus that place in Paul was for me truly the gate to para-dise. Later I read Augustine's *The Spirit and the Letter*, where contrary to hope I found that he, too, interpreted God's righteous-ness in a similar way, as the righteousness with which God clothes us when he justifies us. Although this was heretofore said imper-fectly and he did not explain all things concerning imputation clearly, it nevertheless was pleasing that God's righteousness with which we are justified was taught.[3]

To be sure, Luther here described a decisive point in his devel-opment, but this event dare not be isolated.[4] He himself empha-sized frequently and emphatically that he did not learn his the-ology all at once, but rather had to dig ever deeper into it.[5] This was true not only in the years after 1517, but also for the advances in his biblical understanding after assuming his professorship in 1512. His new understanding of Rom. 1:16 was above all else the result of an intense exegetical effort. The Reformation understanding did not grow out of visions or irrational experiences, but rather out of scholarly work. Luther examined the text thoroughly and thereby recognized an apparent contradiction: If the gospel reveals God's righteousness, how can it possibly be a power for our salvation, as well as declare the just shall live by faith? Luther found that the solution to this dilemma lay in the fact that the expression, "the righteousness of God," should not be understood actively as a subjective genitive, but rather passively as a *genitive auctoris*.[6] The righteousness of God is that which we are given (passively). In lecturing on Gen. 42:19 Luther was even more explicit in clarifying the difference between active and passive righteousness.[7] The righteousness of God understood passively corresponds to the mercy of God. In the same lecture Luther introduced a number of parallels in support of this linguistic usage, which, in distinction from Latin and Greek grammar, he considered characteristic of the biblical idiom.

Already in the September Testament of 1522 Luther translated as follows: "The righteousness that is valid before God."[8] This translation represents an interpretation of the original Greek text. It understands the act of making righteous or justification as the attribution of righteousness. Theologically one speaks of this as imputed righteousness or forensic justification. The expression *forensic* is borrowed from the judicial realm; God passes sentence on the sinner: "You are righteous; the righteousness of Christ is 'attributed' to you." In his exposition of Rom. 1:17 in the lectures on Romans of 1515 Luther did not mention this imputative interpretation[9] (which Luther himself, according to the preface to his Latin writings, also identified from Augustine), but he did mention it in his discourse on Rom. 3:7.[10]

According to Luther, one must even say that those persons declared righteous are not righteous in themselves, but rather by means of the righteousness that God confers on them. The act of making righteous consists of declaring righteous, and to declare righteous is to make righteous. Insofar as Christians look to themselves, they must condemn themselves as sinners; yet through faith in the attribution and promise of God they are righteous.[11] This is the meaning of Luther's famous formula, "simultaneously a righteous person and a sinner"—*simul justus et peccator*." [12]

In recent decades a lively discussion has arisen concerning the correct interpretation of Rom. 1:16f.[13] The outcome seems to be that Luther indeed focused his attention on that which was decisive, but remained somewhat one-sided in his interpretation. The phrase "righteousness of God" can certainly be understood as a subjective genitive. The "righteousness of God" is not merely a gift, but rather also a predicate of God himself (a truth, incidentally, that Luther never denied). God creates both righteousness and salvation. The *iustitia activa* and *iustitia passiva*, that which is created and that which is given, belong together. In this Luther recognized the content of the gospel.[14] In his exposition Luther placed primary emphasis on the individual; his exegetical insight was decisively oriented toward his personal dilemma. But one need not stand opposed to Luther today when one accentuates the worldwide dimensions of God's gift of salvation.

Though Luther's new understanding of the expression "the righteousness of God" was the result of intense scholarly investigation, it was much more for Luther than an academic insight. It was the decisive answer to the basic problem of his life — the search for a gracious God. Luther was a monk and a professor, but he was a professor in the original sense of the word—someone who *professed* something. His theology was more than an academic exercise; it was a confession of faith. For this reason Luther's exegetical discovery became for him an entry into "paradise itself."

The search for a "gracious God" is foreign to our modern age. Today we question instead the existence of God and the meaning of life. Yet in doing this we are not as far from Luther's problem of guilt and grace as we might think. The eradication of life's meaning inevitably confronts us in the forms of fate and guilt. The power that destroys meaning is human sin. Yet, in addition, there are tragic and senseless misfortunes that continue to occur through no fault of our own. The discovery of meaning in these events is possible only when we recognize the features of a benevolent power behind fate, a power that gives us the courage to attribute meaning to our lives despite the circumstances in which we find ourselves. Luther called this power *grace*. At its core, the question of God's existence is a question of grace. Only when the "ground of being" is grace is there something stronger than guilt and fate, and only then does life have meaning. Without "grace" we are overwhelmed by the burden of guilt that rests on this world; without "grace" the riddle of fate remains impenetrable. Without "grace" our lives are never straightened out—we are not "justified."

Luther's search for a gracious God and the answer he discovered are clearly stated in the following Lutheran teaching: We become righteous, that is, right before God, "by grace alone, through faith alone, by the will of Christ alone."

"By grace alone" means that there is nothing we can do to achieve our own salvation; it is absolutely and entirely God's gift. The uniqueness of Luther's doctrine of grace lies in this exclusiveness. During the Middle Ages persons believed they had to complete the work of grace with human accomplishments. Luther considered it to be an attack on God's honor to think that we had to "complete" God's action. We are also not capable of doing so. We all find ourselves in the situation of the lost son, who was no longer in a position to claim anything. Luther's faith was a radical renunciation of every form of achievement-oriented religion and a resolute affirmation of a religion of grace. At the heart of the gospel is God's amazing love for sinners. Of course this does not mean that faith abandons works; there is no faith that is not active in love. Our relationship to God, however, does not depend on our performance, but solely on God's loving will.

For this reason "faith alone," the second affirmation, does not extend beyond "grace alone." Faith itself is neither something we "earn" nor a "good work" that grace must complete. Even more disastrous is the misunderstanding that equates faith with intellectual assent to particular teachings or biblical traditions and sees the "sacrifice of reason" as a special form of merit. To believe is to fear, love, and trust in God above all things. Faith is the unconditional and absolute acceptance of God's offer. Faith is the radical renunciation of any attempt to flaunt one's achievements before God. Faith means restoration as a child in God's family. Every religious achievement, every legalistic form of piety is slavery and leads to bondage. The religion of grace, the piety of faith, means becoming a child again and leads to "the glorious liberty of the children of God." [15] Luther's painful experience of the servitude of legalistic piety led him to oppose, with holy zeal, any attempt to transform the state of being God's child into a condition of slavery.

The third affirmation is "by the will of Christ alone." This is where the truth and reality of the religion of grace and the piety of faith are determined. Without the revelation of Jesus Christ, Luther would never have risked believing in God's unlimited forgiveness. Jesus not only taught about God's love for sinners, he lived it and died for its realization, and God affirmed his death. In a world devoid of grace he displayed a love that, despite all outward appearances, remains stronger than any other power. On the cross sin apparently triumphed; yet that same cross became God's victory. God revealed his power in great weakness; he concealed himself in order to make himself known. In order to overcome sin, Jesus took upon himself the lot of sinners; everything he did was done for the sake of his brothers and sisters. The Son of God wants to make us into God's children. Luther grounded his proclamation of the justification of sinners "by grace alone" and "through faith alone" in his theology of the cross (a subject we will deal with at a later point). In faith the Christian is united with Christ and is shaped according to his likeness.

With this threefold "alone" Luther opposed the "and" of Catholic piety: grace *and* reward, faith *and* works, Christ *and* the church, Christ *and* the saints. We do not say this in order to pass judgment. Synthesis has its place in life. But it can easily lead to compromise. Luther sought to avoid this through his vehement statement of "alone." "Alone" excludes all boasting.[16] The righteousness we call our own is not really ours, but Christ's, which is imputed to us as "alien" righteousness. The self-righteousness that so often reigns in pietistic circles cannot call on Luther for support.

Authentic experience confirms Luther's insight that we remain both righteous and sinful (we are God's children and yet still sinners), even if we attempt to do what God desires of us, namely seek daily to overcome the sin that lives in us. Luther did not condemn Christian growth, but he did call us to a sober realization of our actual situation before God. Luther's doctrine of justification appears abstract and complicated to some; in reality it is quite simple and concrete. It is nothing other than a faithful representation of the real situation of a Christian before God.

When did Luther arrive at his new understanding of the "righteousness of God"? The impetus to provide an answer came in 1904 from Father Heinrich Denifle, an extremely learned man, yet someone filled with an intense hatred of Luther. He is credited with leading Protestant researchers to an energetic investigation of this question. Subsequent decades saw the publication of critical editions of the most significant writings of the young Luther: his lectures on Romans, Galatians, and Hebrews. The first document of his lecture activity, the *Dictata super Psalterium*, had already appeared in 1885 and 1886.[17] Scholars eagerly scoured these documents, seeking to uncover signs of the gospel's rediscovery. Traces were readily apparent, at least from his lectures on Romans onward. But difficulty was created by the fact that Luther, in the foreword to his Latin works, spoke of his "discovery" as occurring in 1518, immediately before his second exposition of the Psalms.

It was the opinion of some that the discrepancy could be attributed to a simple lapse of memory; Luther had merely confused the first and second expositions of the Psalms. But this highly improbable assumption is unnecessary. Luther wrote, "I had indeed been captivated with an extraordinary ardor . . ." (see above). With this "double pluperfect"[18] Luther looked back on a time before the beginning of his second lectures on the Psalms. Therefore this does not prohibit us from looking for signs of Luther's breakthrough in the *Dictata super Psalterium*. The period previous to the *Dictata* is quickly ruled out. The discovery must have taken place during his first lectures on the Psalms,[19] perhaps in connection with Ps. 32:1[20] or Ps. 36:7.[21] Erich Vogelsang's[22] opinion, that it occurred during Luther's exposition of Ps. 72:1,[23] has gained widespread support. At any rate, by following this line of thought one can conclude that the actual turning point for the Reformation was already established before the beginning of Luther's lectures on Romans in April 1515.

This thesis appeared to remain intact until Ernst Bizer questioned it anew in his book *Fides ex auditu*.[24] According to him, Luther's foreword does indeed point to a later date, namely the time around 1518. The texts after 1513, in this view, including those of the lectures on Romans, show that Luther had not yet attained the height of his reforming insight. To be sure, he had already rejected meritorious works, but he still did not know the certainty of salvation, and he still advocated a theology of humility as a means of appropriating grace. Not until 1518 did he actually come to the truly reforming conclusion that the only means of grace is the Word that is appropriated by faith alone.

Heinrich Bornkamm has investigated Bizer's thesis in an extremely thorough study.[25] Bornkamm concludes that Luther based justification on faith in the gospel when he gave his lectures on Romans as well (Rom. 1:17).[26] According to Bornkamm it is just as difficult to assert that there is no explicit theology of the Word in Luther's early lectures as it is to restrict him to a theology of humility. Moreover it was never the intention of the foreword to distinguish between a theology of the Word and a theology of humility. It focused only on the understanding of the "single word" —the righteousness of God. On the basis especially of Luther's personal witness in his letters, Kurt Aland has decided in favor of a later dating, specifically the time between February 15 and March 28, 1518.[27] So far the most extensive discussion of the question, both prior to and after Bizer, has been provided by Otto Hermann Pesch.[28] No definite answer has yet been given. My personal opinion is that the "discovery" took place within the period of the *Dictata super Psalterium.*[29]

The question of *where* Luther made his exegetical discovery is also still under discussion.[30] Luther refers to the place in five different table talks. In TR 3, no. 3232a it is localized "in this tower, in which the secret chamber of the monks is found." He meant the garden tower on the southwest corner of the Black (Augustinian) Cloister. It is for this reason that the discovery is often referred to as his "tower experience." In TR 3, no. 3232c the tower with its heated room *(hypocaustum)* is mentioned. In TR 2, no. 1681 we read, "This skill was inspired in me by the Holy Spirit *auf diss Cl.*" Georg Rörer, to whom we owe thanks for a great many transcriptions of Luther's sermons and lectures, deciphered the phrase, *"auf diss Cl"* as "on this *cloaca"* (with the superscription, "in the garden").[31] The word *cloaca* appears again in TR 3, no. 3232b.

The tradition is therefore not uniform; it has also been corrected. However, the earliest version might have been *"auf diss Cl." "Cl"* can only be an abbreviation for *cloaca,* not *"clarissimum"* or *"capitulum."* Grisar concluded from this that the Reformation discovery took place on a toilet. Of course psychoanalysis drew psychosomatic conclusions from this, and John Osborn made the most of it in his drama *Luther*.[32] But did Luther really speak of "this toilet"? Kroker presumed that Luther used the word *Scheisshaus* ("dung house"), which the transcript abbreviated as "*Cl*." But the word *Scheisshaus* can be understood in a figurative sense. Luther used it to mean human life in this miserable world. Kroker pointed to an obvious parallel:[33] How beautiful eternal life will be, since God has already given us so precious a gift as music in this life, this *Scheisshaus*. Oberman has identified a firm medieval tradition for this usage.[34] With that we should consider this question resolved.

A final question must still be dealt with: Was the discovery of the meaning of Rom. 1:16-17 really a discovery?[35] Denifle asserted that it was not. Of the more than 60 teachers of the Latin church whose writings he examined, none understood the righteousness referred to in Rom. 1:16f as punitive; rather, all understood it, as Luther did, as God's unearned and justifying grace. But in this Denifle overlooked the fact that Luther had primarily systematicians in mind when he used the expression, "according to the usage and custom of all teachers." Karl Holl also examined Denifle's sources. St. Augustine actually did understand the righteousness of God in Romans 1 as the righteousness that God accomplished in human beings, rather than as an attribute of God himself. But the Augustinian tradition was unable to maintain itself clearly in medieval exegesis. It always competed with the predominant tradition that considered punitive righteousness to be an attribute of God, a view espoused especially by scholastic systematicians. Since Luther was trained by scholastics, he read the texts through their eyes. In the school of Gabriel Biel, a clear distinction was drawn between the mercy and the righteousness of God; moreover, mercy was restricted by righteousness.[36] That which Luther referred to as a "discovery" in his foreword was neither an exaggeration nor a "lie" (Denifle).

The Developmental Period
of Reformation Theology

The years 1513-1517 were, in a certain sense, the greatest period of Luther's life.[1] In the tranquility of the cloister, not yet distracted by theological skirmishes or disturbed by polemics, he was able to devote himself to the fundamental principles of his Reformation theology. He gave himself completely to his work as a professor—someone responsible for his students—and to those issues that moved him most deeply.

The result is without parallel: a tremendous theological achievement accompanied by remarkable religious maturation. In his lectures on Romans Luther reached a level with which very little he later accomplished is comparable. Only to a certain degree can one label Luther's theology during these years as "pre-Reformation." Yet the question cannot be avoided whether one ought not give this "pre-Reformation" theology preference over that which came later. If the so-called theology of humility actually stood in contrast with the "theology of the Word," as Bizer maintained, then it would seem more appropriate to affirm the earlier form of the doctrine of justification than the later. We are right before God when we give God what God deserves. This humility, which gives God what God deserves, is no meritorious monastic work; indeed, it is nothing other than faith itself.

The first great document of these years, the *Dictata super Psalterium*, is the result of Luther's first lectures on the Psalms in 1513-1515.[2] It is to be distinguished from the second and unfinished Psalms lectures of 1519-1521.[3] Luther lectured two or three hours every week. The fact that in spite of this he completed the Psalms in just two years is a respectable accomplishment. In the second series of lectures he was only able to reach Psalm 22 within the same amount of time. The *Dictata* are not a unified work. (1) They contain the marginal notations to the *Psalterium Quincuplex* of Faber Stapulensis. (2) The interlinear and marginal comments in Luther's own copy *(Wolfenbüttler Psalter)* are the interpretations that Luther dictated to his students for the edition of the Psalms provided for them (thus the title, *Dictata super Psalterium*). (3) The so-called *Dresden Psalter* contains the textual exposition, the *Scholien,* that Luther delivered without following his own notes verbatim. (4) In the fall of 1516 Luther began work on an edition that was never published. Only two fragments still exist.

The version of the lectures that appears in the Weimar Edition, vols. 3 and 4, no longer meets critical standards; caution in one's evaluation is advisable before the complete appearance of the planned new edition. More recent difficulties have already been taken into account in the selections chosen by Erich Vogelsang and published in the student edition of Clemen.[4]

Luther lectured in the traditionally prescribed manner. First he provided a brief explanation of the words—the so-called glosses, that were immediately recorded by his students between the lines and in the margins of their copies of the text. Then he delivered the *Scholien*—sometimes short, at other times more lengthy expositions of important passages. As a basic text he used the Vulgate; during the course of a lecture he also often consulted the original Hebrew.[5] At that time Luther, like all medieval exegetes, was still convinced that Scripture had a fourfold meaning.

In his lectures on Galatians (1516-1517) he quoted a medieval rhyme about the fourfold meaning in connection with Gal. 4:24.[6] So, for example, in the *literal* sense, Jerusalem is the capital of Judea, in the *allegorical* sense Jerusalem is the church, in the moral or *tropological* sense it is the human soul, and in the *anagogic* sense it is the new (heavenly) Jerusalem. In the church it had long been believed that by applying this method one could extract a richer meaning from Holy Scripture, avoid much that was offensive, and reconcile many contradictions. Of course, not every passage was interpreted in the fourfold sense.

The fact that for Luther Christ was the speaker in almost every Psalm suggests to us today that he allowed the literal meaning of the text to be overshadowed by the allegorical. Of course he did not fail to employ the literal interpretation, especially in the later passages. The most significant meaning for Luther, however, was the tropological. In the Psalms, whenever Christ laments and finds himself in *Anfechtung,* this is understood tropologically as the experience of the Christian soul. Luther depended on this tropological sense.[7] He related Holy Scripture to personal existence. This is the essence of his hermeneutic, his teaching concerning the interpretation of Scripture. It was because he failed to find this point of departure that he distanced himself from the medieval exegete Lyra and from Erasmus. By the way, we may note that he borrowed the Christological meaning from Augustine.

When he wrote the *Dictata,* Luther was still developing, both hermeneutically and theologically. This is why much of what he said was still quite traditional. Nevertheless, Reformation insights grow within the *Dictata* and finally emerge clearly—as we noted in the previous chapter when discussing the exact time of his "tower experience."

The lectures on the Psalms were followed by lectures on Romans (1515-1516), Galatians (1516-1517), and Hebrews (1517-1518). Luther's ability to express himself with theological clarity increased from one lecture to another. Nevertheless, the lectures on Romans, particularly because of their subject matter, remain among the most significant of these witnesses. They were published in 1908 in a special edition edited by Johannes Ficker.[8] In 1938 they were brought out in a new edition in WA 56. Luther's original manuscript was found in the royal library in Berlin, where it had long gone unnoticed. A copy is preserved in the Vatican Library. In addition we also possess student transcripts that provide us with interesting insights into how Luther worked as he lectured.[9]

As in his Psalms lectures, he presented his comments both as glosses and as *Scholien.* Beforehand he consulted a number of sources, among them the commentaries on Romans by Thomas Aquinas, Faber Stapulensis, and Reuchlin. Luther began using the Greek New Testament of Erasmus almost as soon as it appeared.[10] In addition to the old sources, he also used the most recent contemporary literature. Together with his monastic colleague Johann

Lang (who in 1511 had been transferred along with Luther from Erfurt to Wittenberg, and in 1516 was called back to Erfurt), Luther improved his knowledge of Greek and Hebrew. Academically it can be said that Luther's lectures on Romans were among the best of their time.[11]

Yet what Luther offered as exegesis was more than an academic exercise. It was a new religious and theological direction. Luther's Christianity was intense and earnest, complete with treacherous chasms and abysses, yet filled with a passionate devotion to God's gifts and promises. It is, if we may say so, a heroic Christianity, not cozy and comfortable, but radical and strong. It was a flaming torch. One must put aside all subsequent conceptions of Luther as a portly housefather when one thinks of him as the creator of these lectures. As the prophet of a theology of the cross, he himself stood under the cross. This piety was born out of *Anfechtung* and refused even to spare the pious. The certainty of salvation had to be believed; it was not a static possession that stood at one's casual disposal. It existed *"sub contraria specie,"* under the very opposite of that which we accept as true. Those who truly loved God would even be ready to enter hell if such would be God's will.[12] In the pious language of the time, the willingness to enter hell was called *"resignatio ad infernum."* To be sure, those who resign themselves completely to the will of God cannot be far from God; they cannot be in hell, for hell is nothing other than the absence of God.

Through his work on Romans, Luther recaptured the vitality and depth of biblical terminology, which had generally been obscured in scholasticism through the use of Plato and Aristotle. It became clear to Luther that *flesh*, according to St. Paul, did not mean that part of a person which stood in opposition to reason and spirit, the so-called "higher self"; rather, it referred to the whole person, including reason, insofar as the person is apart from Christ. Similarly, sin is not a single act, an expression of sensuality and the "flesh" in the platonic sense, but rather a basic human condition to which reason also belongs. The "higher self" is also affected by sin. "Natural" persons do not recognize their sinfulness; they are hampered by love of self and self-obsession. Only "in Christ," that is, in a faith relationship with Christ, can sin truly be recognized.[13] Admittedly, Luther's discovery of the gracious character of God's righteousness can be dated prior to the beginning of his lectures on Romans.

Several examples may serve the purpose of introduction to this unique document. The letter to the Romans was intended to help persons come to an understanding of their sinful condition and recognize Christ's righteousness. "The whole purpose and intention of the apostle in this epistle is to break down all righteousness and wisdom of our own, to point out again those sins and foolish practices which did not exist (that is, those whose existence we did not recognize on account of that kind of righteousness), to blow them up and to magnify them (that is, to cause them to be recognized as still in existence and as numerous and serious), and thus to show that for breaking them down Christ and His righteousness are needed for us." [14] "For in the presence of God this is not the way, that a person becomes righteous by doing works of righteousness . . . but he who has been made righteous does works of righteousness. . . ." [15]

Schlatter began his critique of Luther's interpretation of Romans by taking issue with this summary. [16] Luther, he said, became entangled in negation, whereas Paul wanted to encourage action. But in the passage quoted, Luther himself affirmed that from Romans 12 on, the theme shifts to how we should act and what we should do on the basis of having received the righteousness of Christ. [17] Yet it is correct to say that Luther was concerned primarily with the elimination of self-righteousness in order to make room for the righteousness of Christ.

Luther explained Rom. 1:20, the familiar passage about the natural knowledge of God, in the following manner: Human beings should have come to know God through the works of creation; in fact, however, they have not done so. Instead of letting God be God (*divinitatem non nudam reliquerunt*), they reconstructed God to meet their own wishes and longings. [18] That is Luther's critique of all paganism, of every form of natural religion, and indeed, even of a degenerate Christendom. Here Luther anticipated Feuerbach's critique of all religion. The sin against the First Commandment, the sin that robs God of divinity, is the original sin. Even "today," Luther asserted, this spiritual and subtle idolatry, in which "they [Christians] worship God not as He is but as they imagine and think Him to be," is spread abroad throughout Christendom. [19] In a rather ingenious way he expanded Paul's critique of ancient paganism into a critique of all religion.

Luther considered Rom. 3:4 in great detail.[20] When we allow God the right to judge us, we are made righteous by God.[21] Note here his exposition of Rom. 4:7f.![22] We are righteous simply on the basis of God's declaration. For this reason our righteousness does not reside in us or in our power.[23] In actual fact we are sinners, but in hope we are righteous.[24] "Now, is he perfectly righteous? No, for he is at the same time both a sinner and a righteous man; a sinner in fact, but a righteous man by the sure imputation and promise of God. . . ."[25] The righteous person is not yet completely healthy, "but he has the beginning of righteousness, so that he continues more and more always to seek it, yet he realizes that he is always unrighteous."[26]

Conceptually there is some lack of clarity at this point. Two ways of seeing things are juxtaposed. On the one hand there is the notion of the "reality" of God's attribution, and on the other, the hope in which we now already have "the beginning of righteousness." But the juxtaposition between a purely attributed righteousness and the beginning of an existential righteousness is also found in the later Luther;[27] therefore one cannot view this as a sign of "pre-Reformation" theology. Concepts that seem to be in conflict can exist side by side in Christian life. Moreover, existential righteousness has its real foundation in the righteousness attributed by God.

The explanation of Rom. 8:26 is particularly impressive.[28] Luther opened with the statement: "It is not a bad sign, but a very good one, if things seem to turn out contrary to our requests. Just as it is not a good sign if everything turns out favorably for our requests."[29] He substantiated this thesis in three stages: (1) God is the Creator; we are creatures. God's thoughts are exalted as high as the heavens above human thoughts.[30] (2) God's will can be done only when our unholy will is broken. ". . . it is the nature of God first to destroy and tear down whatever is in us before He gives us His good things. . . ."[31] This corresponds with Luther's understanding of justification. (3) God is hidden. "For the work of God must be hidden and never understood, even when it happens. But it is never hidden in any other way than under that which appears contrary to our conceptions and ideas."[32] "For in this way He acted in His own proper work, which is the first example of all of His works, that is, in Christ. And then when He wanted to glorify Him and place Him in His kingdom, as the most holy thoughts of all the disciples ardently hoped and expected, He made Him die, be overturned, and descend into hell, contrary to all expectations. . . . And so He deals with all the saints." [33] If we cling firmly and steadfastly to this "alien work" of God, in the end God will give us more than we ever asked for.

This is Luther's theology of the cross, in which he set forth his most profound thoughts and deepest experiences. In this he felt particularly close to the mystic Tauler, who had spoken about the suffering of God with great clarity. [34] In fact he even borrowed expressions that had their origin in mystical thought, though in later years he no longer formulated them in that way. [35] Still, in its emphasis on self-denial and the suffering of God, Luther's theology of the cross did in fact touch German mysticism. [36]

In his treatment of Rom. 2:1 Luther spoke out sharply against worldly rulers who do not hesitate to engage in robbery and plundering, but often go unpunished. [37] Augustine was justified in calling rulers bands of robbers. [38] Frederick the Wise's quest for relics was criticized, [39] but his love for peace was praised. [40] Commenting on Rom. 13:1, Luther asserted that the Christian as such is exalted above everything worldly, but freely submits to earthly systems. [41] Incidentally he also used the same passage to call the leaders of the church to task. [42] Especially from Chapter 12 on, his exposition shows him to have been a critical observer of his time. Luther was conscious of his mission; he pursued his teaching office by virtue of apostolic authority, [43] and he committed himself to using contemporary examples in order to make Scripture understandable to his hearers and clarify his accusations. [44] The troublesome nature of his times, primarily within the church, once led him to sigh, "I am afraid that we shall all perish." [45]

Between October 27, 1516, and March 13, 1517, Luther presented his first lectures on Galatians. [46] We possess these lectures only in the form of a transcript. In 1519 he revised them for publication as the so-called *Small Commentary on Galatians.* [47] A second, abbreviated version appeared in 1523. In 1531 Luther lectured on Galatians for a second time; we have both the transcript by Rörer and the version prepared for publication in 1535. [48] Luther dearly loved Galatians; in a table talk of 1531 he called it his "Katie." [49] The letter provided abundant opportunities for setting forth the inadequacies of legalistic piety.

Immediately following the lectures on Galatians Luther began a series on Hebrews, which presumably lasted until Easter of 1518.[50] Here, too, Luther's original manuscript has been lost. That events during this period forced Luther to exchange the stillness of the cloister for public life is hardly evident from the text. Luther devoted himself completely to the theme, and it may well have been that the energy generated by his studies prepared him for the battles of the coming years. In contrast with the opinion he expressed concerning authorship in the foreword to Hebrews in the September Testament of 1522, at this time Luther still considered Hebrews a Pauline letter.[51]

A comparison with his lectures on Romans reveals that in the interim Luther had become more proficient with philological methods; he referred to the Greek text, and — in the case of Old Testament quotations — the Hebrew as well. He regularly consulted contemporary exegetes such as Faber Stapulensis and above all Erasmus; of the patristic commentators, Chrysostom appears to have been his favorite.

Luther directed the results of his linguistic work against the church's traditional understanding. Luther took a clear stand in the disagreement between Faber Stapulensis and Erasmus concerning authorship.[52] The concept of faith was given ever more prominence as the principal expression of our relationship to God; for some time Heb. 11:1 appeared to Luther to be a straightforward definition of faith. However, it was used not merely in a negative sense; it was also seen as "conformity" with Christ.[53] Christ was both *exemplum* and *sacramentum*, both an example and a sacrament.[54] In Christ's humiliation and death, God destroyed the reign of the devil and through this "alien work" accomplished his "own work."[55] The view that God accomplished his "own work" through an "alien deed" *(opus alienum)* is one of the basic elements of Luther's theology of the cross *(theologia crucis)*. The expression *"theologia crucis"* is found for the first time in the lectures on Hebrews, though the idea was already presented in the lectures on Romans.[56]

In the Hebrews lectures Luther also expressed himself more completely on the Lord's Supper.[57] The sacrament is directed to faith; only in faith does it become a power of salvation. Its gift is the forgiveness of sins. "Therefore it is a great thing to be a Christian and to have one's life hidden, not in some place, as in the case of the hermits, or in one's own heart, which is exceedingly deep, but in the invisible God Himself. . . ."[58]

Contrary to all the polemics, both old and new (Denifle), it has been established that Luther enjoyed the high respect of his fellow monks. In the fall of 1511 he had already been appointed as the monastery preacher, and in 1514 he also assumed the position of preacher in the city church. In May of 1512 he became the sub-prior of the monastery and the dean of its general studies program. In May of 1515 he became district vicar, that is, he was named supervisor of the 10 or 11 cloisters of the Saxon community.

In a letter to his friend Johann Lang, the prior in Erfurt, dated October 26, 1516, he described his heavy work load.[59] Often he could not even find the time to pray his daily breviary, and he had to make up the omissions of three weeks on a later day. Later he attributed the nervousness that often disrupted his sleep to days such as those when he neither ate nor drank.[60]

From the letters that he wrote as district vicar we know that Luther carried out his obligations very strictly; he concerned himself with even the most minute details, and he allowed no deviation from the rules of the order to go unpunished. He admonished Prior Lang to see to it that his cloister did not become a pub, and he demanded an exact report of disbursements from him.[61] He dismissed Prior Michael Dressel in Neustadt on the Orla because he was unable to maintain peace in his convent.[62]

But above all, the letters show him to be a pastoral counselor par excellence. He took his insights concerning the justification of sinners and the theology of the cross seriously, and employed them in his fraternal conversations. These insights were worth practicing both in his own life and in his life together with other monks. These letters are significant enough to be printed in their entirety, but we must satisfy ourselves with a few quotations.

A letter of April 8, 1516, addressed to Georg Spenlein, an Augustinian monk at Memmingen who was previously at Wittenberg, is filled with marvelous thoughts.[63] Luther was worried that this brother might not yet have become sufficiently dissatisfied with his own righteousness to rely solely on the righteousness of Christ. ". . . Learn Christ and him crucified. . . . Beware of aspiring to such purity that you will not wish to be looked upon as a sinner, or to be one. For Christ dwells only in sinners. . . . Accordingly you will find peace only in him and only when you despair of yourself [*fiducialis desperatio*] and your own works." [64] Moreover, he ought patiently to support his wayward brothers, and count their sins as his own. "The rule of Christ is in the midst of his enemies, as the Psalm puts it. Why, then, do you imagine that you are among friends? [65] For a brother who had failed Luther lent his fatherly support.[66]

In a letter to Prior Michael Dressel, dated June 23, 1516,[67] several months before the latter's dismissal on September 25, 1516, Luther counseled him not to "strive for visible peace in the human sense, but for the peace of the Lord, who is hidden under the cross and surpasses all understanding." The words must not be "peace, peace," but rather "cross, cross"; the very words with which Luther concluded the 95 Theses.[68] The true peace of God "cannot be felt, grasped, imagined; only he who willingly bears his own cross experiences this peace." [69] "There is however no better way of seeking it than by cheerfully accepting the *Anfechtung* — as if it were a holy relic — and give up wanting to seek and select peace according to your own discretion and thinking." [70]

That which Luther here called to the attention of his brother monks out of his heart, he expanded for the general public in his first German work: his exposition of seven penitential psalms, published in the spring of 1517.[71] Luther had prepared a new translation, using Reuchlin's insights. In a letter to Christoph Scheurl, dated May 6, 1517, he insisted that the expositions were not intended "for the refined people of Nuremberg, but rather for the coarse Saxons." [72] Nevertheless it was precisely in Nuremberg, where Staupitz had sent them immediately after their publication, that Luther's work received great approval. As an example of the piety expressed in them, the exposition of Ps. 102:8 may be quoted: "To watch is to cling to the eternal good, to look to it and long for it. But in this he [the Christian] is alone; no one is with him, for they are all sleeping. And he says, 'on the roof,' as if he were speaking of the world as a house in which the others are enclosed and sleeping, 'I alone am outside the house, on the roof, not yet in heaven, and yet not in the world. With the world beneath me and heaven above me, suspended between this life and eternal life, I hover in faith.' " [73]

We can gain an impression of Luther the preacher during these years from the nearly 50 sermons that we have from that time. Some are only preparatory notes written in Latin. They press for moral improvement, but are interesting especially because they reveal the fundamental thoughts of Luther's theological development during this period. Again we find the distinction between God's "alien" and God's "proper" works (Isa. 28:21).[74] God hides himself under this alien work in order to accomplish his proper work. "Man hides what is his own in order to conceal it, but God conceals what is his in order to reveal it. . . . And where is there any better will than that which, because it hides itself, removes what impedes the gospel, namely, pride?"[75] "For he who acknowledges himself to be a fool in the sight of God, to him this humility [*humilitas*] will be accounted as the highest wisdom."[76] The knowledge of God and Christ, that which is hidden, is precisely what the wise and the saints find most offensive.[77] "Is everything taken away from us and nothing left to us? Where, then, is wisdom? Where is righteousness? Where is virtue? Not in us, but in Christ. It is outside [*extra*] of us, in God."[78]

This is the famous Lutheran *extra*; our righteousness is an alien righteousness—the righteousness of Christ that is ours only in faith. Human beings reel against this. "For to come to Christ and go out from oneself is the great cross."[79] Human beings love security, spiritual certainty. Indulgences served this end by teaching escape from punishment more than sin.[80] This sermon is from February 24, 1517. Luther had already preached against indulgences on October 31, 1516.[81] The February sermon from which we have quoted closes with the plaintive cry: "Oh, the dangers of our time! Oh, you snoring priests! Oh, darkness deeper than Egyptian! How secure we are in the midst of the worst of all our evils!"[82]

Apart from the exposition of the penitential psalms, Luther's activities during these years were basically confined to his fellow monks, his students, and those who heard his sermons. The hour of the Reformation had not yet arrived. But the Reformation was preceded by a reform of the University of Wittenberg. Those who heard Luther detected that something new was in the offing. Scholasticism had given way to Pauline theology; Aristotle had been replaced by Augustine.

On May 18, 1517, Luther wrote to his like-minded colleague,

Prior Johann Lang in Erfurt, "Our theology and St. Augustine are progressing well, and with God's help rule at our University. Aristotle is gradually falling from his throne, and his final doom is only a matter of time. It is amazing how the lectures on the *Sentences* are disdained. Indeed no one can expect to have any students if he does not want to teach this theology, that is, lecture on the Bible or on St. Augustine or another teacher of ecclesiastical eminence." [83]

With but one exception Luther gained the acceptance and affirmation of his colleagues. In a letter of May 9, 1518, to his former professor Jakob Truttvetter in Erfurt, he named them.[84] The list included the jurist Hieronymus Schurff (1481-1554), Nikolaus von Amsdorf (1483-1565), who had been a professor at Wittenberg since 1511, and Andreas Bodenstein, called Karlstadt (1480-1541). Karlstadt had conferred the doctor's degree on Luther in 1512, but his relationship to him was always chilly. His intensive study of St. Augustine initially led him to join Luther, but later they went their separate ways.

Luther received strong support for his university reform from the private secretary and court preacher to the electoral prince Frederick the Wise, Georg Burckhardt—called Spalatin, after his home Spalt near Nuremberg.[85] Spalatin's historical accomplishment was that he won the electoral prince for Luther's cause. He had already taken a lively interest in Luther toward the end of 1513, and soon became the trusted counselor whom Luther consulted in all important matters. The table of contents for the first volume of letters in the Weimar Edition of Luther's works shows how active Luther's correspondence with Spalatin was.[86] It was through his efforts at reform in the university and through his contact with Spalatin, who stood close to the circle of humanists in Erfurt, that Luther became acquainted with the leading representatives of humanism. He shared his opinions about the Reuchlin debate with Spalatin[87] and corresponded with him about Erasmus.

We have already mentioned how indebted Luther was to the humanists in the field of linguistics. He was united with them in the battle against scholasticism, though much more for religious than for academic reasons. His theological misgivings concerning

Erasmus arose rather early. On October 19, 1516, he asked Spalatin to try to dissuade Erasmus from supporting the opinions of Jerome and attempt to win him for Augustine's understanding of Old Testament law.[88] On March 1, 1517, he wrote Johann Lang, "I am reading our Erasmus but daily I dislike him more and more." He approved Erasmus's critique of monks and priests, but feared that he did not sufficiently emphasize Christ and the grace of God. "Human things weigh more with him than the divine." [89] ". . . not everyone is a truly wise Christian just because he knows Greek and Hebrew." [90] Luther took no pleasure in judging Erasmus, but he was convinced that he had to be read carefully and critically. [91]

Luther's university reform was therefore determined only to a certain degree by humanistic ideas; more decisive was the motivation provided by the recovery of Pauline theology. A significant event was the disputation "On human power and the will without grace." [92] This disputation of September 25, 1516, served as the occasion for Bartholomäus Bernhardi of Feldkirch, a student of Luther's, to receive his *Sententiar* from Dean Karlstadt. The theses were drawn up completely in the spirit and language of Luther, and the disputation resulted in Luther's victory among the faculty. But Luther did not stop there. He planned a frontal assault on the ruling theology.

In connection with the promotion of Franz Günther of Nordhausen on September 4, 1517, Luther put forward a series of theses that he was required to defend, the "Disputation against Scholastic Theology." [93] These affirm Augustine (thesis 1) and condemn the dominance of Aristotle and his logic in scholasticism (theses 41-53). The scholastic doctrine of grace was sharply refuted (passim). In fact, thesis 99 asserted that everything which had been said was truly Catholic and in harmony with the doctrines of the church.

Yet the fact could not be ignored that a sharp attack had begun. Luther was consciously stating his views, and he hoped for discussion. He sent the theses to Christoph Scheurl in Nuremberg, along with the request that he pass them on to Eck at Ingolstadt.[94] He also sent them to Johann Lang at Erfurt and declared himself ready to debate them there; he longed feverishly for an answer.[95] In Nuremberg the theses met with mixed approval, but no debate was scheduled, either there or in Erfurt.[96] These theses contained the principles that could have led to a reformation of the church, yet it was not until the conflict over indulgences erupted that the world took notice.

———————————————————Part Two

THE OPENING YEARS OF THE REFORMATION

The Ninety-Five Theses

In Wittenberg, All Saints' Day (November 1) was an annual festival that attracted large numbers of pilgrims. On that day Elector Frederick the Wise displayed in the castle church the relics he had collected in his collegiate church of All Saints. We still possess the catalog of his collection. The most precious piece was a thorn from the crown of Christ, which he had inherited from his predecessor. In addition, the collection contained a piece of Jesus' manger, fragments of his diapers, some of the gold that the three Wise Men brought from the East, a chip of the rock from which Christ ascended into heaven, a lock of Mary's hair, and much more. A visitor to the exhibit could receive a plenary indulgence of approximately two million years. Luther had already preached against indulgences three times during the years 1516 and 1517, but without visible effect. That was about to change.

Around noon on October 31, 1517, the day before All Saints' Day, Luther, accompanied by his teaching assistant Johann Schneider of Eisleben, called Agricola, walked the short way from the Black Cloister to the castle church and posted on the north door a sheet of paper with 95 theses opposing indulgences. The notice was most likely printed rather than handwritten. In it Luther challenged scholars from Wittenberg and other places to an academic debate on the value of indulgences. Those unable to attend were invited to share their opinions in writing. The disputation was to take place out of love for the truth and in an effort to bring that truth to light.

Luther had advised no one in advance, primarily because he did not want the elector to be drawn into the affair.[1] The posting of academic announcements was a routine matter. The church door served as the university's bulletin board, and every professor had the right to invite fellow academicians to debates. In addition, Luther was under no obligation to provide his ecclesiastical superiors with copies of the theses. Nevertheless, on the very same day he wrote to Albert of Mainz, who was also the archbishop of Magdeburg, and to Bishop Hieronymus Schulze (Scultetus) of Brandenburg. The letter to the bishop has been lost, but more than likely its content did not differ much from the letter sent to Albert of Mainz. In his letter Luther pleaded with the archbishop to admonish Tetzel to cease preaching indulgences and to retract his own instructions concerning the issuing of indulgences. Along with the letter he included a copy of the 95 Theses, in order that Albert might "see how dubious is this belief concerning indulgences."[2]

Luther was obviously aware of the churchly significance of a discussion of indulgences, though he had, for the time being, decided to deal with it on an academic level. Certainly he did not post the theses with the knowledge that they would set "the Reformation" in motion. All that he awaited from Albert of Mainz was the elimination of an ecclesiastical abuse.

Indulgences (*indulgentia*) belonged to the institution of penance.[3] The New Testament speaks of repentance as the one-time turning of the heart (*metanoia*) to enter the kingdom of God. In the early church so-called deadly sins — idolatry, adultery, and murder—excluded sinners from the community of the church. Over the years casuistry gradually transformed these three deadly sins into forgivable transgressions. During the Middle Ages public confession was supplemented by private confession, which was personally made to a priest who provided absolution. This confession consisted of three parts: (1) heartfelt contrition (*contritio cordis*), (2) oral confession (*confessio oris*), and (3) satisfaction by works (*satisfactio operis*). In *satisfactio*, the older institution of repentance lived on.

In 1215 penance (confession) was elevated to the level of a sacrament, with new emphasis placed on the words of absolution spoken by the priest: *ego te absolvo*. In addition there was an effort to lighten the first and third parts of confession. (1) Instead of heart-felt contrition, a contrition of fear would suffice; this would under-score the sacramental character of the priest's absolution; (2) the deeds of satisfaction, which since the 11th century had been car-ried out immediately after absolution, were now understood as a means of reducing temporal punishment. The eternal punishment of hell was remitted by absolution. Since the punishment received in purgatory was also temporal, it became possible to shift most temporal punishment into the hereafter. Indulgence was the final step—the means by which one could attain the lessening of all temporal punishment, including that of purgatory. It is important to note that indulgences provided the remission of temporal pun-ishment and not of guilt; guilt was removed by absolution. Yet many medieval church statements did not maintain this distinction.

Indulgences first appeared during the 11th century in southern France, where they were instituted as a means of financing church construction (special indulgences). In the year 1095, Urban II granted participants in the Crusades a plenary indulgence. Hugo of St. Cher (d. 1263) based indulgences on the so-called "treasure of the church," that is, the surplus merits of Christ and the saints. This treasure of the church (*thesaurus ecclesiae*) was at the disposal of the pope.

Boniface VIII proclaimed a "jubilee indulgence" for the year 1300; all those who during that year visited the Eternal City and carried out certain prescribed acts of devotion would receive it. At first this jubilee indulgence was to be offered every 100 years, but soon the period was shortened to 50, and still later to 25. In 1476 Sixtus IV decreed that one could also acquire indulgence for the dead who were in purgatory; this indulgence was made pos-sible through the intercession of the church (*per modum suffragii*). A 40-day indulgence reduced the punishment of purgatory by the same amount that 40 days of penance would have done under the former penitential regulations. Since this rule was extremely vague, it provided the incentive to acquire as much indulgence as possible.

A certificate of indulgence was like a check that could be re-deemed in an emergency—once in a lifetime and at the hour of death. Contrition and confession were not required at the time an indulgence was acquired; they were only necessary when it was redeemed. Over the course of time indulgences proved to be a lucrative source of income for the church. Their announcement was controlled by the curia. Territorial rulers, however, had the authority to prohibit the implementation of indulgence programs in their regions.

The sale of indulgences was one of the worst ills of the medieval church. It was later prohibited by the Council of Trent (*sessio* XXI). However, one dare not forget that it also served cultural and social purposes. Elector Frederick used indulgence monies to maintain his university, as well as for the construction of a bridge over the Elbe River. The decoration of many famous cathedrals was also financed by the sale of indulgences.

The sale of indulgences by Tetzel, which had prompted Luther to post his theses, had a highly questionable history (though Luther did not know it at the time). Despite a lack of interest in religious matters and a totally unspiritual life-style, Albert of Mainz (1490-1545), a son of the Brandenburg elector Johann Cicero, had become the archbishop of Magdeburg as well as the administrative bishop of Halberstadt. He obtained the diocese of Magdeburg from the Wettin family, to which the electors of Saxony belonged. But that was still not sufficient for the young Hohenzollern prince Albert and his brother, Joachim I of Brandenburg (1484-1535). He also managed to obtain the archdiocese of Mainz (1514), and with it the titles of elector and cardinal (1518).

Even though such an accumulation of offices was forbidden by ecclesiastical law, Albert was able to obtain a dispensation from Leo X. The bribe he paid the pope for this was called a *compositio*. In addition to this *composito*, he was required to send *pallium* funds to Rome regularly, as did every other archbishop. The *pallium* was a cloth band that symbolized the office of archbishop and cost 20,000 gulden.

The total cost of obtaining the dispensation was the equivalent of well over one million dollars. Albert himself was unable to come up with the amount required, and he borrowed it from the Fuggers of Augsburg. In 1515 the pope accommodated him by allowing the sale of indulgences in the territories under his jurisdiction. Officially the proceeds were to go toward the reconstruction of St. Peter's in Rome; but Leo, who was constantly in debt because of his lavish life-style, used some of the funds privately. One-half of the indulgence money was to be sent directly to Rome, and the other half was collected on the spot by a commissioner representing the Fuggers.

In order to carry out this "holy business," Albert had enlisted the services of the experienced indulgence preacher Johann Tetzel, a Dominican father who had been successfully involved in this field for more than 10 years. Tetzel was a large, strong man who knew how to use the loud and vociferous language of the marketplace to accomplish his task. He charged an exorbitant fee for his services; even his servant seems to have received an unusually large allowance. Gossip had it that Tetzel was the father of two illegitimate children in Leipzig; there appear to have been other questionable incidents in his past as well. In his sermons he appealed to the softheartedness of his hearers: "Consider what your parents have done for you! And now, with very little money, you can free them from the punishments of purgatory!"

> As soon as the coin in the coffer rings,
> the soul from purgatory springs.

Such statements in Tetzel's propaganda bordered on blasphemy: the red indulgence cross with the papal coat of arms was as effective as the cross of Christ; he had already saved more souls with his indulgences than St. Peter had with his sermons; even if one had sexually assaulted the mother of God, he could offer forgiveness.[4] After speaking he was usually the first one to go to the coffer and obtain a certificate of indulgence.

Frederick the Wise had forbidden Tetzel to enter his territorial lands; he did not want the monies collected from the sale of indulgences to fall into the hands of the Hohenzollern family. However, when Tetzel moved his campaign to Jüterbog and Zerbst, close to the Saxon border, many of the citizens of Wittenberg went to acquire indulgences. With their certificates in hand, they returned to the parish church and asked Pastor Luther for absolution, without one indication that they were troubled by their sins.

As a serious pastoral counselor, Luther was deeply disturbed. But he did not decide to act until — probably at the beginning of October — he happened upon the instruction manual (*Instructio summaria*) for indulgence preachers, imprinted with the coat of arms of the archbishop of Magdeburg. In this manual Albert promised the complete forgiveness of all sins through the purchase of indulgences; neither contrition nor confession were required, even for those who wished to purchase indulgences for the dead. As a responsible teacher of the church, Luther felt compelled to say something. And so he decided to send the letter to Albert, requesting the repeal of his instructions, and to write the 95 Theses.[5]

The first thesis established in a concise way what penance was. "When our Lord and Master Jesus Christ said, 'Repent,' he willed the entire life of believers to be one of repentance." Penance, in other words, cannot be limited to a sacramental act. It is a basic orientation of the Christian life. The pope cannot remit sin, he can only affirm that it has been remitted by God (thesis 6). The only punishments he can remit are those prescribed by the church; this does not include purgatory (thesis 5). God has made priests responsible for our absolution (thesis 7). Canonical punishments are valid only for the living; one cannot postpone them for purgatory (theses 8-19). Therefore the pope cannot release anyone from the punishments of purgatory (theses 20-29). The pope can only achieve an amelioration of punishment for those in purgatory through intercessory prayer (*per modum suffragii*). It is a human teaching [not divine!] to assert that as soon as the money rings in the coffer, the soul is freed from purgatory (theses 26-27). How are indulgence and true confession related (theses 30-40)? Those who believe that their salvation is assured by indulgence certificates are eternally damned (thesis 32). Thesis 33 was directed specifically against the instruction manual: Persons cannot be reconciled to God through indulgences. So is thesis 35: It is unchristian to teach that contrition is not required to obtain certificates of indulgence. Quite the opposite is true: true contrition receives both the forgiveness of sin and the remission of punishment; it makes indulgences unnecessary (thesis 36). This also makes it impossible for the most learned theologian to commend both indulgences and true contrition to the people (thesis 39). True faith cherishes punishment; indulgences attempt to avoid it (thesis 40). Contrition and indulgences are therefore opposites. Moreover, indulgences also conflict with good works (theses 41-52). Love of one's neighbor and the giving of alms are better than indulgences (thesis 43). "Because love grows by works of love, man thereby becomes better. Man does not, however, become better by means of indulgences but is merely freed from penalties" (thesis 44). Those who have little to spare should not spend their money on indulgences, but ought rather to care for their own (thesis 46). Indulgences are useful only if one does not rely on them (thesis 49). The pope would rather have our intercession than our money (thesis 48); he would rather see St. Peter's lie in ashes than allow it to be built with the skin of his sheep (thesis 50). The preaching of the gospel is more important than the preaching of indulgences (theses 52-55). The "treasure of the church" is neither its earthly wealth, nor the merits of Christ and the saints, nor the poor, as Laurentius maintained, but rather, "The true treasure of the church is the most holy gospel of the glory and grace of God" (thesis 62). The current preaching of indulgences contradicts the gospel (theses 69-80). Theses 81-91, in order to preserve the honor of the pope from the disturbance brought about by the unrestrained preaching of indulgences, address several "shrewd questions of the laity." Why does the pope not decrease purgatory apart from money—purely out of love (thesis 82)? Why are the rules of penance, which have already been abolished, still considered valid for indulgences (thesis 85)? Why doesn't the pope, who is richer by far than wealthy Crassus, build St. Peter's with his own money (thesis 86)? Luther concluded with four powerful theses stated in the spirit of his theology of the cross: "Away then with all those prophets who say to the people of Christ, 'Peace, peace,' and there is no peace! (thesis 92). "Blessed be all those prophets who say to the people of Christ, 'Cross, cross,' and there is no cross! (thesis 93). Christians should be exhorted to be diligent in following Christ, their head, through penalties, death, and hell (thesis 94). And thus be confident of entering into heaven through many tribulations rather than through the false security of peace (thesis 95)."

Luther obviously intended to absolve the pope of responsibility for these abuses (see theses 20, 26, 38, 42, 50, 53, 70, 91). He was thoroughly convinced that he was teaching in the tradition of the church (see also thesis 7). He did not expound the entire riches of his newly acquired Pauline theology in these theses. Nevertheless, one cannot read them without detecting a new theological direction: Luther's ideal church was a church characterized by contrition, the Word, and love.

Over the centuries it has become a tradition to celebrate October 31, 1517, as the birthday of the Reformation. For some time, however, historians have been calling into question not only the date but also the actual posting of the theses.[6] In his letter to Albert of Mainz on October 31, 1517, Luther never mentioned a posting of the theses. The posting and the date (October 31, 1517) are known to us only from Melanchthon's foreword to the second volume of Luther's Latin works in the Wittenberg edition.[7] The foreword is dated June 1, 1546—after Luther's death.

In 1959 Hans Volz challenged the date and the supposition that Agricola accompanied Luther to the church. According to him the posting did not take place on October 31, but on November 1. In support of this Volz cited a letter Luther sent to Amsdorf on November 1, 1527, in which "All Saints'" is referred to as the day of the theses.[8] Others have refuted this position, pointing out that Luther also referred to the Vigil of All Saints, October 31, as "All Saints."

Several years after Volz, the Catholic church historian Erwin Iserloh asserted that the posting itself never took place. Iserloh's contention, which, incidentally, was meant to reinforce Luther's absolute ecclesiastical propriety, initiated an extensive discussion. We cannot present the details here.[9] The following comments must suffice: Luther's letter to Albert did not exclude a posting; the theses were enclosed with the letter as information. They were, from the very outset, developed for the purpose of academic debate rather than for submission to the bishops. Melanchthon was in fact not yet in Wittenberg on October 31, 1517, but in view of their close relationship over several decades, it is very unlikely that they never discussed it. Melanchthon's foreword contains a number of minor errors, yet on the whole it is reliable.[10] The arguments against Melanchthon's comment about the posting of the theses do not appear to me to be strong enough to label his view a legend. And finally, our Protestant celebration of the 95 Theses as the beginning of the Reformation is not dependent on their posting. The once popular view of Luther initiating the new age with resounding hammer blows is unfounded.

Luther waited in vain for someone to inform him of a disputation on the theses. Even the bishops of Brandenburg and Mainz remained silent. On November 11 Luther began to send copies of the theses to others, among them Johann Lang of Erfurt.[11] The result of this action came as the greatest surprise to Luther; it was not at all what he had anticipated.[12] The theses had been written for academic debate, not for the laity. Nevertheless within a few weeks they had been reprinted and circulated throughout all Germany, "as if angels themselves had been the messengers." That was the opinion Luther's contemporary, Friedrich Myconius (1490-1546), expressed in his history of the Reformation.

Luther himself spoke in retrospect (1541) of a mere 14 days passing before the theses were well-known, and he attributed this speed to the fact that the whole world had been complaining about indulgences.[13] No one, however, had "wanted to bell the cat," because the Inquisitors had threatened everyone with burning. "So Luther became famous as a doctor, for at last someone had stood up to fight." [14] "I did not want the fame, because (as I have said) I did not myself know what the indulgences were, and the song might prove too high for my voice." [15] But God had driven him into it like a blinded horse.[16]

By December the patrician Kaspar Nützel of Nuremberg had already translated the theses into German. Out of gratitude Albrecht Dürer sent Luther a collection of his woodcuts and engravings.[17] The old Franciscan Fleck, in his cloister Steinlausig near Bitterfeld, burst forth with the jubilant cry: "Ho, ho, the one who will do it is here." [18] In Luther's own cloister, apprehensive voices were raised. Dr. Schurff warned him, " 'You wish to write against the pope? What are you trying to do? It won't be tolerated!' I replied, 'And if they have to tolerate it?' " [19] Spalatin also had misgivings.[20] Luther would not want the elector to be drawn into the controversy;[21] it should not appear as if Frederick the Wise had commissioned him to attack Tetzel's sale of indulgences out of envy for Albert of Mainz.

But on seeing the theses Tetzel boasted: "I'll have the heretic burned within three weeks and send his ashes to heaven in a bathing cap [his ashes would be put into a bathing cap and tossed into the water]." [22] The powerful Dominican order became Luther's enemy, and Luther's former professor Truttvetter disassociated himself from him. Luther was particularly grieved that Dr. Eck of Ingolstadt also opposed the theses. The two of them had just been introduced to one another in a friendly way during the previous year by Scheurl; now in his writing *Obelisci* (little spear) Eck accused Luther of being a heretic and a Hussite. Wenceslas Link delivered Luther's reply of May 19, 1518, *Asterisci* (little star).[23]

Luther was not pleased with the widespread circulation of his theses among the laity. In order to place something more suitable into their hands he published the German *Sermon on Indulgences and Grace* in March 1518.[24] It was written with far more clarity than the theses: God asks nothing more of sinners than sincere repentance; there is nothing in the Bible about works of satisfaction. Indulgences are only for lazy Christians who do not wish to do good works. One ought not speak for or against indulgences.[25] Yet it was Luther's desire and counsel that no one obtain indulgences.[26] He was not certain whether souls could be freed from purgatory by purchasing indulgences on their behalf, but he did not believe it.[27] Moreover, he didn't place much importance on the fact that those whose business he had destroyed called him a heretic.

Luther had become conscious of the things that needed to be said in this little pamphlet for the laity during his preparation of his *Explanations of the 95 Theses (Resolutiones disputationum de indulgentiarum virtute).*[28] He presented this weighty Latin work to his ordinary, Bishop Schulze of Brandenburg, at the beginning of February 1518, with the request that he review it. The bishop was uncertain as to what action he should take. He waited until the beginning of April before authorizing Luther to have the *Explanations* printed. But because of Luther's trip to Heidelberg, the printing was delayed.

It was not until August 21 that Luther was finally able to distribute the completed copies. The *Explanations* was more than just a commentary; it also expanded the theses and developed them. Luther had studied hard to prepare it. He did not want his statements to be taken as definitive assertions, but as propositions for discussion. He repeatedly declared his willingness to respect ecclesiastical authority. But this did not hinder him from expressing revolutionary thoughts.

In May of 1518 Luther sent a copy of the *Explanations* to Staupitz, accompanied by a letter requesting him to have them transmitted to the pope. He reminded Staupitz of their conversation about penance. He also stated that he was in such poor health that Staupitz should not fear his violent death.[29] This was followed by an appeal to Leo X, to whom the *Explanations* were dedicated.[30]

His call for a debate had been justifiable.[31] He had previously approached several persons of rank within the church, but to no avail.[32] He now wished to submit himself to the judgment of the pope, and would accept the voice of the pope as the voice of Christ. He had not proposed anything that contradicted Holy Scripture, the teachings of the church Fathers, or the law of the church.[33] He might have erred, but he was not a heretic.[34]

In the *Explanations* many of the thoughts in the original 95 Theses are restated and dealt with in greater detail. He reaffirmed his statements on penance in thesis 1: The absolution of the priest assures us of the forgiveness that we have already received.[35] Where there is no faith in the promise of Christ, there can be no forgiveness. Without faith the sacraments cannot effect salvation.[36] The surplus merits of the saints, which are said to be the treasure of the church, do not exist, since no human being has ever satisfactorily fulfilled the commandments of God.[37] Papal authority must be respected and obeyed, but the conscience is not bound by the judicial pronouncements of the pope, including excommunication, if they are unjust.[38] The primacy of the papacy over the whole church did not exist from the beginning.[39] Luther rejected the medieval doctrine of the two swords—the spiritual and the secular—in the hands of the pope.[40] The church is not permitted to use the secular sword, even against heretics.[41] Errors must be disposed of with spiritual weapons. In view of the circumstances within the church, Luther declared near the end of the *Explanations*, "The church needs a reformation which is not the work of one man, namely, the pope, or of many men, namely the cardinals, both of which the most recent council has demonstrated, but it is the work of the whole world, indeed it is the work of God alone. However, only God who has created time knows the time for this reformation." [42] The 95 Theses did in fact introduce the Reformation of the church.

In these few months Luther not only published his *Sermon on Indulgences and Grace* and the *Explanations of the 95 Theses*, but also wrote a short explanation of the Ten Commandments,[43] a manual of instruction concerning the confession of sins,[44] the *Asterisci* against Eck,[45] the *Sermon on Repentance*,[46] the *Sermon on the Proper Preparation of the Heart for the Reception of the Sacrament of the Eucharist*,[47] and various other sermons. Those who are

worthy to receive the Eucharist are not those who consider themselves worthy on the basis of their confession, but rather those who
in faith rely completely on the forgiveness of God.[48]

11

The Heidelberg Disputation

In 1518, the same year in which Luther had published his *Sermon on Indulgences and Grace* and the *Explanations of the 95 Theses*, the Augustinians held their general meeting in Heidelberg. According to the rules of the order Luther, having concluded his term of office as district vicar, was required to attend. The journey had its dangers, for in December 1517 Albert had notified the curia of Luther's activities, and the Dominicans had also formally denounced Luther in Rome. Fearful that his competent professor might be seized by enemies, the elector provided him with a letter of safe conduct.[1] The Augustinians, also, stood by their controversial brother.

On April 11, 1518, Luther set out on foot, accompanied by his fellow monk Leonhard Beier. He arrived in Coburg on April 15, completely exhausted.[2] On April 18 he was received warmly in Würzburg by Bishop Lorenz of Bibra.[3] From there he traveled by wagon, arriving in Heidelberg on April 21. He had been assigned the honored task of presiding over the scholarly disputation that was a customary part of such chapter meetings. The disputation was conducted under his direction on April 26 in the great hall of the Augustinian cloister.

Luther himself presented the theses; Master Leonhard Beier, his traveling companion, defended them. Four parts of this "Heidelberg Disputation" have been preserved: (1) the theses themselves, (2) the arguments in support of the 28 theological theses, (3) an introductory essay, and (4) the arguments *(probationes)* in support of the first two philosophical theses. The subject was not indulgences, but rather much more Luther's views concerning law, righteousness, and the cross. This disputation has been referred to as the principal exposition of his theology of the cross.[4] In his introductory address, Luther called his theses "paradoxes" that he had acquired from St. Paul and his most trustworthy interpreter, Augustine.

The first 18 theses dealt with the law, good works, and freedom of the will. The law is in fact spiritual, but it does not lead to salvation (thesis 1). The good works of natural morality do so even less (thesis 2). Human works always appear to be beautiful and good, but they are nevertheless deadly sins (thesis 3). God humbles us by means of his law and through the sight of our sins, so that we appear to be nothing, and indeed are nothing. Thus humbled, we live in the hiddenness of God; that is, trusting solely in his mercy. So God carries out his "alien work" in us, in order to accomplish his own work. This alien work, through which humility and the fear of God are created in us, is our only merit.[5]

The connection between the doctrine of justification and the theology of the cross is clear. The cross and resurrection of Christ provide the original pattern or image of justification; in justification is realized conformity with Christ—the process of being fashioned in the image of Christ. The Christ event, understood tropologically, is consummated in the event of justification; in both instances the progression is through God's alien work to God's proper work. The righteous are not justified on the basis of their works; their works would lead to death, if they were not recognized and feared by the righteous (thesis 7). "But this is completely wrong *[perversitas]*, to enjoy oneself in one's works, and to adore oneself as an idol."[6] "Arrogance *[praesumptio]* cannot be avoided or true hope be present unless the judgment of condemnation is feared in every work" (thesis 11). "In the sight of God sins are then truly venial when they are feared by men to be mortal" (thesis 12). In Luther's opinion there was absolutely no place for freedom of the will (in questions of salvation): "Free will, after the fall, exists in name only *[res de solo titulo]*, and as long as it does what it is able to do, it commits a mortal sin" (thesis 13). He is only free to sin.[7] "The person who believes that he can obtain grace by doing what is in him adds sin to sin so that he becomes doubly guilty" (thesis 16).

But isn't this moral bankruptcy, ethical nihilism? Are human beings incapable of doing anything good? Luther obviously recognized this crisis for ethics. His response was, ". . . having heard this, fall down and pray for grace and place your hope in Christ in whom is our salvation, life, and resurrection." [8] "To say that we are nothing and constantly sin when we do the best we can does not mean that we cause people to despair . . . rather, we make them concerned about the grace of our Lord Jesus Christ" (thesis 17). For "It is certain that man must despair of his own ability before he is prepared to receive the grace of Christ" (thesis 18). Doing good deeds is humanly impossible in a theological sense, though not in a moral sense. Good works are valid on a human level, but not before God, not before a standard that is absolute. The deeds that God accomplishes through us are good, but not of themselves, because they cannot be separated from our sin. One can say it even more pointedly: The deeds that God accepts are good—that is, those deeds that we acknowledge as sinful and entrust to the mercy of God. In this way moralism and eudaemonism are completely excluded.

Luther's view appears to be complex, but basically it is quite simple. The apparent paradoxes prove to be true in experience. It is a question of honesty whether we acknowledge the reality of this experience or whether we reject it. Luther called this honesty *humility*.

We have already noted the connection between justification and the cross. In theses 19-28 it is even more apparent. Here Luther set forth the implications of his theology of the cross with complete clarity: "That person does not deserve to be called a theologian who looks upon the invisible things of God *[invisibilia dei]* as though they were clearly perceptible in those things which have actually happened" (thesis 19), but the one "who comprehends the visible *[visibilia]* and manifest *[posteriora]* things of God seen through suffering and the cross" (thesis 20).

In his proofs for thesis 19 Luther referred to Rom. 1:20, describing the invisible nature of God as power, deity, wisdom, righteousness, goodness, etc. He concluded, "The recognition of these things does not make one worthy or wise." [9] Of course this approach to understanding ought not be rejected *per se,* but without a theology of the cross the best insights can be applied in the worst ways (thesis 24). True theology holds to the *visibilia* and *posteriora* of God. With the expression *posteriora* ["backside"], Luther alluded to Exod. 33:23, where Moses was not allowed to see the face of God, but was permitted to look at him from behind. The backside of God is his humanity, weakness, and foolishness (1 Cor. 1:25); in other words, that which has become visible in the crucified Christ. "Because men misused the knowledge of God through works, God wished again to be recognized in suffering, and to condemn wisdom concerning invisible things by means of wisdom concerning visible things, so that those who did not honor God as manifested in his works should honor him as he is hidden in his suffering. . . . Now it is not sufficient for anyone, and it does him no good to recognize God in his glory and majesty, unless he recognizes him in the humility and shame of the cross . . . as Isa. says, 'Truly, thou art a God who hidest thyself.' " [10] "Philip [11] spoke according to the theology of glory: 'Show us the Father.' Christ forthwith set aside his flighty thought about seeking God elsewhere *[volatilis cogitatus]* and led him to himself, saying, 'Philip, he who has seen me has seen the Father.' For this reason true theology and recognition of God are in the crucified Christ." [12] These are the most significant statements of Luther's theology of the cross. What do they imply?

(1) The theology of the cross stands in opposition to religious speculation and theological conjecture. True theology is knowledge *a posteriori,* reflection after the fact about that which God has done. It does not live out of ideas but out of experiences. In this sense it is a "theology of revelation."

(2) The knowledge of God obtained from nature and history, often called "natural theology," remains ambiguous. Luther did not reject it, but he clearly recognized its limitations. We need but recall his explanation of Rom. 1:20 in the lectures on Romans. In nature and in history God appears not only as a providential source of life, but also as an agent of its destruction. Moreover, there is also the danger of confusing God with our own ideals. Natural theology is not sufficiently safeguarded from the temptation of constructing a "more appropriate" God. Left to themselves, human beings tend to use religion as a means of insuring their lives in this

world and the next. They worship a God of power, who is there to help them through difficulties and dangers.

(3) Contemplation of the cross of Christ preserves us from these religious distortions and illusions. The reality of the cross does not fit into our religious wishful thinking. It will always be "a stumbling block to the Jews and folly to the Gentiles." [13] The cross appears to reveal God's powerlessness rather than God's power. It is God's "alien work," to use Luther's words—a disguised revelation. But those who learn to look beyond the veil recognize within this "alien work" of God the path to his "proper work." Despite all outward appearances, the cross of Christ proved to be the most powerful disclosure of divine love. For countless people, ready to give up on life, or on ever making sense out of their destiny, the cross of Christ has become a sign of hope. "The longer I contemplate it, the more my burdens are removed from me, until full half are gone; for instead of one, two now endure the hardship, my thorn-crowned brother stands beside me" (Conrad Ferdinand Meyer). The love of God, which cannot reliably be discerned in nature and in history, has shown itself to be stronger than all of the powers of hatred and darkness.

(4) Nevertheless, this revelation of God's love always appears in disguise. It is not obvious to the eyes of all. It can only be seen by "faith." Only those who learn to take up their own crosses can recognize the love that is disclosed in the cross of Christ. Faith focuses on that which is hidden "beneath the contrary image" *(sub contraria specie)*. Faith must therefore always pass anew through *Anfechtung* to God, even as God comes through his "alien work" to us. In Luther's theology of the cross, faith is anything but "security" *(securitas)*. Rather than a "sacrifice of reason," it is the existential acceptance of God's gift.

(5) In the cross of Christ Luther discovered the law of divine activity. He saw the same law at work in the justification of sinners. The event of the cross is the original pattern or image of justification, not merely the foundation that makes it possible. It is in justification that conformity with Christ *(conformitas cum Christo)* occurs. Moreover, justification also moves through God's "alien work" to God's "proper work." God deals with all believers in the same way that he dealt with Christ. The act of justification

can be understood as the tropological meaning of Christ's cruci-
fixion.

Now let us look briefly at the remaining theses. In an exaggerated fashion, thesis 21 asserted, "God can be found only in suffering and the cross." [14] The cross of Christ, which fully comprehends
the knowledge of God, and the cross of the Christian belong together. Just as the works of creation do not lead to the knowledge
of God (thesis 19), but to a wisdom that merely increases vanity
(thesis 22), so too the works of human beings do not lead to the
attainment of righteousness before God (thesis 25). In the Heidelberg Disputation, "works" are understood both as the works of
creation (thesis 19) and as the deeds of human beings (thesis 25).

To Luther, religious speculation was just as reprehensible as
works righteousness. It is for this reason that in the philosophical
theses, which are all directed against scholastic Aristotelianism, he
maintained that philosophizing is dangerous if one has not first
become a fool in Christ (thesis 29).[15] The last of the theological
theses (thesis 28) is a splendid comparison of the love of God
and human love. "The love of God does not find, but creates, that
which is pleasing to it. The love of man comes into being through
that which is pleasing to it." The latter is the opinion of all philoso-
phers. Where the love of God is alive in persons, it reaches out
to sinners, the foolish, and the weak. Luther recognized the difference between *eros* and *agape,* which even Augustine had not
clearly seen.[16] "This is the love of the cross, born of the cross,
which turns in the direction where it does not find good which it
may enjoy, but where it may confer good upon the bad and needy
person." [17] "Sinners are attractive because they are loved; they are
not loved because they are attractive." [18]

The religious significance of the Heidelberg Disputation is far
greater than that of the Disputation Against Scholastic Theology,
in which all of the propositions were formulated negatively. Yet it
is no less forceful in its rejection of scholastic theology, which is
characterized also in the *Explanations* as a "theology of glory" and
contrasted with the theology of the cross.[19]

Luther returned to Wittenberg on May 15. In a letter dated May
18 he described the disputation to Spalatin.[20] The Heidelberg professors had debated with him in a friendly and unassuming manner,
despite the fact that his theology appeared foreign to them. Only

one of them, Georg Niger of Löwenstein, had blurted out angrily: "If the peasants heard that they would stone and kill you." But that remark had only elicited general laughter. Those from Erfurt seemed to find his theology offensive. Even his former teacher Usingen, who in 1512 at the age of 50 had joined the Augustinian order in Erfurt, withheld his approval. When a "doctor from Eisenach" (Truttvetter) received a copy, he placed a Theta (Θ), the first letter of the Greek word *thanatos* (death), before every thesis. Luther looked for him in Erfurt on May 8, during the return journey, but to no avail; a later conversation proved unfruitful.

The younger theologians were exceptionally enthusiastic. Among them were Johann Brenz, Erhard Schnepf, Theobald Billican, and above all the young Dominican Martin Bucer; all were men who later played a role in the Reformation. In a letter to the humanist Beatus Rhenanus of May 1, 1518, Bucer enthusiastically reported the content of the disputation and told of the impressive and winsome way in which Luther conducted himself.[21] He now placed Luther above Erasmus, whom he admired, because Luther openly and freely taught what Erasmus merely hinted at.[22]

It became clear to Luther that he could expect nothing more from the generation of his teachers. He wrote to Spalatin that—like Christ—having been rejected by the Jewish authorities, he would go to the Gentiles.[23] We can sense why the Heidelberg Disputation made a strong and lasting impression. Its concise and powerful formulations serve as a superb introduction to Luther's early Reformation theology.

The Initial Inquiry

Luther's letter to Albert of Mainz was initially delivered to his Magdeburg counselors, who forwarded it to the archbishop on November 17. Albert, who was then residing at Aschaffenburg, then submitted the 95 Theses to the jurists and theologians of the University of Mainz. They in turn recommended that he turn the entire matter over to the curia, since the granting of indulgences was primarily a matter of the papacy. Albert agreed, because he did not desire to get into difficulties with the Augustinians. On December 13 he notified his Magdeburg counselors of his decision; at the same time he instructed them to prohibit the "insolent monk" from making any further pronouncements about indulgences.

But word of this *processus inhibitorius* reached neither Luther nor Tetzel. Albert's petition must have arrived in Rome before Christmas, yet it caused no great stir. It was viewed as one of the "monk's quarrels," which were common occurrences, particularly between the members of rival orders. On February 3 a memorandum was written to Gabriel della Volta, promagistrate of the Augustinian order, instructing him to caution Luther not to make any further statements. We do not know whether Luther ever received these orders. In any case the Augustinians did not hesitate granting Luther the honor of appearing in Heidelberg.

In the meanwhile Tetzel had not remained inactive. On January 20, 1518, the Saxon chapter of the Dominican order met at the University of Frankfurt on the Oder. Tetzel, seeking the title of

Licentiate, debated 106 theses which—according to the custom of the time—had been drawn up by his advisor, a professor named Konrad Koch, also known as Wimpina. These theses were all directed against Luther's 95 Theses, though they displayed little understanding of Luther's concerns.[1] In opposition to Luther's 27th thesis, Wimpina and Tetzel roundly defended the jingle, "As soon as the coin in the coffer rings, the soul from purgatory springs." Moved by Tetzel's attack, the Dominicans formally denounced the impertinent Wittenberger at Rome on suspicion of heresy. This denunciation was far more dangerous than the action undertaken by Albert. The Dominicans were soon boasting that Luther would be burned at the stake.

In March Tetzel had several hundred copies of his theses sent to a Wittenberg bookseller, but the university students got hold of them and burned them. Luther was not amused by the students' action; it could only aggravate the situation.[2] On May 15 he returned from Heidelberg to Wittenberg, physically in much better condition than when he had left.[3] The very next day he entered the pulpit of the city church and preached a sermon on the consequences of excommunication.[4] This immediately caused great excitement. Individual statements were circulated and eventually reached Augsburg, where the Imperial Diet was in session. There they fell into the hands of the legate Cajetan, who dispatched them to Rome. Luther wanted to debate excommunication, but refrained from doing so on the advice of the bishop of Brandenburg. Nevertheless, after receiving a citation to appear in Augsburg, he rewrote the sermon from memory in order to clarify what he had really meant. This must have been published before August 31.[5]

The printed sermon was a milder version. Excommunication, or the "ban," meant expulsion from the church community.[6] However, the communion of believers is twofold: internal or spiritual, and external or physical. Ecclesiastical excommunication could only exclude one from the external community of the church; only those who separate themselves from faith, hope, and love are excluded from the spiritual community. Internal excommunication is decisive; without it the external excommunication of the church cannot exclude persons from the spiritual communion of believers, that is, from communion with God, Christ, and the true treasures of the church. Where repentance and humility are present, outward participation in the sacraments is not an absolute requirement for salvation.[7] If the ban has been imposed unjustly, one should not allow oneself to be dissuaded from doing what is right.[8] Yet one must accept it as an affliction sanctioned by God.[9] Under such circumstances the church still remains one's mother.[10] These thoughts, though revolutionary in their understanding of the church, were expressed by a man who still adhered to his church with deeply traditional devotion.

During this time Luther produced a Latin exposition of the Ten Commandments [11] and a foreword to his *German Theology*.[12] But his major effort was given to preparing the final manuscript of the *Explanations* for publication. They were printed on June 4. In the meantime he received a copy of 50 new theses drawn up by Tetzel, along with Tetzel's refutation of his *Sermon on Indulgences and Grace*.[13]

Luther chose not to reply directly to the theses, even though they threatened him as well as the elector with the stake. As a response to Tetzel's *Refutation*, within a few days he finished writing a work entitled, *Concerning the Freedom of the "Sermon on Papal Indulgence and Grace."* [14] It circulated so rapidly that by the beginning of July a second printing was required. Luther was not particularly satisfied with what he had written. Instead of taking Tetzel on seriously, he had merely played with him.[15] Tetzel, he maintained, had quoted every possible scholastic doctrine, but he had employed Holy Scripture "like a pig with a sack of oats." [16] Tetzel had declared the purchase of indulgences superior to giving alms, a blasphemy far worse than that of the Turks.[17] Any grand inquisitor Tetzel might send to Wittenberg would be welcomed with open arms. Nor should the elector be involved in the matter; he would never encourage heresy.[18] However, by this time the situation had become far more serious than even Luther suspected.

Toward the end of May the general chapter of the Dominican order met in Rome. The general of the order was Cardinal Cajetan. He took that occasion to award Tetzel a doctorate in theology—a sign that the Dominicans stood behind him. For a second time Luther was denounced before the curia by the Dominicans—this time with success. Proceedings were initiated. The papal specialist on doctrinal matters, Sylvester Mazzolini Prierias, was commissioned to prepare a theological judgment. He, too, was a Dominican. His refutation of Luther was very simple. Regarding the matter of indulgences, whoever maintained that the pope did not possess the authority to do what he actually did was a heretic. Then he proceeded to refute the first 92 of Luther's theses, primarily to display his theological superiority over the Wittenberg professor. He called his judgment *Dialogus*.

A citation ordering Luther to appear in Rome was issued to accompany the *Dialogus*. He was to appear for questioning 60 days after receiving it. Both documents were dispatched to Cajetan in Augsburg, and they reached Wittenberg by way of Leipzig on August 7. On the advice of his jurist friends, Luther immediately sent a message to the elector, who was at the Imperial Diet in Augsburg, asking him to intervene, in the hope that the hearing would be held in Germany. On August 8 he also wrote to Spalatin in Augsburg about the matter.[19] Then he prepared a reply to the *Dialogus*, which he completed in two days.[20]

In August he sent his *Reply*, together with Mazzolini's *Dialogus*, to be published by Melchior Lotther in Leipzig.[21] Luther's usual publisher, Grünenberg in Wittenberg, could no longer keep up with his prolific production. The *Reply* concerned itself primarily with Mazzolini's claims about the infallibility of the church, especially the papacy. Theoretically it was possible for the pope as well as a council to err, even if this had not yet actually occurred. Since there was as yet no definitive doctrinal statement of the church concerning indulgences, one could not prohibit their debate. Luther could be declared a heretic only if he opposed an official position.

Meanwhile in Rome Luther was already considered a heretic. This was due to the sermon he had preached on May 16 questioning the power of excommunication. Opponents of Luther who had heard the sermon extracted passages out of context, exaggerated them, restated them in the form of theses, and circulated them.[22] Luther did not discover what had happened until two months later, when he was in Dresden on official business connected with the order. While he was there someone eavesdropped on a private conversation he had with Hieronymus Emser, the court chaplain. On returning to Wittenberg he learned that statements he made had already spread to Augsburg. He then decided to publish what he had actually said in his sermon on the power of excommunication.

In the meantime Cajetan had already received the spurious theses, and he forwarded them to Rome along with a letter of the emperor in which Maximilian requested the curia to place the heretic under the ban. The request was granted, and Luther was declared a "notorious heretic." In his papal brief *Postquam ad aures* of August 23, Leo X ordered his legate Cajetan to arrest Luther immediately. In a second brief issued the same day, he demanded that the elector of Saxony surrender "the son of iniquity" to Cajetan. In a third brief he ordered the abbot of the Augustinian order, Gabriel della Volta, to imprison Luther and bind him hand and foot. Della Volta informed the provincial superintendent of the Augustinians in Saxony, Gerhard Hecker, of this brief, and announced that he too had cited Luther to Rome as a rebel against the order. One could only envision a terrible end to Luther's case.

The Hearing before Cajetan

Things did not happen as anticipated. Power politics intervened, as they did so often in the history of the Reformation. For the papacy of that day, political questions were always more important than purely religious concerns. And so the papacy itself played a major role in keeping Luther's cause alive. *Hominum confusione, Dei providentia;* history has a way of moving forward, impelled by human confusion and divine providence.

It was no secret; the days of Emperor Maximilian (born 1459) were numbered. In fact he died only six months later, on January 12, 1519, in Wels. His last public appearance was in August 1518 at the Imperial Diet in Augsburg. It was rumored that he drank only water, no longer wine, and the worst was anticipated. The Imperial Diet was to decide on a crusade against the Turks; nothing came of it.

Most of Maximilian's grand plans had failed. He now had one last great goal — the election of his grandson Charles (born 1500) as emperor. Charles was already the king of Spain and the duke of Burgundy. The bribes for the princes, their advisors, and other influential persons in order to achieve this were estimated at roughly one million gold gulden. Since Maximilian did not have the necessary funds, the Fuggers offered to finance the venture. The emperor was staying at their palatial mansion.

The curia adamantly opposed the election of Charles; he was considered far too powerful, and could threaten the Papal States from both north and south. The other candidate, Francis I of France, was also considered dangerous. Therefore in Rome serious attention was being given to the candidacy of Elector Frederick the Wise. He was one of the strongest German territorial princes, but held no international power.

On August 27 the elector had refused to endorse Maximilian's proposal for the forthcoming election. The curia could only hope that the elector would hold fast to his decision. The elector used this position to advantage. Several days later he visited Cardinal Cajetan, who was also at the Fugger residence, and requested that Cajetan hear Luther in Augsburg as a "father," not as a judge, and then allow him to return to Wittenberg unhindered. If Luther should be condemned by order of the pope, he himself would see to his punishment.

Obviously the elector had considered Luther's petition of August 8 seriously. Cajetan reported everything to Rome, and on September 11 received instructions to acknowledge the request of the elector. On September 20, Cajetan was able to present this new position before the elector. He in turn issued orders that Luther appear in Augsburg immediately. Luther himself was completely unaware of this background.

On September 26, Luther set out on his journey to Augsburg, accompanied by his traveling companion (*socius itinerarius*) Leonhard Beier—who had also accompanied him to Heidelberg and defended his theses at the disputation. Their first stop was Weimar. The elector, who had left Augsburg on September 22, was residing there. Luther preached in the castle chapel before the royal court, but we do not know whether the elector was among his listeners.

Luther received an electoral letter of safe conduct, several notes of commendation, and 20 gulden for the trip. On October 4 he arrived in Nuremberg and stayed at the Augustinian monastery. The prior, his friend Wenceslas Link, introduced him to several friends of Staupitz. He was disappointed that Christoph Scheurl failed to appear. The elector had requested the city council to send Scheurl along with Luther to Augsburg as legal advisor, but the letter had arrived too late and Scheurl had traveled to Aschaffenburg on business. Luther's monk's habit was in tatters, so Link presented him with a new one. It was important to present a respectable appearance before the high cardinal. Link then accompanied him to Augsburg.

Luther was very depressed at the outset of the journey. All along the way he had been warned that he would be no match for the Italian cardinal; he would be burned at the stake. "Now you must die, I said to myself." "What a disgrace I will be to my dear parents." [1] Yet from Nuremberg he wrote to his Wittenberg friends: "Christ is Lord in Augsburg, even among his enemies! Let Christ live and Martin die!"[2] Just before reaching Augsburg he experienced severe gastric cramps and was forced to take a wagon. On October 7 he arrived in Augsburg. There he stayed in the Carmelite cloister of St. Anna, where Johann Frosch — who knew Luther from Wittenberg — was prior. Luther was completely exhausted, both physically and spiritually. Nevertheless, immediately upon his arrival he had Link announce his presence to Cajetan. But the Saxon counselors who had remained in Augsburg after the departure of the elector forbade him to appear publicly before receiving a letter of safe conduct from the emperor and the Diet.

Luther received many visitors. The famous student of antiquity, Augsburg patrician, and imperial advisor Konrad Peutinger invited him to dinner.[3] On the same day, October 9, an Italian diplomat in the service of Cajetan, Urban de Serralonga, who had previously been an envoy to the court of Frederick the Wise, appeared at the monastery and attempted to persuade him to agree to whatever Cajetan might request. After all, he would only have to speak six little letters of the alphabet, *revoco*, "I revoke." He had taken the question of indulgences far too seriously; their chief purpose was to bring in money. Finally he asked Luther whether he believed the elector would use force on his behalf. "By no means," replied Luther. "But then where will you stay?" "Under heaven," retorted Luther. "Whereupon I dismissed him and he left," Luther wrote to Spalatin.[4] On October 11 the imperial letter of safe conduct arrived, and the next day Luther visited Cajetan in the Fugger mansion. Who was this Cajetan?

Cajetan had been born as Jakob de Vio on February 20, 1469, in Gaeta, north of Naples. He was therefore known as *Gaetano (Cajetanus* in Latin), after his place of birth. His name in the Dominican order, which he joined at the age of 15, was Thomas. He studied Thomistic theology and later became the greatest advocate and reformer of Thomism in the 16th century. In 1494 he had conducted a successful disputation with the celebrated humanist Pico della Mirandola. He received a professorship in Padua and subsequently in Pavia.

In 1502 Cajetan became the general of the Dominican order. In 1511 he defended the authority of the papacy against the reform council of Pisa, which had been instigated by Maximilian and Ludwig XII of France. As a countermeasure he persuaded Julius II to call the Fifth Lateran Council, and he energetically supported the (at that time) unpopular Thomistic doctrine of the infallibility of the pope. In 1517 he was made a cardinal by Leo X. Early in June of 1518 he received the assignment of representing the church as legate at the Imperial Diet in Augsburg. However, he did not achieve his primary goal — the initiation of a crusade against the Turks.

There was not a single word about Luther in Cajetan's instructions. Not until he arrived in Augsburg did he discover he was to interview Luther. The curia had not made a bad choice for this; at that time Cajetan was the best theologian in the service of the curia. He had already begun his commentary on the *Summa theologica* of Thomas Aquinas in 1507; it has been considered so significant that a contemporary edition, the *Leonina* (1888-1906), was commissioned by Leo XIII. Cajetan had concentrated primarily on the doctrine of the church. He was an advocate of the infallibility of the pope, and he maintained that the pope was not subject to any council. Cajetan later admitted that reforms were necessary, but insisted that a true reformation by its very nature had to be a papal reformation.

Not yet aware of Luther's 95 Theses, Cajetan had himself completed a study of the practice of indulgences in December 1517. On many points he came close to Luther, though he still advocated the doctrine of the "treasures of the church" and the right of the pope to dispense them. On receiving the assignment of interviewing Luther, he immediately immersed himself in his writings. Between September 25 and October 29 he had completed writing no less than 15 tracts on Luther's views. Cajetan based his interpretation of the "treasures of the church" primarily on the bull *Unigenitus* issued by Pope Clement VI on January 27, 1343.[5] This bull, he declared, was binding church teaching (*Dogma fidei*), which was actually not yet the case. There was, as Luther had rightly maintained, still no dogma on indulgences. The teaching on indulgences was first declared dogma by the November 9, 1518, bull of Leo X, *Cum postquam*, of which Cajetan himself was the principal author.[6] Only after this bull was it possible to declare Luther's teaching on indulgences heretical.

Before considering Cajetan's examination of Luther, we will look briefly at his subsequent development. He was often called on to serve as papal legate, and under Clement VII he eventually settled in Rome. It was Cajetan who, at Clement's behest, drew up the official documents opposing the divorce of Henry VIII of England. After Augsburg he was frequently engaged in refuting Luther's theology. Having realized that this task had to be undertaken on the basis of scriptural studies, the acknowledged interpreter of Thomas became an accomplished exegete. His goal was to wrest the Scriptures back from the hands of the Reformers.

Cajetan's interpretation was influenced by humanism. He endorsed the literal meaning of the text. He made use of canonical criticism. He recognized the spurious conclusion of Mark, and he questioned the authenticity of the letter to the Hebrews, of James, of 2 Peter, and of 2 and 3 John. After his death his works barely escaped being placed on the index of forbidden books. However, throughout his life he remained convinced that exegesis must agree with church doctrine as it is established by the pope. Therefore Luther's declaration that, "In the end Cajetan became a Lutheran," is not really true.[7] He was never able to accept Luther's principle that Scripture can even be used to judge church doctrine. Yet the serious attempt made by this opponent of Luther to understand Luther's concerns remains remarkable. He died in 1534 and was allegedly buried at the entrance to the Maria sopra Minerva so that, according to his own wishes, persons coming to the shrine would walk over him.

On October 11 Luther wrote a moving and courageous letter to Melanchthon.[8] In it he commended the Hebrew scholar Johann Böschenstein. The thought of giving up, perhaps forever, the company of Melanchthon and his other Wittenberg friends was difficult; but he would rather accept separation than recant. That same day the imperial letter of safe conduct arrived.

On October 12, Luther, accompanied by Link, Frosch, and three other monks, appeared for the first time before Cajetan, who was surrounded mostly by Italians. Luther had been instructed on how to conduct himself in the presence of a cardinal. He prostrated himself before Cajetan. When the cardinal motioned, he rose to his knees. Only after a second sign did he rise to his feet.[9]

Cajetan spoke a few friendly words with him, but then listed three demands: (1) Recant your errors. (2) Promise never to teach them again. (3) Refrain from all activities that destroy the peace of the church. Luther asked, "What do my errors consist of?" Cajetan named the 58th of his 95 Theses, which maintained that the merits of Christ and the saints were not identical with the "treasure of the church," over which the pope had control. This assertion, said Cajetan, was disproved by the bull *Unigenitus*. The second error was found in the *Explanation* to thesis 7 — it is not the sacrament, but faith in the sacrament that justifies.[10] Luther replied, "On this point I cannot recant." Cajetan pressed him: "This you must do today, or you will be condemned." At this the Italians laughed disdainfully, "after their manner." Returning to the first point, Luther explained that for him no bull was authoritative if it contradicted Holy Scripture. Moreover, the Scripture was to be preferred above the opinions of Thomas. Cajetan attempted to instruct him: "The pope is above the council and also above the Holy Scripture. Recant!" In order to put an end to the confused exchange, Luther finally requested time to reflect on the matter until the next morning. This was granted to him.

On the 13th of October Luther again appeared before Cajetan, this time accompanied by a larger group of Saxon counselors, by Dr. Peutinger, and by Dr. Staupitz, who had arrived in the meanwhile. They appear to have considered the situation dangerous. Luther presented a formal statement. He was not conscious of having taught anything against Scripture, the church Fathers, the decretals, or reason. However, as a human being he was liable to error. He would therefore submit himself to the verdict of the church, and was willing to defend his theses in public debate. If that was not acceptable, he wished to have his views submitted to various universities for their judgment.

The cardinal listened attentively, but once more drew Luther's attention to his pet theme, the bull *Unigenitus*. After a lengthy discussion Cajetan, well aware of the assurances he had given the elector, granted Luther's request to express his position in writing. Returning to St. Anna's monastery, Luther immediately sat down and composed a lengthy statement on his two "errors." On October 14th Luther appeared before Cajetan a third time, armed with this written response and accompanied by two Saxon counselors, Rühel and Feilitzsch, who had since come to the conclusion that the cardinal was not committed to conversing with Luther in the "fatherly" manner he had promised the elector.

Cajetan paid little attention to Luther's explanations, but promised to send them on to Rome. He was somewhat angry, and time and again he shouted, "Recant!" Luther also became louder and more vehement. Finally Luther said that if the bull *Unigenitus* actually declared that the merits of Christ were the treasure of the church, he would recant. Cajetan, thinking that he had won, eagerly seized the book and read until he came to the place where it said that Christ had by his passion acquired a treasure for the church. At that point Luther broke in: "Most Reverend Father, you should not believe that we Germans are ignorant even in philology. There is a difference between 'there is' a treasury and 'to acquire' a treasury." Cajetan was disconcerted, and once again yelled at Luther to recant. At that point Luther left. But the cardinal shouted after him, "Go and do not return to me again unless you want to recant." Luther vividly described all this in his letter to the elector, which was to be forwarded to him by Spalatin.[11]

At the time it was Luther's impression that Cajetan had given up all hope of persuading him to abandon his views. Apparently this was not the case. In Augsburg Cajetan is supposed to have said, "This brother has deep-set eyes; that is why he also has strange notions in his head."[12] After dinner the cardinal requested Staupitz and Link to join him in the Fugger mansion, and he deliberated with them for several hours. Staupitz should persuade Luther to recant. But Staupitz diplomatically removed himself from the affair: he had often tried to do just that, but he was no match for Luther in learning or ability. Cajetan was the only one who could deal with this "little brother."[13] Cajetan was not willing to converse with Luther again; however, he was prepared to set out the articles that Luther would have to retract. But he wished to take his time doing this so that Luther might become more amenable.

Meanwhile Luther gave no thought whatsoever to recanting, and he prepared to make a public appeal. On October 14th he wrote Karlstadt concerning Cajetan, "He is perhaps a renowned Thomist, but nevertheless he is an unclear, obscure, unintelligible theologian or Christian, and as incapable of handling this matter as an ass is at playing the harp." [14] Despite their audience with the cardinal, both Staupitz and Link were greatly disturbed by Cajetan's manner. Both of them secretly left the city on October 16. Prior to this Staupitz had solemnly released Luther from his monastic obedience, so that he would have the freedom to act without concern for the order.

Also on October 16, Luther wrote his famous appeal to Leo X,[15] "from the one who is badly informed to the pope who would do better to be informed," [16] as he expressed it. He could not agree to being examined before the tribunal in Rome, where things had become so treacherous that even "our very best pope" Leo had been threatened with assassination.[17] Moreover, the papal commissioners appointed to hear his case were prejudiced and uninformed. In addition, his physical condition would not allow such a strenuous journey.

Luther had his appeal notorized by several witnesses and posted on the door of the Augsburg cathedral. On October 17 he addressed a letter to Cajetan.[18] He apologized for his vehemence; he was prepared to remain silent on the matter of indulgences, provided his opponents also kept the peace, but he could not do anything against his conscience. Then on the next day Luther took his leave of Cajetan by means of a letter.[19] It would be senseless for him to remain in Augsburg any longer, since he could not recant. Cajetan should look kindly on his appeal to the pope.

Luther's friends decided to help him escape. On the night of October 20 he left the city through a small door in the city wall and mounted a horse that had been provided for him. One companion went with him. Years later Luther still recalled with horror that ride on a nag without any suitable clothing. On the first evening he arrived at Monheim (in the district of Donauwörth) and, no longer able to stand, fell on the straw like a dead man.[20] He reached Nuremberg on October 23 and was taken in by a circle of friends that until then had been called the *sodalitas Staupitziana*, but were now renamed *sodalitas Martiniana*. He was invited to

dine with Pirckheimer, and also became acquainted with Albrecht
Dürer. Unfortunately Dürer did not paint his portrait. One need
only compare the portrait of Melanchthon by Dürer with that by
Cranach to recognize what has been lost to us.

While in Nuremberg Luther received a letter from Spalatin, accompanied by a copy of the papal brief of August 23 ordering his
immediate arrest. At first he questioned its authenticity, but then
it became clear to him what danger he had escaped.[21] On October
31, the first anniversary of the posting of the 95 Theses, he returned
to Wittenberg. Within a few days he had prepared his Latin report
about what had taken place in Augsburg, the *Acta Augustana*.[22]
The elector delayed its publication, so it did not appear in print
until the beginning of December.

Luther was now certain that he would be excommunicated. In
order not to make things more difficult for the elector, he planned
to leave Wittenberg and eventually go to Paris, where the university had been able to preserve a certain freedom over against
the jurisdiction of the papal teaching office. On December 1 he
said farewell to his friends. In the meanwhile the elector had received a letter from Cajetan demanding Luther's extradition. But
on December 18 the elector ordered Luther to stay. The arrival of
Karl von Miltitz brought about a new situation.

For Luther the issue of papalism had been overcome in Augsburg. During the debate with Cajetan he had still attempted to find
an acceptable understanding of the treasure of the church in the
bull *Unigenitus* by making a distinction between "being" and
"acquiring." In the *Acta Augustana* Luther dropped all reference to
Unigenitus.[23] Canon law was not always in accord with Holy Scripture. Papalism was a juristic theory that could not be substantiated
by Scripture.[24] The assertion that the pope could not err and stood
above Scripture led to the demise of the church.[25] Luther came
to these insights thanks to his confrontation with Cajetan.

The Leipzig Disputation

While Luther was busy pursuing new theological insights, the intrigues of politics continued. The man who now believed his finest hour had come was Karl von Miltitz (1490-1529). He was born in Meissnischen and since 1513 had worked as a subordinate diplomat in the service of the curia. He had often been involved in purchasing relics for the Wettin princes. As a born Saxon he was confident that he would be able to accomplish more in the Luther case than had the Italian representative of Rome.

Therefore he was quite pleased when, in September 1518, he was given the assignment by the Holy Father of presenting the Golden Rose to Elector Frederick. He was not to bestow this decoration immediately, however, but rather to wait until he was certain how the elector would handle the matter of Luther. To this end he also carried with him a papal bull of excommunication against Luther, as well as a dispensation from the pope annulling the stigma of illegitimacy for the elector's two sons. With that they would be free to pursue higher ecclesiastical posts. Miltitz also carried various other documents, so that he was equipped for every circumstance. Officially he was authorized to act only in accordance with the approval of Cajetan. But when he arrived in Augsburg in mid-November, Cajetan was no longer there. So he set out for Saxony on his own, boasting along the way of the significance of his assignment. At the end of December 1518 he was able to arrange an audience with the elector at Altenburg. It was his intention, he announced, to reconcile Luther with the pope.

On January 4 and 5 conversations took place between Miltitz and Luther. The result was the following: (1) both parties were to refrain from dealing with the question of indulgences; (2) Miltitz would persuade the pope to designate a learned German bishop to specify the articles that Luther should recant. Miltitz attempted to have Archbishop Richard Greiffenklau of Trier appointed, but nothing came of it. At the conclusion of their discussions Miltitz invited Luther to dinner at the castle, embraced and kissed him, displaying tears and great emotion, but this failed to move Luther.

Miltitz had summoned Tetzel to a hearing in Altenburg in order to "wash his head"; he was to receive all the blame. Tetzel, however, would not venture the trip because of the widespread pro-Lutheran mood of the people. When Miltitz passed through Leipzig on his return journey, he arranged a formal meeting with Tetzel and threatened to denounce him in Rome for his immoral life-style and his questionable monetary practices. Tetzel did not recover from this: he retreated to his cell in the Dominican monastery at Leipzig, where he died on August 11, 1519—a broken man. Luther felt sorry for him. Before his death he wrote him a comforting letter, advising him not to worry about the sale of indulgences: "the child had a completely different father."[1]

On January 12, while Miltitz was traveling, Emperor Maximilian died. Now the Lutheran affair became just another means for Leo X to achieve his goal of blocking the election of Charles and winning over Elector Frederick. On March 29 he sent a gracious letter to Luther in which he invited his "beloved son" to Rome in order that he might answer to the pope in person and recant that which he had understandably refused to recant before Cajetan, according to the reports of Miltitz.[2] The brief was addressed to the elector, who did not deliver it to Luther because he thought it unlikely that he would go.

On July 21 Miltitz informed the elector in Frankfurt that he had been commissioned by Orsini, the papal legate, to announce that he would appoint a cardinal from among the elector's friends. The friend the pope had in mind was none other than Luther! The same tactic had been attempted with Savonarola. But the offer arrived too late. In the interim Leo had come to the conclusion that the election of Charles of Spain was inevitable, and further opposition was pointless.

For the time being Luther held "firmly" to the promise he had made at Altenburg. When a derogatory leaflet by Prierias fell into his hands he contented himself by reprinting it along with an ironic preface.[3] At the request of the elector he wrote a "paper" with the title, "Doctor Martin Luther's Opinions on Several Articles That Have Been Attributed to Him by Those Who Begrudge Him."[4] In that work he stated his views about the adoration of the saints, purgatory, indulgences, canon law, good works, and obedience to the church of Rome. The statements were not un-Catholic, though they displayed his liberation from traditional piety. One was to pay more respect to the commandments of God than to the commands of the church. Things were bad in Rome, but that was no reason to separate oneself from the church.

Luther kept silent for two months; only when he became convinced that his opponents were not holding to the pact of silence made at Altenburg did he resume publishing. He was so productive that he used two printers in Leipzig in addition to Grünenberg in Wittenberg. The Kawerau bibliography lists no less than 42 titles for 1519. Among them are the sermons on twofold righteousness, on marriage, on prayer and processions during Holy Week, the German exposition of the Lord's Prayer for simple laity, and the sermon on the contemplation of the holy sufferings of Christ. In addition he published the first volume of his *Operationes in Psalmos* and submitted his commentary on Galatians for publication. His explanation of the Lord's Prayer is among the finest documents ever written on the subject.[5] In his *Contemplation of the Sufferings of Christ*, Luther repudiated overly emotional, sentimentalized passion piety.[6] Reform of the university was making great strides. A Hebrew scholar had been added to the faculty, and since August 1518 Philip Melanchthon had been actively teaching Greek at Wittenberg.

The quiet progress of studies and publications was interrupted by the Leipzig Disputation (June 27 to July 16, 1519). Johann Eck (1486-1543), more precisely Johann Maier of Eck on the Günz in Schwaben, had emerged as a powerful theological opponent of the Reformation. From 1510 until his death he was the leading theologian at the University of Ingolstadt. He had studied in Heidelberg, Tübingen, Cologne, and Freiburg. He had achieved questionable fame through a defense of usury in a disputation at Bologna in 1515. Scheurl had sent him Luther's 95 Theses in an attempt to encourage a friendship between the two men. Instead Eck wrote his *Obelisci* against Luther, and so initiated a lifelong battle against the Reformation.

Both Eck and Luther sought an occasion for a public debate. Beginning in a friendly way, they arranged for a disputation between Eck and Karlstadt, who would take Luther's place. The disputation would be conducted in Leipzig. Karlstadt was in agreement with the arrangements. Despite the fact that the faculty in Leipzig had misgivings and had not yet given its final approval, on December 29, 1518, Eck published 12 theses directed more obviously against the views of Luther than those of Karlstadt. He not only focused on the first of the 95 Theses, but above all on Luther's assertion in his *Explanations* that at the time of Gregory the Great the Roman church did not yet possess supremacy over the churches of Greece.[7] He wanted to portray Luther as an opponent of papal authority.

After his opponent had broken the silence, Luther set forth his own 13 theses in opposition to those of Eck (Eck had in the meanwhile added another thesis to his original 12). Luther's 13th thesis reads: "The very callous decrees of the Roman pontiffs which have appeared in the last four hundred years prove that the Roman church is superior to all others. Against them stand the history of eleven hundred years, the test of divine Scripture, and the decree of the Council of Nicaea, the most sacred of all councils."[8]

Luther prepared for the disputation with intensive historical studies. Increasingly he became convinced of the suspicion already expressed in his conversations with Link,[9] that the Antichrist ruled in Rome.[10] He substantiated his 13th thesis in a special document he had prepared particularly for the event of a disputation with Eck, since it seemed that Duke George of Saxony would more than likely approve his appearance in Leipzig.[11] In it he proposed that the office of the keys was given not only to Peter but to the disciples as a whole. Peter enjoyed a primacy of honor but not a primacy of authority. Christ was the head of the church. The right to exercise authority in the church was only a human right and did not belong to the essential nature of the church.

Luther had determined to go to Leipzig even without the permission of Duke George, but he received it three weeks before the debate was scheduled to take place.[12] Eyewitnesses recorded Luther's arrival in Leipzig on June 24 in detail. The Wittenberg contingent arrived in two wagons; Karlstadt rode in the first, Luther and Melanchthon in the one that followed. Among the officials who had accompanied them were Nikolaus von Amsdorf of Wittenberg and Johann Lang of Erfurt. Some 200 Wittenberg students armed with spears and halberds escorted the wagons on foot, evidently also as a warning. As they entered the city a wheel on Karlstadt's wagon broke and he was thrown to the ground and injured, which was seen as a bad omen by many.

Duke George had made available the great hall of his Pleissenburg Castle for the disputation, and he ordered it decorated with costly adornments. The proceedings were solemnly opened on the morning of June 27. After being welcomed to the university the debators first went in stately procession to Thomas Church, where the choir sang an elaborate 12-part Mass under the direction of the cantor, Georg Rhau. Then they moved to the great hall of the castle, where they listened to a speech by the professor of poetics, Peter Schade Mosellanus, which made everyone drowsy. This was followed by the *"Veni sancte spiritus,"* with the entire assembly kneeling.

The actual debate began at 2:00 P.M. and lasted until 5:00. The lectern to be used by Eck was decorated with the insignia of fighting St. George; that of Karlstadt and Luther was decorated with the emblem of St. Martin. A civil guard was stationed at the castle gates during the entire debate in order to discourage unrest. During the first week only Eck and Karlstadt debated. At issue was the doctrine of the freedom of the human will. The arguments droned on in tiring fashion, both of them drawing extensively on the works of earlier theologians.

Eck was the superior debater. Above all he had a superb memory that allowed him to pepper his opponent with quotations from authorities. The interest of the audience waned as the days passed. However, everyone paid attention when, on July 4, Luther rose to speak.

Mosellanus has left us a report of how the participants struck him:

> Martin is of medium height. He is emaciated from care and study, so that anyone who observes him carefully can almost count every bone in his body. He is in the vigor of manhood and has a clear, penetrating voice. His learning and mastery of Scripture are astounding. In addition, in his life and behavior he is affable and friendly; in no sense is he dour or arrogant. He is equal to anything. In company he is vivacious and jocose—always so cheerful and carefree, no matter how vehemently his adversaries attack him, that one is hard-pressed to believe he could carry on so difficult a task without divine assistance.

Only in the heat of debate was Luther at times somewhat caustic. Concerning Eck, Mosellanus was far less complimentary. "Eck is a tall, square-set fellow with a powerful body and a full voice, equal to that of a dramatic actor or a town crier." He also possessed a marvelous memory. "But his mind is not equally adept. He looks more like a butcher than a theologian. In disputation he is unbelievably audacious and cunning." The Leipzigers appeared to be apprehensive about the fact that Luther, contrary to custom, wore a silver rather than a golden ring; worse yet, the ring contained a capsule that certainly contained nothing but the devil. They were also displeased that Luther had brought along a small bouquet of carnations that he sniffed contentedly whenever the flood of his opponent's words was particularly vehement.

The first day passed without incident. The topic under consideration was the 13th thesis, concerning papal authority and the interpretation of Matt. 16:19. Luther attempted to demonstrate historically that the primacy of the papacy had not been acknowledged in the church at the beginning. Furthermore, a communion of true Christians can exist apart from the church of Rome.

But on the morning of July 5 Eck portrayed Luther's views on papal primacy as being close to "Bohemian heresy," an accusation that was particularly cutting in Leipzig, where people still vividly remembered the horrors of the Hussite wars. Luther protested against this; he had never approved of the Bohemian schism from the one church. But Eck would not back off, and he repeated his accusations. When the assembly reconvened in the afternoon, Luther declared, "Among the articles of John Hus, I find many that are plainly Christian and evangelical, which the universal church cannot condemn; among them, for example, the statement: 'there is only one universal church.' " To this belong also those Christians not obedient to Rome. Articles of faith can be established only on the basis of Holy Scripture; only there can divine right be found.

These words exploded like a bomb. Duke George shouted with a loud voice, "The plague is upon us!" From that moment on he was a fierce opponent of Luther. The argument as to whether Luther could properly be labeled a Bohemian continued on July 6. On the afternoon of July 7 another critical point was reached. Luther had declared that Eck had to prove that a council, for example the Council of Constance, could not err. Hearing this, Eck cut loose: "If you believe that a council, legitimately called, has erred and can err, be then to me as a Gentile and a publican. Here I do not have to explain what a heretic is." Eck was then certain that he had accomplished his objective; he had now obtained proof of Luther's heresy.

After this high point, the succeeding days witnessed discussions of purgatory, indulgences, and penance. On July 14 Karlstadt reappeared to debate various questions concerning the doctrine of grace. On July 16 the disputation was rather hastily concluded, primarily because Duke George was expecting the arrival of a prince.

Luther left Leipzig convinced that Eck had not been able to prove him wrong. However, he was not at all pleased by the direction the debate had taken. "It began badly and ended worse," he wrote to Spalatin.[13] Without a doubt Eck had made more of an impression on the majority of those present than had Luther. The duke himself had sided completely with Eck; he presented him with the gift of a prize stag. Luther, whom he had entertained once during the debate, received nothing. Luther returned to Wittenberg on July 20, somewhat disgruntled.

Eck, on the other hand, remained in Leipzig until July 26 to relish his victory. He received tributes from the city council and from the university faculty. Duke George introduced him to his important guest, the Elector Joachim I of Brandenburg, whom Eck turned sharply against Luther. An attempt to achieve the same thing with Frederick the Wise failed, however. He did succeed in persuading the chief inquisitor—the Dominican Jakob von Hoogstraten (who had achieved dubious fame in the Reuchlin affair)—to join the cause against Luther. On his return to Ingolstadt he was acclaimed once again as a victor; he received a considerable sum of money from his university.

But soon Eck was forced to acknowledge that his "victory" was not as impressive as it had seemed. Polemical pamphlets directed against him began to appear on all sides. The humanists turned away from him in droves. The council clerk Lazarus Spengler of Nuremberg came out in support of Luther. A satire called "The Dressed-Down Eck," most likely written by Willibald Pirckheimer, made a laughingstock of him. Johann Ökolampad (Oecolampadius), at that time a colleague of Erasmus and later a reformer in Basel, wrote against him. More and more students flocked to Wittenberg, among them subjects of Duke George. This included even the chief secretary at the disputation, the rector of the Thomas school in Leipzig, Johann Graumann (called Poliander), the author of the hymn, "My Soul, Now Praise Your Maker!"

Meanwhile the reports of the Leipzig debate had been collected and sent to the universities of Paris and Erfurt for their verdict. The Sorbonne asked such an exorbitant fee (even in retrospect) that Duke George withdrew his request. Erfurt refused to pronounce judgment from the very beginning. In Bohemia Luther gained new allies among the followers of Erasmus. He was called the "Saxon Hus." He put aside several gifts sent to him by the Hussites, including Hus' book on the church, because he had not yet developed a sympathy for the Hussites. It was not until March 1520 that he read it. Deeply moved, he wrote to Spalatin on February 14, 1520, "We all are Hussites and did not know it. Even Paul and Augustine. . . ." [14] It was terrible to think that in Hus the evangelical truth had already been publicly burned for 100 years, and still no one dared confess it. At the time Luther overlooked the fact that Hus had believed in works righteousness. Yet even when he later recognized this, he maintained that Hus had died relying on the grace of Christ.

It was not easy for Luther to free himself from belief in the infallibility of the universal councils, but in taking this step at Leipzig he moved beyond Augsburg. The fact that his appearance at Leipzig won him new followers meant that in the end the disputation was a triumph not for Eck, but for Luther. Nevertheless, Eck had also been able to mobilize new opponents against Luther. The theologians of Cologne and Louvain declared Luther a heretic. This judgment was affirmed by Cardinal Adrian of Utrecht, later Hadrian VI, who as a teacher had previously influenced Charles V. Finally, it was a great detriment to Luther's cause that Eck had won over Elector Joachim I of Brandenburg, who allied himself with the religious positions of Duke George.

15

From Leipzig to Worms

The time between Leipzig and Worms was the high point of Luther's life. After surveying this period it is necessary to catch one's breath. Within approximately two years there would be a religious upheaval of undreamed of magnitude.

Luther's writings during this time made a unique impact on history. That which he had worked out in the quietness of the years before 1517 now reached full maturity. He became the "hero of the nation," though that was not his intention. In the heat of the conflict imposed on him he developed into a virtuoso in the use of crude and often vulgar polemic; yet his primary intent was always the same—the struggle for the grace of God. Even before the year 1517 he had found the only guarantee of faith in Holy Scripture. As the battle began Luther was increasingly forced to state this negatively as well as positively. Final authority resided neither in papal decrees nor in a universal council. This was Luther's path from Augsburg to Leipzig. His Reformation understanding was given its classic formulation in his stand at Worms.

Luther was not satisfied with the course of the Leipzig Disputation. In an attempt to clarify his position and defend himself against the continued attacks of Eck, in August of 1519 he wrote *Resolutiones* (Explanations) of the theses debated at Leipzig.[1] Eck not only responded to, but embraced Hieronymus Emser, whom Luther had taken to task. Then Eck traveled to Rome in order to instigate further action against Luther. Miltitz also surfaced again;

he brought the Golden Rose that he had left with the Fuggers in Augsburg. But his renewed negotiations were unsuccessful. This did not affect Luther, but the growing distance between himself and Staupitz greatly pained him.[2] Far removed from all conflict were the *Fourteen Consolations (Tessaradecas Consolatoria)* Luther wrote for the electoral prince during his severe illness. He was thinking of the 14 saints who played a major role in late medieval piety; Luther replaced them with reliable evangelical reflections on suffering and divine help.[3]

Several other edifying sermons followed: on preparing for death; the Lord's Prayer; penance; Baptism; the Lord's Supper; and excommunication. In the short and long sermons on usury he warned —in opposition to Eck—against charging interest.[4] Luther's advocacy of giving the chalice to the laity aroused the anger of Duke George, who, in turn, exhorted the bishops of Meissen and Merseburg to take prompt action.

When news of Luther's condemnation by the theologians of Louvain and Cologne reached Saxony, Duke George sought to press Luther into making a public offer of peace. But Luther stood firm. In his reply[5] he let it be known that he put as little store in this condemnation as he would in the curse of a drunken woman; both universities had already sufficiently embarrassed themselves in the Reuchlin case.[6] They would have to refute him with Holy Scripture or with rational arguments, and this is precisely what they had failed to do.

Among Luther's many publications during this period, the *Sermon on Good Works* is one of the most important.[7] It is often rightly included as being among the most significant Reformation writings. At the request of Spalatin he dedicated it to Duke John, the brother of the elector. Luther had begun it toward the end of February; on March 25 he wrote to Spalatin that if he continued to make steady progress, it would end up being a small book rather than a sermon—and he believed it to be the best he had written so far.[8] In fact it did become one of the finest presentations of evangelical ethics, as superb in practical matters as it was in theory.

Luther used the Ten Commandments as a framework for expressing his views, expanding them evangelically. In the preface he assured his readers that he was not ashamed of preaching to the "uneducated laity." With his "little *Sexterlin*" he hoped to do more for Christendom than the learned theologians with their thick tomes. "Whether the making of many large books is an art and of benefit to Christendom, I leave for others to judge. But I believe that if I were of a mind to write big books of their kind, I could perhaps, with God's help, do it more readily than they could write my kind of little discourse." [9] Luther chose the theme of "good works" because it brought to the surface many common misconceptions; accusations were being made already at that time that he held good works to be unimportant.[10]

Luther introduced the sermon with two theses: (1) Only those works that God has commanded are good; only those works that God has forbidden are sinful. Therefore one must hold fast to the Ten Commandments, and not seek out those works that human beings have determined to be good. (2) The first and greatest good work is faith in Christ. "For in this work all good works exist, and from faith these works receive a borrowed goodness." [11] There are many who pray, fast, provide endowments for the church, and lead good lives before others; but when one asks whether these deeds are pleasing to God, they do not know. Then the theologians come along and say that such certainty is not really necessary; but without this certainty the works are dead. Without faith, "their works are pointless and their life and goodness all amount to nothing."

When Luther exalted faith in this way and rejected works done without faith, his opponents accused him of forbidding good works; but it was really his intention to teach nothing more than the truly good works of faith.[12] When we rely confidently on God there is no distinction between pious and profane works; every deed is good even if it is as insignificant as picking up a single straw. However, where confidence in God fails, no deed is good, even if we should raise the dead or allow ourselves to be burned at the stake.[13] Since the works please God because of faith and not because of their own nature, they are all equal; there is no distinction between great and small.

Whoever lives by faith, that is, out of the confidence God himself creates, does not need to be instructed in doing good works; he or she already does "whatever the occasion calls for," whatever is at hand.[14] "For faith does not permit itself to be bound to any work or to refuse any work." [15] It is like the love between those who are truly partners in marriage: they do everything out of joyful hearts and without the need of ethical teaching. "Thus a Christian man who lives in this confidence toward God knows all things, can do all things, ventures everything that needs to be done, and does everything gladly and willingly, not that he may gather merits and good works, but because it is a pleasure for him to please God in doing these things. He simply serves God with no thought of reward, content that his service pleases God." [16] Where this trust fails, people turn to St. James, to Rome, to Jerusalem, do penance in this place and in that, yet never find peace.

Yet faith remains small in works; it receives its testing through suffering. There faith is not simply a matter of trusting in God and looking forward to receiving something better from him, as we are prone to think. There God is hidden, and yet he wants to help us. There God stands as though he were behind a wall, but through "the window of dim faith" God lets himself be seen.[17] But the highest degree of faith is to hold fast to God when he appears as if he wants to condemn us forever. "To believe at such times that God is gracious and well-disposed toward us is the greatest work that may ever happen to and in a man." [18] Luther had already spoken of this *"resignatio ad infernum"* in the lectures on Romans.

This then is the work required by the First Commandment, to place our entire trust alone in God. "For you do not have a god if you [just] call him God outwardly with your lips, or worship him with the knees or bodily gestures; but [only] if you trust him with your heart and look to him for all good, grace, and favor, whether in works or suffering, in life or death, in joy or sorrow." [19] The words are reminiscent of Luther's famous explanation of the First Commandment in the *Large Catechism*. Faith is trust in God; this is the heart of Luther's piety. Over against all external churchliness, true Christianity consists of this inner attitude that Luther called faith. Since life never stands still, faith never finds itself without opportunities for doing good works.[20] Indeed, even idleness finds its rightful place only within the activities and practice of faith.[21]

Admittedly not everyone is sufficiently mature to practice the ethics of faith. Many people must still be forced by the law to do that which is good and refrain from doing evil. They must be supported by those who are truly Christian and gently led to faith.[22] And those who stand in faith are not therefore morally perfect. Faith is not an ordinary work like other works; it lives entirely from God's mercy, and it knows that we are God's children and sinners as well.[23] So faith takes refuge in the love of God in Christ.[24] The First Commandment then leads us to Christ.

The Second and Third Commandments flow directly out of the First. We are to praise God's name, practice worship, and hear God's Word.[25] This includes opposing all injustice and combating every misuse of spiritual power. Even trials lead us to call on God's name, and who is not without trials, even for an hour? But the most dangerous trial of all is when there is no trial, and therefore we forget God.[26]

In his exposition of the Third Commandment Luther denounced the excesses of church life.[27] There were far too many festivals that only contributed to idleness and loose living. Absurd fables ought to be banished from sermons. Prayer ought not be mere prattle. One must pray believing that one will be heard, but not "prescribe to him the measure or the manner, the limits or the place" in which God must respond.[28] The disciplines of fasting and self-denial are also among the works called for by the Third Commandment, but they ought not be carried to the extreme of harming one's body.[29] The Old Testament command to keep the Sabbath is no longer binding, but a day must be set aside on which people can go to church to hear God's Word.[30] The Sabbath commandment can also be understood spiritually (allegorically): God wants us to rest from our works and allow his work to occur among us, even God's "alien work." [31] The first three commandments are interlocked like a golden ring.[32]

In his treatment of the Fourth Commandment Luther focused on the duties of parents and children.[33] He discussed evils in ecclesiastical and temporal government and denounced extravagance, prostitution, and exorbitant interest rates. The remaining commandments were expounded much more briefly, though their relationship to faith was constantly emphasized. Good works are the natural outcome of faith. Faith is not one work among others, but the foundation of works. There is no faith without works; nor are there isolated "good works" in the casuistic sense. In this sermon Luther overcame the medieval dualism that distinguished between holy and profane actions and between the ethics of monks and the ethics of the laity.

No less consequential for the existing social order was Luther's work of 1520, *On the Papacy at Rome, Against the Most Celebrated Romanist in Leipzig.*[34] While Luther was still busy with a response to the condemnation issued by the theological faculties of Louvain and Cologne, a new opponent entered the fray—the Leipzig Franciscan Augustine of Alfeld. At the beginning of May Luther heard of his Latin treatise concerning the divine right of the papal monarchy. Alfeld's work was very coarse and presumptuous, but conceptually weak.

Since Luther was already at work on his *Sermon on Good Works*, he instructed his teaching assistant Johannes Lonicer to prepare a refutation. But when Alfeld published his work in German, Luther, noticing that a number of people had been impressed, quickly composed a German response, "against the ass from Alfeld" (as he had called him in a letter to Spalatin).[35] Luther assumed a combative tone in his reply: "What good does it do when a poor frog puffs itself up? Even though he bursts, he will never be like an ox." [36] Evidently there were many persons who wanted to make a name for themselves at Luther's expense and who clung to him "like dirt to a wheel."[37] He could not bear to have the Lord Christ and his holy Word scorned and treated with such mockery.[38]

Luther expressed his views concerning the pope and the church in such fundamental terms that his refutation of Alfeld aroused immediate excitement and rapidly became one of his most important doctrinal writings. Was the papacy a divine or a human institution? Could one name the heretics who, despite their confession of the Christian faith, had been denied papal recognition by their bishops? Luther began by insisting that the papacy was not concerned about divine order, but rather with money above all else.[39] How much longer should the "drunken Germans" continue to put up with this? [40] Alfeld had argued that every community on earth must have a physical head; Christianity is such a community, therefore it too must have a head, and this is the pope.[41] Luther contradicted this. First, reason was not the judge of this question. Second, Alfeld's notion did not even follow reason; there were also republics without a monarchial head, such as ancient Rome or Switzerland.[42] Christendom was not a civic community, but far more "an assembly of hearts in one faith." [43] External unity made persons neither Christians nor heretics.[44]

Christendom was a "spiritual community," [45] whose life, according to Col. 3:3, was hidden with Christ in God.[46] The Holy Scriptures did not say that the external church, where it is by itself, is ordained by God.[47] The true head of Christendom is Christ alone, who resides in the heavens, and not the pope. Nor was the pope Christ's representative, for he did not carry on the work of Christ in the church, namely faith, hope, and love.[48] St. Paul knew nothing of the primacy of Peter.[49] Peter was a messenger [Bote] of Christ, like all the other apostles, for the word *apostle* should be translated into German as *Bote*.[50] "Not Rome or this or that place, but baptism, the sacrament, and the gospel are the signs by which the existence of the church in the world can be noticed externally." Where Baptism and the gospel are, there is the church, even if it rests only on children in their cradles.[51]

The opponents supported papal primacy by quoting Christ's words to Peter in Matt. 16:18-19. Luther did not consider this "proof text" to be valid. According to Matt. 18:18 and John 20:20, the office of the keys was not conferred solely upon Peter, but upon all of the apostles.[52] Moreover, the authority of the keys was something quite different from the authority to govern.[53] The promise, "the powers of death shall not prevail against it," was meant for true faith and not for an external institution. Furthermore the history of the papacy had been marked by numerous instances of subjugation to secular power.[54]

Christ's command to Peter was "feed my sheep." [55] That did not mean "tyrannize them," but "preach to them"; the pope did not do that.[56] Luther had been accused of being excessively "biting"; he was concerned that he had not been biting enough. "I should have pulled even more [at the sheep's] clothing of these raving wolves." [57] Nevertheless the papacy had to be supported, for it did not come into being without God's providence—though it was an angry providence.[58] Yet in spite of this forbearance, two things needed to be held firmly: (1) No one should dare establish new articles of faith such as that of papal primacy; (2) the pope should remain subject to Christ and allow himself to be judged by Holy Scripture.[59] If, however, the pope refused to acknowledge these two points (God forbid), then one needed to say "openly" that he was the Antichrist.[60] Luther concluded with an appeal to the civil authorities to put an end to the robbery of the pope.[61]

No sooner had Luther sent his refutation of Alfeld to press than a new work by his old opponent Silvester Prierias was brought to his attention. Prierias had begun writing a three-volume work against Luther, and he had just released the content of the third volume in advance under the title, *Epitoma responsionis ad Lutherum*. In it he declared that every doctrinal decision of the pope was infallible and that opposition to this deserved temporal and eternal punishment. He also stated that it was a sin to summon a universal council against the pope. Luther was so provoked by this "hellish book" that even reading it almost did him in.[62] It simply convinced him that the papacy itself, not just one particular pope, was the Antichrist. Adding his own marginal notations to the hastily-prepared work, he had it reissued[63] along with a foreword that concluded with the words, "Farewell, you wretched, lost, and blasphemous Rome; the wrath of God is upon you, just as you deserve; you have come to your end."[64] Filled with indignation, he launched into terrible threats: "If we punish robbers with the sword and heretics with fire, why do we not also take hold of these cardinals, these popes, and the whole mob of the Roman Sodom and wash our hands in their blood?"[65] It was the duty of the emperor, the kings, and the princes to take up arms and intervene.[66] By early June he had devised a plan that called on the emperor and the German nobility to engage in open warfare against the Roman tyranny.[67] Out of this plan came the work, *To the Christian Nobility of the German Nation Concerning the Reform of the Christian Estate*.[68]

This treatise was published in the middle of August in 1520 by Melchior Lotther in Wittenberg; by the 18th of August 4000 copies had already been sold. Luther shared this information with his friend, Johann Lang in Erfurt, who had reservations about its publication.[69] Many people liked the book; even in the elector's court there was no evident displeasure. Within a few days a second edition had to be issued. Even Duke George wrote to Rome, "Not everything in this book is untrue, nor does it speak of things that ought not be brought to the light of day. When everyone remains silent, then at last the stones will cry out."

The rapid distribution was no surprise. Luther spoke as an advocate of the German people. The serious struggles for reform of the late Middle Ages and the burdens of the German nation here found expression in the shimmering language and clear tone of the gospel. Luther, in the meanwhile, had become aware of what was happening in the world. He was well acquainted with the crises that threatened the church, the ecclesiastical practices and power; yet he also knew where the failures were among the people, in society, economics, and education.

According to his own declaration, Luther had discovered much about the situation in Rome from a Dr. Viccius, who was in Wittenberg during the time Luther was writing his treatise.[70] Viccius had been Reuchlin's representative in Rome during his dealings with Hoogstraten, and was well-versed in Roman practices. His real name was van der Wick, and he later became a respected evangelical lawyer in Bremen. Luther's counsel in legal matters was his friend and colleague Schurff. Surely Luther must also have read Hutten's dialog, *Vadiscus sive Trias Romana*, which denounced the vices of Rome. But by comparison his own treatise is livelier and much better informed. It is not true that Luther first became consciously German through Hutten. National pride had already been apparent in his appearance before Cajetan, and it grew as Luther became increasingly aware of Rome's presumptuousness.

Shortly before sending his treatise to press, Luther had, on June 23, 1520, sent the manuscript to his friend Nikolaus von Amsdorf for examination. Amsdorf (1483-1565) had been born in Torgau, was a member of the Saxon nobility, and was at the time canon of the cathedral in Wittenberg. He had joined Luther in 1517 and had accompanied him to Leipzig in 1519 and to Worms in 1521. He worked as a reformer in Magdeburg, and in 1541 was installed by Luther as the evangelical bishop in Naumburg. After Luther's death he belonged to the so-called Gnesio-Lutherans who, in opposition to Melanchthon, claimed to represent unadulterated Lutheranism. Luther's letter to him is a masterpiece. "The time for silence is past, and the time to speak has come." "Perhaps I owe my God and the world another work of folly." "I must fulfill the proverb, 'Whatever the world does, a monk must be in the picture, even if he has to be painted in.'" "Since I am not only a fool, but also a sworn doctor of Holy Scripture, I am glad for the opportunity to fulfill my doctor's oath, even in the guise of a fool." "God help us to seek not our own glory but his alone." [71] The content of the letter was included in the book.

Luther opened his treatise *To the Christian Nobility of the German Nation Concerning the Reform of the Christian Estate* by addressing his most illustrious, all-powerful, imperial majesty, and the Christian nobility of the German nation. Since the councils had not accomplished anything, he set his hope on the secular authorities, particularly the emperor, the "young man of noble birth." He warned against self-confident activism when beginning the work of reform: "For God cannot and will not suffer that a good work begin by relying upon one's own power and reason," even if all the power in the world were theirs.[72] This was the very reason the "precious princes," Emperor Frederick I, Frederick II, and so many other German emperors were so "wretchedly" treated by the popes, put down, and trodden under foot. "It may be that they relied on their own might more than on God. . . . We must tackle this job by renouncing trust in physical force and trusting humbly in God. . . . Otherwise . . . [there will be] such confusion that the whole world will swim in blood." This was not a cause that could be helped by war and bloodshed.[73]

Luther did not repeat the threat he made in his response to the *Epitoma* of Silvester. To the contrary, he rejected it as a wrong approach. The Romanists (Luther's term for the papal court) had built three walls with which they had protected themselves against every attempt at reformation.[74] The first wall was the thesis that spiritual power is superior to secular power. The second wall was the thesis that the pope alone had the right to interpret Holy Scripture. The third wall was the thesis that only the pope could convene a council. "May God help us, and give us just one of those trumpets with which the walls of Jericho were overthrown to blast down these walls of straw and paper in the same way." [75]

Against the first wall Luther pitted the priesthood of all believers: "all Christians are truly of the spiritual estate, and there is no difference among them except that of office." [76] The external rite of ordination and priestly garb might indeed make one a hypocrite and a puppet, but never a Christian or a spiritual person. All who had come "out of the water of baptism" had the same spiritual authority, but they assigned it to someone from their midst, who exercised the office in the congregation on their behalf.[77] Priests did not have a *character indelebilis* (indelible character) that was presumably conferred on them through their ordination. When they no longer fulfilled the duties of their office they became farmers or citizens like everyone else. The only distinction was in the office, not in the estate.[78] Civil authorities also held an office, namely that of exercising secular power. When those who exercised this office now saw that spiritual authority was breaking down, they had to come to its aid, even as each member of a physical body supports the others.[79] In such situations the secular authorities were exercising their emergency authority in the church. Occam had already expressed these thoughts in the late Middle Ages; they became a reality with the establishment of the evangelical territorial churches. Church and state together formed the *Corpus Christianum*,[80] therefore the church could not claim special rights or privileges. Crimes of the clergy had to be punished just as those of the laity were. In its existing form Christendom reflected the image of "the Antichrist, or at any rate that [of his] forerunner. . . ."[81]

The second wall was no more than a "fancied fable" for which one could not point to a single letter of Scripture.[82] Had not the pope erred many times?[83] If it were true that the pope was always right, they would have to have confessed, "I believe in the pope at Rome."[84] "It is the duty of every Christian to espouse the cause of the faith, to understand and defend it, and to denounce every error."[85]

The third wall collapsed on its own along with the other two.[86] Neither the Apostolic Council[87] nor the Council of Nicaea were convened or authorized by the pope; the latter was convened by Emperor Constantine.[88] When there is a fire, everyone has the duty of putting it out, even though they may not have been commissioned to do so by the mayor. Since the pope was now an offense to Christendom, it was the duty of the secular powers to convene a just and free council.[89] "There is no authority in the church except to promote good."[90] If a pope used this power to oppose the good and to prohibit the convening of a council, one should not be swayed. Such a council would surely not fail to find plenty of work to do.

In the second part of his treatise Luther outlined a comprehensive program of reform. In the first 25 segments he concentrated on religious problems, and he dealt with the deplorable state of secular affairs in the 26th. The "drunken Germans" paid the bills for the worldly splendor and arrogance of the pope and the curia.[91] But the Germans were now waking up and seeing through the Roman practices.[92] The never-ending payments to Rome had to cease: the *annates,* that is, the taxes paid to Rome by newly-appointed bishops; the palliums, or special payments required of archbishops; the monies paid to the Datarius, the Roman court of justice; the *compositiones,* such as Albert of Mainz had to pay; the indulgence monies; the dispensations; and a host of others.[93] This robbery ruined both the body and soul of Christendom.[94] What could one do against it?

"If we want to fight against the Turks, let us begin here where they are worst of all. If we are right in hanging thieves and beheading robbers, why should we let Roman Avarice go free? He is the worst thief and robber that has ever been or could ever come into the world, and all in the holy name of Christ and St. Peter!"[95] One should "henceforth forbid" the payment of *annates.*[96] The bishops should no longer remain the "ciphers and dummies" of the pope.[97] When the next Roman lackey came with potential appointments for the office of bishop, he should be told "to keep out, to jump into the Rhine or the nearest river, and give the Romish ban with all its seals and letters a nice, cool dip."[98]

Luther would like to have seen the practices of the early church reintroduced. The appointment of a bishop should be made with the approval of the neighboring bishops, and at the head of the bishops there should be a German primate.[99] The pope should have nothing to do with the exercise of secular power; instead he ought to be "the most learned in the Scriptures" and concern himself with the things that pertain to faith and the holy life of Christians.[100] The pope was not the successor of the Roman emperor; the "Donation of Constantine" was an "impossible lie," as Luther had learned through Hutten from the study of the edition prepared by Lorenzo Valla.[101] The papal states had been stolen by the papacy by means of this document.

The kissing of feet was to be abolished; pilgrimages to Rome should cease.[102] There was nothing good to learn there; "The nearer Rome, the worse Christians.'" "They say the first time a man goes to Rome he seeks a rascal; the second time he finds one; the third time he brings him back home with him." [103] Pilgrimages were costly affairs; it would be better and more God-pleasing to use the money for one's own family. Not only the papacy, but the entire life of the church was in need of reform. The number of begging monks had to be reduced; they had become a plague on the countryside.[104] The cloisters ought once again to become Christian schools in which one learned Holy Scripture and Christian discipline, rather than continuing to make "an eternal prison" out of them through the monastic vow.[105] Celibacy should be abolished, at least for parish priests; it was not observed anyway, and it led to a guilty conscience.[106] It was neither biblical nor founded on the traditions of the ancient church.

Luther severely judged the rules and regulations of the church: the interdict, the laws of marriage, the regulations concerning fasting, dispensations, the granting of privileges, and others.[107] Festivals should be abolished and limited to Sundays.[108] Begging was an evil; [109] every city ought to look after its own poor and expel other beggars. It was high time that the schism with the Bohemians be set aside; it needed to be admitted that the burning of Hus was an injustice.[110] Safe conduct was a divine decree. "We should overcome heretics with books, not with fire, as the ancient Fathers did. If it were wisdom to vanquish heretics with fire, then the public hangmen would be the most learned scholars on earth." [111] Reconciliation with the Pickards, the community of Bohemian brethren, was important. The doctrine of transubstantiation was not an article of faith; it was sufficient to believe that the body and blood of Christ are in the bread and wine.[112] One ought to give the cup to the laity.

The universities also needed to be reformed. To begin with, Aristotle needed to be done away with—that "conceited, rascally heathen" who denied the immortality of the soul and knew nothing of the grace of God.[113] Luther knew what he was talking about; he claimed to have studied Aristotle in greater depth than had either Thomas or Scotus.[114] Only his *Logic, Poetics,* and *Rhetoric* were worthy of being kept. Instead of Aristotle, languages, mathematics, and history should be taught. The jurists ought to concentrate on practical reason and forget canon law.[115] The "dear theologians" should, above all, study Holy Scripture and not the *Sentences*.[116]

One became a proper theologian through the Holy Spirit; the study of books alone wouldn't do it. "The number of books on theology must be reduced and only the best ones published. It is not many books that make men learned, nor even reading. But it is a good book frequently read, no matter how small it is, that makes a man learned in the Scriptures and godly." [117] The church Fathers should lead one into the Scriptures, not out of them, as was then the case. For the Scriptures alone are "our vineyard in which we must all labor and toil." In the elementary schools, too, the reading of the gospel ought to be given a primary place.[118] "And would to God that every town had a girls' school as well, where the girls would be taught the gospel for an hour every day either in German or in Latin." Those who withheld the gospel from their youth would be severely judged.[119]

Luther considered secular evils and injustices more briefly, since he had already dealt with them in his *Treatise on Good Works*.[120] He spoke out against luxurious clothing,[121] against the importation of exotic articles, and against excessive interest rates, a subject on which he was very critical of the Fuggers. He did not understand how one could earn 20 gulden on 100 gulden in a year. "I leave this to men who understand the ways of the world. As a theologian I have no further reproof to make on this subject except that it has an evil and offending appearance." [122] Luther declared his support for agriculture: "I know full well that it would be a far more godly thing to increase agriculture and decrease commerce." There was still much uncultivated land in Germany. A dreadful vice of the Germans was excessive "gorging and boozing," which resulted in murder, adultery, robbery, and other crimes.[123] Public brothels were a disgrace.[124] Secular authorities had their work cut out for them in curbing all the deplorable conditions.

In the second edition of the *Letter to the Christian Nobility* there is an additional paragraph inserted immediately after the 25th segment of the second part.[125] In it Luther spoke out critically against the medieval view of the *translatio imperii*, the transfer of the Roman empire—which the pope had supposedly received as a gift from Constantine—to the Germans as a "papal fief." This was nothing but a fabrication of the pope, designed as a means of tyrannizing the Germans. The Western Roman Empire had long since been crushed by the Goths, and the Eastern Empire had been destroyed by the Turks. The pope therefore had nothing to bequeath to the German emperor. The crowning of the German emperor by the pope did not imply that the emperor was subject to the pope. According to Luther, the pope had in fact unjustly assumed the right to give the Western Empire—which had belonged to the eastern emperor—to the Germans in the first place. But God used the malice of the pope to establish among the Germans a second empire after the fall of the first. The Germans should see the providence of God at work in this action and assume responsibility for this empire.

Luther concluded his courageous appeal with these high-spirited, yet confident words: "I know full well that I have been very outspoken. I have made many suggestions that will be considered impractical. I have attacked many things too severely. But how else ought I to do it? I am duty-bound to speak. If I had the power, these are the things I would do. I would rather have the wrath of the world upon me than the wrath of God. The world can do no more to me than take my life." He had previously proposed peace, but his adversaries had given him no rest. "Well, I know another little song about Rome and the Romanists. If their ears are itching to hear it, I will sing that one to them, too—and pitch it in the highest key! You understand what I mean, dear Rome."[126] "God give us all a Christian mind, and grant to the Christian nobility of the German nation in particular true spiritual courage to do the best they can for the poor church." [127]

Luther had indeed "sung high." The book was written in so captivating a style that one would like to quote much more from it. It is packed full of fruitful ideas and practical insights. The proposed program of reform was as comprehensive as it was biblically grounded. In Ranke's opinion, "These few pages both prepare the way for and predict the content of further developments in world history." [128] Johann Lang was disturbed by its "terribly wild" tone, and many agreed with him. Luther himself admitted that he may have "attacked many things too severely," [129] but the situation did not call for a detached academic discussion. It was no unholy passion, but rather a holy zeal for reform of the muddled state of affairs and indignation over outrageous corruption that determined Luther's tone. Without this zeal he might have been a professor, but he would never have become a reformer.

In this work Luther addressed the German nobility; but he had already come into contact with representatives of that estate. On June 4, 1520, Ulrich von Hutten, who was at the time employed by Albert of Mainz, made an appeal to him.[130] Hutten was born on April 21, 1488, in the castle Steckelburg near Fulda, the son of a knighted family. In 1499 he was placed in the monastery at Fulda; he fled six years later, and as a result was disinherited by his father. As a wandering student he led an unsettled life and contracted syphilis. Attracted to beautiful things, he became a humanist and an admirer and student of classical literature. He published Latin indictments of Duke Ulrich of Württemberg, who had been accused of murdering his cousin Hans von Hutten.

After taking up residence in Italy on two separate occasions, Hutten finally returned to Germany in 1517. While in Italy he had become a German patriot, outraged at the arrogance of the Italians. He fought against the Dominicans in the Reuchlin case and, along with Crotus Rubeanus, published the "Letters of Obscure Men." Emperor Maximilian bestowed on him the title poet laureate in Augsburg in 1517. Thereafter he was active in the court of Albert of Mainz.

He had paid little attention to Luther, but that changed as a result of the Leipzig Disputation. Now he saw in Luther the true leader of the "Break-with-Rome" movement he had been planning. It became his goal to stand at Luther's side as a comrade-in-arms. Under the influence of Luther's pamphlets he no longer wrote only in the artful Latin of the humanists, but also in a robust and pithy German. "At first I wrote in Latin; that was unknown to most. Now I write directly to the fatherland, the German people, in their own language, in order to avenge them." Hutten succeeded in winning to his cause the powerful knight Franz von Sickingen, who had taken it upon himself to block the rising power of the princes and restore knighthood to the position of honor and power it had once held. Hutten did not shy away from the thought of taking up arms to break the rule of Rome, and Sickingen was to help him.

Hutten believed that the emperor could be persuaded to support such a reform of the empire. He had already corresponded with Melanchthon, and on June 4, 1520, he wrote to Luther himself.[131] Toward the end of May Luther had written to both Hutten and Sickingen in a roundabout way through Spalatin,[132] but the letters have been lost. In fact the letter to Hutten had already been written early in May.[133] Hutten did not mention these letters. He expressed his concern for Luther's fate and informed him that Sickingen three or four times had asked him to write. He encouraged Luther to join him whenever he no longer felt safe in Wittenberg.

Luther had received a similar overture on June 11, 1520, from Silvester of Schaumberg, a local magistrate in Münnerstadt near Kissingen: If Luther were in danger of losing his life, he could muster 100 knights for his protection.[134] Luther accepted none of these offers. More than likely he had sensed a different spirit in Hutten. Hutten was indeed linked to Luther by means of the fight against Rome, but he was not really moved by Luther's concern for salvation.

Seeing that he could no longer retain his position in the court of Albert, Hutten sought refuge with Franz von Sickingen in the castle Ebernburg near Kreuznach. Following the Edict of Worms he broke with the emperor and continued his denunciation of the priesthood. The ban was imposed on him. Illness forced him to leave the Ebernburg, but eventually Zwingli was able to arrange asylum for him on the island of Ufenau in Lake Zürich, where he died on August 29, 1523. Meanwhile, Sickingen's attack on the archbishopric of Trier ended with his defeat and death in the fortress of Landstuhl near Kaiserslautern (May 7, 1523).

Hutten composed a moving elegy about Sickingen's struggle for life: "I have pondered the risk and bear no remorse; though I may not succeed, I shall remain true to the cause." Because of his lyric poetry Hutten is regarded as the most important literary figure between Walther von der Vogelweide and the German classics. But he never became as proficient in German as Luther.

Luther's appeal to the nobility was not inspired by Hutten, as many have assumed. Nor was his patriotic sense the result of his acquaintance with Hutten; it had already been apparent at Augsburg. Unlike Hutten, Luther never blindly glorified his own people. Hutten was stubbornly courageous, but despite his "we must succeed," he achieved little. His hope for the support of the emperor was never realized. Erasmus, who had earlier commended him, did not hesitate to denounce him when, as an ostracized man, he passed through Basel on his last journey.

The friendship with Luther, which Hutten affirmed to the very last, was never very profound; the two men were too different. Celebrated and treated with disdain, disappointed and yet still dedicated to his goal, he died a lonely man. Luther did not despise his offer of external help, "but I will not take him up on them unless Christ, my protector, be willing, who has perhaps inspired the knights." [135] Nevertheless Luther increasingly distanced himself from them; he did not wish either himself or the gospel to be defended with force. On January 16, 1521, he wrote to Spalatin, who was in Worms at the time, "You see what Hutten is attempting. I am not willing to have anyone fight for the gospel with bloodshed. In this sense I have written to him. By the Word the world is conquered and the church is saved, and by the Word will the church also be restored." [136]

Luther's confidence in the effectiveness of the Word was realistic. Had he entrusted the fortunes of the gospel to the military and political goals of knighthood, the gospel would have floundered with them. Later Luther exhibited precisely the same attitude in his opposition to the Peasants' War. It was Luther's desire that the reformation of the church should not be bound to secular goals or institutional movements.

At the conclusion of his open letter to the nobility Luther announced "another little song about Rome"—the treatise *On the Babylonian Captivity of the Church (De captivitate Babylonica ecclesiae praeludium),* which appeared in print on October 6, 1520.[137] The title was cleverly chosen. True Christians, as well as the sacraments, were being held in a captivity similar to that of the Jews who had been exiled in Babylon. The forced exile of the papacy in Avignon (1300-1377) had also been called a Babylonian captivity, but that was nothing compared with the present captivity of the church. Luther had already spoken of such a Babylonian captivity, for example in the *Resolutions* written to accompany the 13 theses of the Leipzig Disputation.[138]

The immediate cause of the treatise was a new work by Asinus Alveldensis (Alfeld) on Communion, as well as a publication by the Italian Dominican Isidor Isolani, who sought to convince Luther of the primacy of the papacy. The treatise appeared just before the papal bull threatening Luther with excommunication arrived in Wittenberg. It was dedicated to his Wittenberg colleague Hermann Tulichius (Tulken), who taught logic and rhetoric. Unlike the letter to the nobility, this treatise was strictly a theological work, and so was written in Latin. Luther began with an ironic word of gratitude for his opponents: "Whether I wish it or not, I am compelled to become more learned every day, with so many and such able masters eagerly driving me on and making me work." [139] He would really have liked to have burned his earlier writings on indulgences, since in the meanwhile he had been instructed by Silvester Prierias that indulgences were nothing but the deceitful and unworthy invention of haughty Romans. Then Eck and Emser instructed him on the matter of papal primacy. At first he still granted that it was a human right, but then he knew that the papacy was none other than the kingdom of Babylon and the tyranny of the hunter Nimrod.[140]

Now he had been instructed again, this time by Alfeld and Isolani. Alfeld attempted to substantiate his view that the chalice should be withheld from the laity on the basis of Holy Scripture. This "scriptural proof," said Luther, could easily be refuted. A sacrament must be instituted by Christ himself, and an outer sign must accompany the Word. For this reason Luther had to deny that there were seven sacraments and hold that there were but three: Baptism, penance, and the Eucharist, though according to strict biblical usage there was, in his opinion, really but one sacrament, namely Christ himself. The three sacraments were actually sacramental signs for Christ.[141]

Luther began with the Lord's Supper.[142] He had already expressed his views on numerous other occasions. His writings on the Sacrament of the Altar from the years 1518 and 1519 bore an Augustinian character. These were the *Sermon on the Right Preparation of the Heart for the Reception of the Sacrament of the Eucharist* (1518)[143] and the *Sermon on the Blessed Sacrament of the Holy and True Body of Christ, and the Brotherhoods* (1519).[144] In them the Lord's Supper was presented as the sacrament of the *communio*, the community. It was received by faith. Merely receiving the sacrament outwardly was worthless. The *res sacramenti* (content of the sacrament) was the *communio sanctorum* (the communion of saints). The sacrament was a certain sign of this community and an incorporation into Christ. As bread and wine are "transformed" into the body and blood of Christ, so we too are "transformed" into members of the *corpus Christi mysticum*. This is a matter for faith. Both documents are devoid of polemic against the Roman Mass.

A direct precursor of the treatise on the Babylonian captivity was *A Treatise on the New Testament, That Is, the Holy Mass*,[145] which was a revised and expanded version of an earlier sermon. It was published in August 1520. That which was new, by contrast with both of the previous sermons, was the emphasis on the words of institution and on the forgiveness of sins as the real gift of the Lord's Supper.

The Sacrament fit into the framework of *promissio* and *fides* (the Word of promise and faith), into which all of Luther's theological statements fit. According to medieval thought the effect of the sacrament was bound to four prerequisites: (1) A responsible "minister" needed to be present, that is, an ordained priest. (2) That minister was required to have the right "*intentio*," that is, the intention to conduct the sacrament properly. (3) The minister had to make use of the proper elements, for example, wine from the vine. (4) The elements had to be accompanied by the correct "*forma*" (formula), that is, by the recitation of the words of institution during the Mass. The recipient could not be burdened with a deadly sin; so in most cases participation in the sacrament had to be preceded by confession.

Over against these requirements Luther stressed that: (1) The Word confirmed by a sign was the most important part of the sacrament. (2) The Word had to be connected with a sign. (3) The Word, like every word, required only faith. The same was true of the sacrament.

The principal distinctions between Luther's view and that of medieval theology were: (1) For Luther the Word was the gracious promise of God directed to the gathered community, whereas the *forma* was characterized more by its magical effect. In fact the words of institution in the Mass were whispered like a magic formula by the priest. (2) The sacrament was not dependent on the minister and his *intentio*, but solely on the promise of God and the faith of the recipient. With this Luther equated the sacrament with the Word; it was for him, as it was for Augustine, *verbum visibile*, the visible Word.

In his sermon Luther proposed a notable principle for doctrine and for practice: "The nearer our masses are to the first mass of Christ, the better they undoubtedly are; and the further from Christ's mass, the more dangerous." [146] This was a revolutionary principle which, however, Luther himself never completely followed. The "chief part of the Mass" was the words of institution and the gracious gift of the forgiveness of sins they promised.[147] Body and blood were the signs of the reality of the gifts.[148] But "the words are much more important than the signs." [149] "[It is even possible for me to celebrate the mass without the signs, when I] "first grasp and thoroughly ponder the words of Christ." [150]

This paralleled Augustine's *"crede et manducasti,"* (Believe, and you have received the sacrament). The body and blood of Christ were signs that assured the validity of the promise the way a seal validates a will.[151]

For Luther it was the certainty of the real presence of the body and blood of Christ that guaranteed the promise—a stand that was firmly grounded within the Catholic tradition. Luther was far removed from our contemporary difficulties, which are focused directly on the question of the real presence. On the other hand, one is left with the impression that for Luther it was not at all decisive whether one actually received the body and blood or not; rather everything depended on the reality and gift of the Word and the forgiveness of sins. Faith was the crucial foundation. Persons could only receive; they could not contribute anything of their own. Consequently the idea of sacrifice had to be excluded from the Mass.

However, it is questionable whether Luther actually assessed the sacrificial character of the Mass correctly. According to the statements of the Council of Trent, *sessio* XXII, the Mass is the self-sacrifice of Christ and not an action of the church. "It is one and the same sacrifice which he who once offered himself on the cross now offers through the service of the priest. Only the manner in which the offering is made differs." Given this interpretation, the principal point with which Luther took issue no longer applies. But it must be remembered that this formulation was not made until after Luther's death. It was not clearly expressed in earlier doctrinal pronouncements. The wording of the *canon missae* (canon of the mass) as well as common ecclesiastical usage of that day definitely supported Luther's view. In practice the Mass had been turned into a meritorious work. And it was on this practice that Luther rightly focused in his attack.[152]

Where there was no longer a need for sacramental sacrifice, the need for a particular priestly class was also eliminated, and Luther returned to the biblical idea of the universal priesthood of all believers.[153] So Luther set forth the basic principles on which a reform of the doctrine of the Lord's Supper could proceed.

However, it was not until the treatise *On the Babylonian Captivity of the Church* that Luther struck his most radical blow against Catholic sacramental teaching.[154] In the section on the Lord's Supper the basic thoughts of the earlier sermon and treatise were restated and expanded. Luther now saw the sacrament held captive in three ways.

First, the chalice was being withheld from the laity.[155] This was neither biblical nor the practice of the early church. In this regard it was not the Greeks and the Bohemians who were the heretics, but the Romans.[156] Luther no longer merely supported the giving of wine to the laity; he now declared its retention to be sinful. Nevertheless, one ought not compel the administration of the chalice by force. After all, Christ did not command us to use the sacrament; rather, he offered it to us for our delight, and so it is not a sin against Christ when we receive only one form.[157] Only the refusal to offer the chalice to the laity was sinful. The guilt did not lie with the laity, but with the priests.[158] Amazingly, despite Luther's determination to eliminate abuses, he retained a sense of inner freedom. Later on, the practice of giving the chalice to the laity was generally considered a sign that one had sided with the Reformation.

The second abuse by which the Lord's Supper was held captive was transubstantiation.[159] This doctrine was elevated to church dogma by the Fourth Lateran Council of 1215, and was subsequently fleshed out by Thomism. By uttering the words of institution over the bread and wine during their consecration, the substance of the bread and wine were said to be changed into the substance of Christ's body and blood. Only the "accidents" of bread and wine, namely their form, color, and taste remained. Transubstantiation was an attempt to conceptualize the mystery of the sacrament of the altar, perhaps even to protect it from an all-too-crass interpretation. To Luther this appeared to be a pure rationalization concocted by those who refused to accept the mystery. He was also unimpressed by this theory from a philosophical standpoint. The teaching of consubstantiation that he had learned during his earlier studies seemed far more plausible. According to this view the bread remained bread and the wine remained wine, yet the body and blood were present in them. Why should it not be possible for the transfigured body of Christ to be present in the bread? [160] In glowing iron both the iron and heat are present.[161] This view corresponded more closely to the biblical accounts of the first Lord's Supper than did the theory of transubstantiation.

At any rate, transubstantiation should not be made into an obligatory statement of faith.[162] The sacrament was a mystery. "For my part, if I cannot fathom how the bread is the body of Christ, yet I will take my reason captive to the obedience of Christ, and clinging simply to his words, firmly believe not only that the body of Christ is in the bread, but that the bread is the body of Christ. My warrant for this is in the words. . . ." [163] Luther insisted on the real presence rather than on some theory simply because in his view it alone corresponded to the literal meaning of the biblical accounts. Therefore any decision as to the validity of his teaching concerning the Eucharist could be made only on the basis of biblical exegesis.

The third captivity in which the church found itself was the worst: the Mass had been turned into a "good work" and a sacrifice.[164] Here Luther repeated many ideas that are already known to us from his sermon. Again the watchword was to return to the original Lord's Supper and to the words of institution as quickly as possible. "For in that word, and in that word alone, reside the power, the nature, and the whole substance [substantia] of the mass." [165] Body and blood were only signs that confirmed the Word.[166] For "there is greater power in the testament [of Christ] than in the sacrament; for a man can have and use the word or testament apart from the sign or sacrament." [167] At this very point Luther also quoted the "crede et manducasti" of Augustine. In faith a person can celebrate the Mass hourly.[168] The original Lord's Supper was not a sacrifice, not even the self-sacrifice of Christ. "When he instituted this sacrament and established this testament at the Last Supper, Christ did not offer himself to God the Father, nor did he perform a good work on behalf of others, but, sitting at the table, he set this same testament before each one and proffered to him the sign.[169]

Luther expressed his gratitude that in God's mercy, at least Baptism had been preserved by the church.[170] In part he stated the thoughts already expressed in the sermon on Baptism of 1519.[171] Everything depended on the promise and on faith which clings to it.[172] Baptism was the foundation for all sacraments, without which no other sacraments could exist.[173] Those who baptized did not baptize in their own names, but in God's name; they were merely God's agents.[174] There was no secret power in the baptismal water;[175] it was this that distinguished a sacrament from a magical act. God had promised to uphold the sacraments he had instituted. Baptism was the sacrament of justification; but it was not the sacrament as such that justified; rather, it was the faith related to the sacrament that justified.[176] True justification was a matter of dying and rising again; this was also true of Baptism.[177] For this reason one ought not merely sprinkle water on an infant's head but truly immerse him or her, since that corresponded more accurately to the death and resurrection that the sign signified.[178]

Admittedly Satan was also at work here. Baptism had been so overlaid with vows, indulgences, and the like that it had become a matter of little concern to most Christians. Rather than concentrating on all of these outward activities one ought to direct one's entire life to the actualization of baptismal grace.[179] Along with the responsibility of living out of their Baptism, Christians had also been given a glorious freedom; through Baptism they had become children of God, whose consciences dared not be bound to human statutes.[180] Luther had in mind various regulations that replaced the responsibilities of Baptism and made salvation dependent on their fulfillment, such as the vows of parents who dedicated their children to monasticism.[181] The church should not impose vows on persons; individuals who made them did so at great peril themselves. Luther was not yet certain how binding the vows one assumes might be. He would have to give that question more thought. Before reaching a sensible age, no one ought to agree to the vow of chastity. It was Luther's feeling that persons ought to avoid all vows, including both monastic vows and pledges to undertake pilgrimages or complete certain works, and instead live faithfully in the good and effective freedom of their Baptisms.[182]

Penance rested on a divine promise, but it had no outer or external sign, so it was not truly a sacrament.[183] However, it was not the word *sacrament* that was significant, but the matter of repentance itself. In penance everything depended on divine mercy and faith, not on our own sorrow and contrition.[184] Luther fully agreed with private confession, that is, oral confession, but the church had made a tyranny of it.[185] The consciences of the faithful were tortured with reservations. Christians could also hear each other's confessions without the presence of a priest.[186] Absolution ought to follow after the making of amends (*satisfactio*), as it did in the early church.[187] For the moment Luther had nothing more to say about indulgences.

The remaining four sacraments could be retained, but not as sacraments, since either the word of divine promise or the external sign was missing. This was true of confirmation,[188] which was a proper rite of the church but not a sacrament. Some had attempted to base the sacrament of marriage on Eph. 5:25ff. Indeed, the Latin translation said that marriage was a great *sacramentum*, but in the original Greek the word used was *mysterium*, and that meant a secret rather than a sacrament.[189] Moreover, marriage had not been established by Christ but existed ever since creation.[190] Luther vehemently opposed the prohibitions imposed on marriage by canon law.[191] The numerous dispensations served only to fill the coffers of Rome.[192] Luther so detested divorce that even bigamy was more acceptable.[193] Still, Christ allowed divorce where the marriage had been destroyed by adultery. An impotent man might allow his wife to have intercourse with another man.[194] The latter statement and that concerning bigamy were eliminated in later editions.

The church of Christ knew nothing of ordination (*De ordine*); that was a fabrication of the papal church.[195] Luther considered it simply a rite of the church. In his appeal to the German nobility he had already pitted the priesthood of all believers against it. The church could not promise grace; only God could do that. Therefore the church could not institute new sacraments.[196] Those who considered ordination a sacrament appealed to Dionysius the Areopagite, who listed six sacraments, among them ordination.[197] We do not know whether the critical views of Lorenzo Valla concerning the authenticity of the writings of Dionysius were known to Luther. In any case, Luther instinctively detected the unbiblical spirit of those writings. Those who did not regularly preach the Word were not priests.[198] Those who only read the hours and celebrated masses were papists, not priests. "It is the ministry of the Word that makes the priest and the bishop." [199] When the priesthood ceased, Luther believed the papacy would also come to an end, and Christians could once more enjoy their freedom.[200] Extreme unction was based on James 5:14-15.[201] This letter was probably not written by James; at any rate its style was not apostolic. Moreover, even an apostle did not have the right to establish a sacrament; and besides, the passage dealt with anointing the sick, not the dying.[202]

In conclusion, Luther wrote that he had heard that new threats of excommunication had been prepared against him. If that were true, his present book was to be considered a prelude to new declarations of war. He closed with a verse from the Epiphany hymn of Cölius Sedulius (5th century):

> Why doth that impious Herod fear
> When told that Christ the King is near?
> He takes not earthly realms away,
> who gives the realms that ne'er decay.[203]

With the *Babylonian Captivity* Luther attacked the heart of prevailing piety and theology. To be sure, he made concessions in practical matters; many rites and ceremonies could be retained. But he knew nothing of compromise when it came to basic matters. The *Babylonian Captivity* was Luther's most revolutionary writing. The shocked reactions of traditional believers were understandable. In ducal Saxony the work was immediately banned. The papal nuncio Hieronymus Aleander attacked it vehemently at the Diet of Worms in 1521. The father confessor to Charles V, Jean Glapion, said that on reading it he felt as if someone had beaten him from head to toe. Erasmus saw all of his efforts for peace thwarted in Luther's treatise. The Sorbonne in Paris publicly opposed it. Henry VIII of England, who had dabbled in theology before becoming king, wrote a rejoinder with the title, *The Assertion of Seven Sacraments against Martin Luther,* and from the pope won the title, *"Fidei defensor"* (Defender of the Faith), which, incidentally, he continued to use even after his break with Rome. Cardinal Gasparo Contarini, on the other hand, spoke positively of the document.

A contemporary who reconsidered the writing after careful examination was Johann Bugenhagen, called Dr. Pommeranus (1485-1558). In the spring of 1521 he went to Wittenberg to study theology; subsequently he became pastor of the city church and a professor at the university. In contrast to Luther, he was a born organizer and wrote several books on church orders.

With the writing of the *Babylonian Captivity* a whole world crumbled; it was Luther's farewell to medieval piety.

16

Under the Ban

In Rome there was confusion for a long time about the failure
of Miltitz. Finally, in November 1519, the restlessness resulted in
Eck being summoned to Rome to report on the new heresy. Before
resuming official proceedings against Luther, it was decided that
an attempt should be made to persuade the elector to surrender
him. Miltitz was commissioned to make it clear to the elector that
the pope would not hesitate to use harsh measures, even the interdict, if he did not comply with papal wishes. On the advice of his
counselors the elector gave an evasive answer. In a memorandum
he pointed out that he would remain neutral as he had in the past,
and that the matter was entirely in Miltitz's hands. He was not to
blame that Luther had not yet been interrogated by the archbishop
of Trier. He saw nothing criminal in the way in which he had been
conducting himself.

Rome would wait no longer, however. The decision was made to
reopen Luther's case and extend the proceedings to his followers,
including the electoral prince. A papal commission met on February 1, 1520, to prepare a bull of excommunication. From the outset
there was disagreement on the plan of action. Cajetan proposed
that only some of Luther's writings be condemned; the others
ought to be denounced as "scandalous," "false," "insulting to pious
ears," "seductive," or "in conflict with Catholic truth." Luther should
also be urged once more to recant. Eck, who had in the meantime

arrived in Rome, prevailed on the pope to reject this in March of 1520.

A reconstituted commission was given the assignment of simply preparing a bull of excommunication. Eck was able to provide a number of new statements by Luther in which he denounced the papacy. On May 2 the draft was presented to Pope Leo, who had retired to his country residence at Magliano, where among other amusements he enjoyed hunting boar. It was also discussed by the college of cardinals toward the end of May, but with no significant results. On June 15, 1520, the bull was finalized by the papal chancellery and immediately printed.

The bull is known by its opening words, *"Exsurge Domine."* [1] It begins with rousing, solemn phrases: "Arise, O Lord, and judge your cause. Foxes are attempting to lay waste your vineyard, and a wild boar has broken into it," [2] an image most appropriate to the *genius loci* of Magliano. "Arise, Peter . . . arise, Paul . . . arise, all the company of saints and the entire holy church" against those who in the age-old manner of heretics twist the Holy Scriptures to their own intent. To his unspeakable grief the pope had learned that ancient errors that had already been condemned were being sown anew among the noble people of Germany by insolent persons who had no fear of God. It pained him even more since he and his predecessors had always had a special affection for the German people, on whom they had bestowed the Roman Empire. Moreover, the German nation had always shown itself to be a holy warrior against heresy, particularly against the Bohemians.

A listing of 41 errors followed, taken in part from the judgments of the universities of Cologne and Louvain. The most blatant heresies were not included, since Luther's writings of 1520 were not considered. Included were statements on the sacrament of penance, on indulgences, on excommunication, on papal primacy, on the authority of the councils, and on purgatory. Assertions such as the following were condemned as erroneous: "The burning of heretics is contrary to the will of the Holy Spirit," [3] "to oppose the Turks is to oppose God, who is using them as a plague upon our sins," [4] and "Ecclesiastical prelates and secular princes would do well to destroy all beggars' sacks." [5] Much was quoted out of context and consequently misunderstood. No distinction was made between lesser and greater wrongs, since all of them implied that the church could err.

Everyone was to respect this condemnation of Luther. Any religious or secular leaders who presumed to infringe on the bull by defending Luther or promoting his writings would also be subject to excommunication, or at least the loss of their positions, honor, and official status. All of Luther's writings should be burned.

Then the bull turned to the person of the archheretic himself: "Good God, what office of paternal love have we omitted in order to recall him from such errors?" Have we not summoned him to Rome in order to deal with him leniently, and provided him with safe conduct and money for the journey? Surely in Rome he would have recognized his errors. Instead he has had the temerity to appeal to a council, despite the fact that such appeals are punishable as heresy. Even so, he would still be dealt with graciously if he were willing to recant within 60 days of the publication of the bull. This final provision was a formality of the curia. Strictly speaking, the bull was not a bull of excommunication but a bull threatening excommunication, though in reality the distinction meant very little.

Before submitting the bull to the college of cardinals, it was decided that one more attempt should be made to influence the electoral prince. Frederick received letters from both Cardinal Riario and the Mainz chargé-d'affaires in Rome, Valentin von Tetleben. Even though the cardinal had not yet read Luther's works himself, he urged him under threat to take action against Luther. Spalatin sent the letters on to Luther. Luther responded on July 9.[6] He had remained silent as long as his opponents had remained silent. The elector should not be involved. Luther was willing to relinquish his office, but as long as it remained his, he dared not neglect his duty to uphold the truth. The elector should reply that he could not presume to make theological judgments, and so was in no position to make a decision in this case.

But on the very next day Luther was able to inform Spalatin about the content of a letter he had just received from Silvester von Schaumberg.[7] The elector should share Schaumberg's proposal with Cardinal Riario. Luther no longer spoke of relinquishing his office. The cardinal ought to know that the situation would only be aggravated if he were driven from Wittenberg; he would be received with open arms and protected not only in Bohemia, but also elsewhere in Germany, and by persons who were not as conciliatory toward Rome as the elector. "As far as I am concerned the dice have been thrown. I despise Rome's rage as well as her favors. I do not wish to be reconciled with them, nor do I seek their fellowship. Let them condemn what is mine and publicly burn it! As long as there is no shortage of fire, I in turn will condemn and publicly burn the whole papal law — this brood of heresies." (On December 10 of the same year Luther carried out his threat.)

In a subsequent letter Luther proposed that the following suggestions also be included in the elector's response: Luther's teachings have been so widely spread throughout Germany and abroad that they can be refuted only by sound reason and the Holy Scriptures; otherwise Germany will surely be turned into another Bohemia. The Germans are defiant spirits whom the pope can ill afford to irritate, particularly now, when scholarship and the knowledge of languages have reached the point where even lay people are beginning to grow wise.[8]

Elector Frederick made only limited and modified use of these suggestions. He assured the cardinal that Luther was willing to submit to a hearing before the archbishop of Trier; at the same time he encouraged Luther to announce his willingness to participate in such a hearing toward the end of August.[9] Luther promised this in a letter to Charles V, and at the same time requested his safe conduct.[10]

In order to settle matters as quickly as possible, the pope had on July 17, 1520, appointed two new nuncios to implement the ban: his librarian, the humanist Hieronymus Aleander, and Doctor Eck. Aleander's primary task was to assure the wholehearted support of the young emperor. Eck had the thankless job of publishing the bull throughout Saxony, but he was empowered to add other names to the bull. Among those he added were Willibald Pirckheimer, the author of *The Dressed-Down Eck*, and Lazarus Spengler, who had issued a document offering Luther protection.

Eck's mission in the Wettin territories was a disaster. The fact that he had not strictly followed proper procedures governing promulgation was gladly used as an excuse for refusing to accept the bull. He made an impact in only three places: Meissen, Merseburg, and Brandenburg. His greatest disappointment occurred in

Leipzig, where the university, even though it was supported largely by Duke George himself, steadfastly refused promulgation. Posters lampooning Eck had been put up at 10 places in the city, and satirical songs were sung about him. There was no other choice for Eck but to withdraw behind the walls of the Dominican cloister.

Karl von Miltitz, who had not yet been dismissed, saw the failure of the new nuncio, Eck, as an opportunity for himself. His initiatives aimed at mediation should not have been undermined. He renewed negotiations with the electoral court, and he arranged a meeting with Luther and Melanchthon on October 12 in Lichtenberg (between Wittenberg and Leipzig). Luther assured him that he would write a conciliatory letter to Leo X and, in addition, dedicate a small book to him.

Immediately upon his return, Luther set about writing the letter, and most likely also the promised book, even though the actual printing did not take place until later. It was the third time that Luther had written to Leo; the first time he addressed him was in the introduction to the *Resolutiones* of 1518; the second was in a letter following the conversation he had had with Miltitz in Altenburg. The second letter was never sent, however. The third letter was now backdated to September 6; it was not to appear as if it had been written under the pressure of the bull now being published by Eck.[11] The letter and the booklet that accompanied it were issued in Latin and in German.

The letter was as moving as it was defiant. Luther's respect for Pope Leo as a person was genuine and naive. To him Leo appeared to be Daniel in the lion's den,[12] an innocent lamb among raging wolves.[13] But he could not refrain from attacking the curia. "The Roman curia is already lost, for God's wrath has relentlessly fallen upon it." [14] Luther felt badly that "excellent Leo" had to become pope at such a time: "The Roman curia does not deserve to have you or men like you, but it should have Satan himself";[15] Leo lived in the most dangerous of circumstances; he was surrounded by deceptive flatterers.[16] It was out of reverent concern and with a deep sense of responsibility that Luther said these things, just as St. Bernard had done in his book to Pope Eugenius, a work that every pope should know by heart.[17]

Luther would never have begun this battle with Rome on his own, because he saw how futile it actually was. Instead he "gave it a bill of divorce, and said, 'Let the evildoer still do evil, and the filthy still be filthy.' " [18] But then Johann Eck, a "notable enemy of Christ," [19] "with an insatiable lust for glory," [20] challenged him to debate the papacy. Not Luther, but persons like Eck were the real enemies of Leo. He should defend himself against them. "O most unhappy Leo, you are sitting on a most dangerous throne. I am telling you the truth because I wish you well." [21] Luther had taken the advice of his monastic brothers and Miltitz and gladly written this letter.[22] "But let no person imagine that I will recant." He would not be told how he was to interpret Scripture.[23]

Leo should not listen to those who make him out to be "no mere man but a demigod," or say that he is the lord of the world, that he stands above the councils, and that he alone possesses the authority to interpret Scripture.[24] "You are a servant of servants, and more than all other men you are in a most miserable and dangerous position." [25] The popes called themselves Christ's representatives. Luther was afraid they were right, for a representative is present when the master is not.[26] Such a pope is more than likely the Antichrist and an idol.[27] This was truly a remarkable letter that Luther addressed to the pope, as his friend and "your most humble subject," as one Christian brother to another.[28] One cannot help but believe that Luther's confidence in the person of Leo was sincere. Still, the frankness with which he confronted him is remarkable.

In order not to come with empty hands, he concluded by stating that he was sending along a treatise. "It is a small book if you regard its size. Unless I am mistaken, however, it contains the whole of Christian life in a brief form, provided you grasp its meaning. I am a poor man and have no other gift to offer, and you do not need to be enriched by any but a spiritual gift." [29] The enclosed booklet bore the title, *The Freedom of a Christian*.[30] Luther probably wrote the German version on the 13th or 14th of October. He took more time composing the Latin version, which is superior to the German in precision of thought. The German edition of the treatise was dedicated to Hermann (not Hieronymus!) Mühlpfort, the city advocate in Zwickau who had been recommended to him as a friend of the gospel. The German version was by far more influential than the Latin.

The treatise was based on the famous paradox:

A Christian is a perfectly free Lord of all,

subject to none.
A Christian is a perfectly dutiful servant of all,
    subject to all.[31]
In order to understand these two "opposites" one must take into
account that a Christian has a twofold nature, composed of the
spiritual and the "fleshly." No external thing can make the spiritual
person free or righteous. So the soul is not profited when sacred
vestments are placed on the body or when it dwells in churches or
holy places. The soul lives solely on the Word of God, on the
preaching of Christ.[32] It is to the Word that faith is directed; no
other work makes a person Christian—faith alone makes one godly.[33] "This is that Christian liberty, our faith, which does not induce
us to live in idleness or wickedness but makes the law and works
unnecessary for any man's righteousness and salvation." [34]

Faith unites the soul with Christ as a bride is united with her
groom.[35] "Here we have a most pleasing vision not only of communion but of a blessed struggle and victory and salvation and
redemption." [36] "Here this rich and divine bridegroom Christ
marries this poor, wicked harlot, redeems her from all her evil, and
adorns her with all his goodness."[37] Faith is the fulfillment of the
First Commandment, and whoever fulfills the First Commandment
has fulfilled them all.[38] Therefore faith frees one from all the work
of the law.[39] Faith makes all Christians into priests.[40] This is the
freedom of the inner person.

Now we are not only spiritual and internal, but also external
and physical beings.[41] As such we are dutiful servants of all and
subject to everyone. "Here the works begin" and we dare not stand
idle.[42] But the works must not be undertaken in the understanding
that we are made right before God by them.[43] That also holds true
for outward disciplines such as fasting and abstinence. "Good
works do not make a good man, but a good man does good
works." [44] Christ said, "A good tree cannot bear evil fruit, nor can
a bad tree bear good fruit." [45] "So a man must first be good or
wicked before he does a good or wicked work." [46] Faith alone is
capable of making a person good; without faith no work is good.
Good works are not to be despised unless they are undertaken out
of a false understanding.[47]

It could seem as if Luther was of the opinion that works resulted spontaneously from faith. Finding himself in a position of having to oppose legalism, he did indeed put heavy stress on this. But Luther was also realistic enough to know the necessity of preaching the law. He reaffirmed that in a subsequent conflict with the Antinomians, who called on Luther's earliest statements to support their rejection of all preaching of the law. "We must bring forth the voice of the law that men may be made to fear and come to a knowledge of their sins and so be converted to repentance and a better life. But we must not stop with that . . . we must also preach the word of grace and the promise of forgiveness by which faith is taught and aroused," without which all else is of no avail.[48] The Lord Christ should be our example as to how we should serve our neighbor.[49] "I will therefore give myself as a Christ to my neighbor, just as Christ offered himself to me." [50] This also includes having consideration for those who are weak, as well as obeying church regulations, even though these may be wrong-headed.[51]

Luther summed up with this magnificent statement: "We conclude, therefore, that a Christian lives not in himself, but in Christ and in his neighbor. Otherwise he is not a Christian. He lives in Christ through faith, in his neighbor through love. By faith he is caught up beyond himself into God. By love he descends beneath himself into his neighbor. Yet he always remains in God and in his love. . . . As you see, it is a spiritual and true freedom and makes our hearts free from all sins, laws and commands. . . . It is more excellent than all other liberty, which is external, as heaven is more excellent than earth." [52]

This little book is one of the most precious gifts Luther has bequeathed to us. It is a warmhearted testimony to evangelical piety, completely free of polemic. Notes from Christian mysticism are unmistakable, yet the work is free of any unhealthy excesses. The language is noble. However it was not carefully enough safeguarded against misinterpretation. The peasants heard the word *freedom* and understood it as liberation from existing political structures. From the Enlightenment until our own time, freedom has been associated with reason and science. Liberalism saw emancipation from external authorities as the most significant contribution of the Reformation. All of these views have grasped but a part of what Luther understood by Christian freedom. For him, freedom meant being bound to God. Only in this bondage of faith was one free from bondage to worldly powers.

On October 11, one day before he set out for Lichtenberg, Luther informed Spalatin that the bull had arrived in Wittenberg.[53] At first he considered it a forgery drawn up by Eck and refuted it with a tract, *On the New Bulls and Lies of Eck*.[54] But once he was convinced that it had indeed been issued by Rome, he responded by writing, *Adversus execrabilem Antichristi bullam*,[55] and immediately produced a German adaptation for the laity.[56] He defied Leo and the cardinals: if the bull actually came from them, he could only consider the Roman See to be the throne of the Antichrist and match their condemnation with his own. Martyrdom did not frighten him. On November 17 he renewed his appeal from the pope to a council [57] in a publication that was also issued in German.[58] In addition to an appeal to the pope, he had also written appeals to the emperor, the prince, and the German people.

Aleander had more success than Eck. He succeeded in persuading the young emperor to issue an edict against the heresy in the hereditary territories of Burgundy. The first burning of Luther's books occurred in Louvain and Lüttich. But in Cologne Aleander was greeted with defamatory writings. His attempt to enlist the electoral prince Frederick in the cause of the curia failed. Instead the elector turned for counsel to Erasmus. On being asked for his opinion on the Luther affair, Erasmus replied: "Luther has committed two sins. He has grasped the pope's crown and the monks' bellies." Erasmus placed his hope in an impartial dialog. Frederick sent word to Aleander that he could not accept his proposals as long as Luther had not been convicted of any error.

The burning of Luther's works in Cologne backfired; students had secretly provided the executioner with works written by his opponents. When Luther heard of the burnings in Louvain and Cologne, he immediately decided on countermeasures. On the morning of December 10 the students and "all friends of evangelical truth" found a notice posted on the door of the parish church. They were to assemble at 9:00 at the Elster gate and there, according to ancient apostolic practice, assist in burning the godless books of papal law and scholastic theology.[59] A detailed report of this has been preserved.[60] "A well-known master of arts" (most likely Johann Agricola) prepared the pyre and lit the fire.

After several works of canon law and some writings of Eck and Emser had been tossed into the flames, Luther stepped forward and, trembling, threw a small volume into the fire while uttering the words, "Since you have struck the Lord's holy one [Christ], may the eternal fire strike you!" At the time few noticed that this volume contained the bull, since nothing had been said about the bull in the posted notice.

If it were not for the report and a note in a letter Luther sent to Spalatin shortly thereafter, we would probably not have known about it.[61] Luther made as little drama of burning the papal bull as he had of the posting of the 95 Theses. He returned quickly to the city along with the other professors. Several hundred students, however, remained behind and celebrated the occasion with great frivolity. After eating they marched through the city pulling a farmer's wagon, played all sorts of pranks, and tossed more writings of Luther's opponents into the fire. This was all completely opposed to Luther's intentions.

The following day he began his lecture to some 400 students with an address in German rather than in Latin, quite against custom. He made clear to them the seriousness of the situation. They, too, were not confronted by an either/or: martyrdom or hell. He himself anticipated martyrdom. The burning of books outside the Elster gate was not enough; the papal see would have to be burned. "If you are not willing to reject the kingdom of the pope with your whole heart, you cannot gain the salvation of your souls."

The burning of the bull was an unprecedented and bold action. Yet in the pamphlet, *Why the Books of the Pope and His Disciples Were Burned,*[62] Luther never mentioned it; nor did he mention it in the *Assertio omnium articulorum M. Lutheri per bullam Leonis X novissimam damnatorum,*[63] or in its German counterpart, *The Basic Reasons Why All of the Articles of Martin Luther Have Been Wrongly Condemned in the Roman Bull.*[64] In reality the burning of canon law had almost greater significance than the burning of the bull. During the Middle Ages canon law held the same authority as the Talmud did for Judaism or the Koran for Islam. It was not merely ecclesiastical law, but served simultaneously as the basis for all civil legislation and social order.

What particularly outraged Luther in canon law was the excessive idolatry of the pope. One of the books that was burned stated that, "The pope is a god on earth, above all heavenly and earthly powers, and all things belong to him." He was not to be worshiped, but he deserved the same religious adoration as the mother of God, the angels, and the saints. The jurists, admittedly even those who favored Luther, were not in agreement with his burning of the canonical books. "How dare this mangy monk show such audacity?" said one of his Wittenberg colleagues.

The reaction of the general public to the events of December 10 was even more lively. Appalled, Aleander wrote to Rome on February 8, 1521: "All of Germany is in turmoil. For nine-tenths of the people the battle cry is 'Luther,' and for the rest it is at least, 'Death to the Roman Curia.'" On January 2, 1521, the actual bull of excommunication itself (*Decet Romanum Pontificem*) was published; it reached Aleander in Worms on February 10. Its publication was hardly noticed.

In Worms before the Emperor and the Empire

Rome had spoken; but that did not put an end to the matter. Much now depended on the position the emperor and the various estates of the empire would take. The plan to have Luther appear at the next imperial diet had already been proposed by Frederick the Wise at the time of the Leipzig Disputation. On November 28, 1520, the young emperor, on the advice of his counselors, agreed to the elector's request.

The Diet was to be convened on January 6, 1521, in Worms. In the meanwhile Aleander, who was not at all pleased with Luther's possible appearance at Worms, protested the action. One ought not accord Luther the honor of appearing publicly before the Diet. On December 17 the emperor withdrew his consent, declaring that Luther would first have to recant. Frederick then informed Luther that plans for his appearance at Worms had fallen through. But when Frederick arrived in Worms on January 5 and consulted with the emperor about his change of mind, the emperor again reversed his decision. The monk was to be heard and not harmed. However, the motives behind this new pledge were not completely honorable. New proposals had come from the emperor's father confessor, the French Franciscan Jean Glapion. The details of these need not be described here. At any rate, the elector was able, at least temporarily, to thwart Aleander's attempt to have Luther declared an outlaw of the empire.

In mid-March Emperor Charles signed the letter of safe conduct, which was to be delivered to Luther by the imperial herald Kaspar Sturm (called Teutschland) of Oppenheim. However, the emperor's grand chancellor, Gattinara, together with Aleander, hurriedly devised a new intrigue to frighten Luther out of coming to Worms. They had a mandate printed that ordered the burning of all Luther's books and maintained that the Diet had ordered Luther to Worms only to make him recant. This mandate was circulated not only in Worms, but also in many other places, especially electoral Saxony.

While these games of political intrigue were being played out in Worms, Luther continued his work. He wrote his tracts on the burning of papal books, he exchanged angry letters with Hieronymus Emser and with the Franciscan Thomas Murner from Alsace (1475-1537), and he composed a "response" to the book by the Italian Dominican Ambrosius Catharinus, which had been dedicated to Charles V.[1] In this "response" he attempted to furnish proof that the papacy was the Antichrist predicted by Scripture. He described his book as the *Postludium* (Postlude) to the *Praeludium* (Prelude) provided by the *Babylonian Captivity*.

Luther also worked on a series of Latin Advent postils, and on his marvelous interpretation of the Magnificat, which he dedicated to the electoral prince John Frederick, the son of Duke John.[2] Mary was portrayed not as the sublimely exalted mother of God, but as a supreme example of God's grace, which chose that which was lowly and sought nothing for itself.[3] In addition Luther continued to carry on his professional duties in the pulpit and in the classroom. He no longer felt bound to recite the prescribed prayers; during the preceding years he had found little time for them anyway. On March 26 the long-awaited imperial summons arrived. It said nothing of recanting; he was merely to appear for a hearing. Therefore on April 2, the Tuesday after Easter, he set out for Worms.

Accompanying Luther were the imperial herald Kaspar Sturm, Nikolaus von Amsdorf, the student Peter von Suaven, and as *Socius itinerarius* (traveling companion), brother Johann Petzensteiner of Nuremberg. The wagon in which they traveled had been loaned to him by the Wittenberg city council. In Weimar the imperial edict was shown to him. At first he was alarmed, but he soon realized that it had been intended as a deterrent. His friends warned him not to go farther, but Luther would not be swayed from his decision.

Everywhere people ran out to see and greet the courageous "miracle man" who had risked everything to defy the pope. Local authorities presented him with honors. In Erfurt he was met at the outskirts of the city and greeted like a prince by the entire university, led by the rector. On the following day, Whitsunday (April 7), he preached in the Augustinian church, which was so crowded with people that a panic nearly erupted.[4] He also conducted services in Gotha and in Eisenach, where he became severely ill of an intestinal disorder. He was still suffering from it when he arrived in Frankfurt on April 14, two days before the expiration of his safe conduct. He had not lost his courage. "I am coming," he wrote to Spalatin on April 14, "although Satan has done everything to hinder me with more than one disease. . . . Of course I realize that the mandate of Charles has also been published to frighten me. But Christ lives, and we shall enter Worms in spite of all the gates of hell and the powers in the air."[5]

The report of Sturm that Luther was indeed coming and that the journey had turned into a triumphal procession struck the imperial leaders gathered in Worms like a bombshell. Nervously they explored various options that might minimize the effect of Luther's arrival, but they were unable to reach a satisfactory agreement. Yet one last attempt was made to derail him. In the town of Oppenheim, the Dominican Martin Bucer unexpectedly appeared, whom Luther knew from the Heidelberg Disputation, and who was Sickingen's chaplain at the Ebernburg castle. Luther, he said, was to come to the Ebernburg straight away; Glapion would meet him there with very important news. Luther saw through the trick. Whatever Glapion wished to say he could say in Worms. Had Luther followed this advice, to which Hutten and Sickingen had also given their support, his safe conduct would have expired before reaching Worms, and his enemies would have been able to move against him immediately.

It seemed as if everything was bound to keep him from coming. At the very last even Spalatin warned him to stay away. Elector Frederick did not want him to come and would not be able to protect him; he had already been condemned. Luther, as he later recalled, responded from Oppenheim in this way: "If I had known that as many devils as there are tiles on the roofs of Worms .had taken aim at me, I would still have entered the city." [6] He expressed the same thought to the elector in a letter of March 5, 1522.[7] Later, in 1540, he confessed, "I was not afraid; God can make one insanely daring. I am not sure I could be that daring today." [8]

Early Tuesday, April 16, about 10:00 A.M., while the citizens of Worms sat at their midday meals, a trumpet signaled the imminent arrival of the archheretic. Immediately following the imperial herald came Luther's wagon, with Amsdorf, Petzensteiner, and Suaven. The Erfurt professor Justus Jonas, who had in the meanwhile joined Luther, rode behind the wagon. He was followed by approximately 100 nobles on horseback, primarily from Saxony. There was such a crowd that the wagon could move forward only at a snail's pace. When it stopped in front of the Johanniterhof on Kämmerer Street, a priest embraced Luther, holding him as if he were a precious relic. It was during his stay there that a woodcut of Luther with a halo was created.

The Johanniterhof was filled from top to bottom, so Luther had to share his bedchamber with two nobles. Across the street was "The Swan," the inn at which the elector was lodged. As was his custom, the elector remained in seclusion, but assigned Professor Schurff and two of his own counselors to serve as Luther's legal advisors. Instead of the anticipated hearing before the archbishop of Trier, the imperial counselors decided to present Luther before the Diet. Dr. Johann von der Ecken, an outspoken opponent of Luther who was an official in Trier (and who was rooming with Aleander), was to conduct the interrogation.[9]

On the forenoon of April 17 the imperial marshal Ulrich von Pappenheim informed Luther that he was to appear before the emperor and the empire at 4:00 that afternoon. Luther was escorted by Pappenheim and Sturm on a roundabout route to the bishop's palace near the cathedral, where the Diet was assembled. The streets were so packed with curious onlookers that they were impassable. Luther then waited until 6:00 to be summoned. During the two-hour wait he was given many words of encouragement and advice. The often-quoted words by the famous mercenary commander Georg von Frundsberg, "Little monk, you have chosen a difficult path," are from a late tradition.

At last he was ordered to appear and was ushered into the hall in which the Diet was assembled. Pappenheim had previously impressed on him that he was to speak only when he was asked to speak. As he entered the room, all eyes were fixed upon him. Everyone noticed his lively dark eyes. The Spaniards found him lacking in dignity. Aleander, who was not present, was of the opinion that Luther had entered the hall laughing like a fool and kept moving his head back and forth while he was speaking. Actually he had been instructed to stand still before the emperor, with one knee slightly bent. At first sight the emperor is reported to have said, "He will never make me into a heretic."

Dr. Ecken directed two questions to Luther, first in Latin, then in German. Pointing to about 20 volumes, he asked, "Do you acknowledge these books lying here? Are you prepared to retract them as a whole or in part?" Before Luther could respond, Dr. Schurff broke in: "Let the titles of the books be read!" Luther acknowledged that the books were his. But he asked for time to think about the second question. Faith, the soul's salvation, and the Word of God were all involved; it would be presumptuous for him not to prepare a precise reply in advance.

After a brief consultation this request was granted, though reluctantly, "out of the natural goodness of his imperial majesty." He would have one day to think over the matter, but only on condition that he would not read his answer, but reply directly. Much thought has been given as to why Luther did not respond immediately; he knew that he would not recant, and he surely had not become uncertain of his views. But the point was that he did not want to be limited to a simple yes or no. He wanted to gain the opportunity to express himself clearly and to make distinctions. He may even have been directed to take this approach by the elector's counselors. Moreover it could also have been (and understandably so) the overwhelming responsibility of the moment that led him to make his request.

Even though Luther had been forbidden to read his response, he prepared his speech carefully in writing. The original page containing his outline still exists. On April 18, a Thursday, he was again summoned to appear at 4:00, this time in the larger, great hall of the palace. The emperor and the princes did not arrive until about 6:00. Torches had to be lit. Despite the size of the hall, there was terrible crowding. Luther and his Saxon counselors had to stand just below the princes, some of whom had themselves not been able to find places to sit. Again Doctor Ecken asked whether Luther was prepared to recant.

In contrast to his quiet manner on the preceding day, Luther responded with brave and strong words. First he apologized in case he might fail to use the proper title when addressing any of the lords, or in any other way offend courtly custom. His life had been spent in a monk's cell and not at court. Then he divided his books into three categories. First there were those works that were purely edifying, in which even his opponents could find nothing offensive. To recant those would be to damn the truth confessed alike by friends and foes. The second category comprised writings against the papacy. To recant them would be to strengthen tyranny and open not just a window, but the very doors, to un-Christian conduct. The third category included his writings directed against private individuals who defended the tyranny of Rome and condemned godly teaching. In these latter writings he was often more caustic than was seemly for a member of a holy order.

Luther did not consider himself a saint, nor did he wish to defend his own life, but only the teaching of Christ. If one could prove that he had erred on the basis of the prophetic and apostolic writings, not only would he recant, but he would be the first to burn his books. He was aware of the trouble and dissension that could arise from his teachings; but Christ himself did not come in order to bring peace. Those who sought an easy peace in these matters would only bring God's judgment; there were abundant examples of this in Scripture. Besides, that would be an inauspicious beginning to the reign of the noble young emperor. Luther did not presume to instruct such mighty princes, but he could not escape his duty to the German people. He asked the emperor not to allow himself to become prejudiced against Luther by his enemies. After he had spoken for about 10 minutes, he was asked to repeat it all in Latin. He did so immediately, even though he "was very hot because of the press of the crowd."

Luther's speech produced uncertainty among the princes; they had heard him answer not only with a no, but also with a conditional yes. Therefore they went to consult among themselves. They would not allow a disputation to take place, but they did not want to condemn him without hearing more. It was decided that the official should ask Luther to state unequivocally whether he would recant or not. With some degree of anger, Dr. Ecken told Luther that he had not answered the question. He was not to expect a disputation of established articles of faith. What was required of him was a clear yes or no concerning whether he wished to recant.

Luther then gave his famous reply (in Latin): "Since then your serene majesty and your lordships seek a simple answer, I will give it in this manner, neither horned nor toothed: Unless I am convinced by the testimony of the Scriptures or by clear reason (for I do not trust either in the pope or in councils alone, since it is well known that they have often erred and contradicted themselves), I am bound by the Scriptures I have quoted and my conscience is captive to the Word of God. I cannot and I will not retract anything, since it is neither safe nor right to go against conscience." To which he added in German, "God help me! Amen." Early printed versions included the expanded affirmation, "Here I stand, I cannot do otherwise." It is also found in the second volume of the 1546 Wittenberg edition of Luther's works. A more forceful expression of Luther's famous stance, this phrase soon took on great symbolic weight.

Luther had given the clear answer that had been demanded, but Ecken made one more try: "Abandon your conscience, Martin, for your conscience errs. You will never be able to prove that the councils have erred in questions of faith; at most they have erred in questions of discipline." Luther retorted: "I can prove it." But the emperor brought the interrogation to a close and had Luther taken out by the imperial herald. Some thought that Luther should be arrested. The Spaniards shouted after him, "Into the fire!" On reaching the Johanniterhof, Luther threw his hands in the air and exclaimed, "I made it through! I made it through!"

The confession at Worms was a fateful hour in the religious history of humanity. For the first time, the principle of freedom of conscience was expressed publicly before the highest ranking representatives of the church and of the world. One could make demands of everything else, but not of faith, for faith was a matter of the conscience. Of course, one dare not forget that Luther considered his conscience bound to God's Word. Luther's freedom of conscience was not autonomy, but *theonomy*. Yet the subjective point of departure is unmistakable. Luther risked setting his understanding of Holy Scripture against the highest religious authority of his time. His scriptural principle was critical of authority. His attachment to God's Word occurred in the inner freedom of personal perception and personal decision. Luther's freedom of conscience has not even always been realized in the Protestant church. Modern dictatorships will not allow it to be practiced. But once it had been expressed, this ideal could never be lost completely.[10]

On the morning of April 19 Charles V delivered his judgment. He had it read to the princes from a statement written in his own hand. As successor to the German emperors and the kings of Spain, he had determined to place everything under the protection of the Catholic faith and the Roman church. He considered Luther to be a heretic, and he no longer wanted to listen to him. He would honor his safe conduct as long as he did not preach or cause a disturbance on his way. The emperor was a man who had no understanding of Luther's religious concerns, and for whom the German nation remained completely foreign. He was barely acquainted with the German language. His mother tongue was French. He had also learned Spanish, and had only a passing knowledge of Latin. He had summoned Luther to Worms only because at the time of his election he had promised not to place any citizen of the empire under the ban without a hearing.

Of course it was amazing that a person already under excommunication was even allowed to appear before the Diet. But the princes could not simply dismiss the mood of the German people, since they themselves were moved by the complaints of the German nation. During their afternoon session they were not able to reach a consensus concerning the decision of the emperor. Elector Frederick spoke against it, even though he found Luther "far too cocky."

Meanwhile another incident occurred. On the night of April 19, two placards were posted. One was directed against Luther, and the other contained unmistakable threats against his opponents. Four hundred nobles had sworn not to abandon Luther: "I write poorly, but I intend great damage. I will fight with 8000 men. Bundschuh! Bundschuh! Bundschuh!" (*Bundschuh* was a rebellious peasants' movement.) The archbishop of Mainz felt particularly threatened. He pleaded with the emperor to have Luther examined again; others joined him. Against his will, the emperor agreed; he gave them three more days to attempt to persuade Luther to recant.

Therefore on April 24 the chancellor of Baden, Dr. Vehus, conducted a friendly discussion with Luther before an elected commission, but was unable to move him to recant. The conversation was continued in private by Dr. Ecken and the Frankfurt dean Johann Cochläus. They too achieved nothing. After the meal Cochläus appeared again and reported that Aleander was prepared to make certain concessions. The previous conversation had been somewhat stormy; Cochläus never forgave Luther for that. Luther rejected every proposal; to personally recant would achieve nothing, for others would continue the cause better than he. He cited Melanchthon as an example. Nevertheless, Luther's permission to remain was extended for another two days. At this point the archbishop of Trier himself intervened; but he was unable to come to an agreement with Luther about the Council of Constance.

The negotiations of April 24 and 25 proved very trying for Luther, particularly because for the first time he experienced accommodation as well as confrontation. But he held firm against both. On April 25, at about 6:00 P.M., he received orders to leave. He was guaranteed 25 days of safe conduct. Shortly thereafter he was given a secret message by two counselors of the elector stating that during the journey he would be "seized." The elector himself did not want to know where this would take place; he could then later say with a good conscience that he had known nothing of it. In fact, however, it was through this secret order that Frederick saved Luther and the Reformation.

Sometime after 10:00 A.M. on April 26, Luther left Worms. On May 1 he was in Eisenach. He had already taken leave of Kaspar Sturm; now he also dismissed Schurff and Suaven. With Amsdorf and Petzensteiner he rode on to Möhra and was surprised at the number of his relatives living in the area. He had confided in Amsdorf concerning what was to happen, but he was careful to say nothing to Petzensteiner. On May 4 near the castle Altenstein the prearranged attack took place. Petzensteiner turned tail and ran. Amsdorf screamed loudly. Luther was torn from the wagon and had to run alongside the riders for a while. They rode for several hours in various directions, arriving about 11:00 P.M. at the Wartburg, where the drawbridge closed behind them. The captain of the castle, Hans von Berlepsch, gave Luther a friendly reception, but immediately warned him that his transformation into "Squire George" would have to be completed before he would be allowed to leave his two rooms. So Luther let his hair grow and developed a heavy beard. He had wisely taken along his Hebrew Bible and his Greek New Testament.

The news of the attack and disappearance of Luther caused great excitement throughout Germany. Generally it was assumed that he had been eliminated by his enemies. The moving lament of Dürer in the journal of his travel through the Netherlands is well-known: "O God, Luther is dead. Now who will preach the holy gospel to us so clearly?" His hope that Erasmus would carry on Luther's work was admittedly naive. On May 29 Duke John of Saxony still thought Luther was in one of Sickingen's castles. Only the shrewd Aleander suspected that the "Saxon fox" (Frederick the Wise) had hidden him.

The Diet slowly dispersed. On May 23 Elector Frederick left. On May 25 the emperor publicly proclaimed the planned edict. He signed it on May 26, but had it backdated to May 8 in order that it might appear that a majority of the princes had still been present for its publication. The edict declared Luther to be an outlaw of the empire. No one was to provide Luther refuge or give him food or drink. He was to be captured and turned over to the emperor. His books were no longer to be printed. From 1521 until his death Luther lived as an outlaw under excommunication. Embroiled in foreign political affairs, the emperor did not return to Germany for some nine years. The Edict of Worms was not generally respected, and it was not able to hinder the progress of the Reformation.

THE CONTINUATION
OF THE REFORMATION

The Wartburg

During the autumn of 1777 Goethe spent some time at the Wartburg.[1] On Sunday, September 14, he wrote to Frau von Stein, "This is the most marvelous place I have ever experienced; it is so high and exhilarating that one must be a guest only. Otherwise one would be unnerved by its elevation and cheerfulness." On September 28, 1777, he wrote to Kestner, "I am staying at Luther's Patmos, and I feel as happy as he did here." Actually Luther never felt quite that happy, though he did occasionally close his letters with, "in the kingdom of the air," or "in the kingdom of the birds," and once wrote even more explicitly: "In the land of the birds that sing sweetly in the branches and praise God with all their power night and day." [2] But the magnificence of nature could not take his mind off of his cares and concerns. After the hectic battles of the previous years, he had suddenly been condemned to compulsory idleness. The solitude only increased his distress and raised new doubts. "Are you alone wise? Has the church erred for so many centuries? What if you are in error and are taking so many others with you to eternal damnation?" [3] Yet at the very next moment he would accuse himself of not having been sufficiently firm in Worms and of yielding too easily to his friends.

Outwardly Luther was now compelled to lead the life of a knight. He let his hair grow and developed a beard. He wore a sword at his side and a gold chain around his neck. A noble lad brought him meals, and Luther was accompanied by a servant who was required to keep an eye on him. When his transformation into a knight was complete, he was allowed to leave the castle, to wander through the forests and go riding in the surrounding area.

He was taken along on the hunt, "this bittersweet pleasure of heroes," that "worthy occupation indeed for men with nothing to do," as he wrote to Spalatin on August 15, 1521.[4] Hunting provided him with a new image: the devil sicked his dogs, the bishops and theologians, on defenseless little creatures, on simple souls. Luther had managed to save a little rabbit and hide it in the sleeve of his coat, but the dogs came over and bit it to death through the cloth. In a similar way Satan and the pope would destroy the souls who appeared to be saved. He was sick of that kind of hunting and preferred hunting more dangerous beasts of prey. Luther seldom made it easy for his companion to protect his identity. Wherever he saw a book he would reach for it, or he would even take one along with him. Then he would have to be warned that riding and reading were not compatible. When he encountered monks or priests along the way he would invariably get involved in conversations about church matters and the Lutheran affair, and his companion would have a real challenge to tear him away quickly.

Good food and drink were never lacking, but even that proved disastrous. The change from the frugal fare of a monk to the heavy meals of a knight did not agree with him. Already in Worms Luther had suffered from indigestion and constipation. At the Wartburg these became unbearable. By the middle of July he was on the verge of going to Erfurt for medical assistance; only the outbreak of the Plague stopped him. Spalatin sent him pills that alleviated the condition, but Luther did not fully recover until October. In the meantime he had so overtaxed himself with reading and writing that even minor irritations vexed him. Writing to Melanchthon he complained, "Already eight days have passed in which I have written nothing, in which I have not prayed or studied." [5]

Luther's physical and spiritual grievances were certainly related. They gave him far more to worry about than did the fear of the devil, about which tradition loves to speak. As a person who had been nurtured in medieval piety, superstition was not foreign to him. One night while preparing for bed he heard rumbling noises in a chest in which he stored hazelnuts. The reformer heard a thudding sound on the ladder as if kegs were being thrown down it, and he called out, "If it is you, so be it." He then entrusted himself to the care of Christ and got into bed.[6] On another occasion he told of throwing a large black dog that bothered him out the window.[7] Luther admitted that, in contrast to Osiander, he believed in such "Poltergeists."[8] His table talks include even more such ghost stories from his Wartburg days. Natural hallucinations caused by the winds that often buffeted the castle, or the creaking of the floorboards, as well as a heightened sense of fantasy, may have generated them. By comparison, the story of the ink spot on the wall is a legend that has also been attached to other Luther sites, including Wittenberg, Eisleben, and Coburg. According to the oldest version of the legend (1591), it was not Luther who threw the inkwell at the devil, but the devil who threw it at Luther.

According to his own statements, Luther lived in a single room with an adjoining chamber that was accessible only by a ladder that could be removed at night.[9] The furnishings we see in the room today are not original; they are antiques that have been collected since the beginning of the 19th century. And of course Cranach's portraits of Melanchthon and Luther's parents did not hang in the Wartburg at the time of Luther's stay.

Luther entered the Wartburg on the night of May 4. But he did not remain completely isolated for very long on his "Patmos" (as he called it in many of his letters from the Wartburg).[10] By means of trusted messengers it was possible to have written correspondence with Wittenberg. The first known letter is addressed to Melanchthon and dated May 12, 1521.[11] Luther had an almost moving confidence in Melanchthon; he believed Melanchthon would be able to fulfill his role in Wittenberg better than he himself would. Melanchthon had been recommended by his great uncle Reuchlin, and had been installed as professor of Greek in Wittenberg on August 25, 1518.[12] Only a few days later he had delivered his famous inaugural address on university reform, and with that single stroke he had not only aroused the enthusiasm of many of his listeners, but also won the highest admiration of Luther. Luther became his eager student of Greek; but under Luther's influence Melanchthon—who had previously been purely a humanist—became a converted adherent of Paul. The extent to which Melanchthon was converted from an Erasmian to a student of Luther during his first few years in Wittenberg is astonishing. In his will Melanchthon later gratefully acknowledged, "I learned the gospel from him."

The mature fruit of Melanchthon's transformation was his *Loci* of 1521, the first evangelical dogmatics. In that masterpiece Melanchthon made use of his great gifts of learning to draw together Luther's fundamental ideas. Luther praised it profusely, putting it on the same level as the Bible. On May 26, 1521, at the Wartburg Luther impatiently asked Melanchthon for printed sheets of the work. "Even though I should perish, the gospel will not lose anything. You surpass me now and succeed me as Elisha followed Elijah with a double portion of Spirit." [13] Under Luther's gentle pressure Melanchthon not only served throughout his life as a Greek scholar on the faculty of arts, but also as a professor on the theological faculty.

As a theologian Melanchthon later followed his own path; his humanistic heritage once again became more prominent. Nevertheless Luther continued to cherish his friendship—a friendship that proved even more productive in the history of ideas than that between Goethe and Schiller. The development of the Reformation, particularly in the area of learning and education, is unthinkable without Melanchthon. Luther characterized the differences between their natures in his preface to the German edition of Melanchthon's interpretation of Colossians: "I have been born to battle with packs of dogs and devils; therefore my books are far more warlike. I am the rough woodsman who must blaze the trail. Master Philip, having been so richly endowed by God, proceeds neatly and quietly and sows and waters with joy." [14]

During the Wartburg interlude Melanchthon carried many concerns—as he often did—about Luther, about the progress of the Reformation, and about the disturbances that were beginning in Wittenberg. Luther had to encourage and console him constantly. If only Melanchthon would learn to rely on God's grace; he sounded like he thought he had to do everything himself. It is in this connection that Luther used the much maligned expression, *"Pecca fortiter"* (sin boldly). On August 1, 1521, Luther wrote a letter to Melanchthon in which he told him, "If you are a preacher of grace, then preach a true and not a fictitious grace; if grace is true, you must bear a true and not a fictitious sin. God does not save people who are only fictitious sinners. Be a sinner and sin boldly, but believe and rejoice in Christ even more boldly, for he is victorious over sin, death, and the world. . . . Pray boldly—you too are a mighty sinner." [15] Melanchthon had forgotten that "as long as we are here we have to sin. This life is not the dwelling place of righteousness." [16] To see these words as a thoughtless appeal to keep on sinning is to completely misjudge Luther's pastoral intention. As in the other Wartburg letters to Spalatin, Amsdorf, Justus Jonas, and Johann Agricola, Luther was concerned about how to overcome particular difficulties.

While at the Wartburg Luther heard that the Edict of Worms had been issued. His initial response was sorrow for the young emperor, whom he believed had been misled by the counsel of his pernicious advisors.[17] But the gospel would continue to spread. Wittenberg was fortunate that Justus Jonas (1493-1555) had arrived to assume the position of provost at All Saints Church. Jonas had known Luther from Erfurt and had accompanied him on his trip to Worms. Originally trained as a jurist, he had in the meanwhile earned his theological doctorate. Throughout the following years he was of great help in carrying out the Reformation. He accompanied Luther on his last journey, was present at his death, and preached the sermon at his funeral in Eisleben. Johann Agricola was called to the university as a lecturer. On hearing that his wife had given birth, Luther sent both mother and child a gold coin from the Wartburg. Agricola had been Luther's student assistant at the time of the posting of the 95 Theses. Later he had a falling-out with Luther over the preaching of the law and moved to Berlin.

In his Wartburg letters Luther often complained that he felt isolated and useless; there was nothing to do and nothing to study. However these were only passing periods of depression. Actually he also used this time of enforced solitude to bring forth an astounding literary output. On June 10 he wrote to Spalatin, "I am both very idle and very busy here; I am studying Hebrew and Greek, and am writing without interruption." [18] He wrote an explanation of Psalm 68 and finished the commentary on the Magnificat, which he had put aside because of his trip to Worms. He continued working on a Latin exposition of the Psalms, the so-called *Operationes in Psalmos*, which he had begun in 1519, completing it through Psalm 22.[19] He dedicated a little tract to his "special lord and patron" Franz von Sickingen, in which he maintained that private confession was indeed precious and beneficial, but that it ought not be made obligatory.[20] In fact, one could just as well make one's confession to a Christian brother as to a priest. To the "poor little flock of Christ in Wittenberg" he sent an explanation of Psalm 37.[21] "By God's grace I am still as courageous and defiant as I have ever been. I have been overtaken by a minor bodily irritation, but that matters little. Rest assured and fear no one." [22]

One of Luther's most significant theological works, his refutation of the tract by Latomus, also originated at the Wartburg.[23] In a work published on May 8, 1521, the Louvain theologian Jakob Masson (called by the Greek name Latomus) attempted to expand and strengthen Luther's condemnation by the Louvain faculty. Luther obtained a copy on May 26 and immediately, though somewhat reluctantly, began a reply. He had no resources at his disposal other than the Bible and his excellent memory. Nevertheless, this effort resulted in one of Luther's most systematic statements of his teachings on justification and his principles of scriptural interpretation.

Luther concentrated his defense on the recognition that all our actions are sins—including our so-called good works—when they do not stand under grace. Even after Baptism there exists not just weakness, but also sin. No one can become righteous through their own attempts at justification, but only through God's mercy. It is only believers whose sins are not counted against them. If you take away God's mercy, then they are sinners. Those who believe are both righteous and sinful at the same time. There is no such thing as "merit." Grace is not a quality of the soul, but the gracious gift of God *(favor dei)*. The whole person stands under grace and the whole person stands under wrath. "Everything is forgiven through grace, but as yet not everything is healed through the gift." [24]

In support of his position Luther pointed to Romans 7, where, according to his understanding, Paul was speaking of himself as a Christian. Throughout the work he attempted to clarify the correct use of Scripture over against scholastic and allegorical misinterpretations. One should refrain from introducing any new theological concepts that are not in accordance with Scripture. In this connection Luther did not at all like the word *homoousion* (of one being or essence) [used in the Nicene Creed]; but this opinion surely did not make him a heretic.[25] One ought to beware of scholastic theology and philosophy. It was very doubtful that Thomas Aquinas was saved, because one could thank him for the reign of Aristotle, that "destroyer of godly doctrine." [26] In a brief overview we can only touch on the wealth of thought to be found in this treatise. Luther never responded to a later rejoinder by Latomus (1525).

Hieronymous Emser continued the literary feud that had begun after the Leipzig disputation, and therefore provoked a short response from Luther.[27] On April 15, 1521, the theological faculty in Paris issued a decree condemning a series of 104 statements from Luther's writings as pernicious heresies. Melanchthon composed an apology on Luther's behalf. Luther contented himself with translating this apology and the decree and adding his own strongly worded preface and epilog.[28] At the Wartburg Luther also learned that his name had been inserted into the bull *In coena domini* (In the Lord's Supper). This bull of 1364 called for the names of all those who had been excommunicated by the pope to be publicly read and damned every Maundy Thursday, which had the liturgical name *In coena domini*. Luther translated the bull into German and reissued it along with his own comments.[29]

Another matter, however, disturbed Luther more than these renewed animosities. He was preoccupied with it for months. Albert of Mainz, who had caused the whole uproar in the church with his indulgence sales in 1517, had again dared to display his immense collection of relics in his residence at Halle. He promised great indulgences for those who visited. Albert was in constant need of money to maintain his lavish life-style. When he discovered that Luther was planning to publish a treatise *Against the Idol of Halle,* the archbishop worked through his advisor Capito to obtain an order from Elector Frederick commanding Luther to keep silent.[30] But Luther gave no thought to compliance. He sent his manuscript to Spalatin, who was to have it printed.[31] When Spalatin refused, he fired off an impassioned reply "in *Anfechtung* and anger." [32] It was not the public peace, but God's peace that was at stake. "Not so, Spalatin! Not so, Elector!" For the sake of Christ's sheep one had to resist that hideous wolf [Albert of Mainz].

On December 1 Luther addressed a letter to Albert that could not possibly have been more candid.[33] He had already written the cardinal twice without success, first on October 31, 1517, and again on February 4, 1520. This third and last warning was based on Matt. 18:17. Albert ought to leave the poor people alone and behave like a bishop rather than a wolf. God could also oppose a cardinal from Mainz; he takes special pleasure in cutting down the tallest cedars. The cardinal ought not be lulled into thinking that Luther was dead. God would begin a game with him that few people expected. Moreover, Albert should leave in peace those priests who had married. Luther gave the cardinal an ultimatum: If he did not receive a positive reply within 14 days, he would publish his booklet attacking him. In such a manner an excommunicated and banned monk wrote to one of the most powerful princes of the empire. But the unbelievable happened: the cardinal wrote the "dear respected Doctor" a gracious and friendly letter and assured him that the cause of the trouble had been eliminated.[34]

Capito dispatched the letter on December 21, but attached a note of his own suggesting that since the cardinal was so well-disposed toward Luther, he ought not be antagonized any further.[35] Capito himself had been successful in persuading Albert to initiate reforms in the manner indicated by Erasmus. Luther answered this letter on January 17, 1522.[36] He was not at all pleased with what he read; Capito's comments had detracted from the credibility of Albert's letter. The gospel could not be served by false modesty and flattery. Love ought not fail, but faith dared not be infringed upon. Compromise accomplished nothing. Nevertheless Luther did not publish his attack on Albert. Instead he asked Melanchthon to hold it in safekeeping.

In this manner Luther continued from a distance to work effectively in pastoral care by means of publications and letters. He carried on his exchanges with his theological and ecclesiastical opponents. Luther concerned himself with the movement toward religious renewal in Wittenberg; that we will discuss in due course. But the two most valuable contributions he made during his time at the Wartburg were the German church postils (homiletical expositions) and the German translation of the New Testament.

Luther received the initial stimulus for the postils from Elector Frederick in October 1519; he had suggested the project as a way of shifting Luther's attention from more "biting and turbulent polemics" to "peaceful studies." [37] Luther in turn dedicated the collection to the elector. Since it was intended for priests, Luther wrote it in Latin. The piece took some time to complete. It did not appear until March 7, 1521, and was titled, *Enarrationes epistolarum et euangeliorum, quas postillas vocant.*[38] It contained only the sermons for the four Sundays in Advent. While at the Wartburg Luther decided to work on them some more and bring them out first in German. On May 14 he asked Spalatin to send him the original work. Since this was delayed, he began working on the Christmas portions, that is, on the sermons from Christmas to Epiphany.[39] He worked on these until mid-September. From November through February he translated and reworked the original Advent section. The two segments were published separately. The section between Epiphany and Easter did not appear until 1525.

The postils consisted not only of model sermons, but also introduced each Gospel. They were intended to help preachers overcome prevailing custom of using sacred legends or moralisms in their sermons. It was the one gospel of Christ to which the entire Scripture bore witness; by comparison all human words were nothing but idle prattle. Luther was not opposed to having the postils read in public worship; in later years he discovered that the book had also become popular among the laity for devotional use.

Luther's German translation of the New Testament remains the most significant accomplishment of the Wartburg period. He received the stimulus for it during a secret visit to Wittenberg early in December. "[It is] an undertaking our friends request," he wrote in a letter to Lang on December 18.[40] But their desire corresponded to his own. "I am born for my Germans, whom I want to serve," he wrote (in Latin!) to Nikolaus Gerbel in Strasbourg on November 1, 1521.[41] Among other things he was thinking of the postils. The greatest service he contributed to "his Germans" was the translation of the Bible. Luther had the Bible to thank for everything. He could not keep it to himself; he had to pass it on to the laity so they could draw from it and so realize the priesthood of all believers.

It is understandable that Luther did not immediately attempt the whole Bible, but rather began with the New Testament. The completion of the translation took him a mere 11 weeks—an incredible achievement. His translation differed from previous German versions in two ways: it was based on the original Greek text rather than on the inaccurate Latin Vulgate, and it made use of a style of German the people could understand. The task was not easy. All his life Luther had relied on the Vulgate more than on the Greek text. He was not a Greek scholar as Melanchthon was. In addition to the Vulgate, which he knew virtually by heart, he also had close at hand the Latin translation that Erasmus had included along with his Greek edition of the New Testament. Apparently he did not use any of the medieval German translations. The Greek text he used was Erasmus's second edition, published in 1519.

In a table talk of 1532, Luther spoke of the style of German he had selected for the translation: "The language I used was the language of the Saxon chancellory, used by every prince and king in Germany, and so it was the German language common to everyone." [42] Luther was aware that under Emperors Maximilian and Frederick a movement had begun to establish a standard German language; this was to prevent divisions between those who spoke high and low German. Therefore Luther did not create New High German, but it was by means of his Bible that New High German became a connecting link between different groups and was first heard in all its strength and beauty. No one less than Goethe was amazed by the power of Luther's German. Nietzsche was similarly astounded.

After his return to Wittenberg Luther continued to work at perfecting his translation, assisted by much good counsel from Melanchthon and Spalatin. In September 1522, the *German New Testament,* often called the "September Testament," was printed in Wittenberg by Melchior Lotther. Luther's name did not appear on the title page; Luther never requested royalties for any of his books. The Revelation of John was illustrated with woodcuts by Lucas Cranach.

Luther's preface to the entire volume and his introductions to the individual books are gems.[43] The gospel was "a good story and report, sounded forth into all the world by the apostles." Romans was truly the chief part of the New Testament. Luther explained that book's most important concepts. Faith is "a divine work in us which changes us and makes us to be born anew of God. . . . O it is a living, busy, active, mighty thing, this faith. It is impossible for it not to be doing good works incessantly." Luther did not hesitate in assigning each of the individual books a different rank. The gospel of John was rightly "the one, fine, true, and chief gospel."

Compared with John and the most important of Paul's letters, James was "an epistle of straw . . . for it has nothing of the nature of the gospel about it." [44] In his preface to James, Luther especially criticized that book for teaching justification through works and saying nothing about Christ.[45] The "true test" for all books was whether or not they "inculcate Christ." "Whatever does not teach Christ is not yet apostolic, even though St. Peter or St. Paul does the teaching. Again, whatever preaches Christ would be apostolic, even if Judas, Annas, Pilate, and Herod were doing it." Even though Luther did not consider James one of the major books of the Bible, he admitted that there were many good sayings in it.

Luther also looked critically at Hebrews; although the author could not have been Paul, he was nevertheless a learned man. Yet the book's rejection of the possibility of a second repentance after Baptism was a "hard knot" to unravel and contrary to all of the Gospels and to Paul.[46] Concerning the Revelation of John, "My spirit cannot accommodate itself," because the book dealt with pictures and visions, and he found it difficult to learn rightly about Christ from it.[47] In a later preface to the Apocalypse Luther expressed himself more positively, having in the meanwhile accepted the church-historical interpretation.[48]

In his day Luther stood alone in his completely free and varied judgment of the biblical canon; only since the Enlightenment have we been able to recapture his spirit. After completing the New Testament Luther continued to work on his Bible translation, enlisting an entire staff of learned assistants. In 1534 the entire Bible was published in German. Each of the individual books of the Old Testament had already been issued upon its completion. The full German Bible of 1534 was primarily Luther's work, though one should not overlook the contributions and support of his colleagues. Revised editions of the completed work continued to appear during Luther's lifetime. The last edition, issued before his death, was the 1545 Bible. Down through the years the Bible's printers and publishers have varied and its format and organization have changed, but the text of the Luther Bible remained basically unchanged until the time of modern Bible revisions.

Luther defended his translation in *On Translating: An Open Letter,* published in 1530.[49] He took issue with various criticisms that had been leveled by persons such as Hieronymus Emser. When translating it was no use asking the letters of the Latin language how to speak German. "Rather we must inquire about this of the mother in the home, the children on the street, the common man in the marketplace. We must be guided by their language, the way they speak, and do our translating accordingly. That way they will understand it and recognize that we are speaking German to them." Where Matt. 12:34 literally says, "Out of the abundance of the heart the mouth speaks," Luther had translated, "What fills the heart overflows the mouth." The angelic greeting, "Hail Mary, full of grace" was best translated, "Dear Mary." To Rom. 3:38 he had added the word *alone* after *faith* because only then did the correct sense of the passage become clear. His opponents had accused him of distorting the Bible with this addition; a modern catholic exegete of our own day maintains that Luther was correct. Luther had good reason to remark that his enemies were "stealing" his language. In fact the grim Duke George himself had said, "if only the monk would translate the whole Bible into German, and then go to the place he ought to go." [50]

The Old Testament gave Luther the most trouble. "It has often happened that for two or three or four weeks we have searched and inquired for a single word." At times in translating Job they took four days to complete only three sentences. "Now that it is translated and finished, everybody can read and criticize it . . . without realizing what boulders and clods had once lain there where he now goes along as over a smoothly-planed board. . . . The plowing goes well when the field is cleared. But rooting out the woods and stumps, and getting the field ready — this is a job nobody wants." [51]

In order to visualize the 12 pearls of the new Jerusalem Luther visited a jeweler.[52] Before describing the sacrifices of Leviticus he visited the butcher. "Translating is not every man's skill as the mad saints imagine. It requires a right, devout, honest, sincere, God-fearing, Christian, trained, informed, and experienced heart." [53]

Luther was guided not only by what was being spoken by the common people, but also by what was in the heart of the saints.[54] He translated the Bible into German, but his translation was not a distortion.

Luther was not only an unparalleled master of words who possessed a finely tuned musical ear for the rhythm of a sentence, he was also a person who was immersed in the spirit of the Bible in a way that has seldom been equalled. He lived in the Scriptures. He himself once said, "The Scriptures are a vast forest, but there's no tree in it that I haven't shaken with my hand." [55] His translation was not a slave to the letter but rather served the spirit. Luther had the gift of discerning the divine heart of Scripture and of couching it so totally and completely in human forms that the words came to light and life. For that we cannot sufficiently thank him.

Unrest in Wittenberg

Up until this time Luther had conducted his battle for the re-formation of the church solely with the Word. Outwardly, the practices of the church remained as they had been. But while Lu-ther sat alone at the Wartburg, others felt called to complete his work. They wanted words to be followed by actions. Although this goal was understandable, the result was that the Reformation threatened to become a revolution. There was a danger that the old legalism would be replaced by a new one. The primary issues were celibacy and the celebration of the Mass, as well as the adora-tion of images.

In his appeal *To the Christian Nobility* Luther had rejected obligatory celibacy for priests, but not for monks — since they took their vows voluntarily. Now Luther discovered that his former stu-dent Bartholomäus Bernhardi of Feldkirchen, at that time provost in Kemberg, had married. Others followed his example. On Febru-ary 10, 1522, Justus Jonas also was married. Then Karlstadt de-clared that monks also had the right to be free from celibacy.[1] Melanchthon was inclined to agree; the monastic vow could not be binding if one was unable to fulfill it. Luther could not go along with this; by means of such an argument one could set aside every command of God. He would have to give the matter further thought.

In September 1521, Luther wrote the first theses on celibacy. Those who took a vow of celibacy in order to be saved acted wrongly. Luther soon followed this first set of theses with a second set.[2] Meanwhile, more Wittenberg Augustinians left the cloister, among them the fiery preacher Gabriel Zwilling. In order to clear his conscience, Luther wrote a long Latin work entitled *The Judgment of Martin Luther on Monastic Vows* (November 1521).[3] It was published in February 1522, despite the reservations of Spalatin. We have already mentioned the preface to this work in connection with Luther's first Mass; it was written in the form of a letter to his father. In this book Luther developed the major thoughts of his theses on vows. To make a vow with the intention of earning salvation was an abomination.

Taking up Melanchthon's objection that vows incapable of being fulfilled were not binding, Luther contended that marriage had been ordained by God to make true chastity possible. If one were able to fulfill the vow of chastity in marriage but not in celibacy, then the monastic vow had to give way to the divine command. Celibacy required a special gift of God, but there was no special promise attached to it. Luther still valued true celibacy as highly as he ever had. He wrote to Spalatin that he would not let a wife be imposed on him.[4]

Bugenhagen's judgment concerning Luther's treatise *On Monastic Vows* was correct: "This will revolutionize public life. The teachings that preceded it could not have done that." Melanchthon added, "This is truly the beginning of liberation for the monks." [5] After it was published the monks began to leave the monastery in what was, at least in part, a tumultuous exodus. At any rate that was Luther's judgment in his letters to Lang and Link of December 18. No one should be forced to remain, but neither should anyone be forced to leave. Luther himself intended to remain a monk.[6]

About the time of Epiphany in 1522, one of the Augustinian communities in Wittenberg made the following decisions: Those who wished to continue living as monks and hold to the gospel were welcome to stay; those who wanted to leave could do so freely, but not to serve the desires of the flesh. Those who remained in the cloister should study Holy Scripture or engage in useful employment. Begging should be abolished.

Meanwhile the practical reform of the Lord's Supper and the Mass were also being undertaken, primarily by the Augustinians. In *The Babylonian Captivity* Luther had advocated giving the chalice to the laity and had rejected the sacrificial nature of the Mass. But he did not consider lay reception of the wine to be necessary for salvation. Karlstadt, however, soon after issuing his statement on celibacy, also declared that whoever participated in the Lord's Supper without receiving the wine had sinned; it would be better to refrain from the Supper altogether.

Karlstadt had grasped very little of what Luther meant by Christian freedom; he thought legalistically. Luther was gracious and open about matters that did not affect salvation; Karlstadt was in favor of coercion concerning details. For Luther the question of the sacrificial nature of the Mass was far more significant than whether or not the laity were offered the chalice. This sacrificial character was most apparent in the so-called private masses celebrated by priests alone, in the absence of the eucharistic community. Luther had already written to Melanchthon on August 1, 1521, "I also will never say another private mass in all eternity." [7]

In Wittenberg, Gabriel Zwilling was the chief opponent of the concept of sacrifice. He called for a return to the agape meals of the early church. On October 13 the service of the Mass was discontinued in the cloister church and replaced by preaching only. Elector Frederick requested counsel on this matter from the university and from the canons of the castle church. The report of October 20 recommended that the elector continue the reforms, only with some care. But the elector was unable to make a decision. Therefore unrest continued to grow, intensified by the departure of the monks.

Luther attempted to clarify the situation with his work on the abolition of private masses, *De abroganda missa privata*, at the beginning of November 1521. [8] A German edition appeared under the title, *The Misuse of the Mass*. [9] Once again Spalatin initially hesitated giving his approval for publication, but eventually he bowed to the request of Luther. Luther dedicated the work to his "dear brothers, the Augustinians in Wittenberg." He was truly happy that they wished to abolish the Mass and reform the liturgy, but he wondered whether their consciences were clear and their wills strong enough to withstand the hostility that would surely be directed against them. In the beginning of his battle with the pope his own heart had often "quavered" and the question kept coming back, "Are you alone wise?" His primary reason for writing the present work was to strengthen their consciences.

Luther attempted to develop his teaching on the office of the priesthood, the sacrament of the altar, and the provisional nature of human ordinances on the basis of Holy Scripture. He directed his attack against the *Winkelmessen*, that is, against the private masses that had been financially endowed for the benefit of departed souls; they were nothing but works of the devil. He could not approve of self-communion without the presence of another priest or the participation of a believing community. He hoped that all the privately endowed masses at All Saints Church would be abolished. This favorite institution of the elector had become a temple of abomination, a house of idolatry.[10] Indeed the Wittenbergers ought to continue their reforms. However, they were by all means to avoid discord and give due consideration to those who were weak.[11]

When reports of quite a different nature reached the Wartburg, Luther decided to pay a secret visit to Wittenberg. Priests who wanted to say Mass had been driven away by force. The Barefoot Cloister had been threatened, and stones had been thrown through the windows at the home of several cathedral canons. On December 2 Luther set out, still disguised as "Squire George." He risked riding through Leipzig, where he was almost recognized. In Wittenberg he stayed for three days at Amsdorf's house, where Melanchthon was living at the time. There Luther was visited by a number of his friends. It was at this time that Lucas Cranach painted him in his knightly apparel.

Luther was satisfied by what he saw and heard in Wittenberg. Therefore he was all the more angry that Spalatin had held back his last three manuscripts—those on the Mass, monastic vows, and the planned indulgence sales of Albert of Mainz. While still in Wittenberg he wrote to Spalatin and obtained their release.[12] Luther himself was of the opinion that one should not only continue to debate, but at times also follow this with action.[13] But he must already have had misgivings about the direction in which reform was moving.

No sooner had Luther returned to the Wartburg than he wrote *A Sincere Admonition by Martin Luther to All Christians, to Guard against Insurrection and Rebellion*.[14] He sent the manuscript to

Spalatin on December 12; it was not published until January 1522.[15] The papacy would surely be condemned; the last judgment was at hand. But rabble-rousers had no right to intervene and use violence. It was the task of the authorities to bring about change. "Insurrection lacks discernment; it generally harms the innocent more than the guilty." [16] "Hence, no insurrection is ever right, no matter how right the cause it seeks to promote." [17] If those who were in authority were not willing to carry out the needed reforms, one would simply have to suffer through. "I am and always will be on the side of those against whom insurrection is directed, no matter how unjust their cause; I am opposed to those who rise in insurrection, no matter how just their cause, because there can be no insurrection without hurting the innocent and shedding their blood." [18] The Word had done it all in the past, and one should build on the Word in the future. What had already been accomplished ought not be credited to Luther. "I ask that men make no reference to my name; let them call themselves Christians, not Lutherans. What is Luther? After all, the teaching is not mine. Neither was I crucified for anyone. . . . How then should I— poor stinking maggot-fodder that I am — come to have men call the children of Christ by my wretched name?" [19] When reforms were initiated one needed to take stock of the persons involved. "With wolves you cannot be too severe; with weak sheep you cannot be too gentle." [20] Luther was in favor of reform, but in an orderly fashion—without violence or rebellion.

The electoral prince concluded from the differing opinions expressed in Wittenberg that the time for thoroughgoing reform had not yet come. Karlstadt, who felt called to be a practical reformer (and who in Luther's absence had assumed leadership of the movement), thought otherwise. Originally a Thomist, he had become an ally of Luther. Now he took a different path, certainly with personal ambition as one of his motives. On Christmas Day 1521, Karlstadt preached on the correct reception of the sacrament and then distributed both the bread and the chalice into the hands of about 2000 worshipers. He officiated without vestments, omitted the Eucharistic Prayer, and spoke the words of institution in German. He declared that prior confession was not required for participation in the sacrament. On the following Sundays he repeated the same service. At that time this must have had a shocking effect.

Karlstadt also became engaged, and he was married on January 19, 1522.

Unrest increased when on December 27 three men from Zwickau appeared with Melanchthon: two weavers, Nikolaus Storch and Thomas Drechsel, and the former student Markus Thomae Stübner —the Zwickau "prophets." They claimed to have had personal revelations. Melanchthon, who sought in vain to have the electoral prince return Luther to Wittenberg, got himself into difficulties when the three men expressed their doubts about infant Baptism.

Zwickau was a place known for its religious and social unrest. This was prompted on the one hand by Waldensian and Hussite influences, and on the other by its weaving and silver mining industries. The views of Luther had also been readily accepted there. Since May of 1520 Thomas Müntzer had served in Zwickau as the preacher in St. Mary's church.[21] One could detect Luther's influence on his theology as well as that of the mystics. Müntzer was a fanatical and passionate agitator, though he was also an educated man. It was Luther himself who had recommended Müntzer for Zwickau, where he had already become the center of controversy. He had been drawn into a relationship with Nikolaus Storch and his secret society. After several blowups he had been expelled from the city.

The new year began turbulently in Wittenberg. In the Augustinian monastery, oil that had been blessed for anointing the sick, and religious images, were burned. All of the secondary altars were removed. Shortly before this Karlstadt had advocated the removal of images. He based his views on Exod. 20:4, according to which the making of "graven images" was condemned. Storch claimed that the Archangel Gabriel had appeared to him and had promised him, "you will sit on my throne." The entire social order was to be changed, all clerics were to be killed, and the godless eradicated. By means of "solitude" and perfect stillness one could achieve unity with God. Like Müntzer, Storch's mysticism was linked with a fanatic abhorrence of established order and a bloodthirsty apocalypticism.

In the midst of this confused situation, the city council on January 24, 1522, issued a *Praiseworthy Order for the Princely City of Wittenberg*—based in part on Luther's directives for reform. According to this, the principal goal of the city ought to be a fight against poverty. Those in various types of needs should be aided out of a "common chest." Begging, including that by the monks, would no longer be tolerated. Prostitutes should be banned. The worship service was to be celebrated according to Karlstadt's new order of service, and all images should be removed.

In spite of this, on February 6 there was an iconoclastic riot that was condemned by the elector and criticized by the city council. But neither Karlstadt nor Gabriel Zwilling would let themselves be deterred from their reforming passion. The elector declared that the new order of worship was contrary to his will, but he did not risk interfering. And so the disturbances continued. Part of the student body left the university. They were no longer interested in the study of the humanities. The *Schwärmerei* (enthusiasts) were opposed to education. Karlstadt also was overtaken by this mood. Misinterpreting Matt. 11:25, he rejected theological education and allowed uneducated laity to interpret Scripture. Later he also discarded his own doctor's title, because in Matt. 23:8 Jesus said, "You are not to be called rabbi, for you have one teacher."

Luther called those who espoused this form of Christianity "enthusiasts," and he was astonished that Melanchthon himself had been taken in by them. The Zwickau prophets did not impress him. In a letter of January 13, 1522, he sought to free Melanchthon of his lingering doubts.[22] The Zwickau prophets could not prove their "calling." They knew nothing of *Anfechtung*, which was "the only touchstone of Christians." Their arguments against infant Baptism did not appear to be sound.

The turmoil in Wittenberg continued, and the electoral prince found himself completely at sea. When at last the city council sent a call for help to Luther, he could no longer stay at the Wartburg. In a short letter of February 24, he informed the elector of his departure.[23] He never mentioned the personal peril of such a venture, referring instead to the difficulties his move might cause the elector.

Elector Frederick was not only undecided about what he should do concerning the recent changes in Wittenberg, but as territorial lord he also felt threatened by the mandate that had been issued in Nuremberg by the imperial government on January 20, 1522. On the initiative of Duke George, the territorial rulers had been ordered to take firm action against the innovations. It was primarily

Frederick whom they had in mind. Though he was not intimidated, Frederick was disturbed by this development. Another imperial diet had been set for March 26; what would happen if it insisted on a strict enforcement of the Edict of Worms? Would that not threaten a resolution? As soon as he received Luther's letter he sent instructions to the reformer.[24] He informed Luther of the situation in Nuremberg, of the hopeless confusion in Wittenberg, and of his own indecision. It would be better if Luther would postpone his return at least until after the next imperial diet. If he were asked to hand Luther over, he did not know what the outcome would be for his land or for his people.

Luther received this notice on the evening before he left the Wartburg. He knew then that he would be acting on his own authority. With trusting faith he left on March 1. There was no way he could avoid traveling through the territory of his enemy, Duke George. Still, he retained his sense of humor. On March 3 two Swiss students met him in an inn called "The Black Bear" in Jena. Neither of them recognized the knight who displayed so many unusual insights and interests, and who instructed them to take greetings to Wittenberg from "someone who is coming." They took him to be Hutten. But Luther had his fun when, shortly afterward, he met them again in Wittenberg in the company of their fellow countryman, Hieronymus Schurff.

It was not until May 5 in Borna that Luther was able to respond to the elector's instructions and justify his decision to return.[25] In this letter, one of the most splendid documents penned by Luther, he referred to the note he had sent on February 24. In almost every sentence he respectfully addressed Frederick as "Your Electoral Grace," yet there was a sense of roguishness in the repetition. He knew that the elector had acted with the best of intentions toward him; he did not want to hurt his feelings or instruct him in how he ought to conduct himself with his hasty note of February 24. Rather, he had written out of concern for the elector and in order to comfort him about "that untoward movement" in Wittenberg. Indeed he himself had almost lost heart; the situation in Wittenberg was the worst that he had encountered.

Luther said the gospel he proclaimed was not from human beings. It came from heaven only, through the Lord Jesus Christ, "so that I might well be able to boast and call myself a minister and evangelist." He had asked for a hearing not because of doubt, but out of excessive humility, in order to persuade others. But if this humility had detracted from the gospel, then it ought to cease. One year of hiding at the Wartburg was enough. He had stayed there not because of cowardice, but in order to please the elector. He would also have gone into Worms even though there were as many devils there as tiles on the roof.

For Luther, Duke George was far from the equal of one devil. Even now (the next day!) he would ride into Leipzig, though "it rained Duke Georges for nine days." Luther had prayed more than once that God would enlighten the Duke. "I have written this so our Electoral Grace might know that I am going to Wittenberg under a far higher protection than the Elector's. I have no intention of asking Your Electoral Grace for protection. Indeed I think I shall protect Your Electoral Grace more than you are able to protect me. And if I thought that Your Electoral Grace could and would protect me, I should not go. The sword ought not and cannot help a matter of this kind. God alone must do it—and without the solicitude and cooperation of men. Consequently he who believes the most can protect the most. And since I have the impression that Your Electoral Grace is still quite weak in faith, I can by no means regard Your Electoral Grace as the man to protect and save me." The elector should offer no resistance to the emperor on Luther's behalf; it would be enough if he left the door open to retrieving him. In any case the elector ought not suffer for Luther's sake. "Herewith I commend Your Electoral Grace to the grace of God. . . . If Your Electoral Grace believed, you would see the glory of God. But because you do not believe, you have not yet seen. Love and praise to God forever. Amen." Seldom if ever would a servant have dared to write his prince such a letter; yet one dares to call this man a servant of princes!

On March 6 Luther rode into Wittenberg. The elector—a man of great integrity—did not take Luther's letter amiss. Politically the letter was useless to the elector; he could not possibly forward it to the imperial government. Therefore he asked for another letter from Luther, in which he would affirm that he had returned to Wittenberg against the elector's wishes and without his knowledge. With the help of Spalatin's corrections Luther was able to find a formulation that satisfied Frederick.[26] A passage that said, "something absolutely different was decided in heaven than at Nuremberg" was softened in the final version.[27]

Orderly Reform

On the day of Luther's return to Wittenberg, March 6, the city council sent him the fabric for a new monk's cowl, which he wore until October 9, 1524.[1] His first concern was to restore confidence and order. The cowl served him well as a symbol; inner reform was not to destroy externals. The plan was to be evolution, not revolution. The new spirit possessed the inner freedom to maintain continuity in outward forms. Luther was no iconoclast.

The way in which Luther brought the disrupted community back to its senses stands as one of his greatest achievements. On March 9, Invocavit Sunday, he mounted the pulpit in the parish church and preached eight days in a row, once again placing his trust in the power of the Word. He never published these sermons, though they were later printed, using the notes made by persons who were present.[2]

Although none of the sermons was based on a particular biblical text, they were permeated with biblical content. The first one began with a powerful appeal to personal faith and decisions of conscience: "The summons of death comes to us all, and no one can die for another. Everyone must fight his own battle with death by himself, alone. We shout into another's ear, but everyone must himself be prepared for the time of death, for I will not be with you then, nor you with me." [3] The Wittenbergers had indeed made much progress in their faith, but they were to be criticized for two things. First, they had not understood the meaning of love.

With their all-too-hasty reforms they had driven the weak and in-
secure back into the arms of the papacy. They had also failed to
understand the meaning of evangelical freedom. They had made a
law out of the gospel. External forms and ceremonies did not matter, if only the Word was preached. "Loveless liberty" only led to
new constraints.[4]

Only in passing did Luther remind them of the need for order.
The Mass needed to be altered, but that should not have been done
in such a disturbing fashion. They might also have asked Luther
for his opinion, since he still held the office of preacher in the
Wittenberg parish church.[5] Quite frankly, none of his enemies had
hurt him as much as the Wittenbergers had.[6]

Having expressed his principal concerns in the first sermon,
Luther turned to specific questions in those that followed. Since in
love one should refrain from using force in those matters that required reform, was it not even more imperative to refrain from
using force in those things that God had left to human discretion?
"In short, I will preach it, teach it, write it, but I will constrain no
man by force, for faith must come freely without compulsion." The
Wittenbergers should look to him as an example. "I did nothing;
the Word did everything." He could have plunged all of Germany
into a bloodbath and started such a game that even the emperor
would not have been safe. "But what would it have been? Mere
fool's play. I did nothing; I let the Word do its work."[7]

Regulations concerning fasting belonged in the category of *adiaphora* or "free things." Paintings and objects of religious art were
also *adiaphora*, "although it would be much better if we did not
have them at all."[8] One dared not transform freedom into compulsion. Only where images were venerated should they "be put
away and destroyed,"[9] and then only by those in authority.[10] The
fanatic destruction of images would only strengthen their adoration.[11] Here, too, "love is the captain."[12] The worst misuse of
images was not their veneration: no one was so foolish as to think
that an image was a God. A much greater abomination was the
works righteousness associated with images; yet those who had
destroyed them had not recognized this.[13] The persons who presented these images to the churches in the first place did so to buy
their salvation.

It was certainly not a sin for the laity to take the host in their hands during Communion, but the Scriptures did not command that this be done. Nor ought one make a law of giving the chalice to the laity and force persons to accept the practice. The Wittenbergers should not have eliminated confession, even though it must be given freely. He himself had derived much comfort and strength from private confession. He was well acquainted with the devil; the Wittenbergers, with their "foolish actions," had demonstrated that they did not yet recognize him.

In his sermons Luther established that which is basic to ecclesiastical reform: a loving consideration of the "weak," and freedom in relationship to outward ceremonies. These two principles revealed his noble spirit and his pastoral heart. Because he relied only on the power of the Word, Luther has often been accused of being a naive idealist. In reality his approach did not hinder subsequent reforms. Rather, it was to his credit that he kept the Reformation from turning into an "insurrection." Certainly his consideration for the elector and for the mandate of Nuremberg also played a part in this. Luther was not just an idealist—he was also a realist. He would have risked the whole Reformation if he had not intervened in the Wittenberg disorders of 1522. Much more was at stake than rites and ceremonies.

The testimonies of Hieronymus Schurff, Johann Kessler, the Swiss students from "The Black Bear," of Capito (who had made a brief visit to Wittenberg), and of others lead us to conclude that Luther was able to calm the storm in Wittenberg.[14] Melanchthon was relieved to turn responsibility back over to Luther. Even Gabriel Zwilling admitted that Luther was right. Only Karlstadt remained unconvinced. In his opinion Luther was bogged down with measures that went only halfway. The printing of a document defending Karlstadt's views was prohibited by the rector of the university, and Karlstadt was no longer allowed to conduct services in the city church. He was still allowed to serve in the castle church. Luther attempted in vain to reestablish a friendly relationship with him.

The Zwickau prophets were not in Wittenberg at the time Luther preached his series of Invocavit sermons. However, at the end of April Markus Stübner and another like-minded companion showed up for a discussion with Luther. Nothing came of the conversation. Luther detested their spiritual arrogance. He asked them to demonstrate the authenticity of their "spirit" by performing miracles; they declined, but threatened that Luther would eventually be compelled to believe them.[15] Early in September Nickolaus Storch once again made an appearance in Wittenberg, but was able to accomplish very little. The circle of followers that had gathered around the Zwickau prophets in Wittenberg soon dispersed.

During the week of Invocavit Luther had already decided that he would publish the principles expressed in his sermons for a wider audience. The resulting treatise, *Receiving Both Kinds in the Sacrament,* appeared in April 1522.[16] Luther considered the unrest in Wittenberg a work of the devil. Unable to accomplish his goal through the onslaughts of the papists, the devil had shifted tactics and was now using persons from Luther's own circle of friends.

Despite all of the added rules and practices with which the church has fenced off the sacrament, one should not permit Christian freedom to be taken away. Every person was allowed to receive the wine and to hold the bread in his or her hands. Nevertheless, one still needed to ask whether one should practice this freedom. Luther feared that the "common person" was not yet ready for it. The people did not yet know how to exercise their freedom with good consciences. Therefore for a time one had to continue to put up with this abuse of the sacrament and wait patiently until the gospel had become an inner reality in people's lives. The Mass should continue to be celebrated, yet the priests could refrain from using those words that spoke of sacrifice. The lay people would never notice their omission and so would not be offended.[17] (Admittedly at this point Luther's advice was rather questionable.)

Luther also thought it was acceptable for an individual to follow the custom of a place and receive Communion in either the old or the new manner,[18] or one could choose not to receive the sacrament at all for awhile.[19] Those who refrained from participating in the sacrament because they had been refused the chalice should also be tolerated. Private masses for the dead should be stopped; but one ought not drag those priests who still wanted to conduct them from their altars.[20] Concerning confession and the religious images, Luther repeated what he had already said in his sermons. Priests and monks who could not bridle their sexual desires were to marry; congregations ought not complain about this. They should rather direct their anger at unchastity. Still, whoever married ought to do so with a good conscience.[21] In summary, religious reform should begin with inner rather than with outer matters.[22]

Luther's proposals were carried out. The priests appeared in their customary vestments, the Mass was chanted in Latin, and the host was placed in the recipient's mouth. Those who desired to receive the chalice could do so. The Eucharistic Prayer was omitted. Since it had previously been spoken in Latin and in a very low voice, the omission attracted little notice. Private masses were no longer said in the parish church. In the castle church, however, the priests still clung tenaciously to the traditional liturgy of the Mass and to private masses.

Luther also concerned himself with church conditions in other areas. In Erfurt, for example, the lay people had lashed out against the cult of the saints. On the other hand, Luther had to resist the bishops, who had now been supported by the imperial government in their desire to oppose all reform. In a work entitled *Against the Spiritual Estate of the Pope and the Bishops, Falsely So Called,* Luther denounced them more caustically than ever.[23] In 1523 he asserted the rights of Christian congregations over against bishops in *That a Christian Assembly or Congregation Has the Right and Power to Judge All Teaching and to Call, Appoint, and Dismiss Teachers, Established and Proven by Scripture.*[24] A pastor who had been called and installed by a congregation in this manner was properly installed, *rite vocatus.*[25] In fact, a good bishop should not appoint a pastor without the consent of the congregation.[26]

In the pursuit of an evangelical reform, Luther was active not only in Wittenberg but also preached in a number of places in Saxony: Altenburg, Zerbst, Eilenburg, Weimar, Torgau, and Zwickau. These trips were not without danger, since they often required Luther to travel through the territory of Duke George. Inquiries arrived from many locations concerning the steps that should be taken to initiate reform.

The evangelical movement continued to gain favor throughout the territories of Germany. Luther's program was proving itself in practice. By 1523 the feast of Corpus Christi was no longer celebrated in Wittenberg or in Torgau, the residence of the elector. In the parish church of Wittenberg the saints' days were no longer observed; those festivals related to Mary that could also be understood as honoring Jesus were retained. Frequent masses were replaced by daily worship services consisting of proclamation of the Word and prayer. This new order of service is found in Luther's little tract, *On the Order of Worship in the Congregation.*[27] Everything should be done "to enhance the Word and not again allow worship to deteriorate into the monotonous sing-song that it has been." In his Maundy Thursday sermon of April 2, 1523, Luther announced that in the future, Communion would be offered only to those communicants who had previously been examined.[28] After Easter *The Little German Baptismal Book* appeared; in essence it was a condensed version of the traditional Latin rite. Exorcism was retained.[29] By the end of 1523 the Lord's Supper was celebrated in the parish church only under both kinds. In Luther's opinion the congregation had been sufficiently prepared for the change.

In the castle church, by contrast, there were a number of problems. The treasure of relics had actually been increased since the posting of the 95 Theses. Even indulgences had been announced one more time in 1520. For a year afterward the relics continued to be displayed, though without indulgences. Not until 1523 were they shown only to those who asked to see them. Through Spalatin Luther had made several attempts to persuade the elector to abolish the endowments for private masses. He also called the sexual conduct of the canons a public outrage. Adherents of the gospel—Amsdorf, Jonas, and Karlstadt—were in the minority. As a result they failed in their movement to end the masses. The elector did not feel that he could suspend the endowments of his ancestors.

Luther continued to seek change through exhortations from the pulpit. Even attempts at compromise failed. When toward the end of 1524 the chalice was still denied to the laity, despite an agreement to the contrary, Luther issued an ultimatum concerning the endowments. And on November 17, 1524, he took the matter to the pulpit a second time. This sermon on the first Sunday in Advent was a scathing attack on private masses.[30] It was later reworked into the 1525 treatise, *The Abomination of the Secret Mass.*[31]

All but three canons acquiesced to the demands for change. The three that remained were in danger of complete isolation, opposed by the city council, the rector of the university, and the city pastor. When the elector withdrew his support, they conceded. On December 24, 1524, the new order of service was introduced in the castle church, and the priests who had been connected with the endowment became an evangelical community with corresponding services of worship. Responsibility for the pastoral office in the parish church was shifted from the Augustinian chapter to the city council, and Bugenhagen was appointed to that position. It is to Luther's credit that he was able to uphold his principles of freedom and consideration for the weak as long as he did. On the whole the new order of worship was freely accepted by the congregation. Toward the end of 1523 Luther — at the request of his friend Nikolaus Hausmann, pastor of St. Mary's Church in Zwickau—drew up a detailed description of the new order in his *Formula Missae et Communionis pro Ecclesia Wittembergensi.*[32] Luther emphasized that he undertook nothing with force, but proceeded hesitantly out of consideration for the weak, but also because of the many "thoughtless and presumptuous spirits" whose "sole joy is in new innovations." [33] The designation *Mass* could be retained for the celebration of the Lord's Supper, and the use of Latin could continue. The traditional selection of pericopes was not the best, but it could be used as it was for the time being.

Luther continued his practice of following the traditional sequence of the Mass. In fact the traditional order is still retained in Lutheran worship. The number of collects was reduced and some other parts were shortened. The sermon could be inserted before the Introit, but it would be more appropriate to place it immediately after the Gospel or the Creed. Naturally it had to be in German. The *Offertorium* (sacrifice) and the canon prayers were deleted. The words of institution were to be chanted loudly and distinctly so that they could be heard by everyone in the congregation. Candles and incense were *adiaphora.* Vestments were not of much concern, but they should not be pompous. Repeatedly Luther assured his readers that none of his suggestions were meant to be binding; diversity was allowed. A path toward orderly reform had been established.

Civil Government
and Public Life

Prior to 1517 Luther was able to confine himself, for the most part, to his activities as a professor, although he also fulfilled his monastic obligations. But with the posting of the 95 Theses he came under the glare of public scrutiny.[1] Yet at first he was still the great champion who carried the responsibility for the gospel completely on his own shoulders. After his return to Wittenberg, Luther the champion became Luther the churchman. He remained the guiding spirit of reform, but he no longer stood alone. He became involved with a wide variety of issues and addressed questions of public life. He was frequently sought out for his counsel. What he had begun as an individual had become an evangelical movement. Though he did not bear an ecclesiastical title, he in effect became a bishop, and he became increasingly occupied with new tasks.

Luther had been educated in Occamist political theories. Whereas Thomism advocated the subordination of the worldly order to the churchly, Occamism called for a coordination of the two. The conciliar movement of the 15th century had applied the Occamist view that in an emergency the state had the right to assume the tasks of the church—should the church fail to carry out its responsibilities. In his work addressed *To the Christian Nobility* Luther affirmed this position, and he put it into practice with the establishment of territorial churches. In Luther one does not find the theocratic misunderstanding of Augustine. In his lectures on Romans Luther quoted Augustine's dictum about the state being a band of robbers;[2] in fact he still referred to Augustine's comment in 1529.[3] But even in his early period Luther affirmed the power of civil authority. Yet it was not until the 20s that there was a pressing need for him to examine social and political problems.

In 1521 the emperor condemned the Reformation. In 1522 the enthusiasts began to appear. In 1525 came the shock of the Peasants' War. The task of restructuring the church in the Reformation territories could no longer be postponed. Luther directed his attention toward two fronts: on the one hand he battled against the medieval confusion of spiritual and civil authority; on the other hand he opposed the disruption of all worldly authority by the enthusiasts.

The treatise *Temporal Authority: To What Extent It Should Be Obeyed* (which appeared in March of 1523) is a classic summary of Luther's thought on this subject in the early 20s.[4] The immediate occasion for this work was Luther's correspondence with the well-known Bamberg jurist and lawyer, Johann Freiherr von Schwarzenberg, but it also became a response to the prohibition of Luther's translation of the New Testament in Ducal Saxony and other territories. The work was dedicated to Duke John, the brother of Frederick the Wise, because he had requested a written statement regarding these matters. Luther began with the specific question that was plaguing Duke John: How can the demands of the Sermon on the Mount be harmonized with the necessity for temporal order and powers? [5] Luther rejected the medieval notion that the Sermon on the Mount was not a set of general commandments for everyone, but a series of "counsels" for those on the path to perfection—that is, a monastic ethic.[6] Therefore Luther devoted the first part of his work to clarifying the relationship between spiritual and temporal authority.[7] He laid out the following fundamental principles:

1. The temporal sword is ordained by God.[8] The primary biblical basis Luther cited was Romans 13; he also referred to Gen. 9:6 and Exod. 21:23ff.

2. The nonviolent ethic of the Sermon on the Mount seems to contradict this assertion.[9] But the distinction between commandments and "evangelical counsels" was not useful.

3. In its place one must substitute the distinction between the kingdom of God and the kingdom of the world.[10] All those who truly believe in Christ belong to the kingdom of God. They need no temporal sword nor outward government; they do that which is

right on their own accord, without outward coercion; and when necessary they "willingly and cheerfully" suffer wrong.[11]

4. All those who are not truly Christians (that means most people) belong to the kingdom of the world.[12] For them the "sword" is necessary. Its task is to restrain evil and secure earthly peace. It would be irresponsible fanaticism to attempt to govern the world "by the gospel," that is, according to the radical standards of forgiveness of Matt. 5:39. That would mean opening the gates and doors of the world to every evil and setting aside every form of protection for the weak. "Just so would the wicked under the name of Christian abuse evangelical freedom, carry on their rascality, and insist that they were Christians subject neither to law nor sword." [13]

Luther's principle that one cannot govern the world "by the gospel" has often been misconstrued and misused. It does not mean that Luther left the world to be "governed by its own laws." The opposite of gospel is not self-determination, but God's law. The world must be governed by the law of God, that is, according to God's will. Further, the statement did not mean that Christians should not have influence on legislation. Christianity is thoroughly involved in politics.

Corresponding to these two "kingdoms," God has instituted two "authorities"; the spiritual, "to produce righteousness," and the temporal, "to bring about external peace and prevent evil deeds." [14] Each must be clearly distinguished from the other, but both are necessary in this world. The spiritual authority requires the temporal sword in order to restrain evil.

5. Why should Christians be subject to civil authority when they do not need the temporal sword for themselves? [15] They remain subject to temporal authority out of love for their neighbors, in order that their neighbors might be protected. Christians freely and obediently serve for the sake of those who cannot do without secular order.

6. This, however, means that Christians are willing to engage in positive cooperation with temporal authority.[16] This was an honest and level-headed consideration. If Christians are given civil offices, they should accept them with clear consciences. "Therefore, if you see that there is a lack of hangmen, constables, judges, lords, or princes, and you find that you are qualified, you should offer your services and seek the position, that the essential governmental

authority may not be despised and become enfeebled or perish. The world cannot and dare not dispense with it." [17]

With this argument Luther believed he had successfully harmonized temporal authority with the spirit of the Sermon on the Mount. "In what concerns you and yours, you govern yourself by the gospel and suffer injustice toward yourself as a true Christian; in what concerns the person or property of others, you govern yourself according to love and tolerate no injustice toward your neighbor." [18] Christ himself had not wielded the sword for two reasons: it was not his calling, and he wanted his own life to show clearly that God's kingdom has nothing to do with the sword.[19] But Christ did not forbid or suspend the use of the sword, rather, he confirmed it. Those who on principle want to avoid participating in civil affairs should logically also refrain from eating, drinking, or marrying, for those too are "God's work and ordinance." [20]

In the second part of his work Luther turned to the question, "How Far Temporal Authority Extends." [21] He called that section "the main part" because it was there that he sharply defined the limitations of the state.[22] His primary principle was that temporal authority held sway only over the body and outward affairs, not over the soul. With this principle Luther rejected the "totalitarian" state. To be sure, in his day the threat of totalitarianism was more apparent in the church than in the state. The essence of totalitarianism was the confusion of the two authorities. In opposition to this Luther emphasized that only God can rule over the soul. It was neither permissible nor possible to force anyone to believe.[23] When true faith was forbidden by the government, one had to disobey and suffer the consequences.[24]

Among the enemies of the gospel Luther named the lords of Meissen, Bavaria, and Brandenburg. He was not surprised at that.

> You must know that since the beginning of the world a wise prince is a mighty rare bird, and an upright prince even rarer. They are generally the biggest fools or the worst scoundrels on earth. . . . They are God's executioners and hangmen; his divine wrath uses them to punish the wicked and to maintain outward peace. Our God is a great lord and ruler; this is why he must also have such noble, highborn, and rich hangmen and constables. . . . If a prince should happen to be wise, upright, or a Christian, that is one of the great miracles, the most precious token of divine grace upon that land.[25]

It was with such language that the so-called servant of princes wrote to a prince! One is reminded of Luther's letter of March 5, 1522, to the elector.

Luther said it was the duty of bishops to avert heresy, but they were to do this with the Word of God and not with temporal power. "Heresy is a spiritual matter which you cannot hack to pieces with iron, consume with fire, or drown in water." [26] With these words Luther completely rejected the medieval approach to heresy and inaugurated a new age, even though the treatment of heretics in the evangelical territories did not at once reflect this new insight. It should be remembered that among the propositions condemned in the bull that threatened Luther with excommunication had been Luther's statement, "It is against the will of the Holy Spirit to burn heretics."

In the third part of the work Luther painted a picture of what a prince ought to be.[27] The office of a prince ought not be one of dominion but of service.[28] All boasting of one's own rights is reprehensible. "Reason [is] the master of all administration of law." [29] The highest law ought to be the good of one's subjects; a prince should follow the example of Christ in serving them.[30] "Where wrong cannot be punished without greater wrong, there let him waive his rights, however just they may be." [31] This applies not only to the enforcement of the law but also to the waging of war.

Regarding war, Luther proposed the following principles: (1) War is not allowed against one's own government, and therefore not against the emperor.[32] (2) War is allowed against equals or foreigners, but only if an offer of peace has been rejected. But even then the decisive issue ought to be the welfare of one's subjects and not one's own honor.[33] (3) Subjects must commit their lives and possessions to such a war. "In a war of this sort it is both Christian and an act of love to kill the enemy without hesitation, to plunder and burn and injure him by every method of warfare until he is conquered (except that one must beware of sin, and not violate wives and virgins)." [34] In victory one should show "mercy and peace." (4) Should one's own prince be in the wrong, Christian subjects must refuse to follow him. However, if they are uncertain, they can participate "without peril to their souls." [35]

It goes without saying that today we think differently about the destructive capacity of war and the problem of the so-called "just war." It is no longer possible to conduct a war without incurring great guilt. Luther was still bound to a highly individualistic view of war.

Luther's distinction between the two authorities can also be observed in his attitude toward the war with the Turks.[36] Above all, the Turkish threat should have led Christians to repent. This was the intention of the 34th thesis condemned by the bull threatening excommunication, and Luther repeated it in two writings of 1529, *On War against the Turks* [37] and *Sermon on Military Action against the Turks*.[38] When the Turks stood at the gates of Vienna, he publicly called for resistance. However, he emphasized that this war was not to be understood as a crusade. The emperor was not to conduct it as the "head of Christendom" but as the God-appointed defender of Germany. Without repentance and prayer the battle against the Turks, the enemies of Christ, would not be blessed.

In 1526 Luther used the same approach he had used in *Temporal Authority* when he replied affirmatively to the knight Assa von Kram's question in *Whether Soldiers, Too, Can Be Saved*.[39] In fact, he referred to the earlier work [40] and wrote, "Indeed, I might boast here that not since the time of the apostles have the temporal sword and temporal government been so clearly described or so highly praised as by me." [41] When a war was declared solely to punish wrong and evil, then the craft of war was a Christian work, and a deed of love.[42] Indeed, such a war was but a brief interlude of discord by comparison with the infinite and eternal discord it controls.[43] The rest of the work is devoted to insurrection and government, and our criticism of Luther's view need not be repeated.

Luther did not stop with the thoughts expressed in his *Temporal Authority*. Already in that work one notices the juxtaposition of two pairs of concepts: on the one hand Luther spoke of the kingdom of God and the kingdom of the world, and on the other of spiritual and temporal authority.

Behind the first pair of opposites still stood the Augustinian dualism in which the world was seen as being in opposition to God's kingdom. According to this view temporal authority exists only because of evil; the true Christian actually does not need it. Later, however (for example, in his exposition of Psalm 127),[44] Luther included all of the earthly orders (particularly marriage and the right to own property) under temporal authority — not just the power of the "sword" (the authority to punish).

With this expansion of temporal authority Luther's teaching of the two authorities was freed of the dualism in the Augustinian concept. "Temporal" was no longer equated with "sinful," but was conceived of as being earthly in a neutral sense. "Temporal reality" was the same as external order. By contrast with the tract on *Temporal Authority* of 1523, Christians were seen as belonging also to the kingdom of the world and as subject to temporal authority, not simply out of love for their neighbors, but also for their own sake—because they are social beings. In this sense Christians are "citizens of two worlds"; they belong not only to the kingdom of God, they are also citizens of this world. Christians require temporal authority for themselves as well as for others. Luther's rather "enthusiastic" statement of 1523—that Christians could get along without the temporal order—was thereby overcome. Not until this later interpretation of the two authorities do we have the mature form of Luther's "doctrine of the two kingdoms" before us.

In his sermon on December 15, 1532, Luther called temporal authority "God's government with the left hand." [45] Usually one quotes Luther imprecisely and speaks of "God's kingdom on the left," which can lead to misinterpretation. This form of Luther's statement suggests the separation of the sheep from the goats at the last judgment (Matt. 25:33). The kingdom on the left is then equated with the realm of evil, the kingdom opposed to God. In reality the expression "God's government with the left hand" means something entirely different. The kingdom governed with the left hand is God's realm as well, but not God's "proper" realm. God accomplishes the goals of his proper kingdom—the realm of the gospel, of reconciliation and redemption—with his right hand. With the left hand (only incidentally, so to speak) God preserves creation and earthly order. The government with the left hand is therefore not the kingdom of wrath, but God's rule over creation.[46] It is the kingdom of divine preservation of order. It is a transitory kingdom, but nevertheless a "divine arrangement." [47] Temporal order cannot be maintained without distinctions of persons and classes. These necessary distinctions are not a result of sin; they are ordained by God.

When the "two kingdoms" are understood as "two authorities," then the following statements hold true:

1. The two authorities have their unity in God's decree. God

rules in both with his goodness, love, and mercy; and the wrath of God, as well, functions in the service of God's mercy.

2. The two authorities are distinct from each other. They are related to one another like heaven and earth, like righteousness before God and civil righteousness, like love and justice, or like gospel and reason (where reason is understood in a positive sense).

3. The two authorities are dependent on each other. The kingdom of Christ could not endure in this world without temporal authority—without defense against evil and efforts made toward earthly peace. On the other hand, spiritual authority assists temporal authority by proclaiming God's will to government and to all classes.

4. The two authorities must not be confused with each other. This was Luther's chief concern. He accused the papacy (but also the enthusiasts and the peasants) of confusing the two—of wanting to derive laws for the temporal realm and societal advancement directly from the gospel.

So God rules in both kingdoms (through both authorities). Together they are a bulwark against the kingdom of the devil, who directs his attacks against both. In both realms God and Satan battle each other. Christians live in both kingdoms. They must serve two lords, not God and mammon, but God and the emperor.[48] And yet in all of these relationships we basically have only one Lord.

For Luther, believers are "two distinct persons in one being"; they are both Christians and citizens of the world. They act as private persons and they serve in various positions and offices. As Christians they are willing to suffer wrong; in their positions of responsibility they must oppose evil, punish offenders, and use force to further the victory of that which is right.

This distinction between the office and the person is a dangerous one. Luther has been accused of holding up a double morality, of transferring the medieval dualism between perfected and average Christians to *each* individual person. This accusation is well-aimed and identifies a problem; yet it is not completely justified. The form of action one takes in one's official capacity can indeed differ from what one does as an individual; yet the guiding intention should be the same in either case.

A position or an office dare not be considered arbitrary in the sense of being morally free, a law unto itself. Offices are for service in love. It is possible for love to be operating through the harsh realities of justice, punishment, the death penalty, "wrath," and the "sword." In a similar manner, responsible parents discipline their children; and for the most part it causes them pain that they cannot simply "forgive" their children. Thus a judge must punish without personal involvement, vengefulness, or egoism. The tension between personal attitudes and objective actions can be very great, but it can be managed. In fact the ability to deal with such stress is a practical necessity in daily life. According to Luther, the tension we experience points to a tension in God's own actions. Even God must at times carry out his "proper work" only under the form of his "alien work"—his love under wrath, his grace under judgment.

So the ethic related to one's position and the ethic one adheres to personally have their unity in the intention of love; therefore one ought not speak prematurely of a "double morality." Karl Holl fought passionately against Troeltsch on this issue. But Holl's attempt to demonstrate the absolute unity and consistency of Luther's thought is not convincing. Two points need to be considered:

1. The regulations and laws of temporal authority should indeed be applied from an attitude of love, but one cannot always derive them directly *from* love; much more often reason and "natural law" are the points of departure. Both reason and natural law belong to God's creation and therefore are not separated from God's will. To begin with, reason is responsible for external order and for temporal affairs. Admittedly, neither reason nor "natural law" can be equated with self-determination. "Natural law" has found expression in the Ten Commandments and therefore is in agreement with God's will. In the end reason conforms to the command of love, though in terms of content the command protects it from a certain independence. The rational and "natural" motives in "temporal authority" dare not be overlooked.

2. It is true that love can also appear in the form of "wrath." But do love and wrath really fit together so neatly that one can practice justice, exert force and power, wage war, etc., all out of a desire to love? [49] Is this not an underestimation of the danger of demonic perversion involved in all exercise of the sword? Carried to its extreme this could lead to the absurdity of considering a nuclear weapon to be a tool in the service of love. It borders on illusion to see the realization of love in the exercise of power. Luther did not

avoid this problem, and engaged in prophetic criticism of temporal authority. Abstract theory and actual practice are seldom identical. In this respect the outbreak of the Peasants' War served as a painful lesson.

Many criticisms have been directed against Luther's doctrine of the two kingdoms. The most important objections are: (1) Luther removed temporal authority from Christ's claim to lordship. (2) Luther did not sufficiently underscore the otherworldly character of the kingdom of Christ. He understood it as a present reality: where the Word is proclaimed, the kingdom of God is present. (3) Luther's view led to the corruption of politics. (4) It imbued people with a blind obedience to authority. We do not consider these objections convincing, though there is some truth in them. They do point to dangers that have surfaced often enough through misinterpretation of this teaching.

Luther's conception of the state was limited by the circumstances of his time. He thought in terms of "rulers and subjects." He did not recognize that, under some circumstances, a class had the right to secure advancement by means of force. The repeated references to Romans 13 introduced a static element into his thought. The insight that governments are not merely "established by God," but arise historically, was marginal. Luther only reluctantly admitted the legitimacy of resisting the emperor, after the jurists pointed out that he was not a ruler established by God, but one elected by the princes. He was never able to carry out a "demythologization" of Romans 13.

The doctrine of the two kingdoms is a serious attempt to provide a theological foundation for Christian existence in the midst of worldly reality. It seeks as much to avoid a lordship of the state over the church as it does to avoid a lordship of the church over the state. It impels Christians to be actively involved in the structures of the world, but does not give the world license to determine its own destiny. It does not wish to minimize the radicality of the Christian command to love, but concerns itself with the realization of love within the actual conditions of the earthly world. It does not fail to recognize the fragmentation of all earthly reality, but neither does it overzealously wish to extricate Christian existence from the provisional nature of earthly reality. The undeniable paradoxes of Luther's doctrine of the two kingdoms reflect the paradox of Christian existence itself—the tension between creation, sin, reconciliation, and fulfillment.

The Christian existence of each person is fulfilled in the context of his or her own station in life. A Christian is a father or mother, servant or maid, lord or subject. Luther spoke of three principal estates: the priesthood, marriage and/or family (which included economic life), and civil government: *ecclesia, oeconomia,* and *politia.* All three estates are parts of the divine order, established by God in his Word. Each estate has the same honor, and the estates are dependent on one another in their diversity. To be sure, Luther was conservative, but he did not want to provide a religious blessing for the existing structures. The criterion for the estates is whether or not they fulfill a service to one's neighbor.[50]

It belongs to the original wholeness of Luther's ethic that he directed individuals to the fulfillment of their duties within their stations. For example, in the section on the office of the keys of *The Small Catechism* Luther said, "Consider your estate according to the Ten Commandments, whether you are father, mother, son, daughter, etc." Luther did not put much stock in people who distinguished themselves apart from their life station but neglected their duties to those closest to them. In addition to "estate" Luther also spoke of "calling" or "vocation": "Every individual should concentrate on that which is required of him, and take his calling seriously." [51] The vocational ethos of earlier times was Lutheran in origin.

But the fulfillment of service in love to one's neighbor is not limited to one's vocation.[52] Apart from the duties of our calling we are summoned to engage in various acts of Christian love and works of mercy. Luther also knew that God could require extraordinary forms of service from a person. But as long as God did not confront people in that way, they should remain in their callings.[53] Luther rejected self-selected tasks and works and directed us to our vocations; yet even our callings do not free us from sin; in them, also, we need forgiveness. The ethos of vocation does not dispense with justification.

Work was commanded by God.[54] According to Gen. 2:15, Adam also worked in paradise.[55] Work does not belong to the order of sin, but is part of God's creation. Admittedly, according to Gen. 3:17 work also exists under a curse. Luther did not wish to deny that, but for him it was far more decisive that the work of a Christian is blessed by God.[56] To be sure, one cannot use Luther's translation of Ps. 90:10 as an example of this. There we read: "Life at its best is toil and trouble." Work is equated with toil, in accordance with the double meaning of the Latin word *labor,* which in addition to "work" can also mean "affliction." Therefore Luther meant that even the best life is toil and affliction.

Luther himself always worked. But he did not lose his soul in that which he did. He knew that God also wants us to rest. On May 12, 1530, he wrote this wonderful sentence to Melanchthon: "One also serves God by resting, indeed by nothing better than by resting." [57] In his Luther sermons Johann Mathesius reported that when Luther and Melanchthon stopped to visit Spalatin on their way home from Coburg, Melanchthon worked and wrote continuously throughout the entire meal. Finally Luther stood up and took the pen from his hand, addressing him with similar words.

Luther considered the ownership of private property a sensible arrangement. It is a prerequisite for carrying out one's calling and for the functioning of a regulated common life. If the entire world tried to live by begging, it would not be able to endure. For this reason Luther supported the Leisnig common chest ordinance and wrote a preface for it.[58] It contained rules similar to the Wittenberg Order of 1522. The possessions of the monasteries and churches that had been released were to be placed in a "common chest." From these funds payments were to be made for the preacher, sexton, and church building, for education and for the poor. The Leisnig Order served as a model throughout Saxony. Without it, individual communities would have faced external regulation.

Luther rejected the communism espoused by the enthusiasts and, in part, also by the peasants. The sharing of possessions by the early Christian community [59] was not compulsory, but a work of Christian love freely given.[60] When the need of our neighbor requires it we are not to hold fast to our possessions.[61] We must be ready, for the sake of the gospel, to surrender our possessions.[62] The accumulation of goods without concern for one's neighbor is sin.[63]

Luther considered interest on loans to be unchristian. He had already expressed this in his letter to the German nobility.[64] Whoever lent money and demanded more in return than was lent practiced usury. Only those who themselves had nothing to spare were allowed to take interest, but only about four percent.[65] This applied to Christians. In the structures of secular life, however, interest on loans had become well-established and could not simply be done away with. Yet one ought, at least, charge interest with "love and justice." This was how Luther expressed himself in an opinion offered to the Danzig city council in May 1525.[66]

For the most part Luther saw the economy as being ruled by an exorbitant striving after profit. Therefore he spoke out against usury in various writings and many sermons. In his work on *Trade and Usury* of 1524 he provided concrete suggestions.[67] Merchants should not take advantage of the plight of their customers, but calculate their costs and in doing so include the risks involved. Luther, the descendant of peasant stock, could not completely suppress his mistrust of the merchant class; basically he was still an advocate of an agrarian economy. He repeated his sharp condemnation of the practices of companies and their monopolistic management of business that he had already stated in his letter to the nobility.[68] "We must put a bit in the mouth of the Fuggers and similar companies." [69]

Luther was not versed in national economy, nevertheless he observed the economic enterprise with great interest. His suggestions, however, were for the most part generally limited to the sharpening of people's consciences. He placed economic life under the norm of "love and justice."

Education was also part of public life. In his letter to the nobility Luther had already affirmed schools, particularly public schools.[70] Under the influence of the enthusiast movement the educational system had experienced a severe setback. The schools in Wittenberg had suffered greatly. Eobanus Hessus of the University of Erfurt was highly vocal in complaining about the situation. There were theologians who thought it completely unnecessary to learn languages. The number of doctoral graduations had declined.

In this situation Luther joined Melanchthon in a united appeal for education, writing *To the Councilmen of All Cities in Germany That They Establish and Maintain Christian Schools.*[71] Luther saw a special providence of God in the fact that the gospel had been rediscovered at the same time that the ancient languages had been restored. This unique historical hour was a sign of God's grace which ought not be taken lightly. "O my beloved Germans, buy while the market is at your door; gather in the harvest while there is sunshine and fair weather; make use of God's grace and word while it is there! For you should know that God's word and grace is like a passing shower of rain which does not return where it has once been. It has been with the Jews, but when it's gone it's gone, and now they have nothing. Paul brought it to the Greeks; but again when it's gone it's gone, and now they have the Turk. Rome and the Latins also had it; but when it's gone it's gone, and now they have the pope. And you Germans need not think that you will have it forever, for ingratitude and contempt will not make it stay. Therefore, seize it and hold it fast, whoever can; for lazy hands are bound to have a lean year." [72]

The cities paid large sums for defense, for streets, paths, and dams; they ought not spend less on "foolish young people." [73] Parents are often not wise and clever enough or are too burdened by the duties of work to care for the education of their children; so it must be the task of the magistrates and the authorities. [74] The welfare of a city does not lie in its walls, houses, and weapons, but in its "many able, learned, wise, honorable, and well-educated citizens." [75]

The principal task of the schools ought to be the communication of the gospel. The ancient languages are required for this. The devil "smelled a rat"; where the languages are stressed, his kingdom is pierced and the hole cannot easily be plugged. [76] Most likely God gave Greece to the Turks so that the fleeing Greeks would bring their language to the West. "In proportion then as we value the gospel, let us zealously hold to the languages," [77] for "the languages are the sheath in which this sword of the Spirit [namely the gospel] is contained." [78] The reason the Fathers erred so often in their exposition of Scripture is that they did not know the languages. Those who rely completely on the Fathers in their exposition of Scripture should reflect on this: "As sunshine is to shadow, so is the language itself compared to all the glosses [explanations] of the fathers." [79]

However, Christian schools are as important for "temporal government" as they are for theologians, [80] for the temporal realm also requires good and capable men and women. [81] Not only princes, councilmen, and other regents are needed, but also competent men and women who can be sound examples in their domestic concerns for their servants and children.

Schools were no longer the instruments of torture they had been in Luther's youth.[82] Students should learn not only languages, but also particularly history, singing, music, and mathematics.[83] Luther was especially interested in introducing what we know today as elementary schools. A boy ought to attend school for one or two hours each day, a girl for at least one hour.[84] Later, in a sermon "On Keeping Children in School," Luther even favored compulsory education.[85] "We have been German beasts all too long. Let us for once make use of our reason." [86]

Luther also supported the establishment of libraries, the way cloisters once had them, but with better books.[87] Above all, chronicles and histories should be collected, for they are particularly useful "in understanding and guiding the course of events." [88] Luther deplored the fact that the Germans had for so long given so little consideration to their own history; that is why those in other lands know next to nothing about the Germans, who have had to put up with being called "German beasts who know only how to fight, gorge, and guzzle." [89] Luther also offered the assurance, "I am not seeking my own advantage, but the welfare and salvation of all Germany." [90]

Melanchthon wrote a foreword to the Latin translation of this work.[91] Like Luther, he opposed those who out of confused religious motives scorned scholarship. Luther has rightly been called the "most brilliant student" of Melanchthon in scholarly matters. The letter to the city councilors is Luther's synthesis of humanism and the Reformation. Nevertheless, the differences between Luther and Melanchthon should not be overlooked, for Melanchthon placed a stronger independent value on the humanities than did Luther. In his opinion they were not only a major element of education, but a sort of theological pedagogy. For both Luther and Melanchthon, the study of languages had its highest value in enabling the reading of the Bible; on the other hand even Luther recognized that the content of classical education had its own worth. Luther valued Cicero (more highly than Aristotle) and the ancient poets; he was sorry that he had not read more poets in his youth.[92] Neither did he contest the value of dialectic, rhetoric, and poetics. He praised mathematics and astronomy, but above all he repeatedly emphasized the theological-moral and practical applications of history.[93]

Even though Luther was not a humanist, one cannot accuse him of intellectual narrowness. One need but read the catalog of books which he recommended as compulsory reading in his letter to the city councilors,[94] "regardless of whether they were pagan or Christian." [95] Later on Luther did not oppose Melanchthon's reintroduction of Aristotle into the curriculum, most likely with the assurance (reinforced by Melanchthon's actions) that that which was decisive would remain, and that no concessions would be made concerning the teaching of justification.

The Peasants' War
(Thomas Muentzer)[1]

Luther's view of authority and public life was forced to undergo a difficult test during the so-called German Peasants' War of 1525.

The economic circumstances of the peasants varied widely from place to place. In Saxony, for example, there were many rather well-to-do peasants. But when developments in the monetary economy resulted in difficult circumstances for the landed aristocracy, they in turn exerted great pressure on the peasants. Compulsory labor and the amounts of dues levied were increased. The period of "peasant dispossession" began; the heirs to a farm were forced to sell it at a low price in order to provide cheap land and labor. The rights of landlords were also strengthened. The peasants suffered the most from these changing legal relationships, and they demanded a return to "traditional rights."

Economic and legal claims were frequently intertwined with religious ideas. The peasants directed their accusations against the church, which, as one of the largest landowners, was closely bound to the feudal system. It was the "law of God," they said, which had been violated through the persistent removal of peasant rights. The law of God was set forth in the Bible, which through Luther's reformation had once again been placed in the spotlight. The peasants had learned from Luther's battle with the papal church, and they knew that he appealed to the Holy Scriptures as the only divine norm. It is therefore no wonder that the peasants recognized Luther as their champion. Luther's opponents, on the other hand, placed the blame for the Peasants' War on Luther's shoulders. "How Luther polished the peasant shoe *[Bundshuh]*" was the title of a woodcut in Thomas Murner's polemic work *Concerning the Great Lutheran Fool,* which appeared by 1522.

Toward the end of February 1525 the *Twelve Articles* appeared, a manifesto of the upper Swabian peasants. Its authors were the Memminger journeyman furrier Sebastian Lotzer, who had already become known as a lay preacher through his pamphlets, and the Memminger pastor Christoph Schappeler, a disciple of Zwingli. The *Twelve Articles* were printed immediately and distributed widely. They were moderate in tone, and many of the demands were reminiscent of Luther. The first article called for congregations to have the right to freely elect their pastors, or remove them if they did not preach the gospel loudly and clearly.

The remaining articles also appealed to God's Word. The large, 10% tithe on grain was to be used to support pastors, assist the poor, and provide reserves in case of war. The livestock tithe, on the other hand, was to be abolished, since God created animals for human beings to use freely. Serfdom was contrary to God's will, because Christ had redeemed all people equally and liberated them for Christian freedom. However, the government was to be obeyed. Peasants were to be allowed to hunt and fish freely, since God gave all human beings dominion over animals. The right to use wood for fire and for building purposes had unjustly been taken from the community. The number of demanded "services" was to be reduced to the number previously required. The excessive rents of many estates were to be reduced to a reasonable rate. The requisitioning of hereditary possessions by the feudal lords "in case of death" was to be completely eliminated; it was "opposed to God and honor."

Those demands that were not evangelical would be abandoned. The biblical tone was unmistakable. Even if Luther had not been directly asked for his opinion, he could scarcely have avoided giving one.

Between April 17 and 20, even before Luther had heard of the atrocities committed by the peasants in Swabia and Frankonia, he quickly drafted his *Admonition to Peace, A Reply to the Twelve Articles of the Peasants in Swabia.*[2] He anticipated a favorable response, for the *Twelve Articles* had concluded with an expression of openness toward correction and instruction. Luther wanted to take them seriously, even though he had reservations as to whether the entire band of Swabian peasants was truly Christian.[3] If the rioting should get out of hand, everything would be ruined and all of Germany would be destroyed; therefore he could not be silent.[4]

Luther did not write as a politician, but as a pastoral counselor. He wanted to address the consciences of both parties. In doing so he publicly spoke out more sharply against the princes than he did against the peasants. The entire uprising could be blamed on the lords and princes, primarily the ecclesiastical princes and the cloisters.[5] They oppressed and taxed the poor until they could no longer endure it. The sword was at their necks; their throats would be slit because of their own stubborn insolence. God would no longer look on in silence.[6] Luther would not allow the gospel to become the scapegoat.[7] He had always opposed insurrection. Yet now he could truly laugh up his sleeve at the way the peasants sought to vindicate themselves. In fact he could even take their side. But God would prevent him.[8]

The princes ought to deal reasonably with the peasants. Among the 12 articles, there were several that were completely fair and just.[9] Above all, the peasants' demand that the gospel be freely preached was justified.[10] Luther addressed the peasants as "dear friends." [11] They ought to concern themselves with maintaining a good conscience, or they would accomplish nothing, even if they were to slay all the princes.[12] They should not allow themselves to be misled by false prophets, who called for "disorder and murder." [13] Above all they should not refer to themselves as a "Christian association or union" and so misuse God's name.[14] Yet this is exactly what they would be doing if they opposed the government with force.[15]

Even when government is evil and suppresses the gospel, insurrection is not justified. According to natural and universal right, no one should take the law into their own hands and seek revenge; otherwise peace and order could not be maintained in the world.[16] Where would we be if everyone wanted to be a judge over everyone else? [17] Even the Gentiles, the Turks, and the Jews knew that.[18] If the peasants, however, truly wanted to be Christians, they would acknowledge the command of Christ: " 'Do not resist one who is evil.' " [19] "Suffering! suffering! Cross! cross! This and nothing else is the Christian law!" [20] If they wished to move ahead with force, they should not use the name Christian.

Luther did not want to defend the injustice of the authorities. But if the peasants rebelled against authority, then neither of the parties could call themselves Christians. In such cases God allows one group of rogues to punish the other.[21]

Of the 12 articles, Luther considered the first three. The request of the peasants to hear the gospel and to choose their own pastors should not be denied. If the government did not support the pastors they chose, then the congregations would have to support them at their own expense. If the government would not tolerate them, then they should be allowed to move to another city, and whoever wished should move with them.[22] Luther called their refusal to pay tithes "highway robbery." [23] The demand to give up serfdom "absolutely contradicts the gospel" and made Christian liberty into a "completely physical matter." [24] "This article would make all men equal, and turn the spiritual kingdom of Christ into a worldly, external kingdom; and that is impossible. A worldly kingdom cannot exist without an inequality of persons, some being free, some imprisoned, some lords, some subjects, etc." [25]

Luther did not wish to make any judgment about the other eight articles. He left that task to the jurists.[26] At any rate, the name Christian ought not be attached to any of these demands, whether they were justified or not.

In a concluding warning he reminded both parties that they were not dealing with Christian matters but with worldly rights and temporal possessions.[27] He asked them to think of their children, women, and older people and not to begin the shedding of blood. "It is easy to start a fight, but we cannot stop the fighting whenever we want to." [28] There was still time for peaceful arbitration.

Luther still believed a settlement was possible when he received word of the *Agreement between the Honorable Swabian League and the Two Bodies of Peasants in Bodensee and Allgäu*, agreed to on April 22. He reprinted it immediately, along with a foreword and a conclusion.[29] Though he had in the meanwhile heard of violence, pillaging, and thievery, this agreement gave him renewed hope.

The rebellion, however, was already fully under way. The Peasants' War of 1525 was a collection of individual actions which occurred in four principal regions: in southwest Germany, in Frankonia, in Austria, and in Saxony and Thuringia. It was conducted with terrible cruelty by both sides. In Würzburg alone some 63 castles were breached. Cloisters were burned to the ground. There was much talk about the bloodbath which accompanied their occupation of Weinsburg on April 16, where Count Ludwig von Helfenstein and his troops were impaled on spears.

The troops of the princes proceeded with no less brutality. They massacred the peasants by the hundreds. The leader of the Swabian League, Georg Truchsess of Waldburg, earned dubious fame and came to be called "the peasant hunter." He suppressed the Swabian insurrection at the battles of Leipheim (April 4) and Böblingen (May 12) and the Frankish uprising at Königshofen (June 2). In Thuringia the decisive encounter took place when the peasants were defeated at Frankenhausen on May 15.

Insurrection in Thuringia and Saxony broke out at the end of April. Many people from the towns also joined the peasants. Even a large number of nobles supported them under the pressure of the circumstances. Elector Frederick, who lay ill and awaited death in his castle Lochau, had become uncertain about God's will in the matter. On April 14 he wrote to his brother John: "Perhaps these poor people have been given just cause for such insurrection, particularly with the prohibition of God's Word. If God wants it so, it will indeed come to pass that the common man will rule. But if it is not his divine will, the end will soon be otherwise." Until his death on May 5 he still hoped for a settlement. Duke John judged the situation rather despairingly.

Luther had been in Eisleben since April 19. Undaunted, he traveled throughout the troubled region, preaching against the insurrection wherever he went. Among the towns he visited were Stolberg, Nordhausen, and Weimar. From Weimar on May 3 he wrote to Friedrich Myconius in Gotha, expressing his general attitude with the words, " 'In the world you have tribulation; but be of good cheer, I have overcome the world [John 16:33].' " [30]

In Nordhausen he was mocked by several persons who rang bells as he was preaching, admonishing, and pointing to a picture of the crucified Christ. If a sword had been available to them, blood would have flowed.[31] Concerning his encounter with the Thuringian peasants he wrote: "I was in their midst and passed through them at the risk of life and limb." [32] "It is my own experience with the Thuringian peasants that the more they were exhorted and instructed, the more obstinate, the prouder, the madder they became." [33] On

May 3 he therefore advised Duke John in Weimar not to give in to
the peasants, and he approved of Count Albrecht of Mansfeld's
successful attack on a contingent of peasants in the village of
Osterhausen. On May 4 or 5 he wrote to the Mansfeld councilor,
Johann Rühel, that he should by no means encourage his lord to
deviate from his position.[34]

On May 5 Luther left the Seeburg Castle near Mansfeld; he had
been summoned to Lochau to attend the dying elector—who had in
the meantime already passed away. On May 6 Luther arrived in
Wittenberg, determined once more to speak out against the Peasants'
War, but this time in stronger terms. Since taking his position on
the *Twelve Articles* at the end of April Luther had himself acquired
additional experiences which led him to remind the authorities of
their responsibility to act firmly in restoring order. In the first place,
he had heard of the recent atrocities of the peasants. In the second
place the peasants were in most cases now going far beyond what
the *Twelve Articles* had requested. Their newest demands called
for a complete overthrow of the previous order, not merely legitimate reforms. All distinctions between persons were to be eliminated, all fortresses and castles cleared away, all governments removed, all commerce and industry nationalized, and all godless
people destroyed.

These views were unquestionably connected with the ideolo-
gies being proclaimed among the peasants by radical religious
"prophets." Luther had already sharply criticized their activity in
the "exhortation" and warned the peasants to beware of them.
But he was unable to prevent their influence, even in Saxony and
Thuringia, the area in which he had the most direct contact with
the war. Here it is necessary to consider the man whom many
scholars, influenced by Marxist historiography, consider the actual
reformer: Thomas Müntzer.[35]

Thomas Müntzer was presumably born sometime before 1490 in
Stolberg in the Harz Mountains, the son of a fairly well-to-do
ropemaker. He studied theology in Leipzig and in Frankfurt on the
Oder and acquired a respectable education. He understood Greek
and Hebrew and read the Greek classics and Fathers. He was also
influenced by German mysticism and by Joachim of Fiore (d. 1202),
the prophet of the coming kingdom of the Holy Spirit.

Presumably he became acquainted with Luther during the Leipzig disputation, but one cannot describe him as a student of Luther. At an early point Luther evidently regarded him highly, for in 1520 he recommended Müntzer as preacher to Zwickau. There Müntzer came into contact with the Zwickau prophets, who substituted inner enlightenment for biblical revelation and the experience of the cross for justification by faith.

The social plight of the Zwickau clothiers, among whom a new proletariat was beginning to develop, quickly became apparent to him. His innate passion developed into a prophetic consciousness, and his powerful sermons led to clashes. On April 16, 1521, he was dismissed by the city council; he avoided further arguments by fleeing. In Prague he drew up a manifesto in which his consciousness of having been called by God was unmistakably expressed. God himself had ordained him to reap his harvest, and he had sharpened his sickle. However, the approval he expected did not materialize. In fact near the end of 1521, his propagandistic speeches finally led to his expulsion from Prague.

He returned to Saxony. Through correspondence he also sought to gain the support of Melanchthon and Luther.[36] Luther was not acquainted with the Prague manifesto, but he sensed that the spirit of Müntzer was contrary to his own. Moreover he anticipated that these new prophets would not shrink from using force.[37]

After Easter of 1523 Müntzer was installed as preacher in the electoral town of Allstedt am Kyffhäuser, where he soon established a "league of the elect" among whom he wished to realize the true community of Christ. For this community he developed an order for a German Mass (much earlier than did Luther) for which he no doubt gained acclaim. As in Zwickau, so too in Allstedt, Müntzer acquired an enthusiastic following. When the neighboring Count Ernst von Mansfeld prohibited his people from attending church in Allstedt, Müntzer publicly denounced him from the pulpit. By letter he threatened to cause the count 100,000 times more trouble than Luther had caused the pope.

As more and more were drawn to Müntzer from surrounding areas, Müntzer's goal of ushering in the community of God's chosen became ever stronger. An initial indication of the coming rebellion was the March 24, 1524, destruction of a chapel in Mallerbach, near Allstedt, which contained a miraculous madonna. The support of the town council of Allstedt made Müntzer still more courageous.

His "league of the elect" grew to an organization of 500 members. He directed his tract *Concerning Fabricated Faith* against the "honey-sweet Christ" of the Wittenbergers. A second work, *A Protestation, or the Presentation of Thomas Müntzer's Teachings,* set out his opposition to infant Baptism. Like the "honey-sweet Christ," it provided false consolation.

Luther could no longer stand by and watch. He wrote a public *Letter to the Princes of Saxony Concerning the Rabble-Rousing Spirit,* which appeared in July 1524.[38] This spirit who had made a corner for himself in Allstedt did not hold to the Scripture, but said, "Bible, Bubble, Babel." [39] He called on the voice of God within himself, and on his own cross instead of the cross of Christ. Certainly it was not the task of the princes to fight the teachings of Müntzer. "Let them preach confidently and frankly anything they can and against anyone they wish. Leave the spirits to clash and strike one another and so burst asunder. If some are misled in the process, well, so it goes in the course of a war. Where there is a conflict or a battle, many must fall and be wounded." [40]

These statements of Luther are reminiscent of his earlier condemned thesis that the burning of heretics is against the will of the Holy Spirit. However, where heresy leads to acts of violence, the government must intervene, and that was clearly the case. Nevertheless, Duke John wanted to judge for himself. He requested that Müntzer preach before him in the Allstedt Castle on July 13, in the presence of the electoral prince John Frederick and other notable persons.

For this so-called "prince's sermon" Müntzer selected Chapter 2 of the prophet Daniel as his text. It is the great vision of the golden image which symbolizes the kingdoms of this world that are destroyed by the kingdom of Christ. Müntzer saw the court theologians portrayed among the wise men who were unable to interpret Nebuchadnezzar's dream. Although he did not mention Luther by name, Müntzer certainly counted him among their number and referred to him as "Brother Porker and Brother Easy Life." Daniel, who knew how to interpret the future, was naturally none other than Müntzer himself. The time of reckoning was at hand; there was no longer any forbearance for the so-called weak. Müntzer invited the princes to join the chosen ones; for the godless there was only destruction. If the princes were not willing to participate in his program, he would "turn to the simple laity and peasants."

In vain Müntzer awaited a positive response from the "dear regents." They had in the meanwhile also received Luther's sharp warning. Müntzer was summoned to a hearing at Weimar on August 1, 1524, which proceeded negatively. Believing that it was no longer possible to remain in Allstedt, he secretly left the city on the night of August 7.

Müntzer turned to the free imperial city of Mühlhausen, where he already had numerous followers, and, above all, where he found a very active follower in the former Cistercian monk Heinrich Pfeiffer. The warning which Luther addressed to the mayor and the city council of Mühlhausen arrived too late.[41] Pfeiffer warmly welcomed Müntzer in August 1524.

In September, iconoclasm erupted. The authorities were afraid of moving against the strong following of Müntzer and Pfeiffer. A new council was installed. But not everyone was in agreement. The old council was able to regain power and expel Pfeiffer and Müntzer. The peasants of the surrounding countryside also supported the old council, so Pfeiffer and Müntzer turned to Nuremberg. There Müntzer published his work *An Expressed Exposure of the False Faith*, which he had already written in Allstedt. It was virtually a refutation of Luther. His next tract, *A Highly Provoked Defense and Renunciation of the Spiritless, Easy-Living Hulk of Flesh in Wittenberg*, was an even more obvious attack. It accused Luther of not "earnestly preaching the law."

By December 1524 Pfeiffer had once again succeeded in gaining a foothold in Mühlhausen, where he brought about a turbulent state of affairs. Toward the end of February 1525 Müntzer also returned to Mühlhausen, where he was immediately given a pulpit. After leaving Nuremberg he had traveled through southwestern Germany and had gained firsthand impressions of the peasants' rebellion. He then came to the conclusion that he would be able to carry out his apocalyptic program with the help of the peasants.

One must remember that Müntzer was not first and foremost a social revolutionary, but rather a preacher of apocalyptic judgment who sought to establish the kingdom of God with force through the destruction of all godless people.[42] For him the Peasants' War was a means of realizing the final rule of God on earth at the end of time. Müntzer did maintain that too much poverty can stifle faith. How can persons who are overwhelmed by the battle for daily existence still find time to occupy themselves with the Word of God? Yet it is significant that he introduced a religious rather than an economic argument.

For Müntzer, the usual slogans of the Peasants' War were ultimately of little importance. It was the apocalyptic kingdom of God that would resolve all social injustices. The symbols which Müntzer gave the revolutionaries were not class symbols like a clog, but a red cross, a drawn sword, and a rainbow flag as a sign of God's covenant. What Müntzer struggled for was not so much a social revolution as a theocratic revolution of the elect. One cannot exclude Müntzer's theological motivation and interpret him simply as a supporter of class struggle per se. It was as a fanatical apocalypticist and not as a champion of social justice that he called for war without mercy. "It is high time! If there are but three of you, and you rely on God alone and seek his name and honor, you need not fear 100,000. Now go! Go! Go! Spare not! Don't let yourselves be moved to pity! Don't consider the plight of the godless! Don't let your sword grow cold! Forge your tools on the anvil of Nimrod! As long as men rule over you they can tell you nothing about God. On! On, while it is day. God goes before you! Follow! Follow!"

Müntzer succeeded in overthrowing the city council of Mühlhausen and establishing a dictatorship of the elect, who were to realize his Allstedt plans. Now he could count on the support of a rather significant armed force. He ruled in Mühlhausen like a king, causing an uproar throughout the region. Villages, castles, and cloisters were stormed by fanatic masses, plundered, and burned. All order seemed to have been destroyed. The government was paralyzed. The worst was anticipated.

In this situation Luther again took up his pen. To the second printing of his *Admonition to Peace: A Reply to the Twelve Articles of the Peasants of Swabia* he added an appendix bearing the title, "Also against the Other Murderous and Thieving Hordes of Peasants." [43] This highly criticized short work [44] suffered a double misfortune. Although it was initially intended merely as an amendment to the first work, it soon appeared separately with its own title: *Against the Murderous and Thieving Hordes of Peasants.* By dropping the word "also" and the reference to "the other," the emphasis was drastically altered. In addition, the booklet, which was written on May 4, 1525, first became known after the peasants had already been defeated. This gave the impression that Luther had taken the side of the victor, which in view of the date of authorship was not at all the case. At that time Luther had still considered the victory of the peasants as entirely possible.[45] Indeed, Luther believed that a victory by the peasants might even presage the last judgment, which was not far off. The devil wanted to destroy all order and government and make the world into a wasteland.

It should also be noted that this second work was directed more to the princes than to the peasants; it sought to remind the princes of their duty to reestablish order. In his first work Luther had thought he would be successful in achieving peace; but that was no longer possible. The peasants now behaved like "mad dogs." Above all they had been incited by the "archdevil" who ruled in Mühlhausen and caused nothing but murder, robbery, and bloodshed.[46] Luther accused the peasants of three sins. They disobeyed authority, they caused rebellion, robbery, and murder, and they wanted to cover their evil deeds with the gospel.[47] They illegitimately appealed to the creation account and to the common Baptism of all. The New Testament passages Luke 20:25 ("Render to Caesar the things that are Caesar's"), Romans 13, and 1 Peter 2:13 were still in force.

The communism of the early church was a voluntary community of love.[48] Nothing was taken from anyone by force; the peasants did just the opposite.[49] The government had the right, without prior negotiations, to take up the sword against the peasants.[50] But a Christian government must not forget to consider its own sin. Perhaps Germany had earned such a punishment, and perhaps the overthrow of the princes was God's will. Out of fear for God, the princes—even though they were not required to—should once more demonstrate their willingness to negotiate with the peasants. If they were rejected, they should immediately take up the sword.[51] If they failed to carry out their duty of punishing offenders, they would sin against God and would be guilty of all the murders committed by the peasants. "And there is no place for patience or mercy. This is the time of the sword, not the day of grace." [52] The government might intervene with a good conscience, by contrast with the peasants. "Thus, anyone who is killed fighting on the side of the rulers may be a true martyr in the eyes of God"; but whoever was struck dead among the peasants would be lost, both body and soul.[53] "These are strange times, when a prince can win heaven with bloodshed better than other men with prayer!" [54]

Many pious persons had been forced to join in with the peasants.

The battle against the peasants should also be waged to free them from such terrorization. Should they be taken prisoner, the government should have mercy on them.[55] The often-quoted statement of the last paragraph also refers to them: "Therefore, dear lords, here is a place where you can release, rescue, help. Have mercy on these poor people! Let whoever can stab, smite, slay. If you die in doing it, good for you! A more blessed death can never be yours, for you die while obeying the divine word and commandments in Romans 13,[56] and in loving service of your neighbor, whom you are rescuing from the bonds of hell and of the devil." [57]

To be sure, these words were formulated passionately, but they sound quite different when they are taken out of context (as they usually are). Luther did not write thoughtlessly when he spoke of obedience to the Word of God and of the service of love. Despite a number of offensive formulations, Luther's second work on the Peasants' War was written out of a deep sense of responsibility, without consideration for personal gain. He closed with the sentence: "If anyone thinks this is too harsh, let him remember that rebellion is intolerable and that the destruction of the world is to be expected every hour." [58] Luther was concerned with order; despite his passionate formulations, he was not caught up in a bloodthirsty frenzy.

However, the same cannot be said for his opponent, Thomas Müntzer. We have already noted examples of his style. His appeal to his former congregation in Allstedt, made toward the end of April, was filled with fanaticism, yet was at the same time permeated with a utopian confidence in victory. "The whole German, Italian, and French countryside is awake. The master wants to make sport, and the scoundrels have to do his bidding." His followers were to avoid making agreements. "They will implore you as friends, whimper, plead like children; do not show mercy." The last 10 letters we have from Müntzer, encouraging the deployment of the peasants, were written in a similar tone. He signed them, "Thomas Müntzer with the sword of Gideon."

The peasants had managed to assemble an imposing army at Frankenhausen on the Kyffhäuser. But it was there that they experienced their catastrophe. On May 13 they had sent their requests for help to the city of Erfurt, but in vain. Müntzer preached to the masses and took a rainbow to be a sign of the covenant which God had sealed with him. On May 15 the princes proposed that if the peasants would surrender and turn over Müntzer and his supporters, they would be dealt with leniently. But Müntzer knew how to incite them once again. He would catch the shots of the enemy in his sleeves.

As the firing began, the peasants fled wildly in all directions. The pursuing troops engaged in a dreadful bloodbath. Müntzer hid in an attic and pretended to be an ailing, old man. But he was recognized by letters he carried with him. He was taken prisoner and brought before the princes, who conversed with him. Landgrave Philip of Hesse even disputed with him about the worthlessness of his Old Testament proof texts. On the next day Müntzer was interrogated, at points with the use of torture. Not only did he divulge names, he also recanted his sermon against authority and his deviations from the Roman doctrine of the sacraments. Before his death he took the Last Supper in only one form.

No value can be attributed to the confessions forced from him by torture. But it is worth noting that in his last letter to the elect at Mühlhausen he admitted no personal guilt. They bore the blame for the defeat at Frankenhausen because they thought only of their own earthly advantages and not of the coming kingdom of God. On May 27, 1525, Müntzer, along with 53 others, was executed. Among them was Heinrich Pfeiffer, who had initially escaped, but had subsequently been recaptured. Müntzer and Pfeiffer were beheaded and their heads impaled on stakes in front of the city.

Luther was informed regularly about these events through the letters of the Mansfeld city councilor Johann Rühel. On May 21 he informed Luther of the battle of Frankenhausen, the capture of Müntzer, and the devastation throughout the region of Thüringia and Mansfeld.[59] Still unaware of Müntzer's execution, Luther published Müntzer's writings to the counts of Allstedt and Mansfeld as well as what he had heard of Müntzer's speeches previous to the battle, along with a preface of his own.

The pamphlet bears the title, *A Terrible Story and a Judgment of God on Thomas Müntzer.*[60] "Not that I rejoice at the tragedy that has overtaken him and his followers, for how can that help me, since I do not know what God still has in store for me; but I wish to warn all other revolutionaries and so prevent them from falling under the same judgment of God."[61] This was a time of judgment: "It is not a time for preaching but for prayer; wrath has come and we must defend ourselves with our petitions."[62]

Recently it has rightfully been pointed out that Luther saw something apocalyptic in the events of the time: the last onslaught of the devil against the victory of the gospel. The lords were not to succumb to arrogance if they should win the final battle, but should remain in the fear of God. It would be God who gave the victory, not because of their righteousness and piety, but to subdue the injustices of the peasants. They should be gracious to those who have been taken captive and to those who surrender, otherwise "the weather might change and God could give the victory to the peasants." [63]

On May 23 Luther wrote to Rühel.[64] "It is appalling that the poor people [the peasants] are treated so terribly"; but how else should one deal with the situation? "One tragedy is better than the other." "Do not let yourself be too greatly troubled, for it will be a blessing for many souls, who will be deterred by it and so preserved." [65] On May 26 Rühel thanked Luther for this letter.[66] He conveyed details of Müntzer's capture and of his conversations with the princes. In conclusion he suggested that Luther should once more publicly express himself about his booklet against the peasants. He was being accused of being too harsh; in Leipzig the rumor was being circulated that with the elector's death, he had struck such a harsh tone for fear of Duke George.

Luther replied on May 30.[67] It did not surprise him that he was being depicted as a hypocrite. He would have needed a lot of leather if he had wanted to bind up everyone's mouth. God himself would save the innocent among the peasants; but those who supported the peasants' rebellion were also at fault. They should pray for the peasants, that they listen to the Word; where they refused, there would not be much place for mercy. "Let the muskets roar in their ears, otherwise they will make things a thousand times worse." Luther rightly saw that the Peasants' War had not yet ended. Müntzer had not been asked the right questions. He didn't recognize his own guilt. "Whoever has seen Müntzer can say that he has seen the devil in person." The devil was feeling the approach of the last day; "that's why he stirs up the soup and displays all of his hellish powers at once." [68]

From Nikolaus of Amsdorf in Magdeburg Luther had heard that he was being called "a toady to the sovereigns." [69] But he was convinced in his own conscience that he had acted correctly in his booklet against the peasants. When the princes stepped beyond their bounds, they, at least—in contrast with the peasants—wielded the sword under the authority of God. We also hear something of the criticism leveled at Luther from a letter which Hermann Mühlpfort of Zwickau (the man to whom Luther had dedicated his treatise on freedom) sent to Stephan Roth on July 4. Evidently Luther was also being accused of changing positions: first he had talked of peace, then he demanded that the peasants be put down. Not merely opponents such as Cochläus reproached him, but also many of his friends no longer understood him.

Evidently it was the concern of Stephan Roth which caused Luther to defend his booklet against the peasants in his Pentecost sermon of June 4, 1525.[70] Those who incited rebellion were worse than murderers, for they did not merely turn against individuals, but against order itself. Therefore Luther felt obligated to support the authorities—not with the sword but with the Word, for that was his office. That some persons now called him a toady to the sovereigns did not bother him. The end of the printed version of this sermon published by Stephan Roth referred to another publication related to this matter: *An Open Letter on the Harsh Book against the Peasants.*[71]

It is known that Luther's marriage (June 13), about which we will speak later, occurred about this time. In an invitation to the wedding banquet which Luther sent to the Mansfeld city council on June 15, he took note of their concerns: "Dear Sirs, what a hue and cry I have caused with the little book against the peasants! Everything God has done for the world through me has been forgotten. Now lords, pastors, and peasants all oppose me and threaten me with death."[72] The discussion with them at the wedding celebration on June 27 apparently convinced Luther that he had to express his views once more. The circular letter was dedicated to the Mansfeld chancellor Kaspar Müller and appeared during the first weeks in July.

It was only with reluctance that Luther decided to reply. He was accustomed to being contradicted.[73] Those who now approved of the revolutionaries were more than likely revolutionaries in their hearts.[74] The peasants refused to accept advice; "whoever does not wish to hear God's gracious Word must hear the executioner's harsh word." Some accused Luther of being unmerciful; he answered: "Merciful here, merciful there. We are now speaking of God's Word. God wants kings to be honored and revolutionaries to be destroyed,

and God is certainly as merciful as we are." [75] Who had preached
the mercy of God more than Luther? But one must also proclaim
the wrath of God. [76] When the peasants raged and plundered, no
one spoke of mercy; everyone spoke of rights. Nothing was said of
mercy for the princes and lords. Yet, when the peasants had been
defeated, no one wanted to speak of rights, but only of mercy. [77]
It is not mercy when one allows wrong to go unpunished. [78]

In addition, in his little booklet Luther had asked the princes
to deal graciously with those who surrendered to them. Why didn't
his opponents read that in his booklet? The sayings concerning
mercy belong to God's kingdom and apply to Christians. But the
temporal realm should not be merciful, but strict, serious, and
wrathful in its office and work. [79] "Its tools are not a garland of roses
or a bouquet of love, but an unsheathed sword" to defend the pious
from those who are evil. [80] The peasants and those who defended
them reversed the two kingdoms: first they wanted to fight for the
gospel with the sword and then they expected mercy from the
temporal realm. [81] The temporal sword must "out of great mercy be
unmerciful, and practice wrath and severity out of great goodness." [82] In his booklet Luther had spoken out only against the
stubborn peasants; for the others he had demanded grace. [83]

Luther was not responsible for the misuse of force by the princes
and lords. [84] They would not be able to avoid the punishment of
God. At the appropriate time Luther would attack the princes even
as he had the peasants; "for as far as my teaching office is concerned, a prince is as important as a peasant." [85] If one had from
the beginning followed Luther's advice, taken vigorous action, and
"risked a hundred, one would have preserved many thousands." [86]
He would not accept the excuse of those who claimed they were
forced to commit atrocities by the peasants; those who went along
with them could not excuse themselves. [87] A victory by the peasants
would have given rise to unavoidable misery. [88] If one despised
God's present judgment, something still worse could come. "God
can allow the peasants to rise up again, or allow another situation
to erupt that will be even more troublesome." [89]

Whoever read Luther's booklet properly would know that he
wanted nothing else than to remind the Christian authorities of
their office. [90] He had not turned to "bloodhounds" whose master is
the devil. "I have been concerned with both sides. If the peasants
came to power, the devil would be made an abbot, but if such

tyrants gained control, his mother would be made an abbess." The peasants did not listen and they received their reward; the tyrants would also get theirs.[91] In this "circular letter" Luther did not retract a single point; nor did he diminish the sharpness of the tone. But the impartial reader would surely recognize the true intention of the "harsh little book" and acknowledge Luther's seriousness in writing his three works on the Peasants' War.

The Peasants' War was a tragic chapter in German history. Instead of justifiable social evolution, a revolution developed which ended in a catastrophe. Nevertheless, the modern territorial state was itself interested in an efficient and productive peasant class, and their extreme exploitation and deprivation stood in the way. Thus improvements continued to be made during the 16th century.

In conclusion, the following can be said:

1. The Reformation was not the spark that ignited the fire, but the wind which fanned the flames.[92] Luther's attack on the hierarchy brought with it a disruption of the entire social structure; the "spiritual turmoil" could be fanned into "physical turmoil." Many preachers actively sympathized with the peasants' cause. However, one cannot hold Luther responsible for the Peasants' War, as his theological opponents did. After his return from the Wartburg, Luther continually warned of insurrection, within as well as outside of the church.

2. Luther could not remain silent, since the peasants appealed directly to him. From the very beginning, and even in his second work, he still strove for peace. He affirmed many of the reforms demanded by the peasants, and was certainly a critic of the economic and societal evils of his time. His writings against usury and his fight against economic monopoly are well-known to us.

3. But Luther was absolutely opposed to revolution. For him Romans 13 was an irrefutable word of God. At the same time, purely rational considerations also determined his position. He was convinced that even a less than ideal order was better than chaos. He realized that in a civil war it was the innocent who suffered most, and he saw it as his responsibility to remind the authorities of this. The Bavarian chancellor Leonhard of Eck said at the time that a man was needed who could bring the authorities to a more manly disposition. Luther did not become a lackey of the princes. He was not one previous to 1525, and his position after the victory of the princes demonstrates that he did not become one later.

4. Luther's limitation was his inability to admit that under certain circumstances an entire class, also, must use force in fighting for its rights. What he expected of individual Christians, namely, Christian endurance under pressure, he also wrongly expected of an entire social class. Precisely on the basis of his doctrine of the two kingdoms he should have made this differentiation. In economic as well as in political affairs, according to Luther, one is dealing not with the kingdom of Christ but with the temporal realm, which is concerned with legal rights and punishment.

5. Luther saw with complete clarity that all his work was threatened by the Peasants' War. He had to distinguish between economic and political demands and the task of proclaiming the gospel. It was as impossible for him to ally himself with the peasants as with Sickingen's knights.

6. Luther followed his conscience without consideration for his popularity. Throughout the Peasants' War he retained the same posture he had established at Worms. The severity of individual statements can be understood in the context of the heat of the moment, though they cannot be condoned.

7. The Reformation did not come to a standstill as a result of the consequences of the Peasants' War. It continued to progress in Saxony, Hesse, Frankonia, Schleswig-Holstein, and Prussia as well as in numerous cities and villages. The major impact of the Peasants' War was that the "wild growth" of the Reformation came to an end. Luther had lost his trust in the common folk, the "rabble." The period of ordering the structures of the church had begun.

23

The Dispute with Erasmus

1525 was a critical year in Luther's life. It was encumbered by his intervention in the Peasants' War. It was also the year in which he fought with Erasmus.[1]

We have already met Erasmus several times in our account. At the dawn of the Reformation he stood as the prince of the humanists. His edition of the Greek New Testament was one of the greatest contributions made to the Reformation. Yet at a very early point Luther had sensed a different spirit in Erasmus.

Prior to 1517 Luther had corresponded with Spalatin and Johann Lang about Erasmus, in connection with Luther's university reforms. He concurred with Erasmus's critique of scholasticism, but thought that a religious seriousness was lacking. Nevertheless he was persuaded by Melanchthon and other friends to write a letter of tribute to Erasmus.[2] On November 17, 1520, he wrote to Lazarus Spengler in Nuremberg, "God willing, Erasmus and I will of course remain one." [3] It was all right that Erasmus did not wish to be mentioned by him, and he would not attack Erasmus.

Luther's name appears in the letters of Erasmus after 1518. From the very beginning Erasmus wanted to keep his distance from the Luther affair, even when his opinions were favorable. His letter of April 22, 1519, to Melanchthon is characteristic: "All of us approve of Luther's life, but opinions differ concerning his teachings. I myself have not yet read his books. He rightly reminds us of certain matters—would that things might run their course in as happy a fashion as they are honest."

By comparison with the princes of the church (for example, Campeggio and Leo X), Erasmus understood and praised Luther as a legitimate critic of moral conditions (September 13, 1520). The attacks on Luther were a result of the hatred of scholarly studies. Erasmus assured Leo that he had never been a patron saint of Luther. Luther's opponents bore the major blame for the "tumult" that had arisen. He sharply criticized the bull threatening Luther with excommunication. His own plan was to remove the concerns of the world by means of educated and unprejudiced men. This concept of religious dialog was practiced by the followers of Erasmus during the 1540s.

Erasmus had good reasons for his attempts to distance himself from Luther. People were seeing him as an ally of Luther not only in Louvain and in Holland, but also in Paris, Spain, and Italy. It was even rumored that Erasmus had written works that were being disseminated under Luther's name. Luther's combative writings of 1520 aroused Erasmus's disapproval. He saw a catastrophe approaching. "In this tragedy I will not involve myself," he wrote to Gerhard Noviomagus on September 14. He was rightfully fearful for the peaceful progress of academic study.

At that time, as well as later, many were displeased with Erasmus's attempts to remain neutral. They should rather have attempted to understand him. Yet in the long run he was not successful. Not only the traditionalists, but also the Lutherans eventually mistrusted him. He increasingly found himself caught between both fronts. In a letter to Willibald Pirckheimer of March 30, 1522, he lamented his situation: "The Lutherans publicly threaten me with defamatory writings, and the emperor is as good as convinced that I am the head and source of the entire Lutheran turmoil. So I enter into the greatest danger from both sides, even though I have given service to all." Increasingly he was pressured to write against Luther.

The temptation to free himself from this awkward situation was great. Moreover, it was at this very time that he heard of Luther's opinions that acknowledged his philological accomplishments but disputed his theological qualifications. In addition, in 1523 Erasmus became involved in a conflict with Hutten. In 1523 an ugly exchange of letters had developed between them, and from a moral perspective Erasmus had without a doubt come off badly. That was also the impression in Wittenberg.

A final exchange of letters between Erasmus and Luther was unable to delay any longer the outbreak of public conflict. Erasmus had been understandably hurt by the fact that Luther had criticized him so openly. "Kings and friends on every side pressure me to write against Luther," he reported on July 19, 1524. He had in mind Hadrian VI, Henry VIII of England, and Duke George of Saxony. "The dice have been tossed," he wrote at the beginning of September 1524, when his *Diatribe de libero arbitrio* (An Examination of the Free Will) was published.[4]

Erasmus was not completely satisfied with this work; he realized that he was moving beyond his own area of expertise (see his letter to Theodor Adriani, February 9, 1524). With an ironic view of himself he asserted in a letter to Auerbach on December 10, 1524, "Actually I have lost freedom of the will since I published the work." Early in September 1524 he sent the first copies to several places, including Wittenberg. By September 30 Melanchthon had assured him of its initial reception there.[5] He told Erasmus that the book had been accepted with equanimity; its restraint was particularly welcome. Luther had promised to exercise the same restraint in his reply, and had received the book with respect.

Others had given similar judgments on the work. Yet Melanchthon's letter was obviously governed by the fear that a great dispute might arise, and in fact Luther had an entirely different view of the book than Melanchthon had described. On November 1, 1524, Luther wrote to Spalatin: "It is unbelievable how much the book about the freedom of the will nauseates me; I have not yet read more than two pages. It is irksome for me to have to reply to such an educated man about such an uneducated book." [6]

So Luther delayed his response longer and longer; first he wanted to conclude his debate with Karlstadt by finishing the work *Against the Heavenly Prophets*. Then the peasant disturbances occupied his time. It was not until September 1525 that he began working on a reply. In November he finished, and the work appeared in December.[7] Soon thereafter Justus Jonas issued a German translation.

Erasmus greatly resented Luther's sharp reply, and he responded toward the end of February 1526 with the work *Hyperaspistes* (Protective Shield). Luther did not answer. But he did write to

Erasmus once more. In this letter, lost to us, Luther appears to have apologized for his hot temper; Erasmus dismissed this apology as but an excuse in his reply of April 11, 1526. We might well agree with him; for in fact in Luther's tract Erasmus appears as an enemy of Christ, a blasphemer, an Epicurean, and a skeptic. Similar comments about Erasmus also appear in Luther's table talks. One can also understand why Erasmus placed no importance on Luther's wish that God would lead him to the recognition of the impotence of the human will. On the other hand, it should not be overlooked that in Erasmus Luther clearly recognized that he had found a formidable opponent.

In his personal conclusion to *De servo arbitrio* Luther complimented Erasmus that he was the only opponent of his to have grasped the nerve of the whole matter and understood where the real difference lay. The others had bored him with their arguments about the pope, about purgatory, about indulgences, and other similar "trifles." "You and you alone have seen the question on which everything hinges, and have aimed at the vital spot." [8] This praise was justified. However, Erasmus had selected the theme primarily because he did not wish to defend any of the traditional ecclesiastical matters. In his attack on Luther he did not want to support a particular side.

The progression of Erasmus's *Diatribe* is clear and simple. Following a general and methodical introduction there is an explanation of the Old and New Testament passages which support freedom of the will. In the third part Erasmus attempted to refute those texts that speak against free will, including those Luther had referred to in his *Assertio omnium articulorum* of 1520. [9] In the conclusion Erasmus summarized his position and condemned his opponents.

Free will was defined by Erasmus as "a power of the will, by which a person can turn toward that which leads to eternal salvation, or turn away from the same." [10] Erasmus was above all determined to avoid every extreme. To be sure, he attributed "a few things" to free will, but most things to grace. In the beginning and at the end of the process of salvation stood God's action, but in between human beings also contributed something. For example, a child that is not yet able to walk, falls. The father sets it on its feet again. Close by lies an apple. The child wishes to have it. It cannot reach the apple alone. But by taking the hand of the father it succeeds, and so it receives the apple as a "reward." The father could have carried the child, but the child could have struggled against being carried.[11] This is the "cooperation" between God's grace and the human will. The will plays only a small role. Luther's extreme view of grace made God into the author of evil and a cruel tyrant, one who orders a bound slave to run and then punishes him severely when he does not carry out the command.[12] God's essential attributes, however, are righteousness and goodness.[13]

As for the rest, the question of the freedom of the will belongs to those mysteries which ought to be quietly admired rather than inquisitively explored. What is clear is that the main point of religion is the moral aspect. Morality, however, requires a certain freedom of the will. Luther's determinism did away with moral responsibility. Concerning the major theological questions, Erasmus was inclined to skeptical restraint and therefore gladly submitted to the judgment of the church. He wished to assert nothing new, but merely to assemble (*collatio*) the facts. Tradition—which Luther (according to Erasmus) dealt with so highhandedly—was not to be despised; Luther's insistence on spiritual content lacked a scholarly criterion.

Judged by present theological evaluations, Erasmus generally comes off badly. However, one cannot scoff at the *humanitas Erasmiana*, even in the *Diatribe*. Its superb rejection of extreme radicalism is a superior human achievement. Erasmus knew that in life there is not only an either/or, but also a both/and. A tendency toward personal skepticism, along with the painful yet delightful fruit of a scholarly approach to all questions of life, does not produce an iconoclast who opposes the great forces of tradition. Objectivity is not the same as a lack of character. There is such a thing as the neutrality of greater insight. Even though we must often resign ourselves to various riddles in life, that does not excuse us from moral responsibility. Noble humanity is aware of its limitations, and so open to "grace," but submission is not the same as self-renunciation.

Nor can the theological and religious significance of the *Diatribe* be denied. Erasmus was certainly not an original religious thinker in the way Luther was, but he had a religious aspect to his own humanity. He was seriously interested in the religious reforms of his time. He had a personal relationship to the character of the biblical Jesus. The Gospels were among the "sources" to which he was especially dedicated. In his *Diatribe* he endeavored to provide scriptural proof for his theses, and he was not without success in this. In more than a few places his exegesis was more accurate than Luther's. His doctrine of grace was firmly grounded in the teachings of scholasticism: grace did not displace nature, but rather completed it. The answer discovered by Goethe's Faust (Act 2) was the same. For the average modern Protestant this doctrine of grace has become self-evident. It is both religious and rational at the same time. It makes sense. Why then did Luther so vehemently oppose it?

Luther's response to Erasmus, *De servo arbitrio* (The Bondage of the Will),[14] takes up and attempts to refute the *Diatribe* point for point. The conciseness of Luther's flow of thought suffered from this approach, as did the readability of the work. Nevertheless, these shortcomings are more than offset by the significance of the content. In the midst of the polemical give-and-take, Luther revealed the depths of his faith experience.

The arrangement of Luther's material followed that of Erasmus. First he responded to the general and methodological introduction. After this twofold prelude he turned to the scriptural proofs: (1) a refutation of passages offered in support of free will; (2) a defense of his own Scripture passages used against free will; (3) new passages, primarily from Paul and John, against free will. These are followed by concluding remarks.

By way of introduction, Luther separated himself from the skepticism of Erasmus, which he could not bear. A Christian had to take pleasure in firm assertions *(assertiones),* or else he or she was not a Christian.[15] "The Holy Spirit is no Skeptic." [16] A Christian had to know the facts about the question of free will. The reference to honoring mystery did not impress Luther. There are many mysteries in God, but Holy Scripture is clear.[17] Christ is the central content of Scripture. "Take Christ out of the Scriptures, and what will you find left in them?" [18] Yet in the presentation of his case Erasmus had left Christ completely out of the picture. This was going "much too far." [19] The moralistic Christianity of Erasmus was ice-cold.[20]

All Christians ought to know this about their salvation: (1) What we can and what we cannot do;[21] and, (2) whether God sees things in advance or whether we do everything out of necessity.[22] The answer is: "Here, then, is something fundamentally necessary and salutary for a Christian, to know that God foreknows nothing contingently, but that he foresees and purposes and does all things by his immutable, eternal, and infallible will. Here is a thunderbolt by which free choice is completely prostrated and shattered. . . . Hence the proposition stands, and remains invincible, that all things happen by necessity."[23] Only in this way can faith rely on the divine promise.[24]

Erasmus was always afraid of causing offense. Luther did not have a heart of stone,[25] but he knew that God's Word brought conflict along with it. "The world and its god cannot and will not endure the Word of the true God, and the true God neither will nor can keep silence; so when these two Gods are at war with one another, what can there be but tumult in the whole world?"[26] Erasmus considered the paradox of the bondage of the will to be morally questionable; who then "would correct his life?"[27] But in Scripture this "paradox" is clearly attested.[28] No one is able to improve his or her life. It cannot be done, because that comes only through the Holy Spirit.[29] The proclamation of this paradox, however, serves both humility and faith.[30]

To know that our salvation is not in our power is humbling. Since we are unable to comprehend how God, who determines all things, can be merciful and just, we need faith. But faith always focuses on that which is hidden "under an object, perception, or experience which is contrary to it."[31] "This is the highest degree of faith, to believe him merciful when he saves so few and damns so many, and to believe him righteous when by his own will he makes us necessarily damnable."[32] In their bondage, human beings are like animals used for riding, upon which either God or the devil is mounted. It is not in our power to choose which of the two riders we will serve. Rather, the two riders fight for possession of us.[33]

Concerning the second, methodological part of the introduction to the *Diatribe*, Luther made the following comments:[34] Not tradition, but rather Scripture, is decisive! When Erasmus asked if it were possible that God had allowed the church to remain in error so long,[35] Luther answered: The church? No! But one must first accurately determine what the church is. "The Church is hidden, the saints are unknown."[36] The church of God dare not be identified with the historical manifestations we usually refer to as the church. In fact, the discrepancy between the two can almost be spoken of as a normal state of affairs.[37] Therefore the appeal to tradition is not a valid dogmatic criterion. There is only a single (but twofold) measure for dogmatic truth: the inner testimony of the Holy Spirit and the outer clarity of Holy Scripture.[38] In those things that pertain to salvation the Scriptures are clear.

After this twofold introduction, the three-part listing of scriptural proofs begins.[39] It is often overwhelming in its detail. Luther interpreted both the Old Testament and the Synoptic Gospels (Matthew, Mark, and Luke) from a Pauline perspective. From the standpoint of philological-historical exegesis, Erasmus was correct here and there. Luther interpreted individual passages from the whole of Scripture. The *centrum scripturae* (heart of the Scriptures) was for him the work of Christ in the sense of Paul's teaching of justification. He related the various individual expositions to this center. By doing so he achieved a wholistic view which is as historically problematic as it is religiously impressive.

According to Luther, by citing Ezekiel 18:32 in support of free will,[40] the *Diatribe* in the first place failed to recognize the distinction between law and gospel.[41] This passage was not law, but rather gospel. In the second place Erasmus failed to recognize the distinction between the revealed and the hidden God, between the Word of God and God himself.[42] "God does many things that he does not disclose to us in his word; he also wills many things which he does not disclose himself as willing in his word. Thus he does not will the death of a sinner, according to his word; but he wills it according to that inscrutable will of his. . . . God hidden in his majesty neither deplores nor takes away death, but works life, death, and all in all. For there he has not bound himself by his word [*neque definivit sese*], but has kept himself free over all things." [43]

In the second part of his scriptural proofs Luther devoted his attention primarily to the hardening of Pharaoh's heart (Exodus 9)[44] and the Malachi passage,[45] "I have loved Jacob but I have hated Esau" [1:2-3].[46] In his exegesis Erasmus finally went so far as to maintain that human beings are saved or damned "without God's knowledge." This was not the true God, but the sleeping God of Aristotle.[47] "Since, then, God moves and actuates all in all, he necessarily moves and acts also in Satan and ungodly man." [48] In such cases God acts with "evil instruments." [49] God cannot suspend his effectiveness simply because people have evil wills, so by the power of God evil persons do evil things, despite the fact that God can do nothing evil. That is hardening of the heart. God cannot cease being God on account of the desires of evil persons.[50] But why then does God not make evil wills good? "This belongs to the secrets of his majesty, where his judgments are incomprehensible. It is not our business to ask this question, but to adore these mysteries." [51] Why did God allow Adam to fall? "He is God, and for his will there is no cause or reason that can be laid down as a rule or measure for it." [52] Luther himself had often been driven into the depths of despair by this insight, until he recognized "how salutary that despair was, and how near to grace." [53]

In his third section of scriptural proofs Luther cited passages from Paul and John that opposed free will.[54] It is here that he disclosed his deep interest in the teaching of the bondage of the will.[55] If we make the slightest contribution to our own salvation by means of a free will, then there can be no certainty of salvation.

Admittedly there are some insolvable mysteries that remain, even concerning the doctrine of grace. So the treatise concluded with the reference to the "three lights."[56] Job's question—"Why must the righteous suffer?"—is insolvable for the "light of nature." The answer to that question is provided by the "light of grace." And yet it remains incomprehensible, even to the light of grace, that God should damn those who, in spite of all their efforts, are not able to do anything but sin and become guilty. Yet the "light of glory" will allow us to recognize God's righteousness. The reference to the "light of glory" was Luther's last word on the teaching of the bondage of the will. The doctrine of grace leads to eschatology and to reverence in the face of mystery.

We must attempt greater clarification of three questions: (1) What about Luther's "determinism"? (2) How did Luther understand the hidden God in *De servo arbitrio?* and (3) In what sense did Luther affirm predestination?

Concerning the first question, "Everything that comes into being does so necessarily." [57] "Free choice is plainly a divine term, and can properly be applied to none but the Divine Majesty alone." [58] Even the heathen know that everything is predetermined by an unalterable destiny.[59] The illustration of the animal to be ridden is even more blunt.[60]

Luther was obviously a consequent determinist. Nevertheless, he attributed to a person a psychological freedom of will "with respect to what is beneath him," which they can use in the way they wish.[61] He was not interested in the philosophical questions related to determinism. He concentrated exclusively on the question of salvation. Only in relationship to this question did he uncompromisingly affirm the bondage of the will, and only in this respect can one speak of Luther's determinism. Yet one can ask whether Luther's notion of the bondage of the will does not abolish personalism. In this sense the illustration of the ridden animal appears to cross the boundary of the permissible. Still, it is merely an illustration and should not be pressed too far. There is also a precedent for it in Catholic tradition,[62] as well as a related scriptural reference (Psalm 73:22).

Luther did not wish to abolish personhood by means of this illustration. He spoke from experience, for he was filled with the awareness of the hidden powers that seek to control our wills. But our wills do not cease to exist under their influence. Luther's view relied in part on a distinction between necessity and compulsion. The person who has not been grasped by God can only sin. "By 'necessarily' I do not mean 'compulsorily' . . . . he does not do evil against his will, as if he were taken by the scruff of the neck and forced to it, like a thief or a robber carried off against his will to punishment, but he does it of his own accord and with a ready will." [63] Experience also teaches this.[64] Correspondingly, the will which has been taken over by God is a "liberated will"; this possession is "royal freedom." [65]

Therefore the teaching of the bondage of the will does not seek to abolish personalism. Luther even admitted that human beings are suited for being gripped by the Spirit of God and fulfilled by grace; we have a "disposing quality" and a "passive aptitude" for it.[66] It is precisely this disposition that distinguishes us from animals and plants. The teaching of the bondage of the will interprets human existence but does not negate it.

Concerning the second question, the idea of the hidden God is familiar to us from Luther's theology of the cross. It received its clearest expression in the early lectures and sermons and above all in the Heidelberg Disputation. The hidden God of the *theologia crucis* is none other than the crucified God, and therefore a manifestation of the revealed God. These thoughts are also present in *De servo arbitrio,* where the concept of faith as it is used in the theology of the cross is given an almost classic definition.[67]

But this is not the only view that we encounter in the exposition of the Ezekiel passage.[68] Here the hidden God *(Deus absconditus)* is not a manifestation of the revealed God and is not the crucified God, but rather appears to be a *Deus absolutus,* a God "for himself" *(per se)* who is neither revealed, proclaimed, nor worshiped. God is rather the God who effects all things, who does not mourn the death of the sinner, but instead causes it. "Hidden in his majesty," God does not become comprehensible in the Word, but remains free and above all things. When it is said of God, "Things above us are no business of ours," that can certainly not mean God has nothing to do with us. For God's "inscrutable will" is still to be feared and worshiped.[69] Even though we are to hold on to the Word of the revealed God,[70] Erasmus's failure was that he did not take his *hidden* God into account. "Your thoughts about God are all too human," Luther admonished him.[71] By making this distinction did Luther abandon his own basic theological conviction, that God is called Jesus Christ, and there is no other God? Did not Luther himself later warn his followers about *De servo arbitrio,* for example in Chapter 26 of his Genesis lectures? [72] Where is the certainty of salvation?

To declare that the whole treatise is a polemic aberration is not satisfactory. Luther spoke so convincingly of a hidden God that one must assume that an actual religious experience lay behind it. For Luther, God is completely different from a concept, idea, or postulate; God is in fact a vast, living reality. God is "unrestingly active . . . in all his creatures." [73] Like all of life, this life in particular mocks all human classification.

Luther's experience of God was profound. His faith in the revealed God of salvation was surrounded by the awe of that which is eternally incomprehensible. Luther did not always allow us to peer into this abyss, but here he did. The harmless Christianity of the spiritual prince Erasmus drove him to an eruption of his volcanic experiences of God, an inner fire that he—out of pastoral wisdom—

usually restrained in his encounters with simple Christians. It did
not bother him that this eruption reduced systematic theology to a
pile of rubble.

From a distance one can imagine what it meant for the same
Luther to describe himself as "rejoicing in the grace of God." [74] To
speak of an intrusion of philosophy into theology in *De servo arbitrio*
is to completely misunderstand Luther. Luther's experience of the
hidden God was derived from an entirely different dimension than
theoretical reflection of a philosophical and systematic-theological
nature. Luther was not an ordinary theologian.

Concerning the third question, Luther taught the completely unlimited, independent, and efficacious activity of God in the world.
This view was in part based on reason, but for Luther it was also
based on both terrifying and uplifting experience. Luther was conscious of the living reality of God in a way that few others have
been. It was not his Occamist tradition which led Luther to assert
the inaccessibility and incomprehensibility of God's will,[75] but
rather his own religious experience.

The entire treatise against Erasmus has to be understood from the
perspective of this experience. This includes the doctrine of "predestination." Predestination had a dual source in Luther's religious
experience. On the one hand it was related to the question about
the certainty of salvation. Only if our salvation lies completely in
God's hand and is in no way determined by our cooperation can
we be sure of our salvation. On the other hand it is connected with
his experience of the living reality of God. It is not consistent with
God's living reality to speak only of God's foreknowledge (pre-
science).[76] No limits can be set for the reality of the living God;
it cannot be confined in the least even by Satan or the godless.[77]

The logical conclusion to this affirmation of the unlimited activity
of God is that God is also the creator of sin. This conclusion has at
times in fact been drawn in theological circles. Characteristically,
however, Luther did not go that far. He also avoided the teaching
of double predestination in *De servo arbitrio*. This teaching is the
product of a form of logic which is not legitimate in theology.
Its scriptural basis is more than questionable (despite Romans 9),
and it is incompatible with religious experience. If double predestination were actually the case, then the work of Christ would
be in vain and the central declarations of the gospel would lose their
sense. This teaching appeared in theology because precedence was

given to rational construction of an apparently closed system of religious thought and the existential aspects of religious thought were distorted.

Luther took the logical incongruities of his position in stride. He also rejected the related question: Why doesn't God in his omnipotence and goodness direct the evil will of persons to good results? Indeed, why did God ever allow Adam to fall? "This belongs to the secrets of his majesty, where his judgments are incomprehensible." [78] This was not the awkward evasion of someone who had become hopelessly enmeshed in his own polemics. Proper theological thinking stops short at that insolvable antinomy which can be formulated quite simply as, *Godliness is the result of grace*. In the end it is impossible to explain why one person is godly and another is not, no matter how many provisional answers one may come up with. It is to Luther's credit as a theological thinker that he abstained from providing the answer.

With Erasmus everything was reasonable, but this very reasonableness made his solution questionable. Luther's last reference to the "light of glory" should not be seen as a way out of the dilemma but rather as a practical necessity. To a certain extent, Luther's earlier argumentation collapsed and he in effect admitted that he had no solution. Nevertheless, this was still more than polemical obstinacy—though Luther demonstrated that as well when he concluded his argument against Erasmus by declaring, "I for my part in this book have not discoursed, but have asserted and do assert." [79]

Luther stated those things that could be brought to bear on the problem from both sides of the argument, and he also stated those things that needed to be said based on the experience of religious reality. He drew the lines as far as he could possibly draw them, given our earthly vantage point; but their point of intersection, so to speak, lies in infinity. Genuine theology maintains an awareness of its own provisional nature. In doing so it becomes a true reflection of human existence before God.

Luther's dispute with Erasmus was concerned with the reality of God and humanity. In Erasmus he saw this reality concealed behind a congenial, rational theory. Twelve years later he wrote to Capito: "I acknowledge none of them to be really a book of mine, except perhaps the one *On the Bound Will* and the *Catechism*." [80]

Theologically, much of *De servo arbitrio* remains problematic, and one ought not dispute that. Yet the work ranks first among the witnesses to Luther's religious genius.

Luther's Marriage
and Home Life
(the Table Talk)

In the middle of 1525, a year of crisis for the Reformation, an event occurred which initially affected only Luther's personal life, but eventually attained wide-reaching historical significance. On the evening of Tuesday, June 13, 1525, shortly after five o'clock, Luther was secretly married to the former nun Katharina von Bora. The officient at the ceremony was Bugenhagen, the pastor of the Wittenberg parish church.

The ceremony took place in Luther's living quarters in the Black Cloister, with the Cranachs and professors Jonas and Apel present as witnesses.[1] Marriage practices were strictly regulated at that time, and so two weeks later, on June 27, there was another, much larger celebration to which many guests came, including Luther's parents. This served as the public and legal confirmation of the marriage, and therefore included a public procession to the church.

Was this event simply a sunny idyll in the midst of the flurry of those months? Absolutely not! Luther's marriage was considered a scandal not only by his enemies, but in part by his friends as well. We can see this in a letter written by Melanchthon on June 16 to his friend Camerarius. Melanchthon considered Luther's marriage to be a degradation of the great man just at the moment in which his authority was most needed. Melanchthon had not been present at the June 13th ceremony.[2] The jurist Schurff wrote, "If this man takes a wife, the whole world will laugh along with the devil, who will destroy everything he has accomplished."

For Luther's opponents, the marriage between a former monk and a runaway nun must have been a welcome scandal. In confessional polemics it was even claimed that Luther had begun the entire Reformation just because he wanted to get married. That it took him eight years to reach this presumed goal is almost as absurd as the insinuation itself. Even Luther had no illusions about the effect of his decision. On June 16 he wrote to Spalatin, "By marrying I have made myself so lowly and contemptible that I hope the angels will laugh and all the devils weep." [3]

As early as his treatise *To the Christian Nobility,* Luther had argued against mandatory celibacy of priests.[4] Noting that celibacy was not part of the divine order, but an arbitrary rule of the church, he also approved the marriage of his friend Bartholomäus Bernhardi of Feldkirch, provost at Kemberg.[5] Initially he had reservations as to whether celibacy for monks also ought to be abolished, but both in this treatise and his treatise on monastic vows, he came to a radical conclusion. He himself publicly discarded his monastic habit on October 9, 1524, and from then on he preached in his academic gown. He rejoiced over the marriage of Bugenhagen (Oct. 13, 1522) and his monastic brother Wenceslas Link (April 15, 1523), but he himself remained single. As late as November 30, 1524, he assured Spalatin that he had no intention of marrying.[6]

Katharina von Bora, the woman Luther chose, was born on January 29, 1499. She was the child of a somewhat well-to-do aristocratic family in the region south of Leipzig. While still a child of 10 she was placed in the Cistercian Convent of Nimbschen near Grimma. According to the customs of the time, convents often provided for the daughters of noble families; the bewildered girls were seldom asked whether life in a convent appealed to them. An aunt of Katharina's named Magdalene von Bora, who spent her final years in the Luther home as "Aunt Lene," also lived in Nimbschen. Katharina was consecrated as a nun on October 8, 1515.

Before Luther's teachings reached Nimbschen, it seems that Katharina had not found life in the convent to be oppressive. There she was well cared for and had an orderly life. She learned the fundamentals of Latin and so was, to a certain extent, able to understand church texts. We also know that later, as Luther's wife, Katie occasionally used Latin phrases in conversations with their table guests.

The elector's city of Grimma was approximately one-half hour from Nimbschen. Most of its citizens were evangelicals, and there were many followers of Luther in the local Augustinian monastery. In 1522 the prior had voluntarily relinquished his position and left the order, along with a number of like-minded brothers. Two relatives of his lived in the Nimbschen convent. Apparently it was through these contacts that Luther's teachings were introduced there. At any rate, the nuns came to a religious crisis point; they lost the support of their order that they had previously received in gratitude for their service.

Nine of the nuns, including Katharina and a sister of Johann von Staupitz, decided to break their vows and leave Nimbschen. At first they turned to their parents and relatives and pleaded with them to help them leave, since for reasons of conscience they could no longer live in the convent. No help came, however. Then they turned to Luther himself for counsel and help.

Luther did not hesitate to come to their assistance. Since a voluntary release from their vows was out of the question, they would have to proceed secretly. The situation was dangerous, for the punishment for abducting a nun was death. Nevertheless Luther was able to enlist the aid of a respected Torgau citizen, Leonhard Koppe, who had business contacts in Nimbschen. On Easter Eve, April 4, 1523, the escape succeeded in an unlikely and adventurous manner *(mirabiliter)*, as Luther reported in a letter to Spalatin on April 10, 1523.[7] Presumably Koppe had taken the nine nuns out of the convent in a covered wagon with which he usually transported barrels of herring. The legend was later told that each of the nuns had been hidden in an empty herring barrel.

On April 7 the nine women, without the barest of necessities, arrived in Wittenberg. Now the responsibility for their support rested on Luther. It was impossible for them to return to their relatives, since they lived in the territory of Duke George of Saxony, so Luther turned to the Wittenberg congregation and, through Spalatin, to the electoral court.[8] In an open letter to Leonhard Koppe, which appeared under the title *The Reason and the Answer Why Virgins May Rightfully Leave Convents,*[9] Luther acknowledged his part in their escape and attested to the good reputation of the nine nuns, whose names he listed individually. As far as we know, all nine women were eventually married.

Katharina, whose father apparently had already died, was equally unable to return to her relatives. She remained in Wittenberg and found lodging in the home of Lucas Cranach and his wife (who took part in the wedding ceremony on June 13, acting as representatives for Katharina's parents).

In the Cranach household Katharina acquired skills which later became quite useful as Luther's wife. Of course this setting also provided her contacts among the leading Wittenberg circles. Even before her marriage, Katie became acquainted with the Melanchthon household. In later years she did not have a very good relationship with Melanchthon's wife.

Katie met several men who would have suited her as marriage partners. She was not a particularly beautiful woman, but she had a certain charm about her and therefore experienced love and heartbreak. Early in 1523 the young Nuremberg patricion's son Hieronymus Baumgartner, who had studied in Wittenberg from 1518–1521, returned to visit Melanchthon. There he and Katie became acquainted and fell in love. Luther was overjoyed. For the time being there was no engagement, but Hieronymus promised to return to Wittenberg soon. At home he met with opposition. A runaway nun, poor as a beggar, did not live up to the expectations of the Baumgartner family.

On October 12, 1524, Luther wrote to the young man: "If you want to hold on to Katie von Bora you had better hurry before she is given to someone else who is already at hand. She has not yet gotten over her love for you. It would make me very happy to see the two of you united." [10] But Baumgartner kept his distance, and on January 23, 1526, he married Sibylle Dichtel, the 15-year-old daughter of the senior magistrate Bernhard Dichtel of Tutzing. Katie later remembered Hieronymus without resentment, and Luther retained his relationship with him. Occasionally he teased Katie about her first love.

The suitor who was hinted at in the October 12 letter was certainly not Luther himself. It was rather a certain Dr. Kaspar Glatz, a theologian who was serving as rector of the University of Wittenberg during the summer of 1524. But Katie refused her hand. Eventually her mistrust of him found vindication. Two years later the elector accused him of fraudulent financial schemes and neglect of his congregation.

In her predicament Katie took Nikolaus of Amsdorf into her confidence. At the end of September 1524 she went to him and candidly asked him not to let Luther match her with Glatz against her will. She could marry Luther himself or Amsdorf, if either one of them might desire her, but never Glatz.

One must assume that this admission led to the change in Luther's attitude. Initially he had had no liking for Katie; in fact he considered her arrogant. Now, however, it appeared to him that it was God's will that he "take pity on the abandoned," as he later put it in one of his table talks.[11] He also said that at first he had thought of Ave von Schönfeld, one of the other Nimbschen nuns. "But God wanted me to have pity on her [Katie], and, praise God I was successful, for I have a godfearing, faithful wife in whom, as Solomon says,[12] a husband's heart can trust." [13]

Why did Luther marry? Certainly not out of a youthful sense of infatuation. According to several witnesses, Luther longed for familiarity and security; he gradually became dissatisfied with his miserable bachelor existence in the Black Cloister. Moreover, he wanted to underscore with his own actions what he had taught about marriage and the celibacy of priests; and since he expected an early death, he intended to make this witness before it was too late.

Finally, however, there was also pressure to fulfill his father's heartfelt wish. From the very beginning Hans had opposed his son's becoming a monk. But the real motive behind Luther's choice of Katie remained his compassion for the forsaken.

Katie brought new life into the rooms of what had previously been the Black Cloister of the Augustinian Friars. "I feel neither passionate love nor burning for my spouse, but I cherish her," Luther wrote in his wedding invitation to Amsdorf on June 21, 1525.[14] This sense of devotion provided a more solid basis for a happy marriage than a romantic infatuation could ever have done. In any case, a man of Luther's age and position would have found sheer romanticism quite foreign.

From the start he found their sense of togetherness to be enjoyable. "Man has strange thoughts the first year of marriage. When sitting at table he thinks, 'Before I was alone; now there are two.' Or in bed, when he wakes up, he sees a pair of pigtails lying beside him which he hadn't seen there before." [15] Numerous witnesses offer us statements from Luther's own lips about how happy he was in marriage. "I wouldn't give up my Katie for France or for Venice—first, because God gave her to me and gave me to her." [16] "I love my Katie; yes, I love her more dearly than myself; that is certainly true. I would rather die myself than have her and the children die." [17] "The greatest gift and grace on earth is a devout, friendly, godfearing and home-loving spouse with whom you live in peace and to whom you can entrust all your treasures and whatever you possess, even your body and life." "Katie," he added, "you also have a devout husband who loves you; you are an empress." [18]

Because of her diligence and because she always rose very early each morning, Luther called her "the morning star of Wittenberg." [19] When Cranach painted Katie, Luther was delighted and said, "I think I'll have a husband added to that painting, send it to [the Council called to meet in] Mantua, and inquire whether they prefer marriage." [20]

Some persons openly hoped that Katie would have a calming influence on blustery Luther. Melanchthon expressed this view in a letter of June 16. Erasmus wrote, "Dr. Martinus begins to grow milder after his marriage; he no longer rages with his pen." On this point Erasmus was just as mistaken as Melanchthon was.

It was certainly not easy for Katie to be married to such a temperamental man as Luther. But the love and faithfulness the two showed for each other enabled them to overcome their many tensions. Katie did not intrude into her husband's work, though she took an interest in it. Yet she knew very well how to exercise leadership alongside him, and Luther welcomed her governance of their household affairs. She was strong-willed. In his letters Luther often teasingly addressed her as "Lord Katie," or called her "my master and Moses Katie."

Six children were born to the Luthers; three boys and three girls. The first, little Johannes, was born on June 7, 1526, one year after the wedding. He was nicknamed Hans after his grandfather. Later in life he studied jurisprudence and became a chancellory counselor to Duke John Frederick in Weimar. The second child, Elizabeth, born on December 10, 1527, lived only eight months. The third child, Magdalene, was born on May 4, 1529. She died on September 20, 1542, at the age of 13. After Magdalene came Martin (Nov. 9, 1531), Paul (Jan. 28, 1533), and finally Margarethe (Dec. 17, 1534).

Martin studied theology but did not become a pastor. He lived in Wittenberg as a private person, and he died there at the age of 34.

The most talented of Luther's sons was Paul. In his childhood he was physically somewhat weak, but eventually he became a skilled physician. He was court physician in Gotha, then personal doctor to the elector of Brandenburg. Finally he was employed at the court of Elector August in Dresden. After her father's death, Margarethe married a man from Kunheim.

Despite the many demands on his time, Luther took great interest in the lives of his children, and he recorded many precious and detailed observations about them. It did not bother him to have the children romp at his feet while he worked. In fact he saw many aspects of childhood existence as parables for the kingdom of God and of world events. Children were "the finest mockingbirds" and talked "naturally and honestly." [21] They were God's "little jesters"; [22] they had "such splendid thoughts about God." [23] Seeing little Martin clinging to his mother's breast, Luther said, "The pope, the bishops, Duke George, Ferdinand, and all the demons hate this child, yet the little child isn't afraid of all of them put together. He sucks with pleasure at those breasts, is cheerful, is unconcerned about all his enemies." [24]

Those who want to know Luther well should become acquainted with him as a father. Luther's letter to his son Hans, sent from the Coburg Castle, is widely known. There he wrote of the merry garden where the children play and like to pray and learn and be good.[25] Each time we sing the Christmas carol *"Vom Himmel Hoch"* (From Heaven Above) we are honoring Luther as a father.

The death of his little Elizabeth was difficult for him, but he suffered deeply at the death of his 13-year-old daughter Magdalene.[26] "I am joyful in spirit but I am sad according to the flesh. The flesh doesn't take kindly to this. The separation troubles me above measure. It's strange to know that she is surely at peace and that she is well off there, very well off, and yet to grieve so much!" [27] The picture of a man, strong in faith, weeping at the bedside of his dying daughter is deeply moving.

Luther loved his children above all else, but he took discipline seriously. Once when his little Hans did something wrong he would not allow the boy to come to him for three days—until he had asked in writing to be forgiven. When the boy's mother and friends in the household interceded for him, Luther replied, "I would rather have a dead son than a disobedient son."[28] But he also recognized that different children could not be treated in exactly the same way. He avoided the childrearing methods used by his own parents. Praise and blame needed to be apportioned equally. In bringing up a child the apple had to lie by the rod.[29] Too much grace was better than too much punishment.[30]

All in all, a cheerful tone pervaded the Luther household. Music was enthusiastically encouraged. After evening meals Luther often picked up some music and his lute, and the family sang together. Luther had a resonant tenor voice.[31] If they made "a few blunders" while playing and singing, it was not the fault of the composer.[32] For his table guests, Luther set up a game of skittels in his garden (a game in which he himself often participated). He was also an enthusiastic chess player. In leisure hours he worked with his lathe, and in remembrance of his bachelor days, he mended his own pants. After all, it was said that even the electors Frederick and John did the same. Katie was not quite so enthusiastic about the practice. Luther's special joy was his garden, and he worked in it with enthusiasm.

And so there was much life in the Luther home. Besides the children and the servants, several permanent guests lived under Luther's roof: "Aunt Lene," whom we have already mentioned, three nieces of Luther's, an occasional student assistant, various nephews, people passing through who needed a place to stay, and the regular "table guests"—mostly older students of theology who, according to the custom of the times, took their meals with their professor for a small remuneration. There were always a number of them at Luther's table.

It is this group that we can thank for the so-called *Table Talk* of Luther, an indispensable source for understanding the person of the reformer and the history of the times. Admittedly, these talks must be used with a critical eye. They were collected and edited between 1912 and 1921 by Ernst Kroker, the head librarian and director of the archives in Leipzig, and issued in six thick, folio volumes, with more than 7000 entries, classified according to the names of the recorders.[33] In the *Luther-Jahrbuch* of 1919 Kroker thoroughly analyzed these table talks as "historical sources," and on the whole assessed them quite positively, particularly when one can have some critical control by comparing parallel accounts.

The recorders were not young "foxes," but were honest men whom we must trust to have avoided conscious falsification or irresponsible mistakes. Quite frequently they quoted Luther verbatim, and the reformer himself alternated between German and Latin in his table conversations. In fact many of Luther's Latin expressions are based on stenographic Latin transcripts; there were as yet no abbreviations for the German. Luther himself may have made errors. Occasionally he started false rumors; his memory would fail him, or he would intentionally exaggerate. At times he would also keep a monastic silence at the table. More frequently he would turn to his table companions and ask, "Well, gentlemen, what's new?" Or he might open a new topic himself.

We are grateful that Luther's table guests considered such discussions important enough to record. The earliest notes are from Konrad Cordatus, a religious refugee from Austria who was a guest in the Black Cloister in 1531 and 1532. The notes of Veit Dietrich (born in 1506 in Nuremberg), who later became the preacher at St. Sebaldus in his home city, and Johann Schlaginhauffen, later pastor in Köthen, also come from about the same time. The recorders who followed in the years 1536 to 1539 were: Anton Lauterbach, later a pastor in Pirna; Hieronymus Weller from the mountain city of Freiberg, whom Luther often had to console because of his depressions; and Ludwig Rabe, who had fled from Halle. From 1540 until 1542 Johann Matthesius was a table guest of Luther's. He later became the reformer of Joachimstal and is best-known for his Luther sermons—the most well-known, early presentation of Luther's life. In addition there were a number of other men, not all of whom need to be named here.

During the last weeks of Luther's life his student assistant, Johann Aurifaber (Goldschmid, 1519-1575) prepared a collection of notes which were printed in 1566 under the title, *Tischreden und Colloquia Dr. M. Lutheri*. In this compilation the content is organized according to various subjects and the character of a daily journal is completely lost. Aurifaber's work had the greatest impact, for it was in this form that the *Table Talk* has been known through the centuries. Historically it is less dependable than the individual transcripts. By comparison, the Lauterbach collection simply repeats the texts recorded by others. Aurifaber, on the other hand, translated everything into German and occasionally included sayings of his own. Those who simply want to enjoy the *Table Talk* and are not interested in scholarly studies will still do well with the version of Aurifaber.

Luther confronts us personally and directly in the *Table Talk*. The talks are not works of art like Goethe's conversations with Eckermann, but for that very reason they are much more original. There are few areas of life in which Luther did not take a lively interest: everyday theological and practical concerns, historical and personal events, deep religious experiences, and proverbial wisdom were all graphically presented. The richness of thought and formulation never ceases to amaze the reader. We encounter both a lovable sense of humor and a passionate temper. Many of his expressions are too coarse and frank for our contemporary taste. The normal occurrences of life were never glossed over, but one will not find obscenities in Luther. It is remarkable how we are able to examine Luther's life in minute detail. He was not a saint; yet, despite all his contradictions, he deserves our respect and love.

As Luther's wife, Katie had the daily responsibility of caring for a large number of people. Her husband was of little help in this; he generally had no dealings with finances. Once, when a needy person asked him for help and he didn't have any more cash on hand to draw from, Luther immediately wanted to give away the golden goblets given to his children by their godparents. He never received a penny of remuneration for any of his lectures or his countless writings; had he wanted to, he could have become a very wealthy man.

Sometimes Katie would resort to clever ways of curbing her husband's generosity. Behind his back she retained the 20 gold gulden that his old opponent, Albert of Mainz, had (curiously) sent them as a wedding present. Luther had been indignant and had repudiated the gift. When Luther married, the elector had increased his salary to 200 gulden. In later years he received 300 gulden. On special occasions the elector or the city would give him contributions of produce. His income was actually not that bad, but it was still barely sufficient for the large household. In Luther's household accounts for January 2, 1542,[34] this notable verse appears:

Keeping a household requires much.
If you truly want to reckon the bill
You'll find more going out, than into the till;
At least in my house the case is such.[35]

We know that Katie was able to acquire some property. In addition to the cloister garden, Luther owned three other gardens. In 1539 he was able to lease the Boos steading, a small farm southeast of Wittenberg. In 1540 Katie purchased the small, mismanaged farm at Zulsdorf near Borna from her brother, Hans von Bora, for 610 gulden. Most of the money—600 gulden—was contributed by the elector. There were many domestic animals: cows, pigs, goats, chickens, geese, ducks, doves, and a small dog named Tölpel. Fish could be caught from the fish pond, and Katie brewed her own beer. So Katie was constantly occupied as a businesswoman as well as a homemaker. Luther was deeply grateful for all her work, and also occasionally made humorous comments about it.

Her husband's frequent illnesses brought Katie much grief. In 1537, when Luther lay close to death in Smalcald, he asked Melanchthon to console her: "Comfort my Katie. She should endure the pain and remember that these 12 years with me have been happy ones; she has served me not only as a wife, but as a maid. May God reward her for it!" [36] During his last trip to Eisleben he tried again and again to dispel her justified worries with humorous, yet touching letters.

The news of her husband's death was conveyed by Melanchthon. It came as a severe blow. The remaining six-and-a-half years of Katharina's life were exceedingly difficult in every respect. Even though she experienced no direct physical hardships, she suffered from many setbacks and much ingratitude. The times of war were very hard on her. Her own tragic death occurred in 1552; while fleeing from the plague in Wittenberg, she was thrown so hard from the cart she was riding in that she never recovered. Her gravestone is in the church at Torgau.

By becoming Luther's wife, Katharina von Bora entered the pages of history. Even though Luther was not the first evangelical theologian to be married, and his home bore a special character because of the impact of his unique position, one can still say that his marriage marked the birth of the Protestant parsonage. The significance of this event for the cultural history of Germany cannot be denied, even by opponents of the church.

Luther expressed himself on the proper place and meaning of marriage innumerable times in his letters, table talks, sermons, and other writings. The following should especially be noted: *A Sermon on the Estate of Marriage*, 1519;[37] *The Estate of Marriage*, 1522;[38] *The Wedding Booklet*, 1529;[39] *On Marriage Matters*, 1530;[40] and his lectures on Psalm 128 of 1532-1533.[41] Here, too, Luther proved himself to be a reformer of Christian thought. The love of the sexes for each other was part of creation, even though it could not be separated from the principle of original sin. Marriage was willed by God before the fall into sin; it served the propagation of the human species. However, it had also become a remedy for sexual licentiousness. For this reason enforced celibacy was against God's will.

As a monk, Luther had apparently not suffered under the temptations of the flesh. After his own wedding he viewed intercourse within marriage as healthy and normal, and he rejoiced in it. The estate of marriage was "supported by God's Word and has not been devised or established by human beings." [42] It was a "divine and blessed estate." [43]

This biblical-religious foundation for marriage did not stand in opposition to the fact that Luther, at the same time, described it as "an outward, physical or temporal matter." [44] This meant that marriage belonged to the natural order and not to the order of salvation. It was not a sacrament, as the Roman church concluded from a misunderstanding of Eph. 5:32. Therefore secular authorities and not the church were to be responsible for establishing a marriage. The responsibility of the church was not the external legal order, but rather the counseling of consciences. Marriage was a public estate; therefore it was to be entered into publicly, with witnesses, before the community. Luther was opposed to secret engagements. In his opinion they were invalid, though his position aroused the opposition of even the evangelical jurists. Marriage also was not to be entered into without the knowledge and consent of the parents. But neither were parents to force their children into a marriage, nor prevent them from marrying if they loved each other.[45]

Marriage provided for the propagation and rearing of children, but this was not its essence. Marriage was primarily a moral partnership of mutual, self-giving love. Sexual intimacy did not need to be limited to those measures necessary for procreation; it was also an expression and fulfillment of marital love. As grounds for divorce Luther acknowledged adultery (at least if it continued), impotence, and the denial of the marriage relationship.[46]

Luther could never praise motherhood highly enough. As a mother a woman became the instrument of God. If in giving birth she lost her life, she would die "in a noble deed and in subservience to God." [47] In this connection we should not sidestep one particularly shocking assertion: "And even if they [women who bear children] bear themselves weary—or ultimately bear themselves out— that does not hurt. Let them bear themselves out. This is the purpose for which they exist. It is better to have a brief life with good health than a long life in ill health." [48] These words seem cruel and insensitive to our ears, but they were not intended that way. When Katie was seriously ill, Luther cried out fervently, "Dear Katie, don't die and leave me." [49] The passage quoted merely expresses in an exaggerated form the thought that motherhood is the purpose and glory of a woman. Luther was indeed a man of the 16th century. Today we think differently about the roles and significance of women.

Parents had a spiritual office to exercise in relationship to their children. They were not simply to allow them to live "according to the flesh," but above all were to consider the salvation of their souls. "O how perilous it is to be a father or mother where only flesh and blood are supreme!" [50] Parents deserved the authority they had, for they were God's representatives. It was not enough for children to love their parents; they were also to honor them. Where parenthood was understood as an assignment of God, however, parental authority would not be misused.

Luther, who himself did not marry until his later years, knew that it was impossible to build a marriage on the first "intoxicating" love. "It's easy enough to get a wife, but to love her with constancy is difficult." [51] For this reason Luther did not hold early marriages in high regard.[52] On the other hand, because of the danger of immorality one ought not wait too long. He considered a person of 20 old enough to marry.[53] Everything depended on whether one entered marriage with or without God. "O what a truly noble, important, and blessed condition the estate of marriage is if it is properly regarded! O what a truly pitiable, horrible, and dangerous condition it is if it is not properly regarded!" [54]

June 13, 1525, was a date that made history. In the face of ascetic hostility to the body, Luther restored a good name to marriage. Since that time new problems have arisen and new solutions are required. We do well, however, not to overlook Luther's basic principles.

Opposition to Karlstadt and Zwingli

The dispute with Karlstadt did not come to an end when Luther returned to Wittenberg. Initially Karlstadt was still professor at the university and archdeacon of the collegiate church. The circumstances surrounding his departure are not clear, but he soon withdrew to the parish of Orlamünde, which was connected with the collegiate church. When he was dismissed from that position he sought a conversation with Luther.

On August 22, 1524, the two men met at the Black Bear Inn in Jena, the same inn at which Luther, some two-and-a-half years earlier, had happened upon the Swiss students. Luther was aware of the differences between Karlstadt and Müntzer, but he still considered Karlstadt one of the "new prophets." To some extent Karlstadt confirmed his suspicions. Finally Luther handed him a gulden and invited him to write a tract against him.

Two days later Luther had a discussion with the congregation at Orlamünde. This did not go well. The main topics were the removal of images and Karlstadt's "prophesying." Karlstadt was then living as a peasant and asked the community to call him "neighbor Andres." The situation continued to grow worse, so on September 18, 1524, Duke John decided to banish Karlstadt from the electoral territories.

Karlstadt went first to Franconia and then to Strasbourg. He issued a series of tracts against Luther, taking issue primarily with his views on the Lord's Supper. These disturbed the Strasbourgers, who turned to Luther for counsel. In response, Luther wrote a pastoral *Letter to the Christians in Strasbourg in Opposition to the Fanatic Spirit.*[1] In this letter we find Luther's straightforward admission that he, also, had found the symbolic view of the Lord's Supper to be a great temptation, for "I realized that at this point I could best resist the papacy. . . . But I am a captive and cannot free myself. The text is too powerfully present, and will not allow itself to be torn from its meaning by mere verbiage."[2] Karlstadt's manner of writing about the subject could do little but repel Luther. His iconoclasm turned liberty into law.

In the important treatise *Against the Heavenly Prophets in the Matter of Images and Sacraments,* Luther thoroughly repudiated Karlstadt.[3] The first part of the treatise was published toward the end of December 1524. The second part did not appear until the end of January 1525. The conflict with his one-time associate was painful for Luther, but he pursued it with considerable acumen. He was successful in directing the discussion of law and gospel back to fundamental principles.

In the first part Luther dealt with the matter of images.[4] Images first had to be torn from one's heart; then they would not injure one's eyes.[5] The veneration of images would disappear together with works righteousness.[6] Luther had nothing against the removal of images when it was done "by the proper authorities."[7] Exodus 20:3-4 did not deal with the making of images but with their adoration.[8] In itself the fashioning of images was a "minor, external thing"; but when their prohibition was made binding on the conscience, it became "the most important of all," since it "destroys faith."[9] Karlstadt wanted to "capture [consciences] with laws and burden them with sin without good cause."[10] As memorials and witnesses, images were not merely to be tolerated, they were to be seen as praiseworthy and honorable."[11] The destruction of images at pilgrimage sites was to be praised, for those were "the devil's hospices";[12] but it was not a sin to let them stand.[13]

Moreover, Christians no longer needed to pay attention to Moses.[14] According to Karlstadt, the New Testament set aside only the ceremonial and judicial laws of the Old Testament; not the Decalog and its prohibition of images.[15] According to Luther, this traditional view was incorrect; the Decalog also contained ceremonial and judicial regulations,[16] namely the prohibition of images and the command to keep the Sabbath,[17] both of which were abrogated in the New Testament.[18] Only those regulations of the Decalog were to be retained which were in agreement with "natural law"[19] or "the law of nature."[20] Everything else had been set aside as optional,[21] though one might learn much from it.[22] Insofar as the law of Moses was the "*Sachsenspiegel* [an early Saxon legal code] of the Jews,"[23] it had as little jurisdiction over Christians as the *Sachsenspiegel* had over the French.

The clearest summary of this position is found in Luther's 1525 sermon entitled, *[Instruction on] How Christians Should Regard Moses.*[24] The evangelical freedom with which Luther approached the Old Testament was unique and has not yet been surpassed. The iconoclasts gladly used Luther's German Bible with its many illustrations; why shouldn't people be allowed to paint such pictures on walls?[25] When Luther heard or read about the works of God, he always carried a mental picture of them in his mind and heart. "Whether I will or not, when I hear of Christ, an image of a man hanging on a cross takes form in my heart, just as the reflection of my face naturally appears in the water when I look into it." Why was it a sin to have such an image before one's eyes?[26]

In connection with the debate concerning images, Luther attempted to prove that Karlstadt was rightly banished from Saxony.[27] Even though he had distanced himself from Müntzer, they were still of the same spirit. In addition he had become involved with the rabble, the "disorderly populace," who were not to be trifled with.[28] In conversations with Melanchthon and with Luther himself Karlstadt had not been open to reason. This segment of the sermon is not very convincing, yet for the most part this work by Luther was written with care.

The first part concluded with one final section entitled, "Concerning the Mass."[29] Karlstadt refused to speak of the sacrament as "the Mass"; he wanted to abolish the elevation of the host and the chalice, as well as the use of Latin. Luther defended all three, in opposition to Karlstadt and in an attempt to curb the mob spirit that made sins out of things that were not sins. It was not until 1542 that the elevation of the host was completely abolished in Wittenberg.

The entire second part dealt with the nature and meaning of the Lord's Supper.[30] In the year 1521 the Dutch humanist, Kornelis Hoen, developed a symbolic interpretation of the words of institution.[31] The Bohemians espoused a similar view that was related,

however, to Wycliffe. Luther was introduced to Hoen's interpretation by Franz Kolb, preacher in Wertheim, in a letter of August
27, 1524.[32] Karlstadt had adopted this position.

In the letter to the Strasbourgers, Luther confessed that the
symbolic interpretation had been a temptation for him as well. Yet
the form in which Karlstadt presented it was not very enlightening:
with the words "This is my body" Jesus was referring to himself.
But before focusing his attention on this peculiar exegesis, Luther
offered a general refutation of the Spirit-centered Christianity of
the enthusiasts. According to them, true Christians did not require
any external authority, not even the Bible; their hearts were illumi-
nated directly by the Holy Spirit. Luther was much too level-headed
and critical to accept this notion. By what criterion could one be
sure that this alleged spirit of God is not really a controlling manifestation of one's own spirit? Such a criterion could be provided
only by being in agreement with the Holy Scriptures. So the Spirit
pointed back to the Word. God dealt with us in two ways: outwardly through the spoken word of the gospel and through material signs (sacraments), and inwardly through the Holy Spirit
and faith. But the external elements had to come first.[33] "For [God]
wants to give no one the Spirit or faith outside of the outward
Word and sign instituted by him." [34]

In this way a new basis was provided for the sacrament; Word
and sacrament were drawn more closely together and put on the
same level—as "outward elements." The "outward nature" of the
sacrament, which always remained the "visible Word," did not
make the sacrament into something superficial; it is impossible to
speak of Luther's view as "magical." The indispensible relationship between sacrament and faith remained fully intact. The words
of institution required the physical presence of Christ; not only
the presence of the person, but also the presence of body and blood.
For Luther, a mere personal presence of Christ in the Lord's Supper
appeared to contradict the text, which spoke precisely of the separation of body and blood.[35] (A marginal note should be made that
one can hardly agree with this exegesis.) According to Luther,
Karlstadt's interpretation arose from the darkness of reason, which
Luther mockingly referred to as "Frau Hulda, shrewd reason." [36]

But Luther himself did not refrain from rational arguments.
Along with the theory of consubstantiation, which he illustrated

with the image of glowing iron, he offered the rhetorical concept of synecdoche.[37] Synecdoche is a form of expression which uses the whole to speak of a part or vice versa. So a mother points to a cradle with a sleeping child in it and says: "That is my child." [38] In the same way Jesus could say of the bread, which was at the same time his body, "This is my body." Admittedly, to us this argument appears artificial.

For Karlstadt the Lord's Supper was only a memorial meal. In Luther's opinion such a view destroyed everything; then the power of the sacrament would not reside in the gift of Christ, but in one's own piety. "Even if I followed the Karlstadtian teaching and preached the remembrance and knowledge of Christ with such passion and seriousness that I sweated blood and became feverish, it would be of no avail and all in vain. For it would be pure work and commandment, but no gift or Word of God offered and given to me in the body and blood of Christ." [39] The gift of the Lord's Supper, however, was the forgiveness of sins.

At this point we can hear Luther's heart beating. He even made this remarkable statement: "Even if only bread and wine were there present, as they claim, as long as the word, 'Take, eat, this is my body given for you,' etc., is there, the forgiveness of sins, on account of this word, would be in the sacrament." [40] In other words, that which was decisive to the Lord's Supper would continue to exist, even if the real presence of body and blood were gone. It is clear that in this section Luther was dealing with questions that were only marginally important to him. His decisive interest was in the gift of the forgiveness of sins; by comparison, his interest in the real presence of body and blood was only secondary.

By the middle of March two refutations by Karlstadt of Luther's book appeared; others followed. Hoping to set up a meeting at which they could discuss their differences, Luther attempted—but failed—to obtain a safe-conduct for Karlstadt from the elector. Karlstadt moved his activities to Rothenburg, where he continued to preach iconoclasm. The Peasants' War drove him out of that city.

In a letter written from Frankfurt am Main on June 12, Karlstadt asked Luther for pardon and for a word of recommendation so that he might return to electoral Saxony with his wife and children.[41] He said that he was sorry he had written against Luther's work *Against the Heavenly Prophets*. He had sustained severe injuries from the rebellious peasants as well as from the mercenary soldiers. Shortly thereafter he sent a public "apology" to Luther, in which he explained that he had nothing in common with Müntzer and the peasant uprising.[42] At that point Luther took pity on Karlstadt. He wrote a foreword to Karlstadt's "apology" and secretly took him into his own house for a number of weeks.[43] While he was there Karlstadt drew up a theological "explanation" with which Luther was not entirely in agreement. Nevertheless Luther saw that it was published with a foreword.[44]

On September 12, 1525, Luther turned to Elector John with a plea for a residence permit for Karlstadt. One was subsequently provided. But Karlstadt was not able to endure life in electoral Saxony very long. Early in 1529 he left the city suddenly and without notice; this was because he had a miserable existence there and had been required to be silent. By way of Holstein, Ostfriesland, and Zürich he arrived in Basel, where in 1534 he found a position as preacher and professor. In 1541 he died there of the Plague.

Karlstadt's view of the Lord's Supper did have an impact in Strasbourg, the cities of southern Germany, and in eastern Switzerland. His dispute with Luther over the Lord's Supper was just a prelude to the great dispute over the Lord's Supper between Luther and Zwingli.

In Zürich, the principal location of Zwingli's activity, a type of evangelical Christianity had developed which sought to maintain its independence over against Luther's teachings. Three distinct influences characterized Zwingli's reformation: the humanism of Erasmus, the politics of the Swiss patriots, and the influence of Luther.

Huldreich Zwingli was born on January 1, 1484, the son of a well-to-do mayor of Wildhaus in the domain of Toggenburg (today the canton of St. Gallen).[45] He studied in Basel, Bern, and Vienna, where he came into contact with humanism; the star of his youth was Erasmus. By contrast with Luther the monk, he did not have to go through the difficult internal struggle of tearing himself away from scholasticism and the traditional faith; his passage into the new was not a painful break.

As a pastor in Glarus (1506–1516), Zwingli studied the new editions of the classics and the church Fathers; he learned Greek and transcribed the letters of Paul. As a military chaplain in the pope's service in 1513 and 1515 he participated in the victory over and defeat of the Swiss. His first publication was political in nature. It was directed against "mercenariness," the military service of Swiss soldiers under foreign contract.

Even as a reformer, Zwingli remained a politician. Together with the Landgrave Philip of Hesse, he later believed that a great, anti-Hapsburg alliance of evangelicals was the essential need. Politics also finally sealed his fate. As a military chaplain, dressed in helmet and armor, he was killed in fighting near Kappel on October 11, 1531.

Luther's mistrust of an alliance between the gospel and politics was alien to Zwingli. In 1516 he became pastor in the famous pilgrimage site of Mariä-Einsiedeln. In the spirit of Erasmus, he preached there against ceremonies and abuses. In 1519 he was called as a lay priest to the Grossmünster church in Zürich. From that point on, Luther's influence on him is discernible. He learned to understand Luther's view of justification by faith. It cannot be denied that it was through Luther that he first became a reformer, even though later, embittered by his conflict with Luther, he did not always admit it. In spite of this, however, he never entirely disavowed the humanistic element in his thought.

The reformation in Zürich began with a dispute concerning the requirement of fasting. It progressed more radically than in Wittenberg. Images were removed, as were many liturgical ceremonies; cloisters were done away with, and government of the church was assumed by the Zürich city council. The initial actions taken by Anabaptists were forcibly suppressed. The Reformation spread from Zürich to St. Gallen, Schaffhausen, Bern, and Basel, finding allies even in the south German cities of Strasbourg, Constance, Memmingen, Ulm, and Augsburg. But in Wittenberg there was opposition.

Zwingli had also become acquainted with the Dutchman Kornelis Hoen's symbolic interpretation of the words of institution, which during the summer of 1523 had been publicized in Germany and Switzerland by Hinne Rode of Utrecht. In this way Zwingli began to sense his kinship with Karlstadt. Through letters he presented Hoen's view to Erasmus Alberus of Reutlingen and to the Strasbourgers. It is therefore no accident that Luther at once sensed the affinity of Zwingli with Karlstadt, and from the start this fatally strained the conflict between them.

On the advice of his Basel friend Oecolampadius and the Strasbourger Capito, Zwingli opened the fray at the end of February 1527 with the work *Amica exegesis* (Friendly Exposition). Influenced by Bucer's desire for unity, Zwingli moved a little closer to Luther. He propounded the symbolic view, yet he acknowledged a presence of the body and blood of Christ in the spirit of those who were gathered. Christ was present in faith. Near the end of April, even before Luther saw a copy of *Amica exegesis,* he wrote a harsh repudiation of Zwingli: *That These Words of Christ, "This Is My Body," etc., Still Stand Firm against the Fanatics.*[46] At the end of June Zwingli responded sharply with the tract, *That These Words, "This Is My Body," Will Forever Retain Their One, Original Meaning.* He countered Luther's anger with his own irony, ridiculing the "baked God" of the Lutherans [47] and calling them "new papists." [48]

The conflict focused on two points: on Christ's "sitting at the right hand of God" and on the expression "the flesh is of no avail" in John 6:63. Since Luther boasted of appealing to Scripture, Zwingli countered by saying that everyone appealed to the Word, but everything depended on the correct meaning of the Word. That was why he (Zwingli) had wholeheartedly returned to the symbolic view. The sacrament was merely a commemorative and confessional meal, an "oath of allegiance." The word *is* actually meant nothing more than "signifies." Faith dealt only with spiritual matters. Eating the body of Christ could therefore only be understood figuratively, as the appropriation of salvation.

Agreement could no longer be expected. Accordingly, Luther's last word of March 1528, in his lengthy work, *Confession Concerning Christ's Supper,* was a flat no to Zwingli, with a strong emphasis on the physical nature of the real presence.[49] The body of Christ was received by the mouth and chewed with the teeth, even by unbelievers.

Nevertheless, one last attempt at agreement was undertaken, in the Marburg Colloquy of October 1–3, 1529. Following the Second Diet of Speyer in April of the same year, the situation of the evangelicals had become desperate, and Landgrave Philip of Hesse initiated a political alliance against the Hapsburgs. But dissension over the Last Supper stood in the way of unity among the evangelicals. In order to eliminate this difficulty, Philip called for a religious dialog.

Luther wanted nothing of it; he was opposed to a confederation, and held that enough had already been exchanged in writing. Melanchthon and the elector feared that an alliance with the left-wing reformers would jeopardize an agreement with the Catholic party. Nevertheless, in the end they gave in to the wishes of the landgrave. Zwingli, on the other hand, immediately supported the plan. He set out from Strasbourg with Oecolampadius, Bucer, and Kaspar Hedio; Luther appeared in the company of Melanchthon, Jonas, Brenz of Württemberg, and Osiander of Nuremberg.

In the publications of Des Vereins für Reformationsgeschichte,[50] Walther Köhler has attempted to reconstruct the Marburg Colloquy.[51] No new arguments were presented by either side. The debate centered on John 6, which, according to Luther, had nothing to do with the Lord's Supper. Naturally, Luther agreed that the Supper was a spiritual meal; but it was at the same time also a physical meal. It was not for them to question the necessity of physical eating. "If [Christ] should command me to eat dung, I would do it. The servant should not inquire about the will of his lord. We ought to close our eyes." [52]

Then the argument shifted to the question of whether one could seriously speak of a body that did not have physical limitations. Luther rejected all such questions. For him the words of institution were sufficient, and he lifted the velvet cloth that covered his table. Underneath he had written and underscored three times with chalk the word *est* ("this is"). At length, Zwingli finally acknowledged Christ's spiritual presence in the Supper, saying, "There are no people on earth with whom I would rather be united than with the Wittenbergers." [53] Luther, however, maintained his initial judgment: "You have a different spirit than we." [54] He said this to Bucer, whom, upon their first meeting in Marburg, he had greeted with a laugh and a raised finger, saying, "you rascal."

The Zwinglians made a concession when they spoke of the "true presence of Christ's body, but in a spiritual fashion." But the Lutherans held fast to a physical presence. In addition, the Zwinglians were forced to admit that Luther was not a "Capernaite," [55] that he also valued spiritual eating. The Lutherans, however, noted that

Zwingli did not totally deny Christ's presence in the sacrament. Though Luther did not recognize the Zwinglians as brothers, he promised to keep peace with them. As a result of the colloquy, Luther, on October 4, drew up the 15 *Marburg Articles*.[56] The first 14 articles stated the items agreed on; the 15th article, after emphasizing points of agreement, stated those points that divided them concerning the Lord's Supper.

In his two long treatises on the Lord's Supper, Luther sought to defend his view. It is impossible to agree with him on every point, but one must admit that in them he expressed the deepest thoughts of his faith. The theological conclusions of the first treatise can be summed up as follows: The words of institution were clear; they plainly affirmed Christ's bodily presence in the sacrament. Reason had to be subject to the Word, not vice versa. According to the Apostles' Creed, Christ sat at the right hand of God. Zwingli concluded from this that the body of Christ could not be present in the Lord's Supper. Luther replied to this primitive view by asserting that the expression "right hand of God" was not to be understood as a location; the concept needed to be demythologized. The right hand of God was "the almighty power of God, which at one and the same time can be nowhere and yet must be everywhere."[57] So God, who was "above body" and "above spirit," was also "present in every single body, every creature and object everywhere."[58] Therefore Christ's body could also be present in the Lord's Supper. Christ's glory was not diminished by his act of humility.

In one of the most profound insights of his theology of the cross, Luther confessed: "The glory of our God is precisely that for our sakes he comes down to the very depths, into human flesh, into the bread, into our mouth, our heart, our bosom."[59] The John 6:63 passage spoke of flesh in general but not of the body of Christ.[60] Luther spoke of a spiritual eating, but one that did not exclude bodily eating. *Spiritual [geistlich]* was not the same as *mental [geistig]*. Zwingli failed to recognize the physicality of revelation; the Holy Spirit had bound itself to the external Word. The effect of the sacrament was the forgiveness of sins. In this work Luther, citing Irenaeus,[61] also spoke of an effect on the body,[62] but he did not repeat this notion in later works. The question as to whether the real physical presence was necessary was beside the point.

Luther did not treat the matter systematically. He simply accepted the real presence because he believed the text required it, and he thereby separated himself from all speculation about the Lord's Supper.

The second treatise on the Lord's Supper, issued in 1528, presented the same thoughts as the first.[63] The first section was directed against the arguments of the "enthusiasts." In the second part Luther attempted to provide scriptural proof for his views. The conclusion summarized Luther's confession of faith.[64] This summary became the basis for the so-called *Schwabach Articles* of 1529, which, in turn, were later used in the *Augsburg Confession*.

In his exegesis Luther did not achieve a valid historical understanding of the original Last Supper. He interpreted it from the perspective of the contemporary congregational celebration, an understanding which, for him, was still burdened by the practices of the Mass. The way in which a priest celebrated the body of Christ at the altar was, according to Luther's view, the way in which Christ celebrated his own body "at the table." And so Luther was driven to use his theory of Christ's ubiquity (universal presence) to interpret the original Last Supper.

It was not simply an exegetical difference, but also a profoundly Christological difference, that existed between Luther and Zwingli. Their mutual point of departure was the so-called dual-nature Christology of the early church, dogmatized by the Council of Chalcedon in 451. The person of Christ consisted of two natures, the divine and the human. Zwingli began with the difference between the natures, while Luther began with the unity of the person. Since Christ in his human nature—that is, in his body—sat at the right hand of God, his body could not at the same time, according to Zwingli, be present in the Lord's Supper.

Luther passionately rejected this separation of the two natures. But in doing so his mind had really moved beyond the two-nature teaching of the ancient church, even though he still formally retained it. The unity of the person of Christ was to be preserved at all costs. "No, comrade, wherever you place God for me, you must also place the humanity for me. They simply will not let themselves be separated and divided from each other. He has become one person and does not separate the humanity from himself as Master Jack takes off his coat and lays it aside when he goes to bed." [65]

At this point the superiority of Luther's position over that of Zwingli is apparent. Yet it does seem somewhat scholastic for Luther to have continued by asserting that Christ, in the power of his divine nature, participated in the ubiquity (omnipresence) of God; and because the human nature was inseparably bound with divine power in the unity of the person, the human nature of Christ, that is his body, also participated in the omnipresence of God. Luther expressed this omnipresence of God, that is Christ, most profoundly in these words: "You must place this existence of Christ, which constitutes him one person with God, far, far beyond things created, as far as God transcends them; and on the other hand, place it as deep in or as near to all created things as God is in them." [66] God was "a supernatural, inscrutable being who exists at the same time in every little seed, whole and entire, and yet also in all and above all and outside all created things. There is no need to enclose him here, as this spirit dreams, for a body is much, much too wide for the Godhead; it could contain many thousand Godheads. On the other hand, it is also far, far too narrow to contain one Godhead. Nothing is so small but God is still smaller, nothing so large but God is still larger, nothing is so short but God is still shorter, nothing so long but God is still longer, nothing is so broad but God is still broader, nothing so narrow but God is still narrower, and so on. He is an inexpressible being, above and beyond all that can be described or imagined." [67]

Put in contemporary terms, Luther here not only clearly stated the problem of God's immanence and transcendence, but at the same time the inadequacy of these alternatives. Christologically, Luther revealed nothing other than his own concern. For him, a Christ confined to heaven would be no Christ at all. Luther rested his entire experience of salvation on this. Of course Zwingli was right when he replied that a body to which one attributes omnipresence is no longer a body in our usual understanding. On the other hand, Zwingli himself remained trapped in spatial conceptions when he denied the presence of Christ in the elements.

The stated differences between the views of Zwingli and Luther cannot be viewed as convincing. Despite his remarkable thoughts on God's immanence and transcendence, Luther was not able to free himself completely from an outdated "substance" metaphysics. Moreover, the logical arguments which Luther used against Zwingli—for example, the reference to synecdoche—are not convincing. They are helpful expressions, but one should not attribute too great a significance to them. It is more important to inquire into Luther's personal religious concern in his battle with Zwingli.

Two things made Zwingli's teaching on the Lord's Supper unacceptable to Luther. First, Zwingli transformed the gift of God into a human task. For Zwingli the Lord's Supper was a commemorative meal. In the second place, according to Luther, Zwingli made reason into a judge of God's Word; he interpreted the text according to his own understanding. Luther thought that both of these were really the deadly sins of theology. Works instead of grace, reason instead of obedience to Scripture—Luther could not make a more severe accusation. For him Zwingli was one of the "confident spirits"; he knew nothing of Luther's despair of himself or of his need as a sinner.

Luther clung to the words of his Savior, as they stood, as if he were a drowning person; Zwingli could interpret them cooly and academically. Therefore Zwingli, with his "clumsy, atrocious German," [68] was for Luther "un-Christian." [69] His designation of Zwingli as "a different spirit" was justified. But Luther did not see that his own exegesis, on which he had based everything, was unsound, and that therefore his accusation of sophistry against Zwingli was not justified. He failed to see the dual metaphor involved in the words of institution, but rather entangled himself in the question of the "elements," in relation to heavenly substance (*materia coelestis*).

For this reason Luther was not satisfied with the real presence of the person of Christ for the believing recipient, but held fast to the real presence of body and blood. Yet in doing so he came dangerously close to affirming the *opus operatum* position — the completion of a miraculous act independent of the faith of the recipient — a position he himself had earlier rejected. It can be asked whether, in the sharpest formulation of his polemic against Zwingli, Luther remained faithful to his original, reforming point of departure. Zwingli was not entirely wrong in challenging him on this and playing Luther off against Luther.

Yet Luther deserves our great admiration, for in the very same year he spoke to this same theme in his *Small Catechism,* and he did so simply and clearly, avoiding all questionable theories. Here we can discover where Luther really came out on this subject. His barbs against Zwingli should not be interpreted on the basis of his lengthy polemical works, but rather these works should be understood from the perspective of the *Small Catechism.* "How can eating and drinking do all this? It is not eating and drinking that does this, but the words, *given and shed for you for the remission of sins.* These words, along with eating and drinking [note: *along with eating and drinking!*], are the main thing in the sacrament. And whoever believes these words has exactly what they say, forgiveness of sins." Forgiveness of sins is the actual gift of the sacrament, not body and blood, and therefore not the *materia coelestis.* "For where there is forgiveness of sins, there is also life and salvation." And "that person is well prepared and worthy who believes these words, 'given and shed for you for the remission of sins' . . . . for the words 'for you' require simply a believing heart."

Here, in fact, as in the earlier writings, the real presence of Christ's body and blood is presupposed: "What is Holy Communion? Holy Communion is the body and blood of our Lord Jesus Christ given with bread and wine, instituted by Christ himself for us to eat and drink." Who would dispute the fact that the emphasis in this fifth section of the *Small Catechism* lies on faith and on the promise of the forgiveness of sins? The secondary reference to body and blood appears to be determined by tradition and the scriptural text. Here we are not far from Augustine's *crede et manducasti*—believe, and you have received the sacrament. While one was not to "split hairs" over the words of Holy Scripture—an accusation unjustly directed against Zwingli—Luther felt bound by conscience to hold fast to the *"est"* (is), without recognizing that in Aramaic, the language of Jesus, there is no copula. According to the account, Jesus said, "This my body," "This my blood." Therefore there is no exegetical obstacle to a symbolic interpretation. The dual metaphor can, without diminution, be expressed in the simple affirmation, "This I am."

So it becomes quite clear that this statement is not about heavenly substance, namely a heavenly body and heavenly blood, but about the presence of the person, who binds himself with the faith of the recipient in this metaphoric action. One can also speak of a real presence within the framework of a symbolic interpretation. Christ is really present, in faith, in the sacrament. Even a commemorative meal mediates a reality. Luther did not see this, because he found the text "too powerfully present." In other instances he was always well aware of the real presence of Christ, of the reality of his Lord in Word and faith.

The Reorganization
of the Church

Luther did not wish to create a new church, but rather to reform the existing church. After Worms it was clear that both the emperor and the ecclesiastical hierarchy would oppose this reform. But the determination to carry through was apparent in individual congregations.

Luther had already pointed this out in his work addressed *To the Christian Nobility of the German Nation*. The priesthood of all believers made reform imperative. So in 1523 Luther addressed congregations in a work entitled, *That a Christian Assembly or Congregation Has the Right and Power to Judge All Teaching.*[1] Following the custom of the early church, he referred to the pastor of each congregation as bishop, but he said this could only be considered an interim arrangement. It was imperative that an organizational structure above the congregation be established.

In the long run it would not work for each congregation to have its own order of worship. Also, the closing of cloisters and the disbanding of collegiate churches had raised many financial questions which could only be dealt with by some higher authority. Many congregations and members of the nobility were neither in a position nor inclined to pay their pastors a sufficient salary; this, too, called for some form of church administration beyond the congregation. In addition, after his experience with the iconoclasts and the Peasants' War, Luther's confidence in the ability of the masses to govern themselves began to wane dramatically.

The demand that secular authorities intervene and help when spiritual authorities failed had been common in the late Middle Ages. After the Imperial Diet of Speyer in 1526, the territorial princes believed they had free reign to carry out the Reformation in their own regions. So it is understandable that Luther and his co-workers turned to the governing authorities with the request that they assume responsibility for the necessary work of reorganizing the church.

From the very beginning, however, Luther considered the sovereign ruler of a given territory as only an "emergency bishop," who was to carry out this task on behalf of the church out of "Christian love." It was in this vein that Luther expressed himself in 1528 in his foreword to Melanchthon's *Instructions for the Visitors of Parish Pastors in Electoral Saxony*.[2] "To teach and to rule in spiritual affairs" was not the task of princes.[3] By contrast, the electoral instructions of 1527 handed over the supervision of the church completely to the territorial ruler.[4] Moreover, it was assumed that each territorial ruler also had the duty of caring for the spiritual welfare of his subjects.

In Melanchthon's opinion, princes were entrusted with the "custodia utriusque tabulae," the guardianship over the first three commandments. For the princes were the "praecipua membra ecclesiae," the superior ones, those members of the church who had been set apart from the others. So the Christian brother who as prince carried out this "service of love" became the "presiding bishop," the "Summus episcopus" of his territorial church. In this way the administration of the church by territorial princes came into being. However, since territorial rulers usually sought the counsel of the clergy in ecclesiastical questions, a "ministerial church" was also established, which was more efficient in dealing with practical matters than we might think.

As a person living in the 16th century, Luther was unable to conceive of a given territory as being anything other than confessionally unified. This view led to the principle later stated in the Peace of Augsburg of 1555: "Cuius regio, eius religio"—"The religion of the prince is the religion of the land."

The new ecclesiastical order was introduced through visitations. In Saxony this began in 1525 with the accession of John as elector. Luther, Spalatin, and Hausmann of Zwickau had requested that the

elector approve the visitations, and so after 1527 the entire territory was visited, region by region. Both theologians and jurists
were represented on the visitation commissions. Melanchthon and
Hieronymus Schurff were often involved; Luther himself participated only occasionally.

The circumstances that the visitors found in the congregations
and among the pastors were sometimes shocking. There were
pastors who could not recite the Lord's Prayer and the Creed.
They were by no means capable of preaching a sound evangelical
sermon. In such instances it was recommended that they use one
of Luther's postils [books of sermons]. Only a few pastors desired
to hold fast to pre-Reformation faith. These were dismissed, but
the welfare of the older ones among them was provided for. One
pastor had been serving both an evangelical and a Catholic region, using the appropriate rite in each. Naturally he was prohibited
from continuing this practice. Parsonages were often in wretched
condition; salaries were frequently in disorder.

In his *Instructions for the Visitors of Parish Pastors*, Melanchthon
provided directives on the most important elements of evangelical
teaching and churchly practice.[5] Among other things, pastors were
admonished to preach the law as well as faith. This elicited the
protest of Johann Agricola, who considered the preaching of the
law unevangelical. However, this initial "Antinomian" opposition
to preaching the law was soon set aside by Luther. To assure sound
teaching and oversee the conduct of pastors, the so-called super-
intendents were established, whose duties included the regulation
of matters related to marriage. The visitation in electoral Saxony
soon became an example for other regions.

The unversity was reformed at the same time. Among other
things, the conferral of degrees, which had been suspended since
1523, was begun again in 1528. The philosophical faculty was expanded, and the theological faculty consisted of three regular professors and one extraordinary professor. Later (in either 1533 or
1546), an oath of allegiance to the *Augsburg Confession* and to the
three ecumenical creeds was required of all doctoral candidates.
After 1535 all candidates for the ministry were required to undergo
a faculty hearing prior to ordination.

The most valuable contribution to emerge from the church visitations was the writing of Luther's large and small catechisms. Since

1518 Luther had repeatedly preached on parts of the medieval catechism, especially on the Ten Commandments. The experiences of the visitation had shown, however, that there was an urgent need for a catechetical textbook. Luther had originally requested that Jonas and Agricola prepare one, but he then assumed the task himself.

In contrast to many of his other works, Luther thoroughly prepared himself for the catechisms. In 1528 he dealt repeatedly with the parts of the catechism in three different preaching cycles. From the transcripts of these sermons he obtained his content and many of his formulations. *The German Catechism,* which later was given the title the *Large Catechism,* appeared in April 1529.[6] It was not intended as a textbook for schools, but rather as reading material for pastors, teachers, parents, and adults.

The *Small Catechism,* initially published in poster form on panels (March 1529), appeared in May 1529 as a book, illustrated with woodcuts.[7] It was indeed intended for instruction, but also to be a book for the home. Children were to memorize it; but as an "old doctor" Luther had not yet mastered it, and he still used the chief parts for his daily devotions.[8] In his preface he spoke at length about the practical use of the book and about the urgent necessity of Christian education.[9] It is characteristic of Reformation piety that it was not satisfied with formal worship alone but required every believer to acquire as much religious knowledge and insight as possible. "The catechism is the Bible of the laity, in which is comprehended all of the Christian doctrines believers need to know for their salvation." [10] Prayers and a table of household duties were eventually added to the five chief parts; then the "Marriage Booklet for Simple Pastors" [11] was attached, and an explanation of the office of the keys (written by someone else) was also included.

The *Small Catechism* is one of the greatest masterpieces of religious literature, equally distinguished for its brevity and its precision, its polished formulation and depth of content. It is not only a book to be memorized, but also to be prayed. Generations have learned from it and been edified by it. It would be irresponsible not to make this unique work available to people today.

The following classical statements from the explanation of the First Commandment in the *Large Catechism* are worth quoting:

"What is it to have a god? What is God? A god is that to which we look for all good and in which we find refuge in every time of need. To have a god is nothing else than to trust and believe him with our whole heart. As I have often said, the trust and faith of the heart alone make both God and an idol. If your faith and trust are right, then your God is the true God. On the other hand, if your trust is false and wrong, then you have not the true God. For these two belong together, faith and God. That to which your heart clings and entrusts itself is, I say, really your God." [12] "Creatures are only the hands, channels, and means through which God bestows all blessing." [13] In the *Small Catechism* this is stated in even simpler fashion: "We are to fear, love, and trust God above anything else."

Ludwig Feuerbach was of the opinion that, on the basis of these statements, he could call on Luther in support of his (Feuerbach's) view that human beings create God in their own image. That certainly cannot be said of Luther, though he did see God and faith bound together in an indivisible correlation. Luther could not speak of God "objectively," that is, purely academically. He only spoke of God in existential devotion. When Luther discussed God he also had to discuss human beings, and vice versa. In the end there was for Luther no anthropology apart from theology, nor could theology ever be apart from anthropology.[14]

Luther's explanation of the First and Second Articles was also completely existential. Luther did not speak in general about creation and redemption, but about what both mean personally, for each individual. Next to his translation of the Bible, the *Catechism* is perhaps Luther's greatest accomplishment. He himself, as we have already mentioned, acknowledged that alongside the treatise on *The Bondage of the Will*, it was the only work that was "really a book of mine." [15]

A new order of worship was also part of the reorganization of the church. Luther wanted nothing to do with the drastic changes Karlstadt had introduced. His reform was carried out cautiously. The Mass continued to be chanted in Latin. The first all-German congregational Mass was celebrated by Thomas Müntzer on Easter in 1523 in Allstedt. It appeared in print in 1524. But the call for a German service of worship was voiced from other quarters as well, so Luther did not want to delay.

On Sunday, October 29, 1525, worship in the city church was conducted for the first time in the form of the German Mass. It was finally adopted on Christmas Day in 1525. It was published on New Year's Day, 1526, within the framework of a longer treatment entitled, *German Mass and Order of Worship.*[16] In his revision of the musical setting Luther was assisted by the electoral cantors Konrad Rupff and Johann Walther. Luther was concerned that the music and the text work together; the musical lines for the Latin text could not simply be transferred to German—a method Luther had previously criticized when used by others (e.g., Karlstadt).[17]

Luther began his book with the warning that one ought not make his order of worship into a law for others to follow. Wherever good orders already existed, they could be retained.[18] True worship was adoration in spirit; it did not require a public ritual. But for the sake of simple persons and, above all, for the sake of younger persons, one needed public services of worship.[19] On their behalf the bells were also to be rung, the organs were to play, and everything sound forth that could give sound.[20] The Latin Mass was also not to be prohibited, primarily out of a concern for the education of youth.[21] One might even consider Greek and Hebrew masses; worship ought not be limited to a single language, as it was among the Bohemians.

Besides his educational considerations, Luther also had in mind the universality of Christian proclamation, which had been made clear on the Day of Pentecost.[22] But for "simple laity" the German service was the right one.[23] In addition to the general Christian congregation [*Volkskirche*], Luther thought there might also be an assembly of "those who seriously wish to be Christians."[24] He considered this later as well. Lambert of Avignon wanted to adopt it for the Reformation in Hesse in 1527, but Luther was of the opinion that he did not have the people for it.[25]

The most important thing for a proper service of worship was religious education. It was important to have a "good 'catechism,'" especially in the first three parts: the Ten Commandments, the Creed, and the Lord's Prayer.[26] Children were thereby to be given the entire sum of Christian knowledge in two little sacks, the golden sack of faith and the silver sack of love.[27] In the section that followed, Luther reported on how worship was conducted in the Wittenberg parish church.[28] Every Sunday there were three sermons, at 5:00 or 6:00 A.M. on the Epistle, at 8:00 or 9:00 A.M. on the Sunday Gospel, and in the afternoon on the Old Testament. The pericope texts were to be maintained, for practical reasons. One could, however, also preach on entire books, text by text. Sermons were preached daily, early in the morning on the first five days of the week, and at Vespers on Saturday.

The chief service on Sunday retained the structure of the traditional Latin order. Luther simply shortened some things, such as the Kyrie, and of course he removed everything that did not conform to an evangelical perspective.[29] In addition to the liturgical parts in the beginning of the service (Introit, Kyrie, and Collect), there were two Scripture readings, followed by the Creed, the Sermon, and the Lord's Supper. Basically, Luther's Mass already had the form with which we are acquainted in our contemporary Lutheran service of Holy Communion. The mass vestments were permitted to be retained, but the celebrant at the altar was always to face the people.[30] The most significant new element was the active participation of the congregation in the drama of the service. For example, instead of the Credo, a hymn of faith was sung.

By 1523 Luther had already translated the Roman baptismal rite into German and added a brief explanation.[31] But in view of the new reforms in worship, in 1525 he issued *The Booklet on Baptism in Revised Form*.[32] There he eliminated such external rites as breathing on the candidate, the use of salt, and anointing with spittle and oil. However, he retained exorcism—the casting out of demons.

Hymns, sung in German, served as the principal way of involving the congregation in the service. As early as his *Formula missae* [Latin Mass] of 1523, Luther had expressed a desire to have German hymns, but at the same time he regretted the lack of poets.[33] He asked for help from friends such as Spalatin and the electoral Saxon marshal Hans von Dolzig, but nothing came of it. So in spite of his own heavily burdened schedule, he set himself to the task and, amazingly, found that he had the gift of poetry.

It is generally known that Luther discovered this gift in himself when he heard of the burning of two young Augustinian monks, Heinrich Vos and Johann van den Eschen. They suffered martyrdom on July 1, 1523, in the Brussels marketplace for their confession of evangelical teachings. In response Luther wrote a *Letter to the*

Christians in the Netherlands[34] and his first hymn.[35] In a popular style he described what had happened, and at the same time achieved a high level of poetic sensitivity.

> *Ein neues Lied wir heben an,*
> *des walt Gott unser Herre*
> *zu singen, was Gott hat getan,*
> *zu seinem Lob und Ehre.*
>
> (A new song we now begin
>   that God our Lord prevails;
>   we sing about what God has done,
>   to his own praise and honor.)

The two monks had withstood the seductive charms of the Louvain theologians:

> *Sie sungen süss, sie sungen saur,*
> *versuchten manche Listen,*
> *die Knaben stunden wie ein Maur,*
> *verachten die Sophisten.*
>
> (They sang sweetly, they sang sourly,
>   they attempted many tricks;
>   the boys stood like a wall;
>   they defied the Sophists.)

The news of their martyrdom would bear witness everywhere to the truth of the gospel:

> *Die Aschen will nicht lassen ab,*
> *sie stäubt in allen Landen,*
> *hie hilft kein Bach, Loch, Grub noch Grab,*
> *sie macht den Feind zu Schanden.*
>
> (Their ashes will not be stopped;
>   they will fly to every land;
>   no stream will help, no hole, crevice, or grave;
>   they bring the enemy to shame.)

It was the springtime of the gospel:

Der Sommer ist hart vor der Tür,
der Winter ist vergangen,
die zarten Blumen gehn herfür.
Der das hat angefangen,
der wird es wohl vollenden.

(Summer is almost here,
winter is gone;
the tender flowers bloom.
The one who made it begin
will indeed bring it to completion.)

Luther did not remain alone in his hymn writing. The first [German] hymnal, the so-called *Achtliederbuch* (Eight Song Book), was printed in Nuremberg at the beginning of 1524. Together with four hymns by Luther, it contained three hymns by Paul Speratus (1484–1551), who at the time resided in Wittenberg. Wittenberg was named as the place of publication.

Two Erfurt enchiridia were also published in 1524, containing 18 Luther hymns. Twenty-four Luther hymns were printed in the *Geistlichen Gesangbüchlein,* published in Wittenberg in 1524. The hymn "A Mighty Fortress" was probably written in 1527. Additional Wittenberg hymnbooks appeared in 1528, 1529, and 1545. Volume 35 of the Weimar edition of Luther's works, a comprehensive book of some 634 pages, contains 35 church hymns by Luther, plus additional German and Latin poems. That volume also provides the most basic historical introduction to Luther's hymn writing.

Two of Luther's Latin poems are known to us. The grim poem "Pestis eram vivens, moriens ero mors tua, Papa" (In living I was your plague, Pope; in dying I will be your death) was composed in October 1530 in Spalatin's home on the journey back from the Coburg castle.[36] On his last trip, to Eisleben in January 1546, Luther stayed with Justus Jonas and dedicated both a toast and a glass to his host with the poem, "Dat vitrum vitro Jonae vitrum ipse Lutherus, ut vitro fragili similem se noscat uterque" (Luther, himself a glass vessel, gives the glass to Jonas, who is also a vessel of glass, that they might both recognize they are as fragile as glass).[37]

Luther's hymns are in the form of poetry; some are even poems of the first rank. Yet in content and purpose they were never intended to be anything other than a proclamation of the Word.

They were to serve the congregation. In this sense they are not religious lyrics, but rather church hymns.

Nor was Luther interested in originality. Almost half of his hymns are poetic adaptations of pieces of Scripture, drawn frequently from the Psalms. "A Mighty Fortress" is a Christian adaptation of Psalm 46. He also published the Creed, the Ten Commandments, and the Lord's Prayer in hymn form to support catechetical instruction. These hymns sometimes lacked artistic aspiration.

Luther made grateful use of good, traditional hymns. He made many old, German hymns usable for evangelical worship by adding new stanzas that deepened the biblical meaning. Among these is the hymn "Gelobet seist du, Jesus Christ." Other hymns are free adaptations of Latin church songs and liturgical chants, for example, "Lord God, we praise you," the old Te deum.

Despite their functional intent, Luther's hymns reveal his whole self. The moods of strength and gentleness, austerity and joy, the euphoria of victory and times of deepest need ("Aus Tiefer Not") all found expression. The melodies are often attributable to Luther himself. "A Mighty Fortress" is one example.

Luther had a living relationship with the arts, especially literature and music. In the preface to the *Wittenberger Gesangbuch* of 1524 he wrote: "I am not of the opinion that the gospel should cause all of the arts to be struck down and disappear, as some super spiritual persons propose; to the contrary, I would like to see all of the arts, especially music, used in the service of the one who has given and created them." [38] Luther's opponents at the time recognized with jealousy that Luther had sung his way into the hearts of the German people and so had led more people to heresy through his hymns than through his writings. Today Luther's German hymns have found their way into Catholic hymnbooks, giving one good reason to rejoice.

The Coburg Luther

Charles V had thought that the Lutheran heresy would be disposed of with the Edict of Worms. He was mistaken. Two factors in particular interfered with the implementation of the edict; foreign affairs and the mood of the people.

Soon after the Edict of Worms the emperor left Germany for a period of nine years. He was completely occupied with his wars with Francis I of France. For a time the pope was also allied with France, and so unintentionally supported the Reformation. An imperial government was established in Nuremberg to represent the emperor. At its head was the emperor's brother, Archduke Ferdinand, an outspoken opponent of the Reformation. Duke George of Saxony, Joachim I of Brandenburg, and the Wittelsbachs were also enemies of the new movement. Frederick the Wise stood pretty much alone.

Had the Reformation been dependent on the favor of the princes, it would have failed. But alongside the princes stood the people. Luther had won their hearts at Worms. Additional support for the Reformation came from the free imperial cities.

So things proceeded differently from what the emperor had planned. At the Diet of Nuremberg in 1522 the German princes declared that the implementation of the Edict of Worms was impossible. Instead they called for a universal German council to be held on German soil. The deplorable state of affairs required immediate attention.

Leo X had died on December 1, 1521. His successor (from January 1522 until September 1523) was Hadrian VI of The Netherlands, the last non-Italian to sit in the Apostolic See until John Paul II. Hadrian VI had been a professor in Louvain and a teacher of Charles V. He was an honest, serious man with good intentions. The inscription on his tombstone in the Church of Maria dell'Anima, the German church in Rome, attests to that. His enthusiasm for reform naturally elicited derision from the Italians. Through his nuncio Chieregati he allowed a list of the sins of the curia to be read in Nuremberg. Nevertheless, he was a determined opponent of Luther.

Hadrian's successor was the illegitimately born Medici Clement VII (1523–1534), a cousin to Leo X. He had personal integrity, but was a purely political pope concerned with the greatness of Italy. He had no interest in German affairs. It was agreed in 1524 at the Diet of Nuremberg to go "as far as possible" in carrying out the Edict of Worms. In practical terms, this meant that a great deal of freedom was granted.

In 1525 the various princes holding to the traditional faith, among them the dukes of Bavaria and the southern German bishops, united in an alliance to suppress the Reformation. Soon thereafter the persecution of evangelicals was begun in these territories. This marked the beginning of the division of Germany along confessional lines. Conscious of the need to respond, in 1526 the evangelical princes found it necessary to conclude a defense pact in Torgau. The spirit behind the coalition was the young, energetic Landgrave Philip of Hesse. Among others, he was joined by the successor and brother of Frederick the Wise, the honorable but insignificant John the Steadfast.

In the territories where it was not obstructed, the Reformation moved forward. It was especially well received in the cities, where for the most part it was promoted by theologically educated preachers. In the year 1525 Nuremberg, the city of Albrecht Dürer and Hans Sachs, implemented the Reformation. This example encouraged other cities in Frankonia and Swabia. In the same year (on the advice of Luther) the grand master of the Order of Teutonic Knights, the Frankonian Hohenzoller Albrecht of Prussia, transformed the Order's territory into a secular dukedom and introduced the Lutheran confession. There were stirrings throughout the entire empire, in the south as far as Tirol, Salzburg, and the near regions of Austria; in the east as far as Mähren and Hungary; in the west in The Netherlands; and in Switzerland.

After initial successes, the year 1526 developed into an extremely critical one for the emperor. The war with France, on whose side the pope stood, erupted once again, and the Turks advanced victoriously through Hungary. The emperor needed the support of the estates. For this reason the outcome of the Imperial Diet of Speyer in 1526 was rather amicable. In Saxony everyone was allowed to follow the dictates of conscience in carrying out the Edict of Worms responsibly before God and his imperial majesty. This decision encouraged the evangelical princes to establish territorial churches, and the visitations were begun.

For Charles the fortunes of war were favorable. In May 1527 his mercenary troops reached Rome and ruthlessly plundered the eternal city. Notable repercussions were felt in Germany. At the Second Imperial Diet of Speyer early in 1529, the action of the previous diet was rescinded by the emperor and the Catholic estates. The evangelicals protested that majority rule did not hold for matters of faith, becoming known thereafter as "Protestants."

Evangelical plans for an alliance fell through due to disagreement about the Lord's Supper and the legitimacy of resisting the emperor. In the meantime, however, the emperor had made peace with the pope and the French. On February 24, 1530, the last crowning of a German emperor by the pope took place in Bologna. After nine years' absence, Charles returned to Germany. The Diet of Augsburg was to consider the religious question as well as enlist help against the Turks. Faced with the Turkish threat, the emperor was not adverse to a peaceful settlement of the religious question; in the announcement received in Torgau on March 11, his desire was expressed to hear "everyone's judgment, opinion, and view."

Elector John the Steadfast called his theologians together; the result of their consultation was the *Torgau Articles,* a rejection of "papal" abuses. These articles were taken along on the journey to Augsburg that began on April 3. In the entourage of the elector were the two chancellors Gregor Brück and Christian Beyer and the personal physician, Caspar Lindemann, as well as Luther and several other theologians: Philip Melanchthon, Justus Jonas, George Spalatin, and Johann Agricola. They arrived in Coburg on the evening of April 15, Good Friday.[1] The elector probably stayed in the court pharmacy, and Luther in the home of the provost.

In the days that followed (April 16–21), Luther preached at least seven times in the Moritz church. On April 23 the elector and his entourage traveled on to Augsburg; Luther, still under the imperial ban, had to stay behind, but he was to stay as close to the scene of action as possible. For this reason the elector had thought first of Nuremberg, and after they had begun their trip he had sent ahead to inquire if that might be possible. But on April 16, shortly after the elector's arrival, a messenger from Nuremberg arrived in Coburg with a formal rejection of his proposal.

Since the presence of Luther in Nuremberg could not be kept secret, the city council had to assume that the emperor would demand that he be handed over. Naturally the council would not want to comply; but to oppose the emperor, their lawful ruler, would be an act of rebellion. It was therefore better if Luther remained in the elector's territory. The elector respected this argument; Luther, also, approved the judgment of the imperial city. He himself would rather have returned to Wittenberg; he didn't expect much from the Diet. But the elector did not agree to that, and he arranged for Luther to stay at Coburg castle, his southernmost, secure residence.

Luther probably arrived at the castle early in the morning on April 24. He gave those who were continuing on some letters for his Nuremberg friends Wenceslas Link and Eobanus Hessus, the Latin scholar at the Nuremberg secondary school. To Hessus he wrote that he would gladly have gone along, but was told, "Be silent, you have a poor voice." [2] So instead of the desired quintet (Jonas, Melanchthon, Spalatin, Agricola, and Luther), only a quartet would be in attendance.

Luther's faithful assistant Veit Dietrich and his nephew Cyriakus Kaufmann stayed with him in the castle. Luther's thoughts were with those who had gone on to Augsburg; he was troubled by loneliness, particularly since his crate of books had not yet arrived. On April 24 he wrote to Melanchthon, "We have finally arrived at our Sinai . . . but we shall make a Zion out of this Sinai, and construct here three huts: one for the Psalter, one for the prophets, and one for Aesop." [3] With those words he outlined his tasks while at the Coburg, though he was not able to see them through to completion:

an exposition of the Psalms, further work on the translation of the prophets, and an edition of Aesop's Fables. He wished the concerned Melanchthon a good night's sleep and went on to describe his own new home in "the kingdom of the birds."

More than 30 persons lived in the castle, including 12 night sentries and two tower guards. Luther occupied two rooms. On the wall of one of them he had written in Latin a phrase from his favorite psalm: "I shall not die, but I shall live, and recount the deeds of the Lord." [4] The story that the ink spot on the wall was (like the story from the Wartburg) from Luther's bout with the devil is actually a legend that arose in the 17th century. The so-called Hedwig's glass, a valuable Egyptian work said to have belonged to St. Elizabeth, was definitely in Luther's possession in 1541. However, we do not know whether he possessed it in 1530 or whether it was later given to the Coburg castle out of his estate.

While at the Coburg Luther grew a full beard like the one he had grown at the Wartburg. He also wore glasses at times, and he complained about their uselessness in a letter to Katie on June 5, 1530.[5] On the same afternoon on which the first letter to Melanchthon was written, Luther also wrote letters to Justus Jonas and to Spalatin, in which he (half in jest, half seriously) depicted the Imperial Diet as a "diet of crows and jackdaws" in front of his window.[6] He had not yet heard a nightingale. He first reported one in his famous and delightful letter of April 26 to his "table guests in Wittenberg." [7] The authenticity of this letter has been challenged because phrases from the two other letters are repeated word for word in German translation. The argument, however, is not completely convincing, for in this very letter Luther's language is so powerfully alive that it is all but impossible to label it a later compilation.

Physically, Luther did not feel at all well. The eternal chirping of the birds, which at first seemed so cheering, soon began to disturb his sleep. The injury to his shinbone, which occurred during the journey, would not heal.[8] In addition he suffered from excruciating headaches. On May 12 he wrote to Melanchthon, "I can't do anything; I can see that the years add up." [9] Luther perceived all of this as an affliction of Satan against which he battled courageously.[10]

In the letter to Spalatin quoted above he described himself as an "idle spectator," and yet during the half year at the Coburg the sheer sum of his accomplishments was incredible.[11] When Luther left Wittenberg the translation of the Old Testament had progressed up to the prophets. He hoped to have all of the prophets completed by Pentecost. At first he took up work on Ezekiel 38 and 39, in which the Gentile prince Gog of Magog is mentioned. Luther saw this passage as a prophecy related to the Turks, who had already advanced to the outskirts of Vienna. As a result, his translation became an interpretation of the two chapters, and was published in May in Wittenberg as a small pamphlet.[12]

In addition to the threat of the Turks, responsibility for the evangelical movement weighed heavily on Luther's mind. This preoccupation found its literary expression in the powerful and passionate work, *Exhortation to All Clergy Assembled at Augsburg*.[13] Even though he could not be present personally, he still had some things to say about the Diet. On April 29 he wrote to Melanchthon that the thoughts raged through his mind like a mercenary army against which he could barely defend himself.[14] On May 12 the polemical tract was already in the hands of the printer in Wittenberg. On June 7 the first 500 copies reached Augsburg and were immediately disseminated. At the order of the emperor the work was banned by the Augsburg city council.

Luther believed that a good offense was the best defense. It was imperative that the deplorable state of ecclesiastical and cultural affairs be held before the eyes of traditional believers; they ought to give thanks to the "Lutherans" for taking remedial action.[15] The treatise was immediately dubbed "Luther's Augustana."

Luther overtaxed his health: "Concerning work I am therefore a lazy, idle ass; but in my heart I take no holidays."[16] Music provided his primary means of relaxation. He also received guests from Nuremberg, and the number of guests began to increase. Among them was Argula von Grumbach, who arrived on June 3 to give Luther advice on weaning little Lene. After a while the visits became burdensome. On June 6 he wrote to Katie, "It is rapidly becoming a veritable crusade here." [17]

His letters to Wittenberg are among the most charming documents of the Coburg period. Katie had sent her husband a portrait of the year-old Lene as a Pentecost gift. "At first I did not recognize the little strumpet, so dark she appeared to me to be." [18] The picture was evidently no masterpiece, but on June 19 Veit Dietrich reported to Katie that Luther had proudly posted it on the wall across from his table.[19] We have already mentioned the letter to little Hans which spoke of the beautiful, cheerful garden to which diligent children came.[20]

On June 5 Luther received the news of his father's death. Veit Dietrich told Katie that Luther was so deeply affected by it that he was not seen for two days.[21] He remained in his room with his Psalter. The letters to Melanchthon and Wenceslas Link on June 5 expressed Luther's dependence on them and his gratitude for their friendship.[22] Nevertheless, during this same time he was able to muster sufficient strength to comfort his young Wittenberg table companion, Hieronymus Weller, who was suffering from severe turmoil of the spirit. Luther tried to help him by referring to his own experience:[23] "You can't keep the birds from flying over your head, but you don't have to let them build nests there."[24]

In the meantime, Luther's physical ailments increased. However, he knew how to overcome them by concentrating on his spiritual tasks. He wanted to prepare a German edition of the Psalms. As preparation for this he developed the "Coburg Psalms"—short explanations of the first 25 psalms, which were dictated to Veit Dietrich, and in which Luther's personal experiences during these months are vividly reflected.[25] He dedicated an exposition of Psalm 117 to the guardian of the Coburg castle, the knight Hans von Sternberg of Callenberg.[26] Psalm 118, Luther's favorite psalm ("the beautiful confitemini"), was dedicated to the abbot Friedrich Pistorius of St. Aegidius in Nuremberg.[27] The preface to this psalm is among the most beautiful of Luther's writings. "This is my own beloved psalm. Although the entire Psalter and all of Holy Scripture are dear to me as my only comfort and source of life, I fell in love with this psalm especially. Therefore I call it my own. When emperors and kings, the wise and the learned, and even saints could not aid me, this psalm proved a friend and helped me out of many great troubles. . . . Would to God all the world would claim this psalm for its own, as I do! Peace and love could not compare with such a friendly quarrel."[28] But the Holy Scripture was not taken seriously: "Its words are not, as some think, mere literature; they are words of life, intended not for speculation and fantasy but for life and action."[29]

In addition, Luther continued his translation of the prophets.

In 1527 Hieronymus Emser had attacked Luther's efforts at translation, despite the fact that he gleaned his best insights from Luther's work. Luther defended himself in *On Translating: An Open Letter*, addressed to Wenceslas Link in Nuremberg.[30]

A Sermon on Keeping Children in School, written in early July, promoted the continued growth of the Reformation.[31] It was dedicated to the Nuremberg city clerk *(syndikus)* Lazarus Spengler, for "Nuremberg truly shines throughout all Germany like a sun among the moon and stars." [32] The *Admonition Concerning the Sacrament of the Body and Blood of Our Lord* was completed at the end of the Coburg period.[33] This work encouraged more frequent participation in the sacrament, but refrained from polemics against Zwingli and the north Germans.

Naturally Luther followed the proceedings in Augsburg quite closely. Communications between Augsburg and Coburg were irregular; it took messengers three to five days to travel the distance. The Saxons, at first expecting that the negotiations would concentrate on liturgical and ecclesiastical abuses, had brought the *Torgau Articles* with them. But as a precaution, the 17 *Schwabach Articles,* dealing with differences in doctrine, had also been brought. Since Luther's old opponent John Eck had drawn up 404 articles against Reformation theology, it soon became apparent that doctrinal questions could no longer be avoided in Augsburg.

Melanchthon reworked the *Torgau* and *Schwabach Articles* together into a first draft of the *Augsburg Confession*. On May 11 the elector forwarded the document to Luther for his evaluation. On May 15 Luther sent the elector his famous, brief reply: "I have read through Master Philipp's *Apologia*, which pleases me very much; I know nothing to improve or change in it, nor would this be appropriate, since I cannot step so softly and quietly." [34] Both agreement on the basics and gentle criticism are detectable in this judgment.

Melanchthon, of course, had hoped to receive detailed comments, and on May 22 he informed Luther that he was continuing to make changes.[35] Luther heard nothing more of further progress. He complained about this to Melanchthon on May 2 and June 7. On June 13 he let it be known through Veit Dietrich that he would not read any more letters.[36] In fact it seems that Melanchthon, his nerves at the breaking point, had left Luther in the dark for three weeks. On June 25 Luther was informed of the presentation of the confession to those assembled in Augsburg,[37] and on June 29 he finally had a copy of it in his hands.[38] But on June 26 Melanchthon had asked Luther what concessions he felt could still be made.[39]

Luther's position in his letters to Melanchthon of June 27, 29, and 30 is clear.[40] "I detest your interminable worries"; they came from lack of faith.[41] "It is your philosophy that drives you to exhaustion, not theology." [42] "Christ lives and rules; why are we afraid of the truth?" [43] "God has placed this cause into a certain paragraph, which you don't have in your rhetoric, nor in your philosophy. This is entitled Faith." [44] But Luther also reassured him: "I pray for you, have prayed for you, and will continue to pray for you; and do not doubt that I have been heard, for I feel the amen in my heart." [45] Enough had now been conceded, and his dearest wish was to go to Augsburg himself.[46]

The negotiations dragged on from July until September. During this time Luther supported his friends with splendid letters. He was pleased that Christ was being publicly confessed in Augsburg.[47] In the beginning of July he wrote an open letter to Cardinal Albert of Mainz asking him to support the cause of peace.[48] Luther's letter of gratitude to Lazarus Spengler for designing the so-called Luther rose was also written during this time.[49] Luther interpreted the seal as a symbol of his theology: a black cross superimposed on a red heart, placed at the center of a white rose, set in a sky-blue field, surrounded by a golden ring. The often-quoted verse, "Des Christen Herz auf Rosen geht, wenn's mitten unterm Kreuze steht" (The Christian heart rests on a rose, when under the cross it finds repose) did not originate with Luther.[50]

Luther was particularly concerned about the absence in the *Augsburg Confession* of a clear rejection of purgatory, the cult of the saints, and the papacy.[51] After hearing once again the phrase, "Tread softly," he wrote *A Refutation of Purgatory*[52] and shortly thereafter his *Articles Against the Entire School of Satan*.[53] The latter work was obviously, though somewhat obliquely, directed against the renewed attempt by Melanchthon to make concessions regarding questions of traditions and rites, a move that Luther had already rejected in a memorandum to the elector.[54]

In the meantime Eck, Faber, Cochläus, and others had drawn up a "refutation" of the *Augsburg Confession,* the *Confutatio.* A moderated version of this was read on August 3. Point-by-point negotiations were then initiated. Luther thought little of this. On July 15 he had written to his friends, "Home, and again, home!"[55] Philip of Hesse followed this advice on August 6.

On August 5 Luther sent a consoling letter to Augsburg that spoke of two wonders of God in the heavens. It was addressed to the Saxon chancellor Gregor Brück.[56] "I have recently seen two miracles. The first: Looking out of the window, the stars in the sky and the whole beautiful vault of heaven, but I saw nowhere any pillars on which the master had rested this vault; yet the sky did not collapse, and this vault still stands fast." People always wanted to see the pillars, lest they shake and tremble. "The second [miracle was this]: I also saw great, thick clouds hovering over us, so heavy that they could be compared with the waves of an ocean. Yet I saw no ground on which the clouds rested, or stood, nor any tubs in which their water could be caught. Nevertheless the clouds did not fall on us but merely greeted us with a sour face, and drifted on. When the clouds had passed by, both the floor and our roof which had held them up—the rainbow—were shining through." Surely it was God who supported the weight of the water; but only the thick and heavy clouds could be seen. "I am having some fun," Luther wrote, "and yet I am serious." He had hoped that at the very least, *pax politica* (political peace) could be retained, "but God's thoughts are far above our thoughts." So let it be right. Should the emperor win the peace, then the emperor and not God would be given the honor. However, "Those men of blood have not yet brought to an end what they are now beginning, nor have they all achieved security, or whatever it is they desire. Our rainbow is frail; their clouds are mighty; but in the end it will be clear which type of music is being played." Master Philip, the elector, and all the rest ought to console themselves.

On August 26 Luther had to buttress the elector's fortitude so that he would not accept the opponents' proposals for a compromise.[57] On the same day he wrote to Spalatin: "I hear that you people, like it or not, have begun a strange project, that is, to bring about unity between the pope and Luther. But the pope will not want it, and Luther sees no possibility of it."[58] Even among those at Augsburg, there were increasing complaints about Melanchthon having too great a willingness to be conciliatory. In the middle of September, Hieronymus Baumgartner of Nuremberg, a representative of his home city to the Diet, wrote to Lazarus Spengler: "Philip has become more childish than a child." [59]

Melanchthon suffered unspeakably under the tremendous responsibility for the unity of the church and the destiny of the West, and this must be offered in his defense. But at times he also lost clear judgment and a firm trust in God. Luther stood up for him, but also tried to stiffen his backbone.[60] At the same time he wrote to Jonas in a deeply disturbed tone: "It is not our task to foresee future wars, but rather simply to believe and confess. I am almost bursting in anger and rage. If war is to come of this, so be it; we have prayed and done enough." [61]

On September 22 and 23 the decision of the Diet to oppose the Reformation was presented to the evangelical estates. They rejected it under protest. On September 23 the elector set out on the journey home by way of Coburg, where he presumably arrived on the night of October 1. The electoral prince John Frederick had already arrived on September 14, two weeks earlier. But more important than either of them was the guest who arrived on September 25, the Strasbourg theologian Martin Bucer. For two days he negotiated with Luther about the possibility of an agreement on the issue of the Lord's Supper, a matter of urgent concern in view of the threatening situation facing the evangelicals.

Luther and his friends left the Coburg on October 4. Shortly before leaving (on either the first or the fourth of October), he wrote his famous letter to the Bavarian court musician Ludwig Senfl in Munich. He extolled the importance of music and requested a setting of the antiphon "In pace in idipsum" for several voices.[62]

Delivery of the letter was entrusted to the previously mentioned Hieronymus Baumgartner, whom he greeted on behalf of Baumgartner's "one-time flame" Katie von Bora.[63] Luther surely must have feared that his letter would not arrive safely in Senfl's hands, but his love of music overcame this concern. He even had to praise the hostile Bavarian dukes because they valued music so highly. There was, "after theology, no art one can place higher than music, for it alone next to theology can do what theology is capable of, namely, make the soul peaceful and happy." The devil fled from the sound of music just as he did from the Word of theology. "My heart overflows with a feeling of thankfulness for music, since it has so often refreshed me and delivered me in times of great need."

Luther was expecting an early death; "The world hates me and cannot tolerate me; and I am weary of the world and curse it." It was because of this that he loved that particular antiphon so much and asked for the composition.

On June 30 Veit Dietrich wrote to Melanchthon: "In these difficult times I cannot help but be amazed at the uniqueness of this man's [Luther's] steadfastness, joy, faith, and hope; he also nourishes them without ceasing, through the diligent study of God's Word. No day passes on which he does not pray for at least three hours—and precisely those hours that are best suited for study." [64] With these words Dietrich put his finger on the profound secret of the "Coburg Luther." This Luther was no less significant than the courageous monk of Worms or the Junker George of the Wartburg. His confident faith grew out of his deep devotion to God and was bound up with a winsome humanity that appreciated everything good and beautiful in art and in nature.

Old and New Conflicts

We have become accustomed to referring to Luther from the time of the Diet of Augsburg until his death in 1546 as the "old Luther." The "old Luther" is then contrasted with the "young Luther" and, for the most part, written off. This judgment needs to be corrected, even though it contains a kernel of truth.

The greatest decisions of Luther's life were made prior to 1525. The drama and conflict of the years 1517–1521 were not repeated. During those years the history of the Reformation all but coincided with the events of Luther's life; this was not the case later. Luther was no longer alone, but rather had a number of colleagues; after 1530 Melanchthon found himself in the center of public life more than Luther himself did. The initial breakthrough of the Reformation was followed by a period of construction. These developments were perhaps less exciting, but they were no less troublesome and no less needed. However, none of Luther's colleagues ever attained his stature. Among the traditional believers he was therefore often grimly depicted as the antipope. At the same time, however, there was no lack of differences within Luther's own camp.

Yet Luther always remained the leading figure. His literary accomplishments continued to be as astonishing as they had previously been, and they reached even greater heights; for example, the large commentary on Galatians, the rich exposition of Genesis, and the academically significant work *On the Councils and the Church.* As preacher and counselor, as professor and "church father," the "old

Luther," also, made outstanding contributions, despite the hindrance of poor health. On the other hand, one cannot deny that there was a certain intransigence in his established positions. The "old Luther" was not spared bitterness and disappointment. It is true that he hoped until the very end for the victory of the evangelical movement, for in it he saw the cause of Jesus Christ himself. But he did not hold out any great hope for the "world"; he longed increasingly for the "beloved last day," which he believed to have been close at hand. Though one may miss the verve of the early years, one ought to acknowledge with gratitude Luther's faithfulness under trial.

The larger political situation had once again become a decisive factor for the progress of the Reformation. Facing the threat of imperial action after the Diet of Augsburg, representatives of a number of evangelical territories met in Smalcald on February 27, 1531, to form an alliance. In the forefront were Saxony and Hesse, joined by some of the north German cities. The jurists were finally able to dispell the reservations on the part of the theologians (including Luther) against armed resistance to the emperor. They argued that the imperial estates were not only subject to the emperor, but were themselves "governing authorities," and as such were responsible for the spiritual welfare of their subjects. Since the threat of the Turks had not yet been removed, the emperor agreed to the Nuremberg accord guaranteeing religious peace until a council could be called.

Charles V once again left Germany for a nine-year period. The result was a continued spread of the Reformation. With the support of Philip of Hesse, Duke Ulrich returned to Württemberg and reformed the church there. Pomerania became another important victory for the evangelicals. After the death of Duke George in 1539, his successor Henry introduced the Reformation in ducal Saxony, and in the same year Brandenburg became evangelical under the leadership of Joachim II. In Halle, the residence of Albert of Mainz, Justus Jonas successfully introduced the Reformation; in Naumburg, Nikolaus of Amsdorf was installed as evangelical bishop in 1542; and Elector John Frederick of Saxony, who had succeeded his father John in 1532, assumed his role as "emergency bishop."

In 1539, following the Nuremberg accord, the Frankfurt accord provided a renewed moratorium and led to a settlement. After the

Protestants who had gathered in Smalcald in 1537 had refused to submit to a council presided over by the pope, the emperor attempted to establish peace by means of religious dialogs. The followers of Erasmus in the episcopal and princely chancelleries supported this plan. The first dialog was held in Leipzig; other negotiations followed in Hagenau, Worms, and Regensburg. The evangelicals were almost always represented by Melanchthon and Bucer. The last of these sessions, held in Regensburg in 1546, admittedly served only to stall off the Protestants. The emperor had actually already decided on a war against the Smalcaldic League. Luther did not live to see the beginning of the war.

Meanwhile, the evangelicals received a severe blow from within their own ranks. On March 4, 1540, in the presence of Melanchthon and Bucer, Philip of Hesse entered a "Turkish marriage" (a second, bigamous marriage) with Margarete von Saale—a maid-in-waiting to his sister—in Rotenburg on the Fulda.[1] As a 17-year-old, Philip had married Christine von Sachsen, a daughter of Duke George. Although he had several children by Christine, he had never felt close to her. Perhaps driven by some physical abnormality, he began one adulterous relationship after another.

After joining the evangelicals, Philip's conscience troubled him greatly. After 1525 he no longer participated in Holy Communion, and in 1526 he began toying with the idea of a second marriage. In 1539 he at last decided to go ahead with his plan, but the mother of the young woman he had in mind would agree only if the second wedding were properly conducted in public, in the presence of witnesses, and if his first wife gave her consent. She also demanded the opinion of several "learned persons."

Bucer therefore discussed the situation with the Wittenbergers. However, Philip presented the case in such a way that Luther heard only about his troubled conscience.[2] Luther generally argued against his plans, but stated that a second, secret "marriage of conscience" was possible.[3] Here Luther was still bound by medieval confessional practice, which allowed private dispensations to be offered for acts that were publicly prohibited. Bigamy was forbidden by imperial law. Luther's counsel presupposed that secrecy be maintained; the second marriage would be valid only in the eyes of God, and not for the world. He based the possibility of such a marriage on the marriages of the Old Testament patriarchs and on an incorrect understanding of 1 Timothy 3:2. In 1531 Luther had used the same argument to support a bigamous marriage for Henry VIII of England, but not his divorce; Pope Clement VII had likewise recommended a double marriage to the king, upon Cajetan's advice.

When the secret was revealed and the affair became a public scandal, Luther called on Philip to remove the matter from the world's eyes with a "good, strong lie." But Philip did not go along. He became determined to receive an imperial pardon. He was offered it by the Imperial Diet of Regensburg on June 13, 1541, provided he promised to do his best to avert an alliance of the Smalcaldic League with England and France and refused to admit Wilhelm of Kleve into the league. Two years later Karl Wilhelm of Kleve attacked and defeated him and forced him to abandon his plans for church reform. And so the most active member of the Smalcaldic League betrayed the cause for personal reasons.

In a letter to the elector, Luther defended the advice he had given, which had not been politically inspired.[4] Philip would not have gotten into political difficulty had he continued his extramarital intercourse; only bigamy was prohibited. Luther had not been told the whole story, and he had heard only of Philip's burden of conscience. To be sure, Luther's request that his confessional advice be kept secret was unrealistic. Only too late did he realize that his naive trust had been abused.

Luther's request that Philip deny his bigamous marriage goes against our modern moral sensitivities. Nonetheless, the reformer was following the common practice of his day when he assumed that confessional advice was to be kept in absolute secrecy, even by the penitent.

One of the most vehement opponents of the evangelicals among the German princes was Duke Henry of Braunschweig-Wolfenbüttel. Quarrels constantly erupted between him and both electoral Saxony and Hesse. Even in the Catholic camp he was considered a violent, morally unbridled man. When a conspicuous number of fires occurred in the territory of electoral Saxony, he was accused of instigating them and charges were leveled against him before the emperor. When Henry published a polemical work directed against the princes who opposed him, Luther responded in 1541 with the book *Against Hanswurst*.[5]

After an almost arrogant personal introduction to this work, Luther proceeded to defend the evangelical church against the accusation of heresy. The evangelical church was the true, ancient church; it possessed pure teaching and celebrated the sacraments in accordance with their institution. It was the papal church that had broken away, he maintained; he provided 12 points to support his thesis, above all, the deviation from the correct, ancient form of Baptism. The life of the evangelical church was not free from sin, but it was the church because it had the Word of God. In his conclusion Luther used the medieval song about Judas against the duke and his companions: "O villainous Harry, is this your deed? . . ." [6] When Duke Henry illegally attempted to enforce a proscription against the city of Goslar, the territories of electoral Saxony and Hesse opposed him with force (in July 1542), drove him from his own lands, and reformed the church there without bringing about intervention by the emperor.

Luther's lifelong conflict with Rome was not limited to attacks on individuals. Far more significant was the attack that he led in 1533 against the Roman church itself with his treatise *The Private Mass and the Consecration of Priests*.[7] In Augsburg the evangelicals had declared themselves willing to have their pastors ordained by the bishops, provided the bishops would acknowledge the authority of God's Word.[8] However, this prerequisite had not been met.[9] Moreover, George Witzel, a lapsed Lutheran, had appeared in Eisleben, speaking and writing against the Reformation; great pressure had been brought to bear on the evangelically inclined princes of Anhalt; and Albert of Mainz had proceeded against the evangelicals in Halle.

Thus several developments at the same time moved Luther to write this fierce work, which Jonas called a "veritable battering ram" against the papacy. Luther no longer hoped to convince his opponents; now his sole purpose was to support his own companions in the faith. He had long since rejected the sacrifice of the Mass; now he asked whether the body of Christ were truly present in private masses, or whether in this instance the bread did not remain bread. During a possibly fictitious midnight debate, the devil confronted him with this argument and thereby troubled his conscience (since Luther himself had celebrated private masses for years).[10] Private masses were contrary to Scripture, for the Bible spoke of the Lord's Supper as a community meal. The bread did not become the body of Christ in such cases. It was reported that in Rome many priests said, "Bread you are, bread you shall remain," when they celebrated Mass.[11]

Nor did Luther place value in the "consecration of clergy." Ordination consisted of the call to public service by the congregation and the church, without anointing by a bishop.[12] Bishops were not distinguished from other pastors by a superior consecration, but only by their position; in the ancient church there was no distinction.[13] Pastors ought not be separated from their congregations by a particular act of consecration, rather, a pastor was "the mouth for all of us." [14] Nevertheless, the true church had not been completely lost in the papal church; Rome still had Baptism, the gospel, the Lord's Prayer, and more, despite all the abuses.[15]

This treatise impressed Luther's opponents as well as his colleagues, but the misunderstanding arose that he had moved closer to the sacramentarians. Luther countered this misunderstanding in *A Letter of Dr. Martin Luther Concerning His Book on the Private Mass.*[16] His belief had always been and still was that Christ's body was also present in the Catholic Eucharist—but not in the private masses. It was for this reason that he now distinguished sharply between *sacrament* and *mass* and used the term *mass* only for private masses.[17]

Luther's last substantial work against the papacy, *Against the Roman Papacy, an Institution of the Devil,* dates from March 1545.[18] In the pronouncement of the Diet of Speyer on June 10, 1544, emperor Charles V had found it necessary to make considerable concessions to the Smalcaldic League. Since it was still a question whether and when a universal, free council would be called, the emperor promised that there would be a German national synod. For doing this he received an official reprimand from the pope, which also reached the Protestants through other channels. Two versions were circulated, one harsh and the other more mild. Luther was given the more severe version, though he also was aware of the moderate one. His treatise was written in response to this papal brief.

The work was distributed with great speed, and it received an enthusiastic response from followers of the Reformation, even though more than just Luther's opponents were shocked by its excessive venom and crudity. However, this was generally attributed to the "peculiar spirit" with which Luther was gifted.[19] There is very little content in this work that goes beyond the great Reformation writings of the 1520s. Luther maintained that the history of the early church spoke against the primacy of the papacy, the recourse to Matthew 16 did not hold water, and the transfer of the Roman Empire to Charles the Great was a bold fabrication. Luther never wrote the second book that he announced was forthcoming.

As a kind of illustration to his treatise, Luther published a series of 11 cartoons insulting the papacy, accompanied by appropriate texts.[20] We may assume that Luther himself originated the illustrations and gave them to Lucas Cranach to develop. They are in the style of the times, coarse and earthy, including references to excrement. However, it has been rightly pointed out that they are free of lewdness.[21] Nevertheless, they are nothing to be proud of.

In the early years of the Reformation Luther had often called for a legitimate and free council. Many of Luther's opponents also saw this as a solution, and even Charles V supported the idea. But because he wanted to see the management of such a council in the hands of the pope, he repeatedly deferred to Rome. Clement VII, however, always found reasons to avoid calling such a council. But in 1533 he was ready. On June 3, 1533, his legate, accompanied by an imperial envoy, appeared before the elector of Saxony with an invitation to a council. But since Luther and his co-workers recognized immediately from the articles which the legate submitted that it was not to be a truly free council, but a purely papal council, the Smalcaldic League members declined.

Luther himself had soon become skeptical of the authority of a council. As early as 1519, in the disputation with Eck, he had attacked the Council of Constance. In 1535 he directed his first academic disputation against the Council of Constance, which he called the "Concilium Obstantiense," since it had, contrary to better judgment, rejected lay participation in the chalice.[22]

The successor to Clement VII, Paul III (1534–1549), viewed the plan for a council more favorably. In 1535 he sent his nuncio Vergerio to Germany to promote the plan and to discern the prevailing mood. Vergerio took this opportunity to meet with Luther in Wittenberg on November 7, 1535, inviting Luther and Bugenhagen to see him at the castle. The reformer prepared to meet the papal representative with a lighthearted sense of superiority. Desiring to appear as young as possible in order to quash all hope of his imminent demise, he carefully shaved, put on an elegant cloak whose sleeves were decorated with satin cuffs, and wore a golden chain around his neck. While riding in a wagon to the castle, he laughed and said to Bugenhagen, "Here ride the German pope and Cardinal Pommeranus, God's instruments." This was the first time since his meeting with Cajetan that he had personally appeared before a senior representative of the papacy; but how significantly the situation had changed!

An account of this meeting is included in the *Table Talk*.[23] Paolo Sarpi (1552–1623) also recorded the event in the first volume of his history of the Council of Trent. Vergerio is said to have assured Luther how much the pope regretted the loss of such an important man; on the other side, Luther is said to have spoken of the current pope as a wise and upright man. The conversation covered a number of different topics and then focused on the question of the council. Luther was of the unfavorable opinion that the council would deal only with ceremonies and other trifling matters, not with the decisive theological questions. Nevertheless he would be willing himself to come to the council, no matter where it was convened. If the pope would like to come to Wittenberg, with or without weapons, he would be welcomed.

In a report prepared five days later, Vergerio expressed himself very negatively about Luther. He said he was the incarnation of arrogance and spitefulness; in his eyes one could detect the look of a man possessed. His mother was an ordinary bathwoman, his father a common day laborer. Vergerio was particularly angered by Luther's statement that the evangelicals needed no council, but that the other side needed it in order that they might finally arrive at the truth. At a meeting with John Frederick on November 30 he was taken aback to hear that the elector was in complete agreement with Luther. The other members of the Smalcaldic League were of the same opinion.[24] There is a certain irony in the fact that Vergerio later converted to Reformation teaching, was excommunicated, and died in the service of Duke Christoph of Württemberg. He was buried in the cathedral church of Tübingen.

In a bull of June 2, 1536, Paul III called the council for May 23 of the following year. Disregarding the wishes of the German princes, it was to be held in Mantua. The emperor supported this decision. The Smalcald members were disappointed because their request for a free council had not been taken into consideration. The elector of Saxony received the text of the bull on July 6. He opposed acceptance of the invitation, and explained his view in a memorandum of July 26, 1536.[25] Acceptance would involve a commitment to the pope. The Wittenberg theologians, however, took the opposite view: one ought to attend the council in order to render an account of the faith. Instructed by the elector, Luther drew up the articles which were later called the *Smalcald Articles*. A theological conference of December 28 proposed a number of additions, and Melanchthon suggested a moderation of the statements concerning the pope.

The conference in Smalcald, which was personally attended by the evangelical princes, began on February 10, 1537. The idea of participation in the council was rejected. Luther was hardly able to take part in the subsequent gathering of the theologians because of a serious attack of stones he had suffered on February 16. The others designated his articles as his own, private work. Melanchthon drew up his own statement on the power of the pope. It received general assent and was included in the final pronouncement of the gathering.

By comparison, Luther's articles were not signed by everyone, and he was in error when in his preface he assumed that all had done so. The 1537 confession of Smalcald consisted of the *Augsburg Confession,* together with its *Apology,* and Melanchthon's tract on the pope. Luther's *Smalcald Articles* were not included. Later these articles were added to the Lutheran Confessions and included in the *Book of Concord.* That is why they are printed in the confessional writings of the evangelical Lutheran church.[26]

Luther stated in his preface that he was having the articles published because he wanted to give one more witness, just in case he should die.[27] He would welcome a proper council for the sake of the other side, though the evangelicals did not need one. He was afraid that Christ might cause "a council of angels to descend on Germany and destroy us utterly, like Sodom and Gomorrah, because we mock him so shamefully with the council." [28] "Dear Lord Jesus Christ, assemble a council of thine own, and by thy glorious advent deliver thy servants." [29] Luther divided this work into three parts.

The first part dealt with the "sublime articles of the divine majesty," the Trinity and Christology.[30] "These articles are not matters of dispute or contention, for both parties confess them," so they did not need to be discussed.[31]

The second part of his work presented the four articles that dealt with the work of Christ and our redemption. It was these articles that the pope would surely reject, especially the first and chief article concerning justification through faith alone in the redemption accomplished by Christ. "Nothing in this article can be given up or compromised, even if heaven and earth and things temporal should be destroyed. . . . On this article rests all that we teach and practice against the pope, the devil, and the world."[32] The second article stated, "The Mass in the papacy must be regarded as the greatest and most horrible abomination because it runs into direct and violent conflict with this fundamental article [Article 1]. Yet, above and beyond all others, it has been the supreme and most precious of the papal idolatries." [33] On this point the two sides would always remain divided.[34] "Besides, this dragon's tail—that is, the Mass—has brought forth a brood of vermin and the poison of manifold idolatries."[35] Luther listed the examples of purgatory, masses for the dead, pilgrimages, fraternities, relics, indulgences, and the invocation of saints.[36] The third article focused on the current state of the cloisters,[37] and the fourth was directed rather explicitly against the papacy.[38] The papacy did not exist *iure divino*, by divine right; it was a historical entity which had not always been universally accepted. It was the Antichrist and worse than the Turks. The pope would never relinquish his "divine right" and be satisfied with merely human rights; nor would it really make much difference if he did so.[39] It was this fourth article that prompted Melanchthon to qualify his signature, adding that papal supremacy *iure humano* could be acknowledged if the pope would recognize the gospel.[40]

In the third part Luther dealt with the articles that "we may discuss with learned and sensible men, or even among ourselves"; the pope and his court would not be interested in them.[41] Here Luther developed his teachings on sin, the law, confession, the gospel, Baptism, and the Lord's Supper, the office of the keys, repentance, excommunication, ordination, the marriage of priests, the church, justification and good works, monks' vows, human traditions, and finally on the "mockery and fraud" of sacramental actions.

Luther warned of that enthusiasm which despised the objective Word; it was not only the enthusiasts who were enthusiasts—so was the pope.[42] Enthusiasm was a form of original sin common to all human beings; it "clings to Adam and his descendants from the beginning to the end of the world . . . . it is the source, strength, and power of all heresy, including that of the papacy and Mohammedanism." [43] Luther rejected the church's use of "greater excommunication," which involved civil punishment; the "lesser excommunication," by which persons were excluded from the sacrament, was the true Christian ban.[44] The Roman church was not truly the church; but among the evangelicals, "thank God, a seven-year-old child knows what the church is, namely, holy believers and sheep who hear the voice of their Shepherd." [45] In conclusion Luther asserted, "These are the articles on which I must stand and on which I will stand, God willing, until my death. I do not know how I can change or concede anything in them. If anybody wishes to make some concessions, let him do so at the peril of his own conscience." [46] In the *Smalcald Articles* we see none of the "soft treading" that Luther observed in the *Augsburg Confession*. That which Luther missed in the *Confession* he stated here all too clearly. He was no longer able to believe in reconciliation with the papal church.

For this reason Luther also expected nothing to come of the religious dialogs conducted during the 1540s, which were usually led by Melanchthon. He felt the same way about the Regensburg Colloquy of 1541, which has been described as the "most favorable opportunity" for a reunion of the two divided confessional parties.[47] Article 5 on justification, especially, seemed to make a settlement possible.[48] There Luther distinguished between two forms of righteousness, one that was ascribed *(iustitia imputativa)* and one that was indwelling *(inhaerens)*. Believers ought to rely entirely on the righteousness that was imputed; but they were also called righteous because of their indwelling righteousness, because they did that which was right.

Article 5 did not go beyond this juxtaposition of imputed and indwelling righteousness. The thought of a "dual righteousness" was not alien to Luther, but he considered the Regensburg formula to be an unacceptable compromise. There were also differences in the conception of the Lord's Supper and in the doctrine of the church. Thus Luther finally perceived the Regensburg negotiations to be only a papal feint. Incidentally, Rome did not accept them either. The cleft was already too deep for the parties to listen to and hear one another.

In his treatise on *Temporal Authority,* written in 1523, Luther had argued categorically against the civil punishment of heretics.[49] In his *Letter to the Princes of Saxony Concerning the Rebellious Spirit* of 1524, one finds this splendid statement: "Let the spirits collide and fight it out"; however, where rebellion resulted, the authorities ought to intervene.[50]

Polemics against infant Baptism had been around since the Zwickau prophets and Müntzer. Despite vigorous measures taken against them, the Anabaptists continually gained followers. As much as their views were confused, immature, and to some degree fanatical, it could not be denied that they represented a valid concern. In distinction to the official Reformation, which was oriented toward territorial churches, they attempted to reestablish early Christianity in doctrine and in life. In the 16th century that was considered unhistorical but not impious. Social factors were also at work here. In general, one could not deny that they led exemplary Christian lives. But their disregard for public life and civil authority necessarily had a provocative effect.

Luther did not succeed in dealing justly with the Anabaptists, but he shied away from using worldly force against them—quite the opposite of Melanchthon, who in this case was less tolerant. In his work of 1526, *To Two Pastors Concerning Rebaptism,*[51] Luther stated, "It is not right and I am truly sorry that these poor people are so deplorably murdered, burned, and hideously killed. One ought to allow individuals to believe what they want; if they believe wrongly, they will receive sufficient punishment in the eternal fire of hell." [52]

In the matter of infant Baptism Luther relied primarily on traditional practice, on the grounds that not everything was wrong simply because it agreed with tradition. There was no convincing reason to oppose the practice. If Baptism depended on the faith of the child, then adults ought not be baptized either, for one could never be certain if they had faith.[53] According to Luther's view, the Holy Scriptures did not argue against infant Baptism or against the faith of children. But Baptism was not founded on faith; it rested solely on the command of God. Luther said many memorable things about infant Baptism, but in the end he did not solve the problem. In the New Testament the faith of those who were baptized is simply assumed, and the faith of children is not seriously discussed. But neither is a biblically-based argument against infant Baptism justified. The practice can certainly be affirmed on the basis of God's affirmation of the baptized person.[54]

In February 1528, shortly after concluding this work, Luther preached four times on infant Baptism.[55] In so doing he presented these ideas, as well as the argument that people did not lose their faith in sleep; therefore faith was not dependent on the use of reason.[56]

Meanwhile, Anabaptists became active in Thüringia, Saxony, and Hesse. Superintendent Justus Menius wrote against them, and Luther added a preface, which was published at the end of September 1530.[57] There he characterized the Anabaptists as treacherous sneaks and rabble-rousers.[58] He referred to his exposition of Psalm 82, which he had completed before his departure for Coburg. There he had attacked the arrogance of the nobles, who, after they had been liberated from the tyranny of the priests, no longer wanted to submit to the discipline of the gospel.[59] "A preacher is neither a courtier nor a hired hand. He is God's servant and slave, and his commission is over lords and slaves." [60]

Luther made the following statements about the duties of rulers. Among other things, they ought to forbid street corner preaching. If those who preached on the streets were troublemakers and public blasphemers, they were to be punished by the authorities.[61] Persons ought not be compelled to believe, for they could believe whatever they wished. But teaching and blasphemy had to be forbidden.[62] Those who wanted to support themselves off of citizens were to obey the law or "buzz off." [63]

In January 1532 Luther directed the short work on *Infiltrating and Clandestine Preachers* against unauthorized preaching and the audacious practice of interrupting the sermons of ordained pastors.[64] But by the end of October 1531 the Wittenberg theologians, at the request of Elector John, had already issued a report concerning the Anabaptists in which they called for their execution.[65] The reason given was that they had "generally" promoted revolutionary articles or condemned public preaching. Those persons who had gone along with them out of ignorance, yet would not let themselves be corrected, were to be expelled from the territory or given some lesser punishment. Luther signed this report with the addition that, "Even though it seems cruel to punish them with the sword, it is even more cruel that they denounce the office of preaching, promote no particular doctrine, suppress correct teaching, and seek to destroy worldly rights." [66]

Landgrave Philip of Hesse favored more lenient treatment of the Anabaptists. He held 10 of them in prison, but could not prove that they had any "malice." He turned to various sources for advice, including the Wittenbergers. The answer he received in the summer of 1536 generally agreed with the report of October 1531.[67] One ought first, through instruction, to attempt to convert those who had been led astray. Their articles dealing with civil government were revolutionary; physical punishment was therefore in order, under certain conditions including the sword.[68] The government could not tolerate the public dissemination of false doctrine.[69] If their false teachings could be incontestably proven, the false teachers ought to be punished according to the laws of heresy of the ancient church.[70] Those who persisted in teaching falsehood, even if they did not instigate rebellion, were to be executed.[71] Those who had been led astray because of their simplemindedness and showed repentance could be punished by exile or imprisonment.

This document was signed by Melanchthon, Cruciger, Bugenhagen, and Luther. Luther added: "This is the usual rule, but may our gracious Lord show mercy along with punishment, depending on the circumstances." [72] According to a table talk of 1540, Luther returned to a view that distinguished sharply between false teachers and revolutionaries.[73] He did not remain faithful to this principle when he condemned the public proclamation of false teaching as well as insurrection. Nevertheless, with his plea for more moderate practice in individual cases he did distinguish himself favorably from his contemporaries.

The reign of terror of the Anabaptists in Münster from February 1534 to July 1535 was a disaster for the movement, because many put the blame for the atrocities committed also on those followers who were peacefully inclined. Luther did not consider the matter in detail; he criticized the events that had occurred in Münster only in two forewords.[74]

The antitrinitarians were also among the new opponents of Luther. In March 1530 Johann Campanus of The Netherlands came to Wittenberg to argue with Luther concerning Campanus's variant teaching on the Trinity. He denied the personhood of the Holy Spirit and the essential unity between the Father and the Son, as well as other evangelical doctrines. He described Luther as a "devilish liar." He found acceptance of his ideas among the Anabaptists. Luther himself did not write against him, but when in 1532 Bugenhagen published a tract on the Trinity that was ascribed to Athanasius, Luther applauded the venture and provided a foreword.[75] After 1539 he wrote a number of theses for disputation on trinitarian doctrine. In his introduction to a doctoral disputation held on December 12, 1544, he cited both Campanus and Servetus (who was burned at the stake on October 27, 1553, in Geneva) as antitrinitarians.[76]

In that decade a larger antitrinitarian movement arose not only in Germany, but also in Italy, Poland, and Transylvania. In opposition to this the Reformation supported the tradition of the ancient church, which in this area also Luther never rejected, but rather defended.

After many negotiations between the Wittenbergers and the north Germans, a satisfying agreement was reached concerning the doctrine of the Lord's Supper. This was recorded in the so-called Wittenberg Concordat of May 29, 1536.[77] Bucer received most of the credit for this, but Luther, also, was conciliatory. His primary concern, however, seems to have been its implementation. According to this agreement the body and blood of Christ were truly and essentially present in the sacrament, together with the bread and wine, even if this presence was not spatial in nature. Christ's body and blood were also received by the "unworthy," but to their condemnation. The expressions "godless" and "unbelievers" were avoided at the request of the north Germans.

The Swiss could not be persuaded to accept this formulation, and after 1539 the conflict with them was rekindled once more. It has been rightly said that the Concordat foundered on the Zwinglianism of the Swiss. After that, Luther no longer held himself back. At the end of September 1544 his *Brief Confession Concerning the Holy Sacrament* appeared.[78] This was prompted by the firm rejection he had given to the Silesian nobleman Caspar von Schwenckfeld on December 6, 1543, because of his teaching on the Lord's Supper.[79] It also served to answer questions that had arisen in Hungary; the abolition in Wittenberg of the elevation of the host after June 25, 1542, had been unsettling because it was not known whether this step meant a consensus had been reached with the Zwinglians.[80]

Luther's treatise was a final rebuff to the Swiss. They had not held to that which they had agreed to in Marburg. In March 1545 the Swiss issued a rebuttal (to which Luther did not reply), stating that it was Luther who had repeatedly broken the peace arranged at Marburg.[81]

In this treatise Luther recounted, for the last time, his earlier arguments against the sacramentarians. A single heresy corrupted the entire teaching. "For this reason we say that everything is to be believed completely and without exception, or nothing is to be believed. The Holy Spirit does not let himself be divided or cut up." [82] "If a bell cracks at one place, it does not chime any more and is completely useless."[83] Luther wanted nothing more to do with the sacramentarians and would no longer pray for them.[84] His opinion of Calvin seems to have been more moderate: "Calvin is a learned man, but I strongly suspect in him the error of the sacramentarians."[85] Luther is also reported to have said that if Zwingli and Oecolampadius had taught as Calvin had, the conflict would never have arisen.[86]

There were also tensions and conflicts within Luther's own camp. During a church visitation in 1527 Johann Agricola had protested the expectation that there be preaching of the law. At the time, Luther quickly resolved the conflict. Later Agricola (who in the meantime had moved from Eisleben to Wittenberg) renewed his opposition. The result was the Antinomian controversy of 1537, Luther's fight against those who contested the preaching of the law. Between 1537 and 1540 Luther pursued the debate by writing six sets of theses against the Antinomians,[87] as well as the 1539 treatise *Against the Antinomians.*[88] Unfortunately, the dispute resulted not only in objective argumentation, but also in personal disappointments and irritations. The old friendship between Luther and Agricola was shattered.

Agricola supported the following thesis: Penitence ought to be taught from the gospel and not from the law; it arose out of love for Christ. He appealed to earlier statements made by Luther, and was not entirely unjustified in doing so.[89] Luther stood by his earlier statements, explaining that the appearance of a change in his view was because the situation had changed.[90] In the first years of his reforming work he had to preach and teach against the legalistic piety of the papists and insist, over against this view, that the gospel freed one from the tyranny of the law. At that time fear of damnation held sway, but now people had become secure, impudent, and "epicurean"; therefore the law once again had to be impressed upon them. Many were not even capable of hearing the comfort of the gospel because they did not feel that they needed it.

Even in the early years of his work as a reformer, Luther had not refrained from stating that the will of God laid claim on people in the law; moreover, he had repeatedly interpreted the Ten Commandments as being the basic rules for Christian life. In other words, Agricola had drawn one-sided conclusions from particular statements of the "young Luther"—statements to which the "old Luther" still held. Law and gospel were to be strictly distinguished; their confusion was the fundamental error of the papists. Yet at the same time it had to be firmly maintained that law and gospel belonged together. The gospel presupposed the law and its proclamation. Since even justified persons were not free of sin in this life, they still needed the law, which enabled them to recognize their sin and revealed the will of God.

Luther viewed the Antinomians as "sweet theologians"[91] who taught only "sweet grace,"[92] an accusation that Müntzer, in his time, had raised against Luther. Agricola (who by the way was quite envious of Melanchthon's position at the university) could no longer remain in Wittenberg. In the middle of August 1540 he left for Berlin, where he was to become the court preacher for Joachim II of Brandenburg.

An internal struggle also erupted over the question of the meaning of good works with regard to justification. It began when Pastor Cordatus of Niemegk, a devoted follower of Luther, accused Cruciger and Melanchthon of describing good works as a *conditio sine qua non,* as an absolute requirement of justification.[93] Luther dealt with this subject in a number of his disputations. It was clear to him that good works were not a requirement for justification, though they were an inevitable result of it. Works were necessary, but not necessary for salvation. Contrition was necessary for the forgiveness of sins, but it was not the cause of forgiveness.

Cordatus, who was inclined to scholastic hairsplitting, took issue with these straightforward religious statements. And Luther's reassurance did not alleviate his theological mistrust of Melanchthon. He wrote one letter after another and petitioned the elector. He viewed Melanchthon's statements as a revival of the synergism of the Roman teaching of justification, whereby works contributed to justification. Cordatus was a conscientious, but intellectually limited, man, and in him the stunted nature of Protestant scholasticism became visible for the first time. After Luther's death such scholasticism led to the battles between his would-be (but inferior) successors—the so-called Gnesio-Lutherans (the "genuine" Lutherans) and the "Philippists" (the followers of Melanchthon). They argued about theological formulations. There was little of the broad-mindedness with which Luther had concentrated on that which was essential and existential.

After Luther's death Melanchthon suffered inordinately from the *"rabies theologorum,"* the "rabies of theologians." Even during Luther's last years, his relationship with Melanchthon was no longer as congenial as it had once been. Over the years the different temperaments of the two men became disturbingly noticeable. On the doctrine of the Lord's Supper they developed different views, and the older Melanchthon was forced to accept the (not unjustified) accusation of tending toward synergism. Luther was unable to accept Melanchthon's all-too-great willingness to negotiate with everyone; Melanchthon in turn suffered under Luther's intransigence toward all his opponents, even Erasmus and the Swiss theologians. Melanchthon shied away from an open debate; he had problems with Luther.

On the other hand, despite their many disagreements, Luther always supported his friend. Neither privately nor publicly did he ever speak out against him. He retained a lifelong respect for Melanchthon's great mental capacities. Luther was well aware of how important this friendship was to the cause of the Reformation, and though he played the dominant role, he was at the same time also the more considerate of the two.

However, toward the end of the 1530s a serious disagreement erupted between Luther and the Wittenberg jurists (particularly his onetime good friend Hieronymus Schurff), because they advocated retaining canonical rights within the evangelical church.

The fight against the Jews that Luther engaged in during his final decade is an unpleasant chapter of his life.[94] The suffering experienced by the Jews in the Middle Ages is well documented. They were not opposed on racial grounds, but for religious and economic reasons. They were viewed as the people who had killed God's Son, and as usurers. There was one pogrom after another. In 1290 they were expelled from England, in 1394 from France, and in 1492 from Spain. Their situation did not improve in the 16th century. They had been expelled from most of the larger cities. Admittedly, regulations regarding Jews varied from one territory to another. In the 15th century they were forbidden from living in Saxony. In practice, however, such measures were not always enforced.

One must view Luther's position regarding the Jews against this historical background. Like most of his contemporaries, he saw the Jewish question not as a racial but as a religious and economic problem, even though national antipathies (similar to those regarding the "southern Europeans") may have played a part. Even in his last sermon, on February 15, 1546, he repeated the prevalent reproaches against the Jews:[95] they blasphemed Christ and Mary, they engaged in usury, they passed themselves off as medical doctors in order to poison people; but if they were to accept Christ, the evangelicals would "gladly consider them as our brothers." [96]

In this regard Luther's attitude did not change, even though a drastic change in his judgment can be observed during the 1530s. In the early lectures on the Psalms he traced the Jewish rejection of Christ to a lack of information.[97] In his lectures on Romans (11:22) he warned against self-assuredly cursing the Jews and attempting to convert them through force and invective.[98] Christians and Jews alike required God's mercy.

It was in 1523 that Luther for the first time expressed himself on the subject of the Jews. He had been accused of denying the virginity of Mary before and after the birth of Jesus, and of considering Jesus to be a natural descendant of Abraham. His work *That Jesus Was Born a Jew* was directed against this charge.[99] With this tract he hoped not only to defend himself, but even more to win some Jews for the gospel. The mission of the papal church could have no success: it treated the Jews as dogs and not as human beings.[100] Until then they had not heard the true gospel.

Luther had himself learned from baptized Jews that they would have remained Jews, under the mantle of Christ, if the Reformation had not brought them the gospel. Now there was hope that things might be different. The Old Testament bore witness to Christ; when Jews became Christians they were actually returning to their own faith. The Messiah had already come in Christ; the Jews ought not wait for another.[101] When the Jews recognized this they would also learn to recognize the divinity of Christ.[102] Luther sent the Latin translation of this tract (prepared by Jonas) to the baptized Jew Bernhard.[103]

Luther's hope that the Reformation would make possible a successful mission to the Jews was not fulfilled. A dialog held in Worms between Luther and two Jews brought no results. Prior to 1536 three learned Jews came to dispute with Luther over messianic texts of the Bible. Not surprisingly, he was not able to convince them of the validity of his exegesis.[104] But he still did not completely give up hope. On August 6, 1536, the elector issued a mandate that the Jews were no longer to be tolerated in the territory and that no safe conduct and protection was to be given them. The leader of the German Jews, Josel von Rosheim, then turned to Luther with the request that he speak to the elector on their behalf.

Luther replied on June 11, 1537.[105] He rejected the request; the Jews had taken advantage of his favorable attitude toward them. Yet he would not cease to exhort them to come to their senses. Then he wrote a new work on the subject, *Against the Sabbatarians: Letter to a Good Friend*, which appeared in March 1538.[106] Luther had heard that the Jews in Mähren were conducting a mission among the Christians, and that Christians had been circumcised and were observing the Sabbath. The "good friend" was probably Wolf Graf Schlick of Falkenau in Nordböhmen, from whom he had received the news. The Jews did not wish to give up their rabbinic exegesis; therefore there was no point in disputing with them any longer.[107] They would not acknowledge that God had already fulfilled [108] the promise of a new covenant.[109] The law of Moses had lost its validity after the coming of Christ and the destruction of Jerusalem.[110] If the Jews still wanted to retain it, they would have to go to Palestine. But that would never happen because there was no divine promise for it; the promise applied rather to the new covenant.[111] God himself would have become a liar if he had not sent the Messiah. God had abandoned the Jews; they were no longer God's people.[112] This work was not received with favor by the Jews. Instead a rebuttal appeared, which Luther received in May 1542. This prompted him to carry out the plan he had already announced to Josel, of devoting even more attention to the Jews.

In the meantime Luther had done some basic study and had occupied himself with rabbinic literature. At the same time, however, he vented his great anger against the Jews in uninhibited fashion. This was especially true of the first of three writings of 1543, *On the Jews and Their Lies*.[113] He no longer wanted to convert the Jews, because that was impossible.[114] In this work, therefore, he no longer wrote *to* the Jews but rather *about* them and their activities, in order that the Germans might be instructed.[115] The Jews took pride in being descendants of Abraham and the patriarchs, and they considered themselves to be God's chosen people.[116] With this boast they sinned against God. [117] Being descendants of Adam and Eve was just as distinguished, but in God's eyes lineage according to the flesh amounted to nothing.[118] They should boast neither in circumcision [119] nor in the law [120] (which since the destruction of Jerusalem they could no longer fully keep).[121]

Luther went on to analyze a number of Old Testament passages which, in his opinion, proved that the messianic hope had already been fulfilled.[122] The Jews would not begrudge him this, for it was the source of their "venomous hatred" against the Goyim, the Gentiles.[123] In great detail Luther then attempted to refute the rabbinic interpretation of the prophecies of Daniel.[124] The Jewish blasphemies against Christ,[125] against Mary,[126] and against Christians in general [127] were unbearable to him. Their atrocities cried out to heaven.[128] They ought to return to their own land.[129] They claimed to be held captive; in reality they held the Germans captive; they loafed about and practiced usury and let others work in the sweat of their brows.[130] What was to be done? "With prayer and the fear of God we must save at least a few from the glowing flames. We dare not avenge ourselves. Vengeance a thousand times worse than we could wish them already has them by the throat." [131]

Luther's "sincere advice," [132] however, was terrible enough: 1. One ought to burn the synagogues of the Jews in which they blasphemed Christ.[133] 2. One should destroy their houses.[134] 3. One should confiscate their prayer books and the Talmud.[135] 4. The rabbis should no longer be allowed to teach.[136] 5. One should refuse them safe-conduct and prohibit them from doing business in the land.[137] 6. One should forbid them from engaging in usury and confiscate the money they had acquired by means of it.[138] 7. The young, strong Jewish men and women were to be put to work to earn their bread "in the sweat of their brow." [139] The best thing, however, would be to do as other nations had done and expel them from the land.[140] It was the duty of the civil authorities to carry out this "sharp mercy"; [141] Luther could not condone private acts of revenge. But the Jews should not be strengthened in their malice, and people should avoid them.[142] They could not be compelled to believe. Luther did not shy away from repeating the medieval fables about the atrocities of the Jews; in his opinion they were reason enough for the judgment of Christ.[143] Yet despite his fury Luther also wrote, "The wrath of God has overtaken them. I am loath to think of this, and it has not been a pleasant task for me to write this book. . . . O God, heavenly Father, relent and let your wrath over them be sufficient and come to an end, for the sake of your dear Son!" [144]

Luther's second work of 1543 on the Jews, *Concerning Schem Hamphoras and the Lineage of Christ*,[145] dealt with a Hebrew alphabet game that Jews used to defame Christ. The second part of the work [146] attempted to harmonize the two genealogies of Jesus in Matthew 1 and Luke 3. A third writing in 1543, *Concerning the Last Words of David*, presented an interpretation that Luther had referred to in *On the Jews and Their Lies*.[147] It introduced a new translation of 2 Samuel 23:1-7 and a Christocentric interpretation of this text. This gave Luther an opportunity to express his views on trinitarian and Christological questions.[148] In his conclusion he encouraged his fellow theologians to a zealous study of Hebrew so that they would not surrender the Old Testament to the rabbis, "with their tortured grammar and false interpretation," but clearly perceive the Lord Christ in it.[149] The degree to which Luther was occupied with the Jews during the last 15 years of his life is shown by glancing at the index to the Weimar edition of the *Table Talk* under the heading, "Jews." [150]

Today we can no longer accept Luther's messianic interpretation that pointed directly to Christ. With the exception of a few passages, the portrayal of the Messiah in the Old Testament does not correspond to our conception of Christ. The historical interpretation of the rabbis is closer to our contemporary understanding than is Luther's Christological exegesis, which admittedly bound him to a tradition that stretched back to the New Testament itself. As early as the second century, Christians accused the Jews of misinterpreting the Old Testament. Though Luther was able to free himself from many other traditions, he did not do so with this one. Therefore he could only describe the opinion of the Jews as stiff-necked obstinacy. Certainly it was primarily on theological grounds that Luther began to oppose the Jews, but these grounds were not sound. It is a deplorable blot on his life that he used these grounds to disseminate such vulgar propaganda against the Jews, and that he did it with such vehemence.

Preacher and Pastor, Professor, and "Church Father"

The previous chapter depicted Luther as a man who was continually involved in old and new conflicts. But our picture of him would be completely distorted if we believed that during the last one and a half decades of his life he was totally wrapped up in these conflicts. The positive achievements of these years claimed as much of his time and effort as did his fights against old and new opponents, and are at least as significant. They can be considered from three vantage points: Luther as preacher and pastor, Luther as professor, and Luther as "church father."

Luther was one of the greatest preachers in the history of Christendom.[1] In quantitative terms alone, his preaching output was astounding. Between 1510 and 1546 Luther preached approximately 3000 sermons. Frequently he preached several times a week, often two or more times a day. About 2000 of his sermons have been preserved. They have been organized chronologically in the *Hilfsbuch zum Luther-Studium* by Kurt Aland, and listed by pericope in volume 22 of the Weimar Edition. In volume 7 of *Luthers Werke in Auswahl* (Clemens), study edition, Emanuel Hirsch has provided a selection of sermons that serves not only as a valuable introduction to Luther's sermons and postils, but also presents Luther's perspective on his own preaching.

The 2000 preserved sermons are either in the form of transcripts (thanks largely to the indefatigable George Rörer) or versions prepared for publication. Reading the transcripts is not a great deal of fun; Luther's German was reproduced in a mixture of German and Latin, since the copyists had only Latin abbreviations at their disposal. So, for example, they often wrote *f* (for *fides*) instead of *der Glaube* (faith), or *pc* (for *peccatum*) instead of *die Sünde* (sin). Moreover, it was impossible to avoid gaps while writing down what one heard. It is therefore understandable that many passages were reconstructed and supplemented when they were prepared for publication.

The two oldest sermons probably come from the Erfurt period, and are still quite scholastic in style.[2] The few surviving sermons from the years prior to 1518 show Luther developing toward his Reformation theology.[3] We have already discussed those in Chapter 9.

The material available to us dated after 1519 is more plentiful; three collections are available.[4] We have already dealt with his work on the *Church Postils* while at the Wartburg. Luther himself never completed more than the winter segment. Stephan Roth of Zwickau volunteered to fill in the gap between Easter and the last Sunday after Trinity. Luther let him do it only because he was unable to finish the task himself. Roth's *Summer Postils* appeared at the end of August 1526.[5] They were reworked versions of transcribed Luther sermons. Encouraged by their enthusiastic reception, in 1527 Roth also published a collection of postils for festival days,[6] and finally, in 1528, a version of Luther's own winter portion of the *Church Postils*, known as *Roth's Winter Postils*.[7]

Because Luther was not completely satisfied with Roth's *Summer Postils*, in 1535 he engaged Caspar Cruciger, who had already proven his ability as an editor of Luther's works, to prepare a new edition. However, this did not appear until 1544.[8] In the same year, Veit Dietrich's collection of *Home Postils* was published.[9] Dietrich dedicated it to the city fathers of Nuremberg. It was a huge success, and within a year it had gone through nine printings. For generations it remained Luther's most popular sermon book.

The *Home Postils* were freely edited sermons preached by Luther between 1531 and 1535. The majority of them are home sermons from the years 1532 to 1534, when because of his poor health Luther seldom preached publicly. Like a true *Hausvater* he had regularly delivered sermons to his family, the servants, and whatever friends were present. Veit Dietrich worked quite freely with Luther's sermons, often combining several and occasionally incorporating his own material as well. Because of their warm style, these sermons were more appealing than those from the period of the *Church Postils.*

The *Home Postils* of the Philippist Veit Dietrich were criticized by the Gnesio-Lutherans for what they considered obvious failings, but theological differences may also have played a role. The Gnesio-Lutherans also issued their own (Jena) edition of Luther's works over against the Wittenberg edition that had been compiled under the auspices of Melanchthon. The young dukes of Saxony in Jena acquired Rörer's transcripts, and there Andreas Poach edited them for publication. These *Home Postils* by Rörer and Poach appeared in 1559. Even though this edition was text-critically superior to the one by Veit Dietrich, it did not rival Dietrich's in popularity in the years that followed.

In addition to the postils and the collections mentioned above, there are a large number of other Luther sermons scattered throughout the Weimar Edition. One of the most distinguished Luther philologists at the turn of the century, Georg Buchwald (1859–1947), who in his later years served as superintendent in Rochlitz, rendered the service of deciphering the difficult Rörer transcripts. There are sermon series on biblical books or on specific chapters, which Luther preached on Sunday afternoons or during the week. There are sermons on the Ten Commandments, on the Lord's Prayer, and on the catechism. There are sermons for festival days and, finally, those preached on special occasions, such as the Invocavit sermons or those that were delivered in outlying congregations.

In his early years Luther usually preached on particular themes, but as a reformer he turned completely to biblical interpretation. This type of preaching is usually referred to as a *homily,* to distinguish it from thematic preaching. Luther's sermons, however, did not hold strictly to the rules of a homily; rather than following the text verse by verse, they often singled out an important word, even though the emphasis still remained on biblical interpretation.

In the process Luther never lost sight of the goal: Christ and faith. A purely historical proclamation of Christ was not enough; the "fruit" of Christ's work had to become visible. Luther dealt with the theme of justification even in connection with texts that did not specifically mention it.[10] His conflicts with the Antinomians showed that he did not reject the preaching of the law.

Luther could even preach biblically without a text, as can be seen in his Invocavit sermons. He believed that simply reading the Bible was not enough; it had to become *"viva vox,"* living speech, which is what the Bible itself originally was. Preaching was the highest office.[11] The church needed preachers more than those who wrote books.[12] A sermon was both teaching and exhortation, but teaching was more important than exhortation.[13] Exhortation took place not only in the sermon, but often also in the dismissal that immediately followed it. Chastisement was also part of exhortation, and Luther did not refrain from it in his preaching.

For Luther, Christ was the supreme example for preachers. He spoke "simply," in ordinary parables drawn from everyday life. To preach so simply was a great art.[14] Nevertheless Luther did not despise the techniques of public speaking; in this area he was a student of Quintilian.[15] But what made Luther's sermons so captivating was not his skill, not his gestures,[16] and not his powerful voice (which, incidentally, he never had),[17] but the fact that he was captivated by the subject [18] and had a simple, folksy style. Luther stated repeatedly that he did not preach for Bugenhagen or Melanchthon, but for his "little Hans and Elsa." [19] The pulpit was not the place to flaunt one's learning; Luther condemned Zwingli for bringing Greek and Hebrew into his preaching in Marburg.[20] Luther said, "Some day I'll have to write a book against artful preachers."[21] He reprimanded Osiander for introducing theological conflicts into his preaching.[22]

Luther said that preachers ought not say everything that popped into their minds, like young women do when they make one stop after another on their way to the market.[23] Luther often stepped from the pulpit disheartened, hearing afterward that he had done particularly well.[24] He also experienced aversion on the part of his listeners; when he preached on the article of justification, people slept or coughed; but when he told stories or gave examples, they listened silently and attentively.[25] Luther also knew what it was like to be nervous before he preached. When Staupitz first introduced him to the pulpit he thought he would die.[26]

Luther was not tied to a manuscript.[27] He prepared only a general outline.[28] He confessed that he often had dreadful dreams of having to preach without notes.[29] He encouraged young preachers by telling them that at first he had been just as frightened by the task as they were;[30] later, as he entered the pulpit, he would think to himself that the people he was going to address were only "clods," and then "go right on speaking the Word of my God." [31] The fear of God was something entirely different, and even the experienced preacher dared never lose it,[32] for he had to preach about the supreme majesty of God;[33] indeed, it was God himself who wanted to speak through the preacher.[34]

In Aurifaber's collection Luther described the attributes of a good preacher: "A good preacher should have these qualities and virtues. First, he should be able to teach well, in a correct and orderly fashion. Next, he should have a good head. Third, he should be able to speak well. Fourth, he should have a good voice. Fifth, he should have a good memory. Sixth, he should know when to stop (on time). Seventh, he should know his stuff and be diligent. Eighth, he should stake his body and life, possessions and honor on what he says. Ninth, he should be willing to let everyone vex and poke fun at him." [35]

In his sermons Luther also endeavored to provide consolation for his hearers. He knew of those who, like himself, needed comfort and assurance for their troubled consciences. Nor did he overlook those who, in the midst of physical need, longed for encouragement and hope. For him the sermon was therefore always a pastoral event, and the offices of preacher and pastor belonged together.

An entire chapter could be written about Luther as a pastor.[36] His entire career had a pastoral character. As district supervisor he comforted troubled monastic brothers; as a concerned pastor he directed his theses against indulgences; to the ill elector he sent his *Fourteen Consolations;* from Coburg castle he supported Melanchthon and his colleagues in Augsburg; and he sent his letter of consolation to his table guest Hieronymus Weller, who suffered from depression – the list could go on and on. Luther sent hundreds of pastoral letters far and wide, to acquaintances as well as to strangers. Again and again we come across such letters in which he interceded for the poor. A number of them are addressed to one of the three electors, under whose jurisdiction Luther lived and for whom he always willingly provided pastoral advice.

In the year 1531 Luther spoke of his visits to those who were ill:[37]

"One must always speak to and deal with those who are ill in a friendly way. Insofar as I am able, I submit to their wishes. Then I ask the ill person about his illness, how long he has been ill, who his doctor is, and what medication he is taking; then I ask him whether he has patience, whether he believes that the illness has overtaken him according to God's will, and whether he is able to accept this will gladly, even if it should mean his death." In other words, Luther began his conversations with those who were ill by addressing them in purely human terms. Only later did he attempt to give them spiritual comfort. If an ill person thanked him for his visit but indicated that he or she did not deserve it, Luther responded: "It is my office and my duty; it requires no thanks."

By contrast with his generally negative assessment of lawyers, Luther valued physicians highly. They were "our Lord God's patcher-uppers." One ought to make use of medicine; it was created by God. "Once our mayor asked me if it were against God's will to take medications, since Dr. Karlstadt had publicly preached that one ought to use no medications but rather entrust the matter to God." In his practical manner of thinking Luther posed a counter-question: Did he also eat when he was hungry? [38] Similarly, in *A Sermon on Keeping Children in School* Luther praised doctors as an indispensable and beneficial estate, whose work was "a service acceptable to God." [39]

Luther used a rather unusual form of therapy on Melanchthon when he became seriously ill in Weimar during the summer of 1540. Matthäus Ratzeberger, the personal physician to Elector John Frederick, described it in detail. Melanchthon had broken down physically and emotionally over the embarrassing matter of Philip of Hesse's bigamous marriage. Luther approached his friend as if he were dying. "God forbid, how the devil has abused this human instrument of truth!" he cried aloud. Then he turned to the window and prayed. "In that moment our Lord God had to put up with me, for I threw the sack at his gates and rubbed his ears with all his promises, in order that he would respond to my prayer." Then he grasped Melanchthon's hand and encouraged him. He was not to succumb to this sorrowful spirit and become suicidal. After this Luther had food brought in and threatened Melanchthon when he refused to take it. "Listen, Phillip! You must eat or I will place you under the ban."

Later, filled with joy, Luther informed his Katie of Melanchthon's recovery, and in order to reassure her about his own condition, humorously added: "I eat like a Bohemian and drink like a German; thanks be to God for this. Amen. The reason for this is that Master Philip truly has been dead, and really, like Lazarus, has risen from death." [40]

Even during the time of the plague, Luther was not afraid to visit those who were ill. He wrote about this in 1527 in *Whether One May Flee from a Deadly Plague*.[41] In the summer of 1527 the Plague broke out in Wittenberg. In August the university moved to Jena. Despite the request of the elector, Luther remained in Wittenberg; the only other person who refused to leave was Bugenhagen, the city pastor. Preachers and pastors were required to remain, wrote Luther. In times of distress one needed them even more. The same held true for those who served in civil offices and others whose duty it was to care for those in need. Otherwise, leaving in such times was not prohibited. It was not wrong to flee from death, and one ought not tempt God. For the same reason one ought not refrain from taking every precaution against infection, should use medications, and should smoke one's house and yard against the deadly mists. Cemeteries ought to be located outside the city. A cemetery should be "a fine quiet place, removed from all other localities, to which one can go and reverently meditate" and pray; on the walls should be devotional paintings.[42] And the maintenance of graveyards was one part of pastoral care.

Another question that troubled many people was the fate of children who died without being baptized. Article 9 of the *Augsburg Confession* makes it sound as though they would be damned. Luther was not of this opinion. In 1542, therefore, he wrote his little book, *Comfort for Women Who Have Had a Miscarriage*.[43] Mothers whose children were lost in premature birth, in miscarriage, or in stillbirth ought to accept the will of God. God would hear their prayers, even if their children could not be baptized. "God has not limited his power to the sacraments, but has made a covenant with us through his Word." [44] This was also the view Luther espoused in his lectures on Genesis; unbaptized children were to be commended to the grace of God, who could also save without Baptism.[45]

The secret of Luther's proficiency in pastoral care was that he himself had known what it was like to experience attacks of despair

[Anfechtung]. Hieronymus Weller reported that Luther was once asked by one of his table companions how it was that he was able to preach and comfort so that each hearer believed the sermons were directed precisely to him; it was as if he knew the concerns of each individual and was able to look into their innermost heart. Luther answered that he had been taught that skill by his own attacks of despair, and added that he did not know whether there was any temptation, with the exception of miserliness, that he had not experienced.[46] Luther spoke more explicitly about these attacks in a table talk of 1533, in which this revealing sentence is found: "The bouts I've engaged in during the night have become much more bitter than those during the day." [47] In pastoral care Luther did not place himself over against those who were under stress, but joined them as one who was himself in need of comfort.

In addition, Luther knew that in pastoral care each instance had to be taken specifically and personally. So, for example, when he addressed the Antinomians he expressed himself quite differently than he did with Melanchthon. Only in this way can one explain the famous *"pecca fortiter"* (sin boldly) in Luther's letter to Melanchthon of August 1, 1521.[48] That statement was repeated in a similar way in the letter of comfort to Hieronymus Weller that we shall consider in a moment.

In the third place it appears characteristic of Luther's pastoral care that, along with all the references to Christ and the Word of God, he did not reject everyday sources of comfort as well as purely practical suggestions. Unhealthy, overly spiritual approaches were also alien to Luther.

Luther extended himself in a particularly protective, pastoral way to Hieronymus Weller, his table companion and the private tutor of his young son Hans. On June 19, 1530, he had written him a pastoral letter from the Coburg.[49] He said that Weller's thoughts did not come from God, but from the devil; for God was not a God of sadness, but of comfort and joy. All believers had had such thoughts, but they had overcome them. Luther said that a wise man had once been asked by a troubled person why such evil thoughts entered his head. He told him to let them fall out again. We have already mentioned Luther's comment that even though the birds fly over our heads, we don't have to let them nest in our hair.

No less gripping is Luther's second letter to Weller, of July 1530.[50]

He told him that his *Anfechtung* came from the devil; he was tormented because he believed in Christ. He was therefore to rejoice in his *Anfechtung* and not get into a disputation with the devil; in this case scorn was the best approach. He was to flee from loneliness and take part in the jokes and games with Luther's wife and the others. Dealing with his *Anfechtung* was more urgent than eating and drinking.

Luther said that Staupitz had spoken to him in a similar fashion when he had walked around the cloister, always looking depressed: God was testing him because he still had great things in mind for him. And sure enough, Luther became a "great doctor." It would be the same with Weller. When the devil plagues you with such thoughts, seek out conversation with others, drink more, joke and jest, or do something else that is fun. Sometimes it is necessary to drink, play, joke, and—in hate and scorn for the devil—even to commit a sin, so that we do not give him an opportunity to give us a guilty conscience about insignificant things. We must put the whole Decalog out of our sight and mind—we, whom the devil seeks out and torments. And when the devil throws our sins at us, this does not mean we are damned. Christ has done enough for us. Where he is, there I shall also be. The interplay of encouragement, light-hearted comfort, steadfast defiance of the devil, and confident dedication to Christ in this letter is unique.

Luther wrote to Weller a third time during the same year, on August 15, hoping to free him from his feelings of depression.[51] He repeated what he had already written, but emphasized that all of us share in our attacks of despair. "As I suffer for you, so also you suffer for me. We all bear with you and we all suffer in you; for we are indeed all one body." In the end, Luther's words of encouragement were not in vain; Hieronymus Weller later became a distinguished pastor.

Matthias Weller, one of his brothers, seems to have been melancholy as well. He was the court organist of Duke Henry of Freiberg in Saxony, the brother of Duke George. Luther wrote to Matthias Weller on October 7, 1534.[52] He advised that when dark thoughts overwhelmed him, he should say to the devil: "Up! I must play a hymn for our Lord Christ on the organ. And strike boldly on the keys and sing out loudly, until the thoughts evaporate." He ought to "punch the devil in the snout" right in the beginning. He should do this like the husband who, "when his wife began to nag and pick on him, took a whistle from under his belt and whistled contentedly until she finally became so tired that she left him in peace." You will recall that Luther had also written to the Bavarian court musician Ludwig Senfl about the power of music to drive away the devil.

A special kind of pastoral service was rendered by Luther in his short work of 1535 dedicated to his barber, Peter Beskendorf, known as Peter Balbier.[53] It bears the title: *A Simple Way to Pray [For a Good Friend]*. Luther had known Balbier for a long time and they had become friends. In a letter of September 11, 1517, to Christoph Scheurl in Nuremberg he had included greetings from him.[54] Peter had asked Luther for advice on how one should pray. Luther told him how he himself went about praying: He went into his room with his Psalter and meditated on the Ten Commandments, the petitions of the Lord's Prayer, the parts of the catechism, and individual texts of Scripture. It was important that one reserve specific times of the day for prayer, preferably morning and evening. Free prayer arose out of meditation on the previously mentioned texts. They were only a suggestion, however; one could use only selections from them. For prayer did not need to be long in order to be good, but rather "frequent and intense."[55]

We have noted Veit Dietrich's report that Luther prayed for long periods of time at the Coburg. But Luther did not prescribe this for others. To be sure, he had learned monastic meditation, but for him this did not involve a mystical absorption into the sea of divinity; rather, it remained bound to the Word and devoid of ecstatic experiences.[56] Peter Balbier's life ended in tragedy. During a dinner at his daughter's home on March 27, 1535, he (presumably while intoxicated) stabbed his son-in-law, a soldier of whom it was said that he could make himself invulnerable. The old man was universally pitied. Because of the advocacy of Luther and the electoral vice-chancellor Franz Burkhard, he was not executed but only banished, losing both his house and his possessions. He took up his trade once again in Dessau, where he died in August 1538.[57]

To Luther the preacher and pastor, the office of teaching and his professor's chair were no less important than the pulpit. The difference between the two was not as great as is usually the case today. Teaching had its place in the pulpit, and a lecture did not neglect edification. Nevertheless, Luther's lectures differed from his sermons. He used much academic material, relied on original texts, and carried on philological exegesis not only in his early lectures before 1518, but also his later ones. Still, it is not the erudition of these lectures that makes them valuable today; rather it is their theological content, which, incidentally, was always Luther's chief priority.

Luther never lectured on dogmatics; that was Melanchthon's task. It is remarkable that after his early lectures of 1515–1516 Luther never again lectured on Romans; that, too, was reserved for Melanchthon. Moreover, Luther did not lecture on the Gospels. However, he did interpret a number of shorter New Testament books for his students, for example, 1 John, 1 Peter, 1 Timothy, Titus, and others.

His "longer" lectures on Galatians of 1531, which George Rörer published in 1535 as a commentary, are a real gem.[58] In these Luther went far beyond the commentaries of 1519 and 1523, not only in detail but also in content.[59] There he distinguished his position from Jerome, and in part from Erasmus as well, with the aid of harsh polemics.

In Galatians Luther found the article of justification, the doctrine of law and gospel, and the battle against works righteousness all presented in outstanding fashion. His explanation of Galatians 2:20, which deals with being bound to Christ in faith, is marvelous. "By [faith] you are so cemented to Christ that He and you are as one person."[60] It almost appears as if Luther valued Galatians more highly than Romans. In a table talk of 1532 he declared: "The Epistle to the Galatians is my dear epistle. I have put my confidence in it. It is my Katie von Bora."[61] In any case, the Galatians commentary is one of the most significant theological achievements of Luther's later years.

The only work of equal importance was his longer lectures on Genesis,[62] which Luther, interrupted by illness and other hindrances, delivered between June 1535 and November 1545.[63] The transcripts by Cruciger, Rörer, and others were prepared for publication by Veit Dietrich, Rector Michael Roting of Nuremberg, and Hieronymus Besold. Luther had already preached frequently on Genesis, and these lectures turned out to be the most comprehensive and complete of his exegetical works. Philologically he borrowed much from Nicholas of Lyra (ca. 1270–1340), who had utilized Jewish exegesis, but he also learned much from contemporary "Hebrew grammarians."

Creation, the fall, primeval history, and the patriarchal history are the great, fascinating themes of Genesis. Abraham, the father of faith, had already become significant for Luther during his work on Romans. In the Joseph story he found a gripping illustration of how God transforms darkness into light. At times he attempted to excuse the moral weaknesses of the patriarchs, but he generally dealt with them candidly. For him they were not moral models, but examples of how God guides the saints. They, too, were very much in need of forgiveness. Luther incorporated into the lectures a wealth of dogmatic and ethical considerations, together with their practical application for preaching and pastoral care. Text-critically, one must attempt to distinguish between statements that are definitely Luther's and the additions of the editors.

In addition to Genesis, Luther also lectured on a number of other Old Testament books: Deuteronomy; Judges; the Psalms (early in his career); Ecclesiastes; the Song of Solomon; Isaiah; and all the minor prophets. There is also a wealth of sermons on the Old Testament, especially on the Psalms.[64] It is for this reason that one could, as some have already done, call Luther an Old Testament scholar. But the distinction between the Old and New Testaments as separate academic disciplines was still unknown.

Luther lectured on the Old Testament as a Christian theologian; he viewed the Old and New Testaments as belonging together as the Holy Scriptures of Christendom.[65] Luther's translation of the Old Testament had already indicated that, for it was a "Christianized translation." One need only note how significant it was that Luther did not use the Hebrew name for God, Yahweh, but instead followed the Septuagint and the Vulgate in substituting for it the designation, "the Lord"!

The Old Testament was understood as a prophecy of Christ and therefore, insofar as it was possible, interpreted Christologically. Very often Christ appeared as the subject of the Psalms. According to Luther, the church's Christology and doctrine of the Trinity were clearly contained in the Old Testament, as early as the first two verses of the Bible (God, the Word, and the Spirit). The fact that rabbinic exposition contradicted this interpretation appeared to

Luther to be obstinacy and a sign of God's punishment of Israel's unbelief. The faithful of the old covenant believed in the promised Christ; in this respect they were already Christians. Adam and Eve belonged to the church.

In his prefaces to the Old Testament of 1523 and 1545 Luther called it "the swaddling cloths and the manger" in which Christ lay. "Simple and lowly are these swaddling cloths, but dear is the treasure, Christ, who lies in them." [66] The New Testament was basically nothing other than an interpretation of the Old.[67] In any case, the Old Testament was to be interpreted Christocentrically, and the critique of individual books was also Christocentric.

For Luther, a Christocentric perspective not only provided the unity of the two testaments, it also revealed the difference between them. The Christocentric interpretation dared not for a moment lose sight of the distinction between "law and gospel." One could not simply equate law and gospel with the Old and New Testaments, yet the Old Testament contained law for the most part, and the New, gospel. Christ, however, was the end of the law.[68]

From this Luther drew virtually revolutionary conclusions. In opposition to Karlstadt and the enthusiasts, Luther held that, since Christ had come, Moses was no longer binding without qualification. The law of Moses was given only to the Jews. The Ten Commandments—the Decalog—also belonged to this law. This law was the "Jewish Sachsenspiegel." [69] The Decalog agreed with "natural law"; it was written in every human heart. As such it was to be kept, but not as the law of Moses.[70] The Ten Commandments were binding not because they were in the Bible, but because they were "natural law."

Christians were, however, entitled and obliged "to make new decalogs," and "these decalogs are much clearer than the decalog of Moses." [71] Luther noted in passing that the law of Moses contained "fine," reasonable rules and regulations, much like the rules which the Romans also had.[72] The Old Testament was also full of "beautiful examples of faith, of love, and of the cross."[73]

For us today, Luther's Christological interpretation of the Old Testament is outdated. Yet we can still learn from his freedom over against the Old Testament and at the same time from his passion for its religious content. In this regard one need only read his 1545 preface to the Psalter:[74] "There again you look into the hearts of the saints." [75]

The task of revising his translation of the Bible was also part of Luther's academic exegetical work. He pursued this with great effort and dedication to accuracy, supported by his staff of co-workers, until the very end of his life. The disputations, as well, were among Luther's academic accomplishments. In the Middle Ages these were a basic component of university life. After the unrest in Wittenberg, but also because of the humanistic critique of the scholastic system, the disputations in Wittenberg were gradually supplanted, until finally they were no longer held. But in the long run their value for academic instruction could not be denied, and they were reintroduced during the university reforms of 1533.

Some of the disputations were for the conferral of doctoral degrees, and others simply served as occasions for students to practice. Many were also held for particular reasons, as was the case with the theses opposing the Antinomians or the disputation concerning the right of rebellion against the emperor. For doctoral disputations the officient drew up the theses, which the candidate had to defend. Practice disputations were sometimes called "circular" disputations. Luther prepared theses for these as well.

In the disputations Luther can be seen as a skillful academic theologian who insisted on conceptual precision. We can also observe him as a dogmatician who moved confidently with exact definitions, despite the fact that this was not his usual style. It is easier to learn precisely what Luther meant theologically by studying his disputations than his sermons or commentaries. To be sure, at times there was also a scholastic meticulousness about him that did not shy away from pedantic logic. It is reported that as a presider over disputations Luther was generous, lenient, and forbearing, whereas students occasionally complained about Melanchthon's impatience and irritability. The disputations after 1533 are available today in two volumes of the Weimar Edition.[76]

It is primarily in the disputations that we find Luther's thoughts about the doctrine of the Trinity and traditional Christology, though we meet them also, at least in part, in the most significant work of Luther's later period—his treatise *On the Councils and the Church* of 1539.[77] In the formative years of the Reformation Luther had hoped that there might be a council. But that hope had already begun to wane after 1523; it became clear to him that the pope would never call a truly free council. We have already traced the progression of this fading hope up to Smalcald in 1537.

The Smalcaldic League had rejected the invitation to a council. In 1537 several cardinals who favored reform, foremost among them Gasparo Contarini, met and issued a memorandum calling for the "improvement" of the church. When Luther heard of it, he responded only with ridicule and scorn. He could no longer believe in the integrity of such intentions. In 1538 he published their *Counsel* along with a preface of his own.[78] "The pope is trailing his poor council around like a cat with kittens. He does not want to have it held in Germany, and he cannot have it in Mantua (or so he claims), and now it is to be in Vicenza, where it cannot be. They have no intention of holding it there either."[79] The pope's experience with the council was like that of the character Markolf in the legend, who couldn't find a tree on which he wanted to hang himself.[80] There were, however, those among the evangelicals who later found it impossible to support the decision of the Smalcaldic League.

It was during this period that Luther would have begun to develop his comprehensive statement *On the Councils and the Church*. He had prepared himself for this through years of study, finally making use of the extensive history of the Councils by the Franciscan, Krabbe. On March 14, 1539, he was able to report to Melanchthon that he had completed the document.

On the Councils and the Church enables us to see Luther not only as a polemicist, but also as a historian of the church and of dogma. The first part is a mainly polemical, but also historically couched, statement of Luther's position regarding the contemporary debate on a council.[81] In promising a council the pope had behaved like a tormentor of animals, first offering a dog a morsel to eat and then striking it on the snout with a knife.[82] The pope had repeatedly held out the promise of a council to the emperor; he had just announced it for the third time. But the decisions to be arrived at had already been determined.[83] The pope opposed every reform.[84] The enthusiasm of the Catholic reformers was in vain;[85] and who could tell if they were really serious, anyway?[86] The evangelicals were concerned with the chief articles of faith,[87] but the Councils had often concentrated on outward things. The Apostolic Council, for example, dealt with dietary regulations.[88] The church Fathers were human beings who could err; their writings ranked beneath the Holy Scriptures.[89] The Councils and the Fathers often contradicted each other.[90] The four chief councils of the ancient church had not been convened by the popes, but by the emperors.[91]

In the second part of the treatise Luther discussed in detail the four chief councils: Nicaea (325), Constantinople (381), Ephesus (430), and Chalcedon (451).[92] Luther had studied their pronouncements thoroughly.[93] At that time the doctrines of the Trinity and the divinity of Christ were dealt with. In Nicaea the faith of the early church was defended against the innovations of Arius.[94] The Nicene formulation was founded on Holy Scripture; otherwise it would have no authority.[95] The other canons of Nicaea—for example, the rules governing the day on which Easter falls—were only "clerical squabbling." [96] The Council of Constantinople had defined the divinity of the Holy Spirit,[97] and at the same time repudiated Pope Damasus' claim to power.[98] The Council of Ephesus had proclaimed the *theotokos* dogma, that Mary was the mother of God,[99] and at the same time condemned Nestorius.[100] Luther gave extended treatment to this latter judgment, for it did not appear self-evident to him. Nestorius had denied neither the divinity of Christ nor his two natures; his error was that he had not included the so-called *communicatio idiomatum,* the communication of human and divine attributes, in the single, divine-human person.[101] Luther said that in his time it was Zwingli who was a Nestorian.[102]

The final formulation of the doctrine of the two natures was made at Chalcedon, and condemned was the teaching that the human nature was absorbed by the divine nature after union with it.[103] The reports about this decision were not entirely clear;[104] those in the early church who followed Eusebius did not go that far. Luther was dependent on the accounts given by the popes, principally Leo I.[105] Luther read himself "into a bad humor" by reading the history of Chalcedon,[106] because there was so much "bickering, confusion, and disorder" there, and the bishops and council participants were "inordinately ambitious, haughty, quarrelsome, and vehement." [107] In spite of this, however, they were able to preserve the truth. But it was good that we now had something better than the Councils on which to base our faith, namely the Holy Scriptures.[108]

From his analysis of the four major councils Luther concluded that no council had the authority to establish new articles of faith; its sole purpose ought to be to defend the apostolic faith against false teaching.[109] It had no right to require new good works or ceremonies.[110] From good beginnings monasticism had evolved into an unbearable system of works, yet without being condemned by the medieval councils.[111] Moreover, councils ought not involve themselves in civil affairs or issue decrees.[112] Basically, the office of a pastor or of a schoolmaster was of no less importance than a council.[113] Augustine, "the poor, insignificant pastor at Hippo" had taught more than all the Councils.[114] Parishes and schools were small, yet "eternal and useful councils." [115] A council ought not condemn according to its own discretion, but only on the basis of the Holy Scriptures.[116] In conclusion, a council ought to limit itself to matters of faith; it had nothing to do with questions of discipline and ceremonies.[117] The council that was truly needed would have to be a council against the pope.[118]

Luther followed his exposition on the Councils with a third part on the nature of the church. The church was the communion of saints, a holy people called by God. Therefore it did not consist of the pope and the clergy.[119] The word *Kirche* (church) was not German and did not convey the right meaning.[120] The church to which the creed referred was not a stone building.[121] Christendom was called "holy" because the Holy Spirit gave it faith, love, and hope.[122] This holiness had nothing to do with the "holier" holiness of the papacy and monasticism.[123] The holy Christian church could be recognized by the Word of God, Baptism, the Lord's Supper, the office of the keys, ordination, the praise of God, and finally by "the holy possession of the sacred cross."[124]

Alongside this church the devil, "God's ape,"[125] had built his chapel and made outward usages the primary concern of the church.[126] But the devil was just as active in the spiritual Christendom of the enthusiasts.[127] God had bound himself to the outer Word and the sacrament, and a spiritual order was necessary in the church.[128] In addition to the church—and the schools, whose responsibility it was to educate ministerial candidates—there was the family and the city hall: "These are the three hierarchies ordained by God, and we need no more." [129]

In his treatise on the Councils Luther confessed the trinitarian and Christological dogmas of the ancient church. He did so as well in the *Smalcald Articles,* where he solemnly stated that there are no "matters of dispute or contention" concerning "the sublime articles of the divine majesty." [130] The confession of these doctrines was expressed in the three so-called ecumenical creeds held to by the Reformation: the Apostles,' the "Nicene," and the "Athanasian." Luther explicitly affirmed (for himself and others) all three in his work *The Three Symbols or Creeds of the Christian Faith,* written in 1538.[131] He described the Athanasian Creed as the "symbol in defense of" the Apostles' Creed.[132] And in a letter to Duke Albrecht of Prussia (1532) he wrote: "It is dangerous and frightening to hear or believe anything against the united witness of the entire holy Christian church, which has from the beginning maintained itself in unity throughout the world for more than 1500 years." [133]

Luther did not want to found a new church, because he highly valued continuity with the true, ancient church. In order to understand this adherence to dogmatic tradition, one had to look at the origin of this tradition. Councils did not have the right to establish new articles of faith; they only had the task of defending the truth of Holy Scripture. In doing this they could also use expressions such as *homousios* (of one substance) or "original sin," which were not found in the Holy Scriptures, provided such expressions could "condense the meaning of Scripture." [134] Luther did not like the word *homousios* (as he had told Latomus [135]); he thought as little of it as he did of the expression "one-in-three." [136]

The significance and the limitation of the Councils was therefore in the clarity of their formulation of scriptural truth. Luther never gave up the primacy of Scripture over against the church and the Councils, despite his high regard for the ancient dogmas. In the disputation on the authority of the Councils he described it as arrogance when a council such as Constance prided itself in having been "legitimately convened by the Holy Spirit." [137] To the objection that Christendom would not know what the gospel was without the authority of the church, Luther answered, the gospel "is not believed because the church affirms it, but because it is recognized as the Word of God." [138]

There is no question but that Luther affirmed the trinitarian and Christological dogmas of the ancient church because he considered them to be proper expositions of the Holy Scriptures. Without this conviction he would have separated himself from them as he did from the traditions of the papal church. Since it has in our day become problematic to view the apostolic dogmas as being in accordance with Scripture, and since we can no longer be convinced of the doctrinal unity of the New Testament, it is impossible for us simply to affirm Luther's position concerning these ancient dogmas, even though we do not want to overlook the elements of truth they contain.[139]

In his youth Luther had expressed a lively interest in history, and in his later years he was occupied with it as well, though in a more limited way. In his preface to a work on the history of Milan translated by Wenceslas Link, he commended the writers of history as "the most useful people and best teachers," who could not be praised enough.[140] He complained that the Germans knew so little about their history.[141] He admitted that a historian had to have "the heart of a lion" [142] in order to record the truth courageously, for no one's sake and to no one's harm.

Luther himself attempted to write some history in his *Supputatio annorum mundi,* known in German as *Chronika,* which appeared in 1541 and in a revised edition in 1545.[143] The work was intended to give an overview of biblical history, but it was extended to include Luther's own time. According to an ancient belief, the world was to last for 6000 years. Since 5500 years had already passed and the last days were to be shortened, one could—according to Luther's opinion—already expect the last judgment.[144] Luther was not, however, interested in the wild calculations of Michael Stiefel, a preacher in Lochau.

Prompted by the Turkish threat, Luther also occupied himself with the Koran. In 1530 he was already acquainted with a refutation of the Koran by the Dominican monk Ricoldus (Ricardus), which was written around 1300. In the spring of 1542 Luther translated it into German and had it published.[145] At the same time he also obtained a Latin edition of the Koran. When a learned man in Zürich by the name of Bibliander ("bookman") sought to issue a new Latin translation of the Koran, accompanied by a refutation, the city council of Basel wanted to prohibit its publication. Luther requested that the council release the work,[146] and he himself wrote a foreword to it.[147] He considered a knowledge of the Koran and of its refutation to be essential.

Luther's collection of proverbs is also worthy of note—a project he started after 1535.[148] He was not the only one who had such an interest; Johann Agricola and the humanists—above all, Erasmus—had similar collections. Luther valued proverbs not only for their popular folk wisdom, but also for their usefulness in improving his German style. In his exposition of Psalm 101 in 1534–1535 have been found no less than 170 proverbs.[149] Luther's collection was intended as a regent's code for Elector John Frederick. In it he recommended that one also read classical authors such as Homer, Virgil, Demosthenes, Cicero, and Livius, since one could learn much from them about the secular realm. This love for the classics went back to Luther's student days. In his admonition *To the Councilmen of All Cities in Germany* concerning the importance of schools, also, he had advocated reading the classical authors.

Luther must have felt particularly exhilarated as he did his work on Psalm 101, for it is written with amazing freshness and descriptive power. In his conclusion he expressed the hope that he had made a good job of it. "I shall call it good if it is well-pleasing to a few people and quite disgusting to many people." [150] He did not spare the elector and his court from bitter truth.

For a long time Luther successfully blocked the publication of a collected edition of his works. However, an index of his books appeared without a preface by him in 1528. A second edition was published in 1533.[151] In his preface to that volume Luther stated that he would gladly have seen all of his books destroyed, because everything depended solely on the Holy Scriptures.[152] The most good that could come from such a listing was that one could see that he had made progress in the knowledge of Christ, as well as in his rejection of the papacy. He appealed to Augustine, who in his own *Retractationes* had provided a sort of self-critique of his literary development.

A few years later the Strasbourgers pressed him with a request for a complete edition. On July 9, 1537, Luther wrote the previously cited letter to Wolfgang Capito.[153] He would gladly have devoured all his books, like Saturn had done to his children; at most he could approve only of *The Bondage of the Will* and the *Catechism*. Nevertheless, he instructed Casper Cruciger to take on the task of a complete edition. In 1539 the first volume of Luther's German works appeared in Wittenberg; it was followed in 1545 by the first volume of the *opera latina*.

In his preface to the first German volume Luther repeated his aversion to the publication of the collection, but hoped that his books might at least lead to a study of Scripture.[154] But in order for this to happen, prayer, meditation, and temptation *(oratio, meditatio, tentatio)* were necessary.[155] Let those who took pride in their own little books grab their own ears; there they would find a beautiful pair of big, long, hairy, donkey ears, on which they could also hang some bells.[156]

In his preface to the first volume of the *opera latina* Luther provided an overview of his theological development up to the Diet of Worms;[157] central to this was his discovery of the *iustitia passiva* in the exegesis of Romans 1:16-17.[158] The second volume of the *opera latina* appeared after Luther's death and included a "Life of Luther" written by Melanchthon.[159]

By means of his public activities, Luther became a type of "church father." His opponents mockingly referred to him as the "Counterpope." But that is not exactly what he was. He never claimed to be the supreme judge in the ecclesiastical questions of his time. For example, his *German Mass* was only a proposal for a new order of worship; he did not want it to be viewed as a law. Luther's religious genius, however, was so outstanding that he involuntarily became an authority in theological and ecclesiastical questions, even to the point of becoming a "church father." In the Lutheran camp one hardly dared contradict him in questions of doctrine; even Melanchthon shied away from controversies.

Publicly Luther did not have a prominent position; he was a professor like his colleagues, even though in the last decade of his life he held the position of dean. In addition to this he often filled the role in Wittenberg of city pastor. In this connection he compared himself to Augustine, "the poor, insignificant pastor at Hippo," who achieved more for the church theologically than did most of the Councils.[160]

Luther's influence extended far beyond Wittenberg; questions came to him from every quarter. He advised the Grand Master Albrecht to transform the lands of his order into a secular duchy. He drew up numerous theological opinions. His correspondence includes well in excess of 4000 items; a great number of these dealt with more than personal matters. He was constantly asked to provide forewords for newly published books; the *Hilfsbuch zum*

Lutherstudium by Aland lists no less than 118, including the prefaces to his own books. This shows how sought-after his authoritative recommendation was and how broad his range of interests was. As theological advisor for his elector, he became involved in the churchly and worldly politics of his time. In a reply to Hans Kohlhase Luther warned him against wanting to be his own judge.[161]

The precious, humorous letter that Luther directed to Provost George Buchholzer in Berlin on December 4, 1539, should also be mentioned.[162] Buchholzer had reservations about the strong, traditional church order that Elector Joachim II wanted to introduce. According to Luther, ceremonies, vestments, rites, and processions did no harm if they were not in conflict with the gospel. He used examples from the Old Testament to illustrate the need for great freedom in dealing with external matters.

It was in this sense that Martin Luther actually became a "church father."

Illnesses and Death

By nature Luther had a healthy constitution. While still in the monastery he survived more than a few severe physical strains without great injury. We need only recall his journeys by foot to Rome, to Heidelberg, and to Augsburg. But apparently the excessive asceticism of the cloister had, over the years, impaired his health. Throughout his lifetime Luther was plagued by restless sleep. In Leipzig he appeared to Mosellanus to be abnormally thin. He had unwisely exposed his tonsure to the blazing sun, only to suffer later from repeated, splitting headaches. Often he had not eaten or drunk anything for three days, and he had forcibly suppressed bowel movements and urination.

The book *Dr. Martin Luthers Krankengeschichte* (Leipzig: 1881) by the physician Friedrich Küchenmeister still provides the best information on Luther's illnesses. By contrast, the previously cited work by Paul J. Reiter, despite its wealth of material, is of less value because of its one-sided judgment of phenomena.[1] Reiter considered even poorly documented, negative reports about Luther as "not inconceivable." He stated that there was "a definite possibility that Luther had syphilis, though it cannot be determined with certainty." [2] "With good intentions [!] one could also consider the possibility that Luther suffered from epilepsy." [3] According to Reiter, "Luther's great attack of mental illness" occurred in the years 1527–1528.[4] The enormous amount of work that Luther nevertheless accomplished was explained by Reiter as "compensation."

But back to Luther's catalog of illnesses! On the way to Augsburg he was overtaken by a severe stomach disorder.[5] At the Wartburg he suffered from constipation, and in January 1528 he had hemorrhoids; for six days he had no bowel movements.[6] Nervous agitation, unusually heavy meals, and lack of exercise may have been the cause. He is reported to have fainted in his cell on the 24th of August [?], 1523. In 1526 he experienced his first attack of stones, which were to trouble him so often; they were kidney stones. At the beginning of January 1527 he had a choking fit brought on by heart trouble.[7] On April 22, 1527, he was forced to break off a sermon because of an attack of dizziness.[8]

Early on July 6, 1527, he was overcome by severe despair. In retrospect he wrote to Melanchthon (on August 2) that he had spent more than a week in death and hell and had completely lost Christ.[9] A terrible buzzing began in his ears, and he passed out. Expecting death, he said goodbye to his wife and his young son Hans. He made his confession to Bugenhagen and received absolution from him. We have detailed reports about this incident from both Bugenhagen and Justus Jonas.[10] Luther thus found that anguish of the spirit was more difficult than physical disorders.[11] It was weeks before he had at least partially recovered. But he did not doubt the validity of his work of Reformation, and "his" Christ had also triumphed in the midst of despair.[12]

In August 1527 the first cases of the Plague appeared in Wittenberg; the epidemic broke out in December. Luther refused to leave Wittenberg, despite the request of the elector.[13] Though he did not personally take ill, he experienced cases of the illness in his immediate surroundings. He was worried about his young son and his wife, who was at the time expecting their second child; little Elisabeth was subsequently born in good health on December 10, 1527, but she died on August 3 of the following year. Since only five of Luther's pigs perished during the Plague, he said, jokingly, that the Plague must have been satisfied with this "census." [14]

On April 14, 1529, he reported to Justus Jonas that he was experiencing severe hoarseness along with anginal and catarrhal troubles;[15] today we would probably call it a serious case of the flu. At the Coburg Luther suffered severe headaches, as already mentioned, and stomach disorders; in addition, his shinbone would not heal properly. After that time the headaches occurred more frequently.

Perhaps the most serious disturbance was an attack of renal colic that occurred while he was staying in Smalcald in 1537. He had already complained of it when he set out from Wittenberg on January 31. On February 8 and 14 he passed stones, but the pains returned. Ratzeberger, the personal physician of the elector, reported this incident in his story of Luther and his times. Luther preached on the morning of February 18, and in the afternoon the pains became unbearable. Urination was impossible, he could not keep his food down, and he could not sleep. His entire body became swollen.

Various physicians were sent to him, and they tried to help by giving him a catheter and a liquid medication to drink that was made from garlic and horse manure. But nothing helped. He placed himself in God's hands and anticipated his imminent death. He entrusted his Katie to the care of his friends. He was worried about the future of the evangelical church. He said that he would have preferred to have died at home rather than in the view of the papal legates in Smalcald.

On February 26 the elector provided his personal wagon for Luther's journey home. The jolting of the ride shifted the stone, and an opening was created through which the urine could slowly pass. That happened on the first night after they had stopped in Tambach. Filled with gratitude to God, Luther immediately (it was about 2:30 in the morning) wrote to Melanchthon in Smalcald with the news.[16] He had been able to urinate no less than eight times, and was so happy that he had collected it in a jug, "completely worthless to others, but of the greatest value to me." Surely God had appeared to him in Tambach, and he called it his Penuel.[17] Shortly afterward, around 3:00 A.M., he also wrote to his wife; through God's grace her husband had been returned to her, and the children once again had their father. "In two hours about one *Stübig* [three to four liters] passed from me, and I feel as if I were born again." [18]

But on the next day, in Gotha, the pains returned. During the night of March 1 he was so miserable that he gave Bugenhagen, who had accompanied him on the journey home, his last instructions, which Bugenhagen later recorded as Luther's "Last Testament." [19] But six stones left him in Gotha, one as large as a bean. So the journey could continue. On March 14 they arrived in Wittenberg, where, after a few days, he again passed two stones. On March 21

Luther informed Spalatin that, after severe weakness, he was once more slowly recovering.[20]

But Luther was never again truly a healthy person. One or another disorder continually plagued him: intestinal problems, colic from stones, rheumatism, and attacks of sciatica or dizziness. On April 12, 1541, he reported to Melanchthon an extremely painful inflammation of the sinuses and a middle ear irritation, so severe that the tears flowed from his eyes (which otherwise seldom happened), until relief was provided by an incision in the eardrum.[21] But then he had to fear the complete loss of his hearing. Luther felt weak, old, useless, and tired of living.[22]

On March 30, 1544, he wrote to Sibylle of Saxony in this vein: "The age has arrived in which one knows that he is old and cold and awkward, ill and weak." [23] In an attempt to relieve his headaches, in the fall of 1543 Luther received a fontanel on his left leg, which he had to keep continuously flowing. At the end he also seems to have developed a cataract in his eye.[24] Death finally came when his heart and lungs gave out.

Luther was not a complaining patient. Much like Bismarck, he had often not adhered to dietary prescriptions. While he was suffering from stones in 1526, Katie wanted to prepare some food for him. To her dismay he asked for a fried herring with cold peas and mustard. On the other hand, Luther did not ignore the advice of the physicians, even though he often found it difficult to comply with it. One year after Smalcald he declared, "I was at that time sufficiently annoyed by the physicians. They gave me as much to drink as if I had been a big ox. They worked over my body until all my members, even my private parts, became lifeless. I had to obey the physicians. I did what I did from necessity, lest I appear to neglect my body." [25]

In June of 1540 the physicians advised Luther to take mineral baths. "I am in agreement, and I am pleased that the doctors are devoted to their methods, but they ought not make people prisoners with their rules." Since the doctors had given different prescriptions at other times, he did not want to swear by their pronouncements. "The doctors want to make a fixed star of me, but I am a planet and irregular." [26] In Smalcald Luther became angry; when the doctors gave him the garlic juice and horse manure mixture to drink, he told them, "Don't show up here again! I would rather die." [27]

Luther said there were many "daring" doctors who treated people without giving careful examinations; "they must own a new cemetery." On the other hand, there were also timid doctors who irritated their patients by their indecision. Doctors dealt only with the "natural" aspect of illness and healing. They didn't take into account the fact that the devil was at work in natural causes. Against him we need a "superior medication," namely "faith and prayer." [28] He also attributed his recovery after the Smalcald attack to the prayers of his friends.[29] "My best prescription is recorded in John 3:16: 'God so loved the world.' That is the best that I have." [30]

Luther did not overlook the role that work played in treatment. At the Coburg, for example, he worked heroically, in spite of his headaches. And he always returned to his activities as soon as he found the slightest relief. He seldom spoke of his pains in detail; for the most part he only touched on them with a few sentences.

There may well be a connection between Luther's physical illnesses and his attacks of *Anfechtung,* but we cannot simply blame these attacks on physical or purely nervous disorders. Such an interpretation reveals the limitations of an exclusively medical or psychological approach. One cannot understand Luther's *Anfechtung* if one does not recognize it also as a religious phenomenon. His earlier, monastic struggle with the question of a gracious God continued to be present in it. For Luther, the "certainty of salvation" never became self-evident. Time and again the question surfaced as to whether "he alone was right"—an accusation that had been leveled against him at Worms. The observation that his work had not been as successful in turning the tide as he had hoped gave rise to inner doubts. He found it painful that others died for the gospel while martyrdom was denied him.

As a pastor Luther had often given practical suggestions for overcoming attacks of *Anfechtung.* The last resort, however, was always to flee to Christ, in whom God's mercy had appeared. In the Gospel for Reminscere Sunday, Matthew 15:21ff., we meet the Canaanite woman who did not allow herself to be discouraged by Christ's apparent rebuke. "This shows us how the human heart feels in its *Anfechtung.* Christ here recognizes and addresses that feeling. The heart perceives nothing but no, and yet that isn't so. The heart must turn from such feelings, grab hold of and cling fast, with firm faith in God's Word, to the profound, yet hidden yes surrounding every no, and accept God's right to judge us. Thus, in the end we are victors, and capture God in his own words." [31]

Luther was at times annoyed and disgruntled during his last decade of life; as his illnesses increased, so did his irritability. There were occasional bursts of anger. The theologians as well as the jurists caused him grief. He thought they lacked necessary moral seriousness. He was disturbed by the theological quarrels within his own ranks. Indecent fashions in Wittenberg outraged him.

By the end of July 1545 Luther had had enough. He was in Leipzig on a trip, and from Zeitz he informed his wife (on July 28) that he did not want to return to Wittenberg.[32] He wrote: "My heart is chilled." Katie was to go to Zulsdorf. The elector would continue to pay Luther's stipend for the rest of his life, even if he didn't live in Wittenberg any longer. It took great effort to persuade Luther to return, though he postponed going back until August 16. He was promised assistance in correcting the abuses there.

Since Lessing in his *Rettungen* later took up his cause, the young humanist and poet Simon Lemnius (at the time a student in Wittenberg) should also be mentioned. In 1538 he had published epigrams which he dedicated to Cardinal Albert and in which he had made derogatory remarks about leading citizens of Wittenberg. He was to have been brought before a university tribunal, but fled before his case could be heard. Luther denounced him in a public notice from the pulpit.[33] Lemnius avenged himself by increasing the printing and distribution of his epigrams, in which he now included Luther among those he defamed.

Luther refrained from any further public attacks, but composed several satirical Latin verses against Lemnius, which he read to his friends.[34] That same year Luther also wrote a new tract against Albert of Mainz, and then had it printed (against the wishes of the elector). As a result the elector forbade him from publishing anything concerning personal affairs without first having submitted it to the electoral court.

The picture would be distorted, however, if one took only these things into account and imagined the old Luther only as an ill, morose, and irritable man. His letters to Katie while on the journey to Eisleben show that he had not lost his sense of humor. His activities had not decreased, and he could still vent himself in an almost frightening way, as he did in his last work against the papacy.[35]

Luther was a genius, and there is always a certain isolation connected with that; but he was definitely not lonely. Around him was a circle of friends and co-workers who respected him and even loved him, though at times they were also afraid of him. He understood himself as a member of the congregation and was thankful for the communion of faith. He hoped the last day would come soon, but he did not withdraw from his daily duties. He worried about the future of Germany and the evangelical church; but he also called for prayers for Germany,[36] and on June 20, 1543, he wrote to Wenceslas Link: "I do not leave our congregations in poor shape; they flourish in pure and sound teaching, and they grow day by day through [the ministry of] many excellent and most sincere pastors." [37]

Luther's life was full of battles; but it concluded with a work of reconciliation. The counts of Mansfeld, to whom Luther had felt particularly bound because of his birthplace, had over the years been engaged in continuing conflicts with one another over various legal rights. Count Albrecht III (1480-1560), the ancestral lord of the region in which Luther was born, was a champion of the Reformation in his territory, but otherwise did not have a very good reputation. He was at odds not only with his cousins, but also interfered with his own brother. His subjects who were employed in the mines also complained about oppression and exploitation because of the count's avarice.

Luther had already appealed to his "dear Lord of the land" [38] on their behalf in May of 1540, and he did so a second time in February of 1542.[39] In 1545 Albrecht announced that he was prepared to accept Luther's mediation. At the beginning of October Luther, Melanchthon, and Jonas traveled to Mansfeld; the negotiations, however, did not reach the intended goal, because the count had to mobilize his forces against Heinrich von Braunschweig. Shortly before Christmas Luther was in Mansfeld a second time, but had to leave early because of his concern for his companion Melanchthon's physical condition.[40]

A third trip was planned for the end of January. This time the meeting was to take place in Eisleben. The journey began on Saturday, January 23, 1546. Luther was accompanied by his three sons (Hans, Martin, and Paul), his assistant Johann Aurifaber (who recorded the table talks of the last days), and his servant and home tutor Rudtfeld.[41] They arrived in Halle on January 25 and were joined by Justus Jonas. They were detained there for three days by flooding and an ice jam on the Saale River. Luther reported this to his wife on January 25, calling the Saale a "huge Anabaptist." Instead of the river's water they drank "good beer from Torgau and good wine from the Rhine." [42]

On the next day, January 26 (the Conversion of St. Paul), Luther preached on Acts 9. On January 28 they undertook the crossing of the Saale. When they came into Mansfeld they were received by an honor guard sent by the count that included more than 100 horsemen. They entered Eisleben on the 29th. Just outside the city Luther suffered a fainting spell. He reported this to Katie in a humorous letter written on February 1 and addressed "To my dearly beloved mistress of the house, Katherine Luther, a doctor, the lady of Zölsdorf [and] of the pig market, and whatever else she is capable of being." [43] He said the spell was his own fault; he had perspired and caught a cold. But he thought Katie would have said that it was the fault of the Jews, for they had to pass through a town close to Eisleben where many Jews lived, and they had perhaps "attacked me so painfully. . . . Such a cold wind blew from behind into the carriage and on my head through the beret, as if intended to turn my brain to ice." Now he was feeling good again. He signed the letter, "Your loving Martin Luther, who has grown old."

On January 31 he was able to preach again. He wrote to his wife frequently in order to ease her worries about him. He also kept Melanchthon regularly informed. The second letter from Eisleben, "To the highly-learned woman, Catherine Lüther, my gracious mistress at the house at Wittenberg," is dated February 6.[44] He said he would feel good, if only their "disgusting business" would get finished.

The third letter was written on February 7.[45] Katie was to forget her worries and read the *Catechism,* a book of which she had once said that everything in it was about her. God had preserved him from the Saale and, on another occasion, from burning during a chimney fire in his lodging on February 2. "Free me from your worries. I have a caretaker who is better than you and all the angels; he lies in the cradle and rests on a virgin's bosom, and yet, nevertheless, he sits at the right hand of God, the almighty Father." [46] There in Eisleben, all the devils had gathered, so bogged down were the negotiations. There were also many Jews there, against whom he preached. He was actually so angry that he could have "greased the carriage," that is, left, but the misery in his homeland held him back. The wine was good, but the beer contained too much pitch, and he felt it on his chest.

The next letter to Katie was sent on February 10.[47] While she was busy worrying about him, he had almost been burned in a fire directly outside the door to his room, and the previous day in the "secret chamber," a stone from the ceiling missed falling on his head by a hairsbreadth. He had left his caustic behind in Wittenberg, which he needed to keep the wound on his calf open. On February 14 he asked Melanchthon to send it as soon as possible.[48]

The fourth and last letter to Katie was sent on February 14.[49] Luther hoped to return home that week. The negotiations for a settlement had almost been completed. Along with the letter he sent Katie trout, which the countess Anna von Mansfeld had given him. With that the correspondence ended. The last letter arrived in Wittenberg on the day of Luther's death.

Luther preached four times in Eisleben, the last time on February 15.[50] He broke off with the words, "I am too weak and we shall let it go at that." The negotiations caused him much frustration, even though he only participated in them for an hour to an hour and a half each day. On February 16 they finally reached a positive outcome. The last note we have from Luther's hand came the same day. It was found on the table after his death. It was written in Latin and reads as follows in translation:

> No one can understand Virgil's shepherd and peasant songs unless he has been a shepherd or a peasant for at least five years. No one can understand Cicero's letters, so I imagine, unless he has spent 20 years in public affairs. No one can claim to have understood the Holy Scriptures adequately unless he has presided over the congregations for 100 years with the prophets. Do not lay your hand on these divine *Aeneids*, but in deep devotion follow their footsteps. We are beggars. That is true.

The exact wording of the text is not reliable, but the two concluding sentences are certain.[51] They have become established as a sort of testament by Luther.

On Wednesday, February 17, a further agreement was reached to which Luther also attached his signature. Then he withdrew to his room.[52] Justus Jonas and Michael Cölius, the Mansfeld court preacher, remained with him. Luther prayed often; in between he said to the two of them: "I was baptized here in Eisleben, what if I should stay here?" During the evening meal he was still jovial, though he felt some pressure on his chest. There were cheerful as well as serious conversations, even about seeing one another after death.

After returning to his room he once again experienced chest pains. He was rubbed with towels and given an expensive medication, after which he slept on a couch from 9:00 to 10:00 P.M. Jonas, Cölius, and his sons kept watch at his side. Luther wanted them to leave him and he went into his bedroom, saying these words of prayer (in Latin): "Into thy hands I commit my spirit; thou hast redeemed me, O Lord, faithful God."[53] He slept until 1:00 A.M., when he again complained of chest pains and lay down on the couch in the room.

The city clerk, in whose house he was living, and two physicians were summoned. Soon Count Albrecht and his wife also arrived, and later the Count and Countess von Schwarzburg. Luther felt death was close. He thanked God for having disclosed his Son to him, and he commended his soul into God's hands. He repeated the verse from Psalm 31 three more times. Then he was silent. Jonas and Cölius spoke loudly into his ear: "Reverend father, are you willing forever to persevere in the Christian faith and doctrine that you have preached?" He replied with an audible "Yes." That was his last word.

Death occurred between 2:00 and 3:00 A.M. on February 18. The (Catholic) pharmacist was summoned, who made a last attempt at resuscitation, but without success. About 4:00 A.M. the remaining counts of Mansfeld, the prince of Anholt, and several other lords and citizens of the city appeared in order to take their leave of Luther. The body was clothed in a long robe of white linen and placed in a tin coffin, past which hundreds of people walked.

An artist from Eisleben painted a portrait of Luther's face before noon, and another, Lukas Fortnagel of Halle, did so after the body had lain one night in the coffin. On the afternoon of February 19, Justus Jonas preached the funeral sermon in the principal church (St. Andrews) on 1 Thessalonians 4:13-18. A night watch in the church was assumed by 10 citizens of the city.

On February 20, after a sermon by Cölius on Isaiah 57:1-2, the transfer of the body to Wittenberg was begun. Everywhere along the way people streamed together to the tolling of church bells. In Halle a wax death mask was made. The procession arrived in Wittenberg on the morning of February 22. Students had told Melanchthon of Luther's death on February 19; he responded with the words: "Alas, the charioteer and the chariot of Israel,[54] who ruled the church in this time-worn world, has passed away." [55]

On February 22, at about 9:00 A.M., the body was received by representatives of the university and the city at the Elster gate. The procession proceeded directly to the castle church, in which Luther was buried. The clergy, professors, and students sang funeral hymns along the way. They were followed on horseback by the representatives of the elector, the two counts of Mansfeld, and their cortege. Behind the coffin, Katie rode in a small, simple wagon, accompanied by several other women. They were followed by the three sons, along with various relatives, university persons, the city council of Wittenberg, and the students and citizens of the city.

In the castle church Bugenhagen preached with great warmth on the same text that Jonas had used in Eisleben. Then Melanchthon, as a representative of the university, gave an address in Latin.[56] He praised the accomplishments that Luther had, by God's grace, been able to achieve for the renewal of the church. He placed him among the series of chosen instruments which God had used since the days of the Old Covenant. He pointed to his courage, his keen intellect, and his unique eloquence. His vehemence came from his zeal for the truth. They had lost a father. He had stood before them to admonish them. Now he was among the throngs of those perfected and was being greeted by the prophets as their companion.

By including Luther among the prophets, in this speech Melanchthon poignantly described his significance. One can point out many things about Luther: he was a brilliant theologian, a creator of language, an artist, a hero, and an outstanding preacher and pastor. And yet it is not saying too much to describe him as a prophet.[57] He had humbly declined this title, but at the same time he was conscious of his prophetic task. "I do not claim to be a prophet, but I do say that the more they scorn me and the higher they regard themselves, the more reason they have to fear that I may be a prophet." God had spoken to Balaam through an ass; God did not respect great skill and power. So God could also use Luther as his instrument. "Even if I am not a prophet, as far as I am concerned I am sure that the Word of God is with me and not with them." [58]

The juxtaposition of his denial of the prophetic title and the certainty of his prophetic task is characteristic of Luther. A prophet is not primarily a person who predicts the future, but rather a person who reveals the will of God; who is called by God to be a herald. Luther was conscious of this calling, even though at the same time he pointed to his orderly and proper calling as a teacher of Holy Scripture. He did not doubt that God had elected him for a unique purpose.

Luther felt a special obligation toward his Germans and often spoke of himself as "the prophet of the Germans." [59] As such, and like the prophets of the Old Covenant, he could not avoid warning the people of the judgment of God. "It is not my purpose to foretell the future for Germany from the stars, but to proclaim the wrath of God from theology; for it is impossible that Germany will continue without great hardship, for daily God is being provoked to destroy us." [60] "Such woe will befall Germany that it will be said: Germany once stood here." [61] Luther's concern for that which would come was a heavy burden on his mind. In this, only prayer and the hope of the last day were of help to him. He had to experience both the heights and the depths of the prophetic office.

Those who concern themselves with Luther's life cannot help but grow fond of him, in spite of many reservations. It is also crucial that our generation carry on his prophetic work.

Chronological Table

1378–   The great schism in the western church, with antipopes in
1417   Avignon and Rome
1453   Conquest of Constantinople by the Turks
1477   Death of Charles the Bold of Burgundy and marriage of
        Maximilian of Hapsburg to Charles' daughter (and heir);
        beginning of the war between the house of Hapsburg and
        France
1483   Birth of Martin Luther on November 10th in Eisleben
1484   Luther's family moves to Mansfeld
1492   Columbus discovers the West Indies
1498   Savonarola executed in Florence as a heretic
1501–   Luther studies in Erfurt, after attending schools in Mans-
1505   feld, Magdeburg, and Eisenach
1505   Luther enters the monastery on July 17
1507   Luther is ordained as a priest
1510–   Luther's trip to Rome; begins lecturing in Wittenberg
1511
1512   Luther receives his doctorate in theology; begins his major
        lectures; is district superintendent of his order
1514   "Poor Konrad's" peasant rebellion in Württemberg
1515   *Letters of Obscure Men* written in conflict with Johann
        Reuchlin
1516   Erasmus of Rotterdam publishes his Greek New Testament;
        Luther publishes *A German Theology*
1517   Conflict over indulgences and Luther's 95 *Theses*

1518   Luther appears before Cajetan in Augsburg in October/November; Philip Melanchthon is called to Wittenberg

1519   Charles V is chosen as emperor; Leipzig Disputation (July); the mission of Karl von Miltitz

1520   Papal bull threatens Luther with excommunication; on December 10th Luther burns the bull and the canon law; Luther publishes his works *Address to the German Nobility, The Babylonian Captivity of the Church,* and *The Freedom of a Christian.*

1521   Diet of Worms and Luther comes under the ban of the empire; Luther at the Wartburg

1522   Unrest in Wittenberg and Luther's return; in September he publishes his *German New Testament*

1523   Collapse of the knights' revolt led by Sickingen; death of Ulrich von Hutten; Diet of Nuremberg

1525   Battle of Pavia; German Peasants' War; death of Thomas Müntzer at Frankenhausen; Luther's writings against the peasants; Luther's work *The Bondage of the Will;* Luther's marriage to Katharina von Bora

1526   Alliance between the pope and France against Charles V; victory of the Turks over the Hungarians at Mohács; Diet of Speyer

1527   Sack of Rome by the troops of Charles V; beginning of church visitations in Electoral Saxony

1528   Conflict between the Wittenberg and Swiss theologians

1529   Diet of Speyer; revocation of stance of tolerance, and "protest" of the Protestants; dialog between Luther and Zwingli in Marburg; publication of the *Large* and *Small Catechisms*

1530   Diet of Augsburg; *Augsburg Confession;* Luther at the Coburg castle

1531   Smalcaldic League (lasted until 1546); Swiss civil war and death of Zwingli at Kappel

1532   "Peace of Nuremberg" concerning freedom of religion; the Turks threaten to move beyond Hungary

1534   Württemberg becomes Protestant; Anabaptists take over Münster (crushed in 1535); England breaks with Rome (Supremacy Act); publication of Luther's complete German translation of the Bible

Bibliography

1. Comprehensive Editions of Luther's Works

Kritische Gesamtausgabe (Weimar Edition). Weimar: 1883ff. 1. Abteilung Schriften. 2. Abteilung Tischreden. 3. Abteilung Deutsche Bibel. 4. Abteilung Briefe. The Weimar Edition currently includes 104 volumes.

The "Erlangen Edition" (1826ff.) was superseded by the Weimar Edition. It is still needed, however, because the literature often cites the *Briefe Luthers* edited by Ernst Ludwig Enders, Gustav Kawerau, and others. 19 vols. 1884-1932.

2. Selected Editions of Luther's Works

a. Original Texts

The so-called Clemen or Bonner Edition. *Luthers Werke in Auswahl.* Multiple editors. 8 vols. New ed. Berlin: 1959-1963. Recommended especially for theologians.

Lutherausgabe in der DDR. Edited by Hans-Ulrich Delius. Vol. 1. East Berlin: 1979. By 1983, five volumes were to appear.

b. Modern High German Translations

Münchener Ausgabe. Edited by H. H. Borcherdt and Georg Merz. 6 vols. and a supplementary volume. 3rd ed. 1948ff.

Berliner Ausgabe. Luther Deutsch. Edited by Kurt Aland. 10 vols., an index volume, and a Luther dictionary. Berlin (later Stuttgart): 1948ff.

Calwer Lutherausgabe. Edited by Wolfgang Metzger. 12 vols. Gütersloh: 1964ff.

See also: Hans Volz. "Lutherausgaben." *Religion in Geschichte und Gegenwart* (RGG). Vol. 4. Cols. 520-523. 3rd ed. 1960.

3. Helpful Resources

A Luther chronology by Georg Buchwald and a catalog of Luther's writings (listing their order of appearance in the Weimar and Erlangen editions) by Gustav Kawerau is found in *Schriften des Vereins für Reformationsgeschichte.* Vol. 47. No. 147. Leipzig: 1929.

Aland, Kurt. *Hilfsbuch zum Lutherstudium.* Berlin: 1957. 3rd ed. 1970. Includes alphabetical and chronological lists of Luther's writings.

Buchwald, Georg. *Beginn eines Gesamtregisters.* Vol. 58, I of the Weimar Edition (see above). Weimar: 1948. A larger version of this is no longer planned.

4. Additional Literature

The most prominent technical, overall biography is still Julius Köstlin, *Martin Luther: Sein Leben und seine Schriften.* Edited by Gustav Kawerau. 2 vols. 5th ed. Berlin: 1903; *Life of Luther* (New York: Longmans, 1912). The less complete biographies by O. Scheel, H. Boehmer, M. Brecht, and H. Bornkamm are listed in the notes.

Stephan, Horst. *Luther in den Wandlungen seiner Kirche.* 2nd ed. Berlin: 1951.

Since 1957 the *Luther-Jahrbuch* of the Luther-Gesellschaft has provided a complete, annual bibliography of all new titles on Luther.

Lutherforschung heute. (Prior to 1938, *Deutsche Lutherforschung.*) Berlin: 1958. Pp. 161-171.

"Martin Luther." I. Leben und Schriften; by H. Bornkamm. II. Theologie; by G. Ebeling. *Religion in Geschichte und Gegenwart* (RGG). Vol. 4. Cols. 480-520. 3rd ed. 1960. Includes bibliography.

von Loewenich, Walther. "Wandlungen des evangelischen Lutherbildes im 19. und 20. Jahrhundert." *Wandlungen des Lutherbildes.* Studien und Berichte der katholischen Akademie in Bayern. Vol. 36. Würzburg: 1966.

von Loewenich, Walther. "Evangelische und katholische Lutherdeutung der Gegenwart im Dialog." *Luther-Jahrbuch 1967.* Pp. 60-89.

Koch, Hans-Gerhard. *Luthers Reformation in kommunistischer Sicht.* Stuttgart: 1967. cf. Franz Lau in *Luther-Jahrbuch 1969,* p. 95.

Wartenberg, Günther. "Bibliographie der marxistischen Luther-Literatur in der DDR 1945-1966." *Luther-Jahrbuch 1968.* Pp. 162-172.

Lohse, Bernhard. "Die Lutherforschung im deutschen Sprachbereich seit 1966." *Luther-Jahrbuch 1971.* Pp. 91-120.

Wolf, Gerhard Philipp. *Das neuere französische Lutherbild.* Wiesbaden: 1974.

The *Luther-Jahrbuch 1977* contains an overview of the most recent international Luther research.

Kremer, Ulrich Michael. *Die Reformation als Problem der amerikanischen Historiographie.* Wiesbaden: 1978.

Wolf, Herbert. *Martin Luther: Eine Einführung in germanistische Luther-Studien.* Stuttgart: 1980.

Lohse, Bernhard. *Martin Luther: Eine Einführung in sein Leben und sein Werk.* Munich: 1981.

Helmut Riege lists selected titles from the vast literature on Luther in the very accessible, short biography by Hanns Lilje, *Luther.* Reinbek: 1965. Pp. 134-153.

References to specialized literature are found in the notes to this volume.

Notes

The following abbreviations are used:

WA   *Kritische Gesamtausgabe.* The "Weimar Edition" of Luther's Works. Weimar: 1883ff.

WATR   *Kritische Gesamtausgabe. Tischreden.* The *Table Talk* from the Weimar Edition.

WADB   *Kritische Gesamtausgabe. Deutsche Bibel.* The German Bible from the Weimar Edition.

WABr   *Kritische Gesamtausgabe. Briefwechsel.* Letters from the Weimar Edition.

AE   *Luther's Works.* American Edition. Edited by Jaroslav Pelikan and Helmut T. Lehmann. St. Louis and Philadelphia: Concordia Publishing House and Fortress Press.

CR   *Corpus Reformatorum*

Tappert   *The Book of Concord: The Confessions of the Evangelical Lutheran Church,* trans. and ed. Theodore G. Tappert (Philadelphia: Fortress, 1959).

Vg   Vulgate

INTRODUCTION: PATHS TO LUTHER
Chapter 1. A Controversial Figure

1. Adolf Herte, *Das Katholische Lutherbild im Bann der Lutherkommentare des Cochläus,* 3 vols. (Münster: 1943).
2. Walther von Loewenich, *Luther und Lessing: Sammlung gemeinverständlicher Vorträge und Schriften,* vol. 232 (Tübingen: 1960).

3. Gerhard Philipp Wolf, *Das neuere französische Lutherbild* (Wiesbaden: 1974).
4. "Die evangelische Kirche in Deutschland nach dem Zusammenbruch des dritten Reiches," in Eberhard Busch, *Karl Barths Lebenslauf* (Munich: 1975), p. 318; *Karl Barth: His Life from Letters and Autobiographical Texts*, trans. John Bowden (Philadelphia: Fortress, 1976).
5. Gorden Rupp, *Martin Luther: Hitler's Cause or Cure* (Cambridge: Lutterworth, 1945).
6. Ernst Bloch, *Thomas Münzer als Theologe der Revolution* (Munich: 1921; Berlin: 1960).
7. Hans Gerhard Koch, *Luthers Reformation in kommunistischer Sicht* (Stuttgart: 1967).
8. Dieter Forte, *Martin Luther und Thomas Münzer oder die Einführung der Buchhaltung* (Berlin: 1971); *Luther, Münzer, and the Bookkeepers of the Reformation,* trans. Christopher Holme (New York: McGraw-Hill, 1972).
9. Cf. "Luther als Bühnenheld," ed. Friedrich Kraft, *Zur Sache: Kirchliche Aspekte heute,* vol. 8 (Hamburg: 1971).
10. See p. 6 of my contribution to the work cited in note 9.
11. See the detailed assessment by Kurt Aland in *Martin Luther in der modernen Literatur* (Witten and Berlin: 1973).
12. Ibid., pp. 359-360; Werke X, 375-376.
13. See Acts 26:24.
14. Kurt Aland, *Luther in der modernen Literatur,* p. 367.
15. Wilhelm Walter, *Luthers Charakter* (Leipzig: 1917).

Chapter 2. On the Eve of the Reformation

1. In addition to the larger works by Ranke, Gregorovius, and Pastor, the small volume by Hans Kühner should be noted: *Lexikon der Päpste* (Frankfurt am Main: 1960). See the bibliography included in that volume.
2. Luke 16:9.
3. Denzinger and Bannwart, *Enchiridion symbolorum, definitionum et declarationum de rebus fidei et morum,* no. 734 (Freiburg: 1928). See also the 33rd edition by Denzinger and Schönmetzer (Freiburg: 1965).
4. Denzinger and Bannwart, no. 735.
5. Denzinger and Bannwart, no. 1641.
6. Alexander III, in 1179, at the Third Lateran Council.
7. Mirbt and Aland, *Quellen zur Geschichte des Päpsttums und des römischen Katholizismus,* vol. 1, no. 780 (Tübingen: 1967).
8. Herbert Grundmann, "Ketzergeschichte des Mittelalters," in *Die Kirche in ihrer Geschichte,* eds. Kurt Dietrich Schmidt and Ernst Wolf, 2nd ed., vol. 2, part G (Göttingen: 1967), pp. 42-43.

9. "Wegbereiter der Reformation," in *Klassiker des Protestantismus*, vol. 1, ed. Gustav Benrath, compiled by Dieterich (Bremen: 1967).

10. Hanns Rückert, *Die geistesgeschichtliche Einordnung der Reformation: Vorträge und Aufsätze zur historischen Theologie* (Tübingen: 1972), pp. 52ff.

11. Johann Huizinga, *Europäischer Humanismus: Erasmus* (Hamburg: 1958).

12. A comprehensive and brilliant depiction of the beginning of the new era is given by Willy Andreas in *Deutschland vor der Reformation* (Berlin: 1943).

PART ONE: THE DEVELOPMENT OF THE REFORMER

Chapter 3. Childhood and Youth

1. Heinrich Fausel has provided sources for Luther's life and work in vols. 11 and 12 of the Calwer Edition, 3rd (paperback) edition of Luther's Works (Gütersloh: 1977). Basic concerning the childhood and youth of Luther are the works by Heinrich Boehmer and Otto Scheel: Heinrich Boehmer, *Der Junge Luther*, ed. Heinrich Bornkamm, 6th ed. (Stuttgart: 1971); *Martin Luther: Road to Reformation*, trans. John W. Doberstein and Theodore G. Tappert (New York: Meridien, 1967) (That volume takes Luther to 1521); Otto Scheel, *Martin Luther: Vom Katholizismus zur Reformation*, vol. 1. (Tübingen: 1921); vol. 2 (concluding with 1513–1514) (Tübingen: 1930); more recently, Martin Brecht, *Martin Luther: Sein Weg Zur Reformation 1483-1521* (Stuttgart: 1981); *Martin Luther: His Road to Reformation 1483-1521* (Philadelphia: Fortress, 1985). Brecht opts for a late dating of Luther's "reforming discovery" and categorizes the theology of Luther prior to 1518 as a "theology of humility." According to Brecht, the posting of the *95 Theses* took place after the 31st of October, probably in the middle of November (see his p. 197). Another recent volume is Helmar Junghans, *Wittenberg als Lutherstadt* (Berlin: 1979).

2. WATR 5, no. 6250.

3. WABr 2, 338, 55; AE 48, 227.

4. WATR 4, no. 4996.

5. H. Hahne, "Luthers Totenmaske," in *Vierteljahresschrift der Luthergesellschaft* 1931, pp. 74ff.

6. Letter of November 1, 1521, to Gerbel in Strasbourg; WABr 2, 397, 34; AE 48, 320.

7. WATR 5, no. 5428.

8. H. E. Matthes, "Luthers mütterliche Abstammung und Verwandschaft," in *Archiv für Sippenforschung*, nos. 5-7, 1935.

9. WA 53, 511, 32; AE 47, 121.

10. WA 6, 81, 30.

11. WATR 3, no. 2888; AE 54, 178.

12. WATR 1, no. 137; AE 54, 20.
13. WATR 2, no. 1559; AE 54, 157.
14. WATR 3, no. 3566A; AE 54, 235.
15. WATR 2, no. 2756a.
16. WA 38, 338, 6.
17. WATR 4, no. 5050.
18. Erik H. Erickson, *Der junge Mann Luther* (Reinbek: 1970); *Young Man Luther* (New York: Norton, 1962).
19. Heinrich Bornkamm, "Luther und sein Vater," *Zeitschrift für Theologie und Kirche* 66 (1969): 38-61; Franz Lau, *Luther-Jahrbuch 1966*, pp. 148-149.
20. WATR 1, no. 137; AE 54, 20.
21. WA 30, II, 576, 13; AE 46, 207.
22. WADB 4, 29, 11.
23. WABr 5, 349, 18.
24. WABr 5, 351, 20; AE 49, 318-319.
25. WABr 6, 103; AE 50, 17-21.
26. WA 25, 460, 10.
27. WA 44, 711, 38ff.; AE 8, 181-182.
28. WA 47, 379, 3.
29. WATR 5, no. 5558.
30. WA 39, II, 167, 20; AE 46, 155.
31. WATR 1, no. 204; AE 54, 27.
32. WATR 2, no. 2370.
33. WATR 4, no. 4617.
34. WATR 3, no. 2982b; AE 54, 188.
35. WA 40, I, 315, 2.
36. WATR 3, no. 2982b; AE 54, 188.
37. Harmannus Obendiek, *Der Teufel bei Luther* (1931).
38. WA 40, I, 531, 24; AE 26, 346.
39. WA 15, 46, 7; AE 45, 369.
40. WATR 5, no. 5571; AE 54, 457.
41. WATR 3, no. 3566A; AE 54, 235.
42. WA 15, 33, 9; AE 45, 353.
43. WA 38, 105, 8.
44. WATR 5, no. 5362.
45. The oldest surviving letter by Luther, written April 22, 1507; WABr 1, 11, 31; AE 48, 4-5.
46. WATR 6, no. 6910.
47. WA 30, II, 576, 12; AE 46, 250.

Chapter 4. Erfurt

1. WATR 4, no. 4714; AE 54, 362.
2. Erich Kleineidam, *Universitas Studii Erffordensis: Überblick über die Geschichte der Universität Erfurt im Mittelalter*, vol. 2, 1460-1521 (Leipzig: 1969).

3. WATR 2, no. 2788b.
4. WABr 2, 91, 141.
5. WA 6, 600, 11.
6. WATR 2, no. 2544a.
7. Otto Hermann Pesch, *Die Theologie der Rechtfertigung bei Martin Luther und Thomas von Aquin* (Mainz: 1967).
8. WA 31, II, 454, 16; AE 17, 250.
9. WATR 3, no. 3608d; AE 54, 243; WATR 1, no. 135.
10. Friedrich Nitzsch, *Luther und Aristoteles* (Kiel: 1883).
11. WATR 2, no. 2412b.
12. WATR 1, no. 135.
13. WATR 5, no. 5440; AE 54, 423.
14. WA 18, 706, 14; AE 33, 171.
15. WATR 2, no. 2413a.
16. WATR 3, no. 2834b; AE 54, 173.
17. WATR 1, no. 116; AE 54, 14.
18. WABr 1, 541, 3.
19. WATR 1, no. 119; AE 54, 14-15.
20. WABr 2, 91, 141.
21. WATR 1, no. 116; AE 54, 13-14; WATR 3, no. 3767; WATR 5, no. 5346.

Chapter 5. Entrance into the Monastery

1. WATR 3, no. 3593.
2. Johannes Mathesius, *Luthers Leben in Predigten,* Ausgewählte Werke, vol. 3, ed. Georg Loesche (Prague: 1898), pp. 18, 20; Johann Matthesius (1504-1565) was a student of Luther and Melanchthon's. He was occasionally a table guest in the Luther household and took notes on the conversations. Later he became the school principal and pastor in the Bohemian silver-mining town of St. Joachimsthal. In 17 sermons he provided his congregation with an edifying portrayal of Luther's life, and so, in the 16th century, produced the first Luther biography.
3. WA 37, 661, 20.
4. WATR 4, no. 4707.
5. WABr 1, 543, 106.
6. WA 8, 513; AE 48, 332.
7. WABr 2, 384, 79; AE 48, 300-301.
8. WATR 4, no. 4707.
9. WA 8, 573, 20; AE 48, 331.
10. WA 49, 322, 12.
11. Otto Scheel, *Dokumente zu Luthers Entwicklung,* no. 533, 2nd ed. (Tübingen: 1929), p. 201.
12. Paul J. Reiter, *Martin Luthers Umwelt, Charakter und Psychose,* vol. 2 (Copenhagen: 1941), p. 556; Erik H. Erikson, *Der Junge Mann Luther,* pp. 24ff.

13. Mark 9:17-18.
14. WA 8, 573, 25; AE 48, 331.
15. WA 44, 213, 5; AE 6, 286.
16. See WATR 5, no. 5375.
17. Christian Georg Neudecker, *Die handschriftliche Geschichte Ratze-bergers über Luther und seine Zeit* (Jena: 1850).
18. See WATR 5, no. 6039.
19. WATR 1, no. 116; AE 54, 14.
20. WA 51, 83, 8; see also WA 40, I, 244, 7.
21. Melanchthon CR VI, p. 159.
22. WATR 4, no. 4174; AE 54, 325.
23. WATR 2, no. 1558; AE 54, 156.
24. WA 43, 382, 1; AE 4, 341.
25. WA 8, 573, 30; AE 48, 332.
26. WATR 4, no. 4414; AE 54, 338.
27. WA 8, 575, 23; AE 48, 334-336.
28. WA 8, 573, 35; AE 48, 335.
29. WA 8, 576, 18; AE 48, 336.
30. WATR 1, no. 116; AE 54, 14.

Chapter 6. Between Erfurt, Wittenberg, and Rome

1. WATR 2, no. 2800b.
2. WATR 3, no. 2871b.
3. WATR 4, no. 4681.
4. Schindanger, WATR 2, no. 2800b.
5. WABr 1, 17, 40.
6. Luther's marginal notes on Peter Lombard and Augustine are published in WA 9.
7. WA 9, 29, 3.
8. WATR 3, no. 3698; AE 54, 260.
9. WATR 4, no. 3984.
10. WA 9, 6, 10.
11. WA 9, 14, 23.
12. WATR 2, no. 2494b.
13. Heinrich Boehmer, *Luthers Romfahrt* (Leipzig: 1914).
14. See Boehmer, *Luthers Romfahrt*, pp. 82ff. and the index to WA 58, I, pp. 29-33.
15. WATR 3, no. 3621.
16. WA 42, 414, 1; AE 2, 215.
17. WATR 4, no. 3956; AE 54, 298.
18. WATR 4, no. 3930; AE 54, 296.
19. WA 54, 166, 12.
20. WATR 4, no. 4925.
21. WATR 5, no. 6059.
22. WA 47, 817, 3.

23. WA 31, I, 226, 9; AE 14, 6 (1530).
24. WA 7, 732, 19.
25. WATR 3, 3428.
26. WATR 5, 5484; AE 54, 427.
27. WA 47, 425, 5.
28. See Scheel, *Dokumente zu Luthers Entwicklung*, no. 539, p. 210.
29. Habakkuk 2:4.
30. WA 51, 89, 20.
31. WATR 5, no. 5484; AE 54, 427.
32. WA 47, 392, 9.

Chapter 7. The Struggle to Find a Gracious God

1. WA 8, 660, 31; AE 44, 387.
2. WA 41, 690, 16.
3. WA 38, 143, 25.
4. WATR 5, no. 4422; AE 54, 339.
5. WATR 1, no. 121; AE 54, 15.
6. WATR 1, no. 518, p. 240, 24; AE 54, 95.
7. Paul Althaus, *Die Theologie Martin Luthers* (Gütersloh: 1962); *The Theology of Martin Luther*, trans. Robert C. Schultz (Philadelphia: Fortress, 1966). I myself have attempted to make the basic thought of Luther understandable to contemporary persons in my little book *Luthers evangelische Botschaft*, in Kirchlich-Theologische Hefte, 2nd ed. (Munich: 1946). (The 2nd ed. is contained in *Christentum und Geistesleben*, vol. 4 [Munich: 1948].)
8. WA 56, 356-357; AE 25, 345-346. Many examples can also be found in Althaus, *Die Theologie Martin Luthers*, pp. 131ff.
9. Galatians 6:8.
10. Proverbs 14:34.
11. WA 37, 274, 14.
12. WA 40, II, 15, 15; AE 27, 13.
13. WATR 5, no. 6017.
14. WA 22, 305, 35.
15. WA 38, 147, 30.
16. Dionysius the Areopagite is a pseudonym for a Christian neoplatonist who lived about 500 A.D. Throughout the Middle Ages he was considered to be the student of Paul mentioned in Acts 17:34, and was accordingly highly regarded. In his treatise *The Babylonian Captivity of the Church* of 1520 Luther said that Dionysius was more platonic than he was Christian. "So far, indeed, from learning Christ in them [Dionysius' writings], you will lose even what you already know of him. I speak from experience" (WA 6, 562, 9; AE 36, 109). In Luther's time Dionysius was still generally considered to have been a student of Paul. It was Lorenzo Valla (1407–1457) who first challenged the authenticity of his works. Luther later adopted this critical

view (WA 42, 175, 1; AE 1, 235 [1535]; WATR 2, no. 2779aa, bb [1532]).

17. WATR 1, no. 644; AE 54, 112.
18. WA 40, III, 719, 20.
19. WA 1, 354, 5; AE 31, 40.
20. WA 1, 354, 11; AE 31, 40.
21. WA 40, II, 316, 32; WA 3, 30, 17.
22. WA 40, II, 331, 27.
23. WA 47, 590, 1.
24. WA 18, 719, 4; AE 33, 190.
25. WATR 2, no. 2654a.
26. WA 1, 557, 33; AE 31, 129.
27. Joseph Lortz, *Die Reformation in Deutschland*, vol. 1 (Freiburg: 1939), p. 176. *The Reformation in Germany*, trans. Ronald Walls (New York: Herder and Herder, 1968). With that volume Lortz (1887-1975), a Catholic church historian, brought about a change in the Catholic view of Luther.
28. WATR 3, no. 3131, p. 180, 9.
29. WATR 1, no. 347; AE 54, 49.
30. WATR 1, no. 122; AE 54, 15.
31. WATR 4, no. 4362; AE 54, 334.
32. WATR 3, no. 3680.
33. Ernst Wolf, *Staupitz und Luther*, Quellen und Forschungen zur Reformationsgeschichte, vol. 9 (Leipzig: 1927).
34. WATR 2, no. 2255a.
35. WA 30, III, 386, 30; AE 34, 103.
36. WATR 1, no. 518; AE 54, 94-95.
37. WATR 6, no. 6669.
38. WA 1, 525, 10; AE 48, 65.
39. WA 1, 525; AE 48, 66.
40. WA 1, 525; AE 48, 66.
41. WATR 1, no. 1017.
42. WATR 2, no. 1490.
43. WATR 1, no. 526; AE 54, 97.
44. Ibid.
45. WATR 1, no. 173.
46. WABr 3, no. 659, p. 155.

Chapter 8. Rediscovery of the Gospel

1. WATR 5, no. 5518; AE 54, 442-443.
2. WA 54, 179; AE 34, 336-337.
3. See p. 195 in this volume.
4. WATR 5, no. 5518; AE 54, 442-443.
5. WATR 1, no. 352; AE 54, 50; WA 54, 186. 25.
6. According to E. Hirsch, "Initium theologiae Lutheri," in *Luther-studien*, vol. 2 (Gütersloh: 1954), p. 16, n. 8, Luther made a dis-

tinction between active and passive righteousness for the first time in *The Bondage of the Will* of 1525 (WA 18, 768, 37ff.; AE 33). Luther understood the phrase, "the righteousness of God" as a Hebraism that Paul often used. In *Martin Luther*, vol. 2, p. 589, n. 3, Scheel indicates that Luther had already used the expression "passive" in his first lectures on the Psalms, in order to exclude the Catholic understanding (WA 3, 174, 31; AE 10, 146; WA 4, 487, 19). Luther also noted the inadequacy of the Latin translation of biblical terms in reference to the concept of *poenitentia* (WA 1, 526, 12; AE 31, 83-84). At an early point Luther had interpreted the expression "the righteousness of God" in a tropological sense (see WA 3, 466, 26; AE 10, 408; WA 3, 463, 1; AE 10, 404), in accordance with his view that the tropological sense was the "primarius sensus scripturae" (WA 3, 531, 33; AE 11, 12).

7. WA 44, 485, 25; AE 7, 250ff.
8. WADB 7, 30, v. 17.
9. WA 56, 172, 3; AE 25, 151-152.
10. WA 56, 220, 11; 56, 221, 18-19; AE 25, 204-206.
11. WA 56, 272, 17; AE 25, 260.
12. Paul Althaus, *Die Theologie Martin Luthers*, p. 211. Luther certainly acknowledged that there was such a thing as progress in "righteousness." The *simul* formula had both a partial and a total application; see p. 212 of Althaus.
13. Bernhard Lohse, *Lutherdeutung heute* (Göttingen: 1968), pp. 23ff; Ernst Käsemann, "Gottesgerechtigkeit bei Paulus," in *Zeitschrift für Theologie und Kirche* 58 (1961): 367ff., or in *Exegetische Versuche und Besinnungen*, vol. 2 (Göttingen: 1964; 2nd ed. 1965), pp. 181-193; Peter Stuhlmacher, *Gerechtigkeit Gottes bei Paulus* (Göttingen: 1965); Eduard Lohse, *Die Einheit des neuen Testaments* (Göttingen: 1973), pp. 216ff.; Paul Althaus, *Der Brief an die Römer*, in Das Neue Testament Deutsch, vol. 6, 10th ed. (Göttingen: 1973), pp. 13-15; Ernst Käsemann, *An die Römer*, in Handbuch zum Neuen Testament, 8 a, 3rd ed. (1974), pp. 18-19; *Commentary on Romans*, trans. and ed. Geoffrey W. Bromiley (Grand Rapids: Eerdmans, 1980).
14. WA 56, 215, 16; AE 25, 200-201.
15. Romans 8:21.
16. Romans 3:27.
17. WA 3; 4; AE 10; 11.
18. Ernst Stracke, "Luthers grosses Selbstzeugnis 1545 und seine Entwicklung zum Reformator," in *Schriften des Vereins für Reformationsgeschichte* 140: 122 ("captus fueram," WA 54, 185, 15) (Leipzig: 1926); Aland (see n. 27) explained the double pluperfect as a Germanism in which the pluperfect becomes something like an imperfect.
19. The Latin Bible, the Vulgate, counts Psalms 9 and 10 as one psalm. This accounts for the discrepancy between the original Hebrew (as

followed by the Luther Bible) and the Vulgate. After Psalm 148 they once again correspond. In WA 3 and 4 both the numbers in the Vulgate and the corresponding numbers of the Hebrew texts are provided (the latter in brackets).

20. Vg. 31:1; WA 3, 174, 19; AE 10, 145-146.
21. Vg. 35:7; WA 3, 199, 18; Hirsch, *Initium*, pp. 26-27.
22. Erich Vogelsang, *Die Anfänge von Luthers Christologie* (Berlin: 1929), pp. 48ff.
23. Vg. 71:1; WA 3, 463, 1; AE 10, 404-405; see also WA 3, 458, 8-11; AE 10, 401-402.
24. Ernst Bizer, *Fides ex auditu*, 1958, 3rd ed. (1966).
25. "Zur Frage der Iustitia Dei beim jungen Luther," *Archiv für Reformationsgeschichte* 52 (1961), no. 1; 53 (1962), nos. 1-2.
26. WA 56, 172, 5; AE 25, 151-152.
27. *Der Weg zur Reformation*, Theologische Existenz heute, Neue Folge no. 123 (Munich: 1965), p. 104.
28. "Zur Frage nach Luthers reformatorischer Wende," *Catholica: Vierteljahresschrift für Kontroverstheologie* 20 (1966), nos. 3 and 4, pp. 216-243 and 206-280.
29. Helpful information is provided by the collection edited by Bernhard Lohse, *Der Durchbruch der reformatorischen Erkenntnis bei Luther*, in Wege der Forschung, vol. 123 (Darmstadt: 1966). It contains excerpts from the most important contributions to the discussion and an introductory foreword by B. Lohse. Also worthy of examination is Welhelm Link, *Das Ringen Luthers um die Freiheit der Theologie von der Philosophie* (Munich: 1940), pp. 6-77.
30. Ernst Kroker, "Luthers Tischreden als geschichtliche Quelle," *Luther-Jahrbuch 1* (1919), pp. 81ff. and esp. pp. 112ff.; a diagram of the various traditions is on p. 115; Otto Scheel, *Martin Luther*, vol. 2 (1930), p. 569, n. 6; Heiko A. Obermann, "Wir sein pettler. Hoc est verum," *Zeitschrift für Kirchengeschichte* 78 (1967): 234ff.; Hartmann Grisar, *Luther*, vol. 1 (Freiburg: 1924), pp. 324-325 and vol. 3 (1925), pp. 978-988; *Luther*, trans. E. M. Lamond (London: Paul, Trench, Truebner, 1914-1917).
31. WATR 2, no. 1681, n. 1.
32. Paul J. Reiter, *Martin Luthers Umwelt* (see p. 51a, n. 12), pp. 321-322; Erik H. Erikson, *Der junge Mann Luther*, pp. 225ff.; John Osborn, *Luther* (Frankfurt am Main: 1963), pp. 17, 22, 27; *Luther: A Play* (New York: NAL, 1963).
33. WATR 4, no. 4192.
34. Obermann, "Wir sein pettler," pp. 237ff.
35. Heinrich Denifle, *Die abendländischen Schriftausleger bis Luther über iustitia dei (Röm. 1:17) und die iustificatio 1905: Quellenbelege zu Denifles "Luther und Luthertum,"* I/2, 2nd. ed. (1905); Karl Holl, *Die iustitia dei in der vorlutherischen Bibelauslegung des Abendlandes*, Festgabe für Harnack (1921); *Gesammelte Aufsätze* 3 (Der Westen) (1928), pp. 171-188.

36. Heinrich Bornkamm, "Iustitia dei in der Scholastik und bei Luther," *Archiv für Reformationsgeschichte* 39 (1942): 1-46, esp. 25.

Chapter 9. The Developmental Period of Reformation Theology

1. Regarding this chapter see Karl August Meissinger, *Luthers Exegese in der Frühzeit* (Leipzig: 1911); Heinrich Boehmer, *Luthers erste Vorlesung: Berichte über die Verhandlungen der Sächsischen Akademie der Wissenschaften in Leipzig, Phil.-hist. Klasse 75, 1923*, no. 1 (1924); Karl Holl, "Die Rechtfertigungslehre in Luthers Vorlesung über den Römerbrief mit besonderer Rücksicht auf die Frage der Heilsgewissheit" (1910), in *Gesammelte Aufsätze zur Kirchengeschichte* 1, Luther (Tübingen: 1927), pp. 111-154 (cf. P. Althaus, *Die Theologie Martin Luthers*, p. 210); Johannes Ficker, *Luther als Professor* (Halle: 1928) (concentrates primarily on the period after 1517); Karl Bauer, *Die Wittenberger Universitätstheologie und die Anfänge der Deutschen Reformation* (Tübingen: 1928); Reinhard Schwarz, *Fides, Spes und Caritas beim jungen Luther* (Berlin: 1962); Hans Hübner, *Rechtfertigung und Heiligung in Luthers Römerbriefvorlesung* (Witten: 1965); Leif Grane, *Modus loquendi theologicus* (Leiden: 1975).
2. WA 3; 4; 55; on the basis of remarks in the work *On the Councils and the Church* (1539) (WA 50, 519, 26; AE 41) Boehmer concluded that there were lectures on Genesis in the Winter of 1512, but his view has not been persuasive. Luther's longer lectures on Genesis of 1535-1545 (WA 42-44; AE 1-8), his last lectures, should be distinguished from these supposed first lectures on Genesis.
3. WA 5.
4. Clemen, vol. 5 (Berlin: 1933).
5. See Siegfried Räder, *Das Hebräische bei Luther, untersucht bis zum Ende der ersten Psalmenvorlesung* (Tübingen: 1961); *Die Benutzung des masoretischen Textes bei Luther in der Zeit zwischen der ersten und zweiten Psalmenvorlesung* (1515–1518) (Tübingen: 1967).
6. WA 57, 95, 23; see also Clemen, vol. 5, 339, 31: "Littera gesta docet; quid credas, allegoria; Moralis quid agas; sed quid speres, anagoge.
7. WA 3, 531, 34; AE 11, 12. Ebeling, in particular, has referred to this in various publications.
8. The second, unaltered edition appeared in 1923.
9. WA 57.
10. WA 56, 400, 15; AE 25, 390 (Rom. 9:19).
11. Contrary to Meissinger, *Luthers Exegese*, p. 36.
12. WA 56, 391, 7; AE 25, 381-382.
13. WA 56, 231, 6; AE 25, 215.
14. WA 56, 3, 6; AE 25, 3.

15. WA 56, 3, 16; AE 25, 3.
16. See Adolph Schlatter, "Luthers Deutung des Römerbriefes," *Beiträge zur Förderung christlicher Theologie* 21 (1917): 7, and his commentary on Romans, *Gottes Gerechtigkeit* (Stuttgart: 1935).
17. WA 56, 3, 12; AE 25, 3.
18. WA 56, 177, 4; AE 25, 157-158.
19. WA 56, 179, 11; AE 25, 159.
20. WA 56, 224ff.; AE 25, 209ff.
21. WA 56, 226, 23; AE 25, 210-211.
22. WA 56, 268-291; AE 25, 257-279.
23. WA 56, 269, 2; AE 25, 257.
24. WA 56, 269, 30; AE 25, 258.
25. WA 56, 272, 16; AE 25, 260.
26. WA 56, 272, 16-20; AE 25, 260.
27. See Althaus, *Theologie Luthers*, pp. 203ff.
28. See Walther von Loewenich, "Gebet und Kreuz: Zu Luthers Auslegung von Röm. 8:26 in der Römerbriefvorlesung des Jahres 1515/16," *Vierteljahreschrift der Luther-Gesellschaft*, no. 1, 1927, pp. 3-13; WA 56, 375, 1-381, 11.
29. WA 56, 375, 1; AE 25, 364-365.
30. WA 56, 375, 6-13; AE 25, 365.
31. WA 56, 375, 18; AE 25, 365.
32. WA 56, 376, 31; AE 25, 366.
33. WA 56, 377, 4; AE 25, 366-367.
34. WA 56, 378, 13; AE 25, 368.
35. WA 56, 379, 1; AE 25, 368.
36. We possess Luther's marginal notes to Tauler's sermons made in the first half of 1516 (WA 9, 95-104). In them Luther praised mystical theology as a wisdom based on experience rather than theory (WA 9, 98, 20). Luther found that the fundamental concepts of his theology of the cross were present in mystical theology. This is true, provided that one sets aside—as Luther did—the metaphysical background of mystical theology. In the same year Luther published excerpts from a mystical work, whose author was unknown, and sent them to Spalatin (WA 1, 79, 58; AE 48, 35-36); at that time he still took them to be the work of Tauler (see WA 1, 153-154; AE 31, 75-76). In 1518 Luther was able to publish a complete edition of the work, to which he gave the title, *A German Theology* (WA 1, 375-379). By then he knew that Tauler was not the author, but he found that the work reflected Tauler's thought.
37. WA 56, 189, 15; AE 25, 171-172.
38. WA 56, 189, 24; AE 25, 172.
39. WA 56, 483, 25; AE 25, 476.
40. WA 56, 448, 25; AE 25, 441.
41. WA 56, 476, 1; AE 25, 468-469.
42. WA 56, 476, 28; AE 25, 469.
43. WA 56, 480, 3; AE 25, 472.

44. WA 56, 480, 5; AE 25, 472.
45. WA 56, 500, 11; AE 25, 494; Johannes Ficker has provided a detailed and valuable introduction to the lectures on Romans in his special edition. It is not included in WA 56.
46. WA 57.
47. WA 2, 436ff.; AE 27, 151ff.
48. WA 40, I and 40, II through p. 185; AE 26 and 27.
49. WATR 1, no. 146; AE 54, 20.
50. WA 57; AE 29, 107ff. a previous edition by Emanuel Hirsch and Hanns Rückert appeared in *Arbeiten zur Kirchengeschichte* 13 (Berlin/Leipzig: 1929); Erich Vogelsang, *Luthers Hebräerbriefvorlesung 1517-1518*, Sammlung gemeinverständlicher Vorträge 43 (Tübingen: 1930); J. P. Boendermaker, *Luthers Commentaar op de Brief aan de Hebreeen 1517-1518*, dissertation (Amsterdam: 1965).
51. WADB 7, 344, 31.
52. WA 57, 117, 10; WA 57, 117, 20; AE 29, 126.
53. WA 57, 124, 9; AE 29, 131-132.
54. WA 57, 114, 12; AE 29, 123.
55. WA 57, 128, 13; AE 29, 135.
56. WA 56, 79, 20; AE 25, 71-72.
57. WA 57, 211, 15; AE 29, 213-214 (Heb. 9:17); WA 57, 191, 19; AE 29, 192-193; WA 57, 169, 23; AE 29, 172.
58. WA 57, 215, 1; AE 29, 216.
59. WABr 1, 72, 4; AE 48, 27-28.
60. WATR 1, no. 495; AE 54, 85.
61. WABr 1, 42, 22; AE 48, 15.
62. WABr 1, 57-58; AE 48, 21-24.
63. WABr 1, 33-36; AE 48, 11-14.
64. WABr 1, 35; AE 48, 12-13.
65. WABr 1, 36, 52; AE 48, 13.
66. WABr 1, 39.
67. WABr 1, 46-47.
68. WA 1, 238, 14; AE 31, 33.
69. WA 1, 47, 38.
70. WA 1, 47, 46.
71. WA 1, 154-220.
72. WABr 1, 93, 6.
73. WA 1, 199, 1.
74. WA 1, 112, 24.
75. WA 1, 138, 13; AE 51, 26.
76. WA 1, 139, 8; AE 51, 27 (Matt. 11:25).
77. WA 1, 139, 27; AE 51, 28.
78. WA 1, 139, 33; AE 51, 28.
79. WA 1, 141, 11; AE 51, 30.
80. WA 1, 141, 22; AE 51, 31.
81. WA 1, 94-99; in his sermon of July 27, 1516 (WA 1, 63-65; AE 51, 14-17), Luther was still uncertain of his view on indulgences.

82. WA 1, 141, 37; AE 51, 31.
83. WABr 1, 99, 8; AE 48, 42.
84. WABr 1, 170, 2.
85. Irmgard Höss, *Georg Spalatin* (Weimar: 1956).
86. See p. VI.
87. WABr 1, 23.
88. WABr 1, 70; AE 48, 24-26.
89. WABr 1, 90, 15; AE 48, 40.
90. WABr 1, 90, 22; AE 48, 40.
91. WABr 1, 90, 19; AE 48, 40.
92. WA 1, 142ff.
93. WA 1, 224-228; AE 31, 3-16; we cite the version of Erich Vogelsang in his student edition of Clemen, vol. 5, pp. 320ff. (1933); see especially Leif Grane, *Contra Gabrielem* (Copenhagen: 1962); Emanuel Hirsch, "Randglossen zu Luthertexten," in *Theologische Studien und Kritiken* (1918), pp. 108ff. (concerning the disputation "Concerning the Powers . . .").
94. WABr 1, 105, 107.
95. WABr 1, 103.
96. WABr 1, 116, 17.

PART TWO: THE OPENING YEARS OF THE REFORMATION
Chapter 10. The Ninety-Five Theses

1. WABr 1, 118, 9.
2. WABr 1, 110, 5; AE 48, 48-49.
3. *Dokumente zum Ablassstreit von 1517*, edited by Walther Köhler, in Sammlung ausgewählter kirchen- und dogmengeschichtlicher Quellenschriften, series 2, no. 3, 2nd ed. (Tübingen: 1934); Kurt Aland, *Martin Luthers 95 Thesen nebst dem Sermon von Ablass und Gnade* (Kleine Texte) (Berlin: 1962); see also the detailed article, "Indulgenzen," by Theodor Brieger, in *Realenzyklopädie für protestantische Theologie und Kirche* (RE), 2nd ed., vol. 9 (1904), pp. 76-94; Gustav Adolf Benrath, "Ablass," in *Theologische Realenzyklopädie* (TRE), vol. 1 (1977), pp. 347-364. Concerning the development of the theory of indulgences, see also the collection of sources by Denzinger and Schönmetzer and by Carl Mirbt.
4. According to Luther in his work, *Against Hanswurst* (against Duke Heinrich von Braunschweig) of 1541 (WA 51, 538ff; AE 41, 185-256). Luther reported what he had heard about Tetzel. He quoted this ominous sentence in Thesis 75; in the *Explanations of the Ninety-Five Theses*, however, he considered it to be a rumor that circulated among the people (WA 1, 622, 1; AE 31, 240-241). It is not found in the official sermons of Tetzel.
5. WA 1, 233-238; AE 31, 17-33.
6. Hans Volz, *Martin Luthers Thesenanschlag und dessen Vorgeschichte*

(Weimar: 1959) (of the 148 pages, 90 are notes!); Heinrich Born-kamm, *Thesen und Thesenanschlag Luthers* (Berlin: 1967) (bibli-ography!); Franz Lau, "Die gegenwärtige Diskussion um Luthers Thesenanschlag," in *Luther-Jahrbuch 1967,* pp. 11-59.

7. CR 6, 161-162.
8. WABr 4, 275, 25.
9. See the sources mentioned in n. 6.
10. Bornkamm, "Iustitia," p. 25, n. 76.
11. WABr 1, 121.
12. Letter to Scheuerl of March 5, 1518; WABr 1, 151.
13. *Against Hanswurst;* WA 51, 540, 25; AE 41, 234.
14. WA 51, 541, 3; AE 41, 234.
15. Ibid.
16. WATR 1, no. 1206.
17. Luther to Scheuerl, March 5, 1518; WABr 1, 152, 1.
18. WATR 5, no. 5480; cf. WATR 2, no. 2619.
19. WATR 3, no. 3722; AE 54, 264.
20. WABr 1, 147, 62.
21. Ibid.
22. WATR 3, no. 3846.
23. WABr 1, 178.
24. WA 1, 243ff.
25. WA 1, 245, 26.
26. WA 1, 246, 11.
27. WA 1, 246, 21.
28. WA 1, 522-628; AE 31, 77-252.
29. WA 1, 527, 6; AE 48, 69-70.
30. WA 1, 527-530.
31. WA 1, 528, 27.
32. WA 1, 528, 20.
33. WA 1, 529, 33; AE 31, 83.
34. WA 1, 530, 11; AE 31, 83.
35. WA 1, 541, 14; AE 31, 107.
36. WA 1, 544, 39; AE 31, 105.
37. WA 1, 605, 33ff.; AE 31, 213.
38. WA 1, 618, 24; AE 31, 239-240.
39. WA 1, 571, 16; AE 31, 152.
40. WA 1, 624, 6; AE 31, 244.
41. WA 1, 624, 35; AE 31, 245.
42. WA 1, 627, 27; AE 31, 250.
43. WA 1, 247ff.
44. WA 1, 257ff.
45. WA 1, 278ff.
46. WA 1, 317ff.
47. WA 1, 325ff.
48. WA 1, 330, 36.

Chapter 11. The Heidelberg Disputation

1. WABr 1, 155, 1; 168, 4.
2. WABr 1, 166.
3. WABr 1, 168.
4. Here I might refer to my book *Luther's Theology of the Cross*, trans. Herbert J. A. Bouman (Minneapolis: Augsburg, 1976); the Heidelberg Disputation is printed in WA 1, 353-374; AE 31, 35-70; with regard to more recent literary-critical investigations (Hirsch, "Randglossen," see Chap. 7, n. 13), see the selected edition of Clemen, vol. 5, pp. 375-404, ed. E. Vogelsang; the new edition by Helmut Junghans in *Martin Luther: Studienausgabe*, ed. Hans Ulrich Delius, vol. 1 (East Berlin: 1979), pp. 186-218.
5. WA 1, 356, 33ff.; AE 31, 35ff.
6. WA 1, 358, 5; AE 31, 46.
7. WA 1, 359, 36; AE 31, 48-49.
8. WA 1, 360, 35; AE 31, 50.
9. WA 1, 361, 34; AE 31, 52.
10. WA 1, 45, 15; AE 31, 52-53.
11. John 14:8.
12. WA 1, 362, 1ff.; AE 31, 53.
13. 1 Corinthians 1:23.
14. WA 1, 362, 28; AE 31, 53.
15. WA 1, 355, 1-25; AE 31, 41.
16. 1 Corinthians 13.
17. WA 1, 365, 13; AE 31, 57.
18. WA 1, 365, 11; AE 31, 57.
19. WA 1, 613, 21ff.; WA 1, 614, 17ff.; AE 31, 227.
20. WABr 1, 173, 23ff.; AE 48, 60-63.
21. WA 9, 160ff.
22. WA 9, 162, 8.
23. WABr 1, 174, 45; AE 48, 63.

Chapter 12. The Initial Inquiry

1. They have been reproduced by Nicolaus Paulus in *Johann Tetzel, der Ablassprediger* (Mainz: 1899), pp. 171ff.; excerpts are also found in Köhler, *Dokumente zum Ablassstreit*, pp. 127ff.
2. WABr 1, 155, 24.
3. WABr 1, 173, 10; AE 48, 61.
4. WA 1, 634.
5. Letter to Spalatin of August 31; WABr 1, 191; AE 48, 76-80.
6. WA 1, 639.
7. WA 1, 643, 11.
8. WA 1, 643, 1.
9. WA 1, 642, 29.
10. WA 1, 642, 38.
11. WA 1, 395-521.

12. WA 1, 375; AE 31, 71-76.
13. WABr 1, 180, 19.
14. WA 1, 382-393; June 1518.
15. WABr 1, 185.
16. WA 1, 385, 19.
17. WA 1, 387, 19.
18. WA 1, 392, 12.
19. WABr 1, 188; AE 48, 70-76.
20. WABr 1, 192, 32; WA 1, 686, 28; AE 48, 79.
21. WA 1, 644ff.
22. WABr 1, 194, 29.

Chapter 13. The Hearing before Cajetan

1. WATR 2, no. 2668a.
2. WABr 1, 208.
3. WABr 1, 209, 21.
4. WABr 1, 209, 24; WATR 5, no. 5349, p. 79, 2ff.
5. Denzinger and Schönmetzer, no. 1025-1027; Köhler, *Dokumente,* p. 19; Mirbt, *Quellen* (1924), p. 224; Mirbt and Aland, *Quellen* (1967), p. 472.
6. Köhler, *Dokumente,* p. 158; Mirbt and Aland, p. 503.
7. WATR 2, no. 2668a.b.
8. WABr 1, 212.
9. WATR 5, p. 79.
10. WA 1, 544, 40; AE 31, 102.
11. WABr 1, 214-215; AE 48, 83-87.
12. WATR 2, no. 2327.
13. WABr 1, 215; AE 48, 86.
14. WABr 1, 216, 39.
15. WA 2, 28ff.
16. WA 2, 32, 32.
17. WA 2, 31, 15.
18. WABr 1, 220.
19. WABr 1, 222; AE 48, 87-89.
20. WATR 1, no. 1203.
21. WABr 1, 225; AE 48, 92.
22. WA 2, 1ff.
23. WA 2, 8, 1ff. (and other places).
24. WA 2, 22, 6.
25. WA 2, 22, 18.

Chapter 14. The Leipzig Disputation

1. WA 54, 184, 34.
2. WABr 1, 363.
3. WA 2, 48ff.
4. WA 2, 66ff.

5. WA 2, 74ff.; AE 42, 15-81.
6. WA 2, 131ff.; AE 42, 3-14.
7. WA 1, 571, 16; AE 31, 152.
8. WA 2, 161, 35; AE 31, 318.
9. WABr 1, 270.
10. Letter to Spalatin of March 13, 1519; AE 48, 114.
11. WA 2, 180ff.
12. Luther gave Spalatin a detailed account of Leipzig in the letter of July 20, 1519 (WABr 1, 420ff.; AE 31, 318-325); in addition see the record of the disputation in WA 2, 250ff.
13. WABr 1, 424, 146; AE 31, 325.
14. WABr 2, 42, 24; AE 48, 153.

Chapter 15. From Leipzig to Worms

1. WA 2, 388ff.
2. Letter of October 3, 1519; WABr 1, 514, 49.
3. WA 6, 99ff.; AE 42, 117-166.
4. WA 6.
5. WA 6, 170ff.
6. WA 6, 194, 30.
7. WA 6, 196-276; the handwritten manuscript by Luther was found in the Staatsbibliothek in Danzig; it is reproduced in WA 9, 226-301; AE 44, 15-114.
8. WABr 2, 75.
9. WA 6, 203; AE 44, 22.
10. WA 6, 202; AE 44, 21.
11. WA 6, 204, 31; AE 44, 24.
12. WA 6, 205, 1ff.; AE 44, 24.
13. WA 6, 206, 8; AE 44, 25.
14. WA 6, 207, 4; AE 44, 26.
15. WA 6, 207, 12; AE 44, 26.
16. WA 6, 207, 26; AE 44, 27.
17. WA 6, 208, 6; AE 44, 28.
18. WA 6, 209, 1; AE 44, 29.
19. WA 6, 209, 27; AE 44, 30.
20. WA 6, 212, 33; AE 44, 34.
21. WA 6, 212, 38; AE 44, 34.
22. WA 6, 213, 15; AE 44, 35.
23. WA 6, 216, 9; AE 44, 37.
24. WA 6, 216, 26; AE 44, 38.
25. WA 6, 217ff.; AE 44, 39ff.
26. WA 6, 223, 30; AE 44, 47.
27. WA 6, 229ff.; AE 44, 54ff.
28. WA 6, 233, 17; AE 44, 59.
29. WA 6, 245, 19ff.; AE 44, 71-72.
30. WA 6, 243, 21; AE 44, 72.

31. WA 6, 248, 1ff.; AE 44, 77.
32. WA 6, 249, 11; AE 44, 79.
33. WA 6, 250, 33; AE 44, 80ff.
34. WA 6, 277-324; AE 39, 49-104.
35. WABr 2, 111, 12; AE 48, 164.
36. WA 6, 324, 3; AE 39, 104.
37. WA 6, 286, 30; AE 39, 57.
38. Ibid.
39. WA 6, 288, 26; AE 39, 58.
40. WA 6, 287, 14; AE 39, 58.
41. WA 6, 290, 20; AE 39, 62.
42. WA 6, 291; AE 39, 64.
43. WA 6, 293, 4; AE 39, 65.
44. WA 6, 294, 16; AE 39, 67.
45. WA 6, 295, 22; AE 39, 68.
46. WA 6, 295, 35; AE 39, 69.
47. WA 6, 296, 30; AE 39, 70.
48. WA 6, 298, 27; AE 39, 72.
49. WA 6, 299, 1; AE 39, 73.
50. WA 6, 299, 31; AE 39, 73-74.
51. WA 6, 301, 3; AE 39, 75.
52. WA 6, 309ff.; AE 39, 86.
53. WA 6, 312, 1; AE 39, 89.
54. WA 6, 315, 5; AE 39, 94.
55. John 21:15ff.
56. WA 6, 316, 20; AE 39, 95ff.
57. WA 6, 320, 27; AE 39, 100.
58. WA 6, 321, 31; AE 39, 101.
59. WA 6, 322, 1; AE 39, 101.
60. WA 322, 18; AE 39, 102.
61. WA 322, 23; AE 39, 102.
62. Letter to Johann Hess; WABr 2, 118, 14.
63. WA 6, 325-348.
64. WA 6, 329, 17.
65. This is the only place where Luther called for an armed attack on the Curia; he did not do so in his work *To the Christian Nobility.* In addition he used a citation from Psalm 58:11. In his work *On the New Bulls and Lies of Eck,* Luther stated that this threat was directed only against the followers of Prierias (WA 6, 585, 2).
66. WA 6, 347, 17.
67. WABr 2, 120, 13.
68. WA 6, 381-469; AE 44, 115-217; cf. the edition with commentary by Karl Benrath (Verein für Reformationsgeschichte) (Halle: 1884).
69. WABr 2, 167.
70. WATR 3, no. 3724, p. 567, 24.
71. WA 6, 404-405; AE 44, 123-124.

72. WA 6, 405, 24; WA 6, 405, 29; AE 44, 124-125.
73. WA 6, 406; AE 44, 125-126.
74. WA 6, 406, 21; AE 44, 126; Capito mentioned the image of the three walls in a letter to Luther of September 4, 1518 (WABr 1, 198, 11). It can be traced to Virgil, *Aeneid* 6, 549.
75. WA 6, 407, 4; AE 44, 127.
76. WA 6, 407, 13; AE 44, 127.
77. WA 6, 408, 11; AE 44, 129.
78. WA 6, 408, 20; AE 44, 129.
79. WA 6, 409, 11; AE 44, 130.
80. WA 6, 410, 6; AE 44, 130.
81. WA 6, 411, 6; AE 44, 133.
82. WA 6, 411, 33; AE 44, 134.
83. WA 6, 411, 30; AE 44, 135.
84. WA 6, 412, 15; AE 44, 135.
85. WA 6, 412, 37; AE 44, 136.
86. WA 6, 413; AE 44, 136.
87. Acts 15.
88. WA 6, 413, 17; AE 44, 136-137.
89. WA 6, 413, 27; AE 44, 137.
90. WA 6, 414, 6; AE 44, 138.
91. WA 6, 415, 19ff.; WA 6, 416, 30; AE 44, 141-143.
92. WA 6, 418, 4; AE 44, 143.
93. WA 6, 418-427; AE 44, 143-156.
94. WA 6, 427, 13; AE 44, 156.
95. WA 6, 427, 16; AE 44, 156.
96. WA 6, 427, 35; AE 44, 156-157.
97. WA 6, 428, 18; AE 44, 157.
98. WA 6, 429, 1; AE 44, 158.
99. WA 6, 429; AE 44, 158.
100. WA 6, 430, 5; AE 44, 159-160.
101. WA 6, 434, 25; WA 6, 435; AE 44, 165-166.
102. WA 6, 435, 25; WA 6, 437; AE 44, 168-172.
103. WA 6, 437, 7; AE 44, 170.
104. WA 6, 438, 14; AE 44, 172.
105. WA 6, 439, 37; AE 44, 175.
106. WA 6, 440, 15; AE 44, 176.
107. WA 6, 445; AE 44, 181-182.
108. WA 6, 445, 33; AE 44, 182.
109. WA 6, 450, 22; AE 44, 189.
110. WA 6, 454, 17; AE 44, 195.
111. WA 6, 455, 19; AE 44, 196.
112. WA 6, 456, 31; AE 44, 198-199.
113. WA 6, 457, 28ff.; AE 44, 201.
114. WA 6, 458, 18; AE 44, 201.
115. WA 6, 459; AE 44, 202.
116. WA 6, 460, 6; AE 44, 204.

117. WA 6, 461, 1; AE 44, 205.
118. WA 6, 461, 11; AE 44, 205-206.
119. WA 6, 461, 25; AE 44, 206.
120. WA 6, 468, 28; AE 44, 216.
121. WA 6, 465, 25; AE 44, 212.
122. WA 6, 466, 31; AE 44, 214.
123. WA 6, 467, 7; AE 44, 214.
124. WA 6, 467, 17; AE 44, 214.
125. WA 6, 462-465; AE 44, 207-212.
126. WA 6, 468, 32; AE 44, 217.
127. WA 6, 469, 15; AE 44, 217.
128. Leopold von Ranke, *Deutsche Geschichte im Zeitalter der Reforma-tion*, vol. 1, p. 316; *History of the Reformation in Germany*, trans. Sarah Austin (New York: Unger, 1966).
129. WA 6, 468, 33; AE 44, 217.
130. WABr 2, 115.
131. Ibid.
132. WABr 2, 111; AE 48, 163-164.
133. WABr 2, 98, 5.
134. WABr 2, 121.
135. WABr 2, 117, 32; WABr 2, 103, 19.
136. WABr 2, 249, 12.
137. WA 6, 484-573; AE 36, 11-132.
138. WA 2, 215, 2.
139. WA 6, 497; AE 36, 11.
140. WA 6, 498, 1; Genesis 10:8-10; AE 36, 12.
141. WA 6, 501, 33; AE 36, 18.
142. See my book, *Vom Abendmahl Christi* (Berlin: 1938).
143. WA 1, 329ff.
144. WA 2, 742ff.; AE 35, 45-73.
145. WA 6, 349ff.; AE 35, 74-111.
146. WA 6, 355, 3-4; AE 35, 81.
147. WA 6, 358, 15; AE 35, 82.
148. WA 6, 359, 1ff.; AE 35, 84-86.
149. WA 6, 363, 7; AE 35, 91.
150. WA 6, 358, 11; AE 35, 82.
151. WA 6, 359, 1ff.; AE 35, 84.
152. Concerning the continued development of this problem in modern Catholicism, see my book *Der moderne Katholizmus vor und nach dem Konzil* (Witten: 1970), pp. 24ff.; *Modern Catholicism*, trans. Reginald H. Fuller (New York: St. Martin's, 1959).
153. WA 6, 370, 25; AE 35, 101ff.
154. WA 6, 484ff.; AE 36, 11-132.
155. WA 6, 503, 9ff.; AE 36, 21ff.
156. WA 6, 505, 21; AE 36, 24.
157. WA 6, 507, 7; AE 36, 27:

158. WA 6, 507, 11; AE 36, 27.
159. WA 6, 508, 1ff.; AE 36, 28-35.
160. WA 6, 508, 14; AE 36, 31.
161. WA 6, 510, 4; AE 36, 32.
162. WA 6, 512, 5; AE 36, 33.
163. WA 6, 512; AE 36, 34.
164. WA 6, 512, 9; AE 36, 35.
165. WA 6, 512, 33; AE 36, 36.
166. WA 6, 515, 22; AE 36, 40.
167. WA 6, 518, 16; AE 36, 44.
168. WA 6, 518, 20; AE 36, 44.
169. WA 6, 523, 22; AE 36, 52.
170. WA 6, 526, 35ff.; AE 36, 57-81.
171. WA 2, 724-737; AE 35, 23-43.
172. WA 6, 527, 33; AE 36, 58-59.
173. WA 6, 528, 18; AE 36, 61.
174. WA 6, 530, 19; AE 36, 63.
175. WA 6, 531, 31; AE 36, 64.
176. WA 6, 532, 29; AE 36, 66.
177. WA 6, 534, 3; AE 36, 67.
178. WA 6, 534, 20; AE 36, 68.
179. WA 6, 527, 9; AE 36, 57-59.
180. WA 6, 535, 27; AE 36, 70.
181. WA 6, 538, 26; AE 36, 80.
182. WA 6, 538, 26; AE 36, 81.
183. WA 6, 543, 4.
184. WA 6, 544, 26; AE 36, 84.
185. WA 6, 546, 11; AE 36, 86.
186. WA 6, 547, 5; AE 36, 88.
187. WA 6, 549, 12; AE 36, 90.
188. WA 6, 549, 20; AE 36, 90-91.
189. WA 6, 551, 6; AE 36, 93.
190. WA 6, 550, 33; AE 36, 92.
191. WA 6, 553, 22ff.; AE 36, 96.
192. WA 6, 554, 13; AE 36, 97.
193. WA 6, 559, 20; AE 36, 105.
194. WA 6, 558, 20; AE 36, 103-105.
195. WA 6, 560, 20ff.; AE 36, 106-117.
196. WA 6, 561, 19; AE 36, 108.
197. WA 6, 561, 34; AE 36, 109.
198. WA 6, 564, 15; AE 36, 113; see also Chap. 7, note 16.
199. WA 6, 566, 9; AE 36, 115.
200. WA 6, 567, 25; AE 36, 117.
201. WA 6, 567, 33ff.; AE 36, 117-123.
202. WA 6, 568, 10; WA 6, 568, 31; AE 36, 118-119.
203. WA 6, 573, 20; AE 36, 126.

Chapter 16. Under the Ban

1. Reproduced with others in Mirbt and Aland, *Quellen*, pp. 504ff. and in part in Denzinger and Schönmetzer, nos. 1451ff.
2. Psalm 80:13.
3. Psalm 80:33.
4. Psalm 80:34.
5. Psalm 80:41.
6. WABr 2, 134.
7. WABr 2, 136.
8. WABr 2, 136, 40.
9. WA 6, 474ff.
10. WABr 2, 172ff.
11. WA 7, 1ff.; 7, 42ff.; AE 31, 334-343.
12. WA 7, 4, 5; AE 31, 334.
13. WA 7, 5, 32; AE 31, 336.
14. WA 7, 5, 7; AE 31, 336.
15. WA 7, 6, 8; AE 31, 337.
16. WA 7, 8, 30; AE 31, 341-342.
17. WA 7, 10, 29; AE 31, 342.
18. WA 7, 7, 10; AE 31, 338.
19. WA 7, 7, 15; AE 31, 338.
20. WA 7, 8, 23; AE 31, 338.
21. WA 7, 69, 18; AE 31, 337.
22. WA 7, 9, 9; AE 31, 340-341.
23. WA 7, 9, 27; AE 31, 341.
24. WA 7, 9, 39; AE 31, 341-342.
25. WA 7, 10, 2; AE 31, 341.
26. WA 7, 10, 17; AE 31, 342.
27. WA 7, 10, 23; AE 31, 342.
28. WA 7, 11, 2; AE 31, 343.
29. WA 7, 11, 4; AE 31, 343.
30. WA 7, 20ff.; Latin pp. 49ff.; AE 31, 343.
31. WA 7, 21, 1; AE 31, 344.
32. WA 7, 22; AE 31, 344-345.
33. WA 7, 23; AE 31, 346.
34. WA 7, 25; AE 31, 349-350.
35. WA 7, 25, 26; AE 31, 351.
36. WA 7, 25, 34; AE 31, 351.
37. WA 7, 26, 4; AE 31, 352.
38. WA 7, 26, 13; AE 31, 353.
39. WA 7, 24, 35; AE 31, 353.
40. WA 7, 27, 17; AE 31, 354.
41. WA 7, 29, 31; AE 31, 358.
42. WA 7, 30, 15; AE 31, 358.
43. WA 7, 30, 31; AE 31, 359.
44. WA 7, 32, 5; AE 31, 361.

45. AE 7, 32, 9; AE 31, 361.
46. AE 7, 32, 15; AE 31, 361.
47. AE 7, 33, 36; AE 31, 363.
48. AE 7, 34, 12; AE 31, 364.
49. Phil. 2:5ff.; WA 7, 35, 2; AE 31, 366.
50. WA 7, 35, 35; AE 31, 367.
51. WA 7, 36-37; AE 31, 368-369.
52. WA 7, 38, 6; AE 31, 371.
53. WABr 2, 195.
54. WA 6, 576ff.
55. *Against the Damnable Bull of the Antichrist;* WA 6; 595ff.
56. *Against the Bull of the Antichrist;* WA 6; 613ff.
57. WA 7, 74ff.
58. WA 7, 83.
59. WA 7, 183.
60. WA 7, 184-186.
61. WABr 2, 234, 6; AE 48, 186-187.
62. WA 7, 152ff.; AE 31, 383-395.
63. WA 7, 91ff.
64. WA 7, 299ff.

Chapter 17. In Worms before the Emperor and the Empire

1. WA 7, 698ff.
2. WA 7, 538ff.; concerning the Mariology of Luther see Hans Düfel, *Luthers Stellung zur Marienverehrung* (Göttingen: 1968).
3. Luke 1:46ff.
4. This sermon was published because of the negative reports that had been made about it (WA 7, 803ff.).
5. WABr 2, 298; AE 48, 198.
6. WA 15, 214, 24.
7. WABr 2, 455, 53; AE 48, 390 reads, ". . . I should nevertheless have leaped into their midst with joy."
8. WATR 5, no. 5342b; p. 69, 15ff.
9. In addition to the actions of the Diet and the dispatches of Aleander. note the record of the proceedings in WA 7, 814ff.
10. Cf. my book, *Luther und der Neuprotestantismus* (Witten: 1963).

PART THREE: THE CONTINUATION OF THE REFORMATION
Chapter 18. The Wartburg

1. Heinrich Bornkamm, *Martin Luther in der Mitte seines Lebens* (Göttingen: 1979); *Luther in Mid-Career, 1521-1530,* trans. E. Theodore Bachmann (Philadelphia: Fortress, 1983).
2. WABr 2, 349, 101; AE 48, 236.
3. WA 8, 412, 2; 8, 483, 2.

4. WABr 2, 380, 56; AE 48, 295.
5. WABr 2, 357, 2; AE 48, 257.
6. WATR 3, nos. 2885; 3814; AE 54, 280.
7. WATR 5, no. 5358b.
8. Ibid.
9. WATR 6, no. 6816.
10. Revelation 1:9.
11. WABr 2, 332; AE 48, 215-217.
12. February 16, 1497–April 19, 1560; Wilhelm Maurer, *Der junge Melanchthon*, 2 vols. (Göttingen: 1967 and 1969).
13. WABr 2, 348, 58; AE 48, 232.
14. WA 30, II, 68, 16.
15. WABr 2, 372, 82; AE 48, 281-282.
16. Ibid.
17. WABr 2, 365, 27; AE 48, 270.
18. WABr 2, 354, 22; AE 48, 255.
19. WA 5, 19-673.
20. WA 8.
21. WA 8.
22. WA 8, 240, 4.
23. *Rationis Latomianae confutatio*, WA 8, 36-128; *Against Latomus*, AE 32, 133-260.
24. WA 8, 107, 21; AE 32, 229.
25. WA 8, 117, 33; AE 32, 243-244.
26. WA 8, 27, 18; AE 32, 258.
27. WA 8, 247-254.
28. WA 8, 267ff.
29. WA 8, 688ff.
30. WABr 2, 393.
31. WABr 2, 399; AE 48, 323.
32. November 1; WABr 2, 402; AE 48, 325-328.
33. WABr 2, 406; AE 48, 339, 343.
34. December 21, 1521; WABr 2, 420.
35. WABr 2, 416.
36. WABr 2, 430; AE 48, 372-379.
37. WABr 1, 538.
38. WA 7, 458-537.
39. WA 10, I, 1.
40. WABr 2, 413; AE 48, 356.
41. WABr 2, 397, 34; AE 48, 320.
42. WATR 2, no. 2758a, b.
43. WADB 6 and 7; AE 35, 335-411.
44. WADB 6, 10; AE 35, 358; 35, 365; 35, 370; 35, 362.
45. WADB 7, 384; AE 35, 396.
46. WADB 7, 344; AE 35, 396-397; 35, 395; 35, 394.
47. WADB 7, 404; AE 35, 399.
48. WADB 7, 406ff.; AE 35, 399-411.

49. WA 30, II, 627ff.; AE 35, 175-202.
50. WATR 2, no. 2790b.
51. WA 30, II, 636, 16; AE 35, 188.
52. Revelation 21:19.
53. WA 30, II, 640, 26; AE 35, 194.
54. WADB 10, I, 103.
55. WATR 1, no. 674; AE 54, 121.

Chapter 19. Unrest in Wittenberg

1. Hermann Barge, *Andreas Bodenstein von Karlstadt,* vol. 2 (Leipzig: 1905); Ronald J. Sider, *Andreas Bodenstein von Karlstadt: The Development of His Thought 1517-1529* (Leiden: 1974).
2. WA 8, 313.
3. WA 8, 564; cf. Bernhard Lohse, *Mönchtum und Reformation* (Göttingen: 1963); Heinz Meinwolf Stamm, *Luthers Stellung zum Ordensleben* (Wiesbaden: 1980); AE 44, 243-400.
4. WABr 2, 377; AE 48, 290.
5. WA 8, 317.
6. WABr 2, 415, 25; AE 48, 356-359.
7. WABr 2, 372, 73; AE 48, 281.
8. WA 8, 398ff.
9. WA 8, 477ff.; AE 36, 133-230.
10. WA 8, 561, 21; AE 36, 227.
11. WA 8, 562, 27; AE 36, 229-230.
12. WABr 2, 409; AE 48, 350-352.
13. Letter to Spalatin of December 12, 1521; WABr 2, 412, 22; AE 48, 352.
14. WA 8, 670ff.; AE 45, 51-74.
15. WABr 2, 412, 31; AE 48, 355.
16. WA 8, 680, 18; AE 45, 62-63.
17. WA 8, 680, 20; AE 45, 63.
18. WA 8, 680, 32; AE 45, 63.
19. WA 8, 685, 4; AE 45, 71.
20. WA 8, 687, 13; AE 45, 73.
21. Walter Elliger, *Thomas Müntzer: Leben und Werk* (Göttingen: 1975).
22. WABr 2, 424; AE 48, 364-372.
23. WABr 2, 448; AE 48, 386-388.
24. WABr 2, 449.
25. WABr 2, 453; AE 48, 388-393.
26. See WABr 2, 457-473; AE 48, 393-399.
27. WABr 2, 461, 74, 94; AE 48, 397.

Chapter 20. Orderly Reform

1. WA 15, 408, 4.
2. WA 10, III, 1ff.; AE 51, 67-100.

3. WA 10, III, 1-2; AE 51, 70.
4. WA 11, 31; AE 51, 74.
5. WA 10, 15; AE 51, 73-74.
6. WA 10, 42, 13; AE 51, 89.
7. WA 10, 18, 10ff.; AE 51, 77-78.
8. WA 10, 26, 6; AE 51, 81.
9. WA 10, 28, 5; AE 51, 82.
10. WA 10, 28, 24; AE 51, 83.
11. WA 10, 29, 7; AE 51, 83.
12. WA 10, 30, 16; AE 51, 84.
13. WA 10, 31; AE 51, 84.
14. WA 10, III, XLVIIIff.
15. WABr 2, 493, 3.
16. WA 10, II, 1-41; AE 36, 231-267.
17. WA 10, 29, 14; AE 36, 254.
18. WA 10, 29, 27; AE 36, 254-255.
19. WA 10, 31, 19; AE 36, 256.
20. WA 10, 32, 11; AE 36, 256-257.
21. WA 10, 35, 1; AE 36, 260-261.
22. WA 10, 36, 28; AE 36, 262.
23. WA 10, II, 61ff.; AE 39, 239-299.
24. WA 11, 401ff.; AE 39, 301-314.
25. WA 11, 412, 30; AE 39, 309.
26. WA 11, 414, 1; AE 39, 311-312.
27. WA 12, 31-37.
28. 2nd version in WA 12, 476ff.
29. WA 12, 38-48.
30. WA 15, 758ff.
31. WA 18, 8ff.
32. WA 12, 197ff.
33. WA 12, 205, 13.

Chapter 21. Civil Government and Public Life

1. Paul Althaus, *Die Ethik Martin Luthers* (Gütersloh: 1965); Walther von Loewenich, "Luthers Stellung zur Obrigkeit," in *Staat und Kirche im Wandel der Jahrhunderte,* ed. Walter Peter Fuchs (Stuttgart: 1966), pp. 53ff.
2. WA 56, 25, 27; 56, 189, 25.
3. WA 30, II, 123, 25.
4. WA 11, 229-281; AE 45, 75-129.
5. Matthew 5:39.
6. WA 11, 245, 19; AE 45, 101-102.
7. WA 11, 245-261; AE 45, 85-104.
8. WA 11, 247, 21ff.; AE 45, 85-87.
9. WA 11, 248, 32; AE 45, 87-88.
10. WA 11, 249, 24; AE 45, 88-90.

11. WA 11, 250, 4; AE 45, 89.
12. WA 11, 251, 1ff.; AE 45, 90-93.
13. WA 11, 251, 28; AE 45, 91.
14. WA 11, 252, 12ff.; AE 45, 92.
15. WA 11, 253, 17; AE 45, 93-95.
16. WA 11, 254, 26; AE 45, 95.
17. WA 11, 255, 1; AE 45, 95.
18. WA 11, 255, 12; AE 45, 96.
19. WA 11, 258, 12; AE 45, 101.
20. WA 10, 258, 21; AE 45, 99.
21. WA 11, 261, 25-271, 26; AE 45, 104-118.
22. WA 11, 261, 27; AE 45, 104.
23. WA 11, 264, 23; AE 45, 107-108.
24. WA 11, 267, 1; AE 45, 111-112.
25. WA 11, 267, 30—268, 14; AE 45, 113.
26. WA 11, 268, 27; AE 45, 114.
27. WA 11, 271, 27—280, 19; AE 45, 118-129.
28. WA 11, 272, 1; AE 45, 118-121.
29. WA 11, 272, 15; AE 45, 119.
30. WA 11, 273, 7; AE 45, 120.
31. WA 11, 276, 21; AE 45, 124.
32. WA 11, 277, 1; AE 45, 124.
33. WA 11, 277, 5; AE 45, 125.
34. WA 11, 277, 18; AE 45, 125.
35. WA 11, 277, 28; AE 45, 125-126.
36. Helmut Lamparter, *Luthers Stellung zum Türkenkrieg* (Munich: 1940).
37. WA 30, II, 107ff.; AE 46, 155-205.
38. WA 30, II, 160ff.
39. WA 19, 616ff.; AE 46, 87-137.
40. WA 19, 625, 14; AE 46, 95.
41. WA 19, 625, 15; AE 46, 95.
42. WA 19, 625, 23; AE 46, 96.
43. WA 19, 626, 12; AE 46, 96.
44. 1532/1533; WA 40, III, 202ff.
45. WA 36, 385, 8.
46. WA 44, 218, 12; AE 6, 293.
47. WA 32, 467, 22.
48. WA 32, 453, 8.
49. WA 11, 255, 12.
50. WA 19, 657, 26; AE 46, 122.
51. WA 10, I, 2, 306, 17.
52. WA 34, II, 313, 6.
53. WA 43, 642, 34; AE 5, 310-311.
54. WA 40, III, 279, 18.
55. WA 7, 31, 24; AE 31, 360.
56. WA 30, I, 149, 32.

57. WABr 5, 317, 40.
58. 1523; WA 12, 11-30; AE 45, 159-168.
59. Acts 2:44.
60. WA 39, II, 59, 25.
61. WA 39, II, 68, 9.
62. WA 39, II, 40, 18.
63. WA 19, 561, 36.
64. WA 6, 466; AE 31, 214.
65. WA 6, 57, 7.
66. WABr 3, 483.
67. WA 15, 279ff.; AE 45, 231-310.
68. WA 15, 365, 19; AE 45, 270-271.
69. WA 6, 466, 31; AE 44, 213.
70. WA 6, 461; AE 44, 206-207.
71. At the beginning of 1524; WA 15, 9ff.; AE 45, 339-378.
72. WA 15, 32, 4ff.; AE 45, 352-353.
73. WA 15, 33, 9; AE 45, 353.
74. WA 15, 33, 25; AE 45, 354.
75. WA 15, 34, 32; AE 45, 355-356.
76. WA 15, 36, 26; AE 45, 358.
77. WA 15, 37, 14; 15, 37, 17; AE 45, 359.
78. WA 15, 38, 8; AE 45, 360.
79. WA 15, 41, 15; AE 45, 364.
80. WA 15, 43, 19ff.; AE 45, 367.
81. WA 15, 44, 13; AE 45, 368.
82. WA 15, 46, 6; AE 45, 369.
83. WA 15, 46, 13; AE 45, 369.
84. WA 15, 47, 1ff.; AE 45, 370.
85. 1530; WA 30, II, 586, 7; AE 46, 256-257.
86. WA 15, 48, 26; AE 45, 372.
87. WA 15, 49, 10; AE 45, 373-374.
88. WA 15, 52, 11; AE 45, 376.
89. WA 15, 52, 18; AE 45, 376-377.
90. WA 15, 53, 6; AE 45, 377-378.
91. CR 1, 666.
92. WA 15, 46, 18; AE 45, 370.
93. WA 15, 52, 11; AE 45, 376-377.
94. WA 15, 52; AE 45, 376.
95. WA 15, 52, 6; AE 45, 376.

Chapter 22. The Peasants' War (Thomas Müntzer)

1. Gottfried Maron, "Bauernkrieg," in *Theologische Realenzyklöpadie* (TRE), vol. 5, pp. 319-338 (see the bibliography!).
2. WA 18, 279ff.; AE 46, 3-43.
3. WA 18, 292, 25; AE 46, 17-18.
4. WA 18, 292, 31; AE 46, 18.
5. WA 18, 293, 27; AE 46, 19-20.

6. WA 18, 294; AE 46, 20-21.
7. WA 18, 295, 30; AE 46, 20-21.
8. WA 18, 296; AE 46, 22.
9. WA 18, 297-298; AE 46, 22.
10. WA 18, 298; AE 46, 23.
11. WA 18, 299, 34; AE 46, 23.
12. WA 18, 300, 26; AE 46, 23.
13. WA 18, 301, 21; AE 46, 24.
14. WA 18, 301, 32; AE 46, 24.
15. WA 18, 302-303; AE 46, 25.
16. WA 18, 304, 18; AE 46, 27.
17. WA 18, 306, 24; AE 46, 27.
18. WA 18, 307, 23; AE 46, 27.
19. Matt. 5:39; WA 18, 309, 20; AE 46, 28.
20. WA 18, 310, 28; AE 46, 29.
21. WA 18, 315, 25; AE 46, 32.
22. WA 18, 325, 20; AE 46, 37-38.
23. WA 18, 325, 36; AE 46, 38.
24. WA 18, 326, 32; AE 46, 39.
25. WA 18, 327, 20; AE 46, 39.
26. WA 18, 327, 28; AE 46, 39-40.
27. WA 18, 329, 28ff.; AE 46, 40-43.
28. WA 18, 332, 23; AE 46, 42.
29. WA 18, 335ff.
30. WABr 3, 478.
31. WATR 5, no. 6429.
32. WA 19, 278, 24.
33. WA 18, 391, 24; AE 46, 72.
34. WABr 3, 479; AE 49, 108-112.
35. Siegfried Bräuer, "Müntzerforschung von 1965 bis 1975," in *Luther-Jahrbuch 1977*, pp. 127ff.; *Luther-Jahrbuch 1978*, pp. 102ff.
36. WABr 3, 104.
37. WABr 3, 315, 12.
38. WA 15, 199.
39. WA 15, 211, 29.
40. WA 15, 218, 19.
41. WA 15, 230.
42. Gottfried Maron, "Thomas Müntzer als Theologe des Gerichts," in *Zeitschrift für Kirchengeschichte* 83 (1972), no. 2.
43. WA 18, 344.
44. WA 18, 357-361; AE 46, 46-55.
45. WA 18, 360, 33; AE 46, 52.
46. WA 18, 357; AE 46, 49.
47. WA 18, 357, 21-358, 32; AE 46, 49-51.
48. Acts 4:32.
49. WA 18, 359, 5; AE 46, 51.
50. WA 18, 359, 14; AE 46, 52.

51. WA 18, 359, 26; AE 46, 52.
52. WA 18, 360, 1; AE 46, 53.
53. WA 18, 360, 12; AE 46, 53-54.
54. WA 18, 361, 4; AE 46, 54.
55. WA 18, 361, 7; AE 46, 54.
56. Romans 13:1-2.
57. AE 18, 361, 24; AE 46, 54-55.
58. AE 18, 361, 33; AE 46, 55.
59. WABr 3, 504.
60. WA 18, 362ff.
61. WA 18, 373, 26.
62. WA 18, 374, 8.
63. WA 18, 374, 15.
64. WABr 3, 507.
65. WABr 3, 508, 14.
66. WABr 3, 509.
67. WABr 3, 515.
68. WABr 3, 516, 34.
69. WABr 3, 517; AE 49, 113.
70. WA 17, I, 265.
71. WA 18, 375; AE 46, 58-85.
72. WABr 3, 531.
73. WA 18, 384.
74. WA 18, 385, 27.
75. WA 18, 386, 9.
76. WA 18, 387.
77. Ibid.
78. WA 18, 388, 13.
79. WA 18, 389, 30.
80. WA 18, 389, 34.
81. WA 18, 390, 6.
82. WA 18, 391, 31.
83. WA 18, 392, 11.
84. WA 18, 393, 13.
85. WA 18, 393, 23.
86. WA 18, 393, 26.
87. WA 18, 394, 14.
88. WA 18, 396, 38.
89. WA 18, 397, 12.
90. WA 18, 400, 13.
91. WA 18, 401, 3.
92. Maron, "Thomas Müntzer," p. 327.

Chapter 23. The Dispute with Erasmus

1. Walther von Loewenich, "Gott und Mensch in humanistischer und reformatorischer Schau: Eine Einführung in Luthers Schrift De servo

arbitrio," in *Humanitas–Christianitas* (Gütersloh: 1948), pp. 65-101. See also the historical introduction by A. Freitag in WA 18, 551-599.

2. WA 28, 3 (1519); WABr 1, 361; AE 48, 117-119.
3. WABr 2, 217, 18; AE 48, 185.
4. The best edition is by Johann von Walter in *Quellenschriften zur Geschichte des Protestantismus*, no. 8 (Leipzig: 1935). Translation by Otto Schumacher (Göttingen: 1940).
5. CR 1, 644.
6. WABr 3, 368, 29.
7. WA 18, 551ff.; AE 33.
8. WA 18, 786, 26; AE 33, 294.
9. WA 7, 91ff.
10. von Walter edition, p. 19.
11. Ibid., p. 83.
12. Ibid., p. 80.
13. Ibid., p. 81.
14. WA 18, 551-787; AE 33.
15. WA 18, 603, 10; AE 33, 19-20.
16. WA 18, 605, 32; AE 33, 24.
17. WA 18, 606, 12; AE 33, 24-26.
18. WA 18, 606, 29; AE 33, 26.
19. WA 18, 610, 5 (German between the Latin); AE 33, 29.
20. WA 18, 611, 5; AE 33, 31.
21. WA 18, 614, 1; AE 33, 35.
22. WA 18, 614, 27; AE 33, 36.
23. WA 18, 615, 12; 18, 617, 19; AE 33, 37; 33, 40.
24. WA 18, 619, 16; AE 33, 42.
25. WA 18, 625, 25; AE 33, 51.
26. WA 18, 626, 22; AE 33, 52.
27. WA 18, 630, 19; AE 33, 58.
28. WA 18, 631; AE 33, 59.
29. WA 18, 632, 3; AE 33, 60.
30. WA 18, 632, 27; AE 33, 61.
31. WA 18, 633, 7; AE 33, 62.
32. WA 18, 633, 15; AE 33, 62.
33. WA 18, 635, 17; AE 33, 65-66.
34. WA 18, 639ff.; AE 33, 71-102.
35. WA 18, 649, 26; AE 33, 85.
36. WA 18, 652, 23; AE 33, 89.
37. WA 18, 650, 26; AE 33, 86.
38. WA 18, 653, 13; AE 33, 90-91.
39. WA 18, 661, 29; AE 33, 102.
40. von Walter edition, p. 34.
41. WA 18, 683, 1; AE 33, 137.
42. WA 18, 685, 1; WA 18, 685, 26; AE 33, 138-140.
43. WA 18, 685, 21; AE 33, 140.

44. Walther von Loewenich, "Pharaos Verstockung," in *Von Augustin zu Luther* (Witten: 1959), pp. 161-179.
45. Malachi 1:2-3; cited in Romans 9:13.
46. WA 18, 699ff.; AE 33, 195-202.
47. WA 18, 706, 14; AE 33, 171.
48. WA 18, 709, 21; AE 33, 176.
49. WA 18, 709, 28; AE 33, 176.
50. WA 18, 712, 19; AE 33, 180.
51. WA 18, 712, 24; AE 33, 180.
52. WA 18, 712, 32; AE 33, 180-181.
53. WA 18, 719, 4; AE 33, 190.
54. WA 18, 733, 22; AE 33, 247.
55. WA 18, 783, 17; AE 33, 288-289.
56. WA 18, 785, 26; AE 33, 292.
57. WA 18, 617, 19; AE 33, 40.
58. WA 18, 636, 28; AE 33, 68.
59. WA 18, 617, 23; AE 33, 41.
60. WA 18, 635, 17; AE 33, 65-66.
61. WA 18, 638, 5; AE 33, 70.
62. Hans Vorster, *Das Freiheitsverständnis bei Thomas von Aquin und Martin Luther* (Göttingen: 1965), pp. 415ff.
63. WA 18, 634, 19; AE 33, 64.
64. WA 18, 634, 33; AE 33, 64-65.
65. WA 18, 635, 16; AE 33, 65.
66. WA 18, 636, 14; AE 33, 67.
67. WA 18, 633, 7ff.; AE 33, 61-62.
68. WA 18, 685; AE 33, 138-140.
69. WA 18, 685; AE 33, 140.
70. WA 18, 685, 29; AE 33, 140.
71. WA 18, 622, 15; AE 33, 47.
72. WA 18, 43, 463; AE 5, 50.
73. WA 18, 711; AE 33, 178.
74. WA 18, 625, 27; AE 33, 51.
75. WA 18, 712, 32; AE 33, 180-181.
76. WA 18, 717, 24; AE 33, 185.
77. WA 18, 709, 21; AE 33, 176.
78. WA 18, 712, 24; AE 33, 180.
79. WA 18, 787, 11; AE 33, 295.
80. WABr 8, 99; AE 50, 172-173.

Chapter 24. Luther's Marriage and Home Life (the *Table Talk*)

1. Heinrich Boehmer, "Luthers Ehe," in *Luther-Jahrbuch* 1925, pp. 40-76; Ernst Kroker, *Katharina von Bora* (Leipzig: 1906; 7th ed., Berlin: 1974); Walther von Loewenich, "Luthers Heirat," in "Luther," *Zeitschrift der Luther-Gesellschaft* 1976, no. 2, pp. 47-60.

2. *Melanchthons Werke,* study edition, vol. 7, part 1, ed. Hans Volz (Gütersloh: 1971), pp. 238-244; includes bibliography; see also Bornkamm, *Martin Luther in der Mitte seines Lebens,* p. 361.
3. WABr 3, 533.
4. WA 6, 440ff.; AE 44, 175-179.
5. Letter of August 1, 1521 to Melanchthon; WABr 2, 371, 13; AE 48, 278.
6. WABr 3, 393; AE 49, 93.
7. WABr 3, 54.
8. Ibid.
9. WA 11, 387.
10. WABr 3, 357.
11. WATR 4, no. 4786.
12. Proverbs 31:11.
13. WATR 4, no. 4786, p. 504.
14. WABr 3, 541; AE 49, 117.
15. WATR 3, no. 3178a; AE 54, 191.
16. WATR 1, no. 49, pp. 17, 24; AE 54, 7-8.
17. WATR 2, no. 1563.
18. WATR 2, no. 2506.
19. WATR 2, 2772.
20. WATR 3, no. 3528, p. 379; AE 54, 222.
21. WATR 4, no. 4364; AE 54, 334.
22. WATR 2, no. 1406.
23. WATR 2, no. 2302.
24. WATR 2, no. 1631; AE 54, 159.
25. WABr 5, 377; June 19, 1530; AE 49, 323.
26. WATR 5, no. 5490-5502; AE 54, 428-434.
27. Ibid., p. 191; AE 54, 432.
28. WATR 5, no. 6102.
29. WATR 3, no. 3566; AE 54, 234-235.
30. WA 51, 206, 13; AE 13, 153.
31. Hans Preuss, *Martin Luther: Der Künstler* (Gütersloh: 1931), pp. 98ff.
32. WABr 7, 154, 18; January 1535.
33. See also WA 48, 365-719.
34. WABr 9, 579.
35. WABr 9, 583, 149.
36. WABr 8, 55.
37. WA 2, 166; AE 44, 3-14.
38. WA 10, II, 275; AE 45, 11-49.
39. WA 30 III, 74.
40. WA 10, III, 205; AE 46, 259-320.
41. WA 40, III, 269.
42. WA 30, III, 75, 15.
43. WA 30, I, 161, 28; Tappert, 393.
44. WA 30, III, 74, 3.

45. WA 15, 163-164; AE 45, 385-386.
46. WA 10, II, 287, 13; 10, II, 290, 5; 10, II, 291, 5; AE 45, 30-35.
47. WA 10, II, 296, 20; AE 45, 40.
48. WA 10, II, 301, 13; AE 45, 46.
49. WATR 2, no. 2764b.
50. WA 6, 252, 27; AE 44, 83.
51. WATR 5, no. 5524; AE 54, 444.
52. WA 32, 374, 8.
53. WA 10, II, 303-304; AE 45, 46-48.
54. WA 2, 170, 35; AE 44, 13-14.

Chapter 25. Opposition to Karlstadt and Zwingli

1. December 1524; WA 15, 391-397; AE 40, 61-71.
2. WA 15, 394, 16; AE 40, 68.
3. WA 18, 37-214; AE 40, 73-223.
4. WA 18, 67-84; AE 40, 84-101.
5. WA 18, 67, 9; AE 40, 84.
6. WA 18, 67, 18; AE 40, 84-85.
7. WA 18, 68, 17; AE 40, 85.
8. WA 18, 69, 1; AE 40, 86.
9. WA 18, 73, 11; AE 40, 90.
10. WA 18, 73, 25; AE 40, 91.
11. WA 18, 74, 3; AE 40, 91.
12. WA 18, 75, 1; AE 40, 91-92.
13. WA 18, 75, 3; AE 40, 92.
14. WA 18, 76, 4; AE 40, 92.
15. WA 18, 76, 13; AE 40, 92-93.
16. WA 18, 76, 23; AE 40, 93.
17. WA 18, 77, 3; AE 40, 93.
18. WA 18, 77, 10; AE 40, 93.
19. WA 18, 80, 29; AE 40, 97.
20. WA 18, 81, 4; AE 40, 97.
21. WA 18, 81, 9; AE 40, 97.
22. WA 18, 81, 18; AE 40, 98.
23. WA 18, 81, 14; AE 40, 98.
24. WA 16, 362ff.; AE 35, 161-174.
25. WA 18, 82, 21; AE 40, 99.
26. WA 18, 83, 6; AE 40, 99-100.
27. WA 18, 85-101; AE 40, 102-143.
28. WA 18, 88, 20; AE 40, 103-104.
29. WA 18, 101-125; AE 40, 118-143.
30. WA 18, 134-214; AE 40, 144-223.
31. Enders, *Luthers Briefwechsel*, vol. 3, p. 412.
32. WABr 3, 331.
33. WA 18, 136, 9; AE 40, 146.
34. WA 18, 136, 17; AE 40, 146.

35. WA 18, 163, 25; AE 40, 171.
36. WA 18, 182ff.; AE 40, 192ff.
37. WA 18, 187, 13; AE 40, 197.
38. WA 18, 187, 30; AE 40, 198.
39. WA 18, 203, 3; AE 40, 213.
40. WA 18, 204, 15; AE 40, 214.
41. WABr 3, 529.
42. WA 18, 438.
43. WA 18, 436.
44. WA 18, 446.
45. Walther Köhler, *Huldrych Zwingli* (Leipzig: 1943). The complete works of Zwingli are found in *Corpus Reformatorum,* vols. 88ff.
46. WA 23, 38-320; AE 37, 3-150.
47. WA 23, 201, 13; AE 37, 22.
48. WA 23, 180, 17; AE 37, 87.
49. WA 26, 241-509; AE 37, 151-372.
50. *Schriften des Vereins für Reformationsgeschichte,* no. 148 (Leipzig: 1929).
51. See also WA 30, III, 92ff.; AE 38, 3-89.
52. WA 30, III, 116, 6ff.; AE 38, 19.
53. WABr 5, 340, 49.
54. WABR 5, 340, 54.
55. John 6.
56. WA 30, III, 160; AE 38, 85-89.
57. WA 23, 132, 19; AE 37, 57.
58. WA 23, 136, 25; AE 37, 60.
59. WA 23, 156, 30; AE 37, 72.
60. WA 23, 170, 9; AE 37, 80-81.
61. WA 23, 228; AE 37, 115-116.
62. WA 23, 204, 11; AE 37, 100-101.
63. WA 26, 241-509; AE 37, 151-372.
64. WA 26, 499-509; AE 37, 360-372.
65. WA 26, 333, 6; AE 37, 219.
66. WA 26, 336, 15; AE 37, 223.
67. WA 26, 339, 34; AE 37, 228.
68. WA 26, 282, 19; AE 37, 180.
69. WA 23, 76, 19; AE 37, 52-53; WA 26, 342, 21-22; AE 37, 231.

Chapter 26. The Reorganization of the Church

1. WA 11, 401-416; AE 39, 301-314.
2. WA 26, 175ff.; AE 40, 263-320; WA 26, 197, 26; AE 40, 269-273.
3. WA 26, 200, 29; AE 40, 273.
4. Karl Holl, "Luther und das landesherrliche Kirchenregiment," *Gesammelte Aufsätze zur Kirchengeschichte* I, Luther, 4th and 5th ed. (Tübingen: 1927), pp. 326-389.
5. WA 26, 201ff.; AE 40, 273-320.

6. WA 30, I, 123-238.
7. WA 30, I, 239-425.
8. WA 30, I, 126, 14.
9. WA 30, I, 264ff.
10. WATR 5, no. 6288.
11. WA 30, III, 74-80.
12. WA 30, I, 132.
13. WA 30, I, 136, 6.
14. Walther von Loewenich, *Wahrheit und Bekenntnis im Glauben Luthers* (Wiesbaden: 1974).
15. WABr 8, 99; AE 50, 173.
16. WA 19, 44-113.
17. WA 18, 123, 19; AE 40, 141.
18. WA 19, 72-73.
19. WA 19, 73.
20. WA 19, 73, 24.
21. WA 19, 74, 4.
22. WA 19, 74, 16.
23. WA 19, 74, 22.
24. WA 19, 75, 5.
25. WA 19, 75, 18.
26. WA 19, 76, 1.
27. WA 19, 77, 14.
28. WA 19, 78, 25.
29. WA 19, 80, 25.
30. WA 19, 80, 26.
31. WA 12, 38ff.
32. WA 19, 531ff.
33. WA 12, 218, 15.
34. WA 12, 73ff.
35. WA 35, 411.
36. WA 35, 597.
37. WA 35, 602.
38. WA 35, 475, 2.

Chapter 27. The Coburg Luther

1. Hans von Schubert, "Luther auf der Coburg," *Luther-Jahrbuch 1930*, pp. 109-161; Walther von Loewenich, "Der 'Coburger Luther,'" in *Martin Luther Ausstellung: Kunstsammlung der Veste Coburg, Juli-Oktober 1967* (Coburg: 1967), pp. 6-12.
2. WABr 5, 283.
3. WABr 5, 285; AE 49, 288.
4. Psalm 118:17.
5. WABr 5, 347; AE 49, 314.
6. WABr 5, 289; 5, 290; AE 49, 292-295.
7. WABr 292.

8. WABr 5, 298, 13.
9. WABr 5, 316.
10. WABr 5, 317.
11. WABr 5, 291, 28; AE 49, 294.
12. WA 30, II, 220-236.
13. WA 30, II, 237-356; AE 34, 3-61.
14. WABr 5, 298.
15. WABr 289, 14.
16. To Melanchthon on May 19; WABr 5, 322, 11.
17. WABr 5, 347.
18. To Katie; WABr 5, 347; AE 49, 312.
19. WABr 5, 379.
20. WABr 5, 377; AE 49, 323-324.
21. WABr 5, 379.
22. WABr 5, 351; 5, 349; AE 49, 316-319.
23. WABr 5, 374.
24. WABr 5, 374, 37; see WATR 6, no. 7075.
25. WA 31, I, 258-383.
26. WA 31, I, 219-257; AE 14, 1-39.
27. WA 31, I, 65-182; AE 14, 45-106.
28. WA 31, I, 66; AE 14, 45-46.
29. WA 31, I, 67; AE 14, 46.
30. WA 30, II, 627-646; AE 35, 175-202.
31. WA 30, II, 508-588; AE 46, 207-258.
32. WA 30, II, 518, 10; AE 46, 214.
33. WA 30, II, 595ff.; AE 38, 91-137.
34. WABr 5, 319, 5; AE 49, 297-298.
35. To Luther on May 22; WABr 5, 336.
36. Bernhard Klaus, "Veit Dietrich," *Einzelarbeiten aus der Kirchen-geschichte Bayerns*, vol. 32 (Nuremberg: 1958), p. 76; also WABr 5, 396.
37. WABr 5, 395.
38. WABr 5, 405, 17; AE 49, 328.
39. WABr 5, 397, 15.
40. WABr 5, 398; 5, 405; AE 49, 326-333; WABr 5, 411.
41. WABr 5, 399, 6.
42. WABr 5, 399, 16.
43. WABr 5, 400, 23.
44. WABr 5, 406, 56; AE 49, 331.
45. WABr 5, 413, 60.
46. WABr 5, 405, 17; AE 49, 332; WA 5, 400, 38.
47. WABr 5, 442, 1; AE 49, 354; letter to Cordatus of July 6.
48. WA 30, II, 391ff.
49. WABr 5, 444.
50. WA 35, 586, 29.
51. To Jonas in Augsburg on July 21; WABr 5, 496.
52. WA 30, II, 360-390.

53. WA 30, II, 413-427.
54. Enders, *Briefe* 8, 72; WABr 5, 453.
55. WABr 5, 480, 21; AE 49, 376.
56. WABr 5, 530; AE 49, 395-399.
57. WABr 5, 572; AE 49, 406-412.
58. WABr 5, 576, 13; AE 49, 413.
59. WABr 5, 625.
60. To Melanchthon on September 20; WABr 5, 627.
61. WABr 5, 629.
62. Psalm 4:8; "In peace I will both lie down and sleep"; WABr 5, 635ff.
63. WABr 5, 640; 5, 641, 23.
64. WABr 5, 420.

Chapter 28. Old and New Conflicts

1. Wilhelm Maurer, "Theologie und Laienchristentum bei Landgraf Philipp von Hessen," in *Humanitas Christianitas,* for the 65th birthday of Walther von Loewenich (Witten: 1968), pp. 106-107.
2. WABr 8, 631.
3. WABr 8, 638.
4. WABr 9, 131 of June 10, 1540.
5. WA 51, 461-572; AE 41, 179-256.
6. WA 51, 570, 28; AE 41, 255.
7. WA 38, 171ff.; AE 38, 139-214.
8. *Augsburg Confession* 28.
9. WA 38, 195, 17; AE 38, 147.
10. WA 38, 197ff.; AE 38, 149ff.
11. WA 38, 212, 1; AE 38, 166.
12. WA 38, 228, 27; AE 38, 166; WA 38, 238, 7; AE 38, 197.
13. WA 38, 237, 22; AE 38, 196.
14. WA 38, 247, 28; AE 38, 208.
15. WA 38, 221, 19; AE 38, 177-178.
16. WA 38, 257ff.; AE 38, 215-233.
17. WA 38, 267, 5; AE 38, 226-227.
18. WA 54, 195ff.; AE 41, 257-376.
19. WA 54, 201; AE 41, 257-376.
20. WA 54, 346ff. and art supplement.
21. WA 54, 357.
22. WA 39, I, 9ff.
23. WATR 5, no. 6384.
24. CR 2, 987.
25. CR 3, 99.
26. The Weimar Edition includes it in vol. 50, pp. 160ff.; Tappert, pp. 287-318.
27. WA 50, 192ff.; Tappert, 289.

28. WA 50, 195, 30; Tappert, 290.
29. WA 50, 196, 32; Tappert, 291.
30. WA 50, 197; Tappert, 291.
31. WA 50, 198, 13; Tappert, 292.
32. WA 50, 199, 21; Tappert, 292.
33. WA 50, 200, 8; Tappert, 293.
34. WA 50, 204, 15; Tappert, 294.
35. WA 50, 204, 25; Tappert, 294.
36. WA 50, 204-211; Tappert, 294-297.
37. WA 50, 211, 13; Tappert, 297-298.
38. WA 50, 213-219; Tappert, 298-301.
39. WA 50, 216; Tappert, 299.
40. WA 50, 253, 11; Tappert, 316-317.
41. WA 50, 220, 22ff.; Tappert, 302.
42. WA 50, 245, 1; Tappert, 312.
43. WA 50, 246, 20; Tappert, 313.
44. WA 50, 247, 5; Tappert, 314.
45. WA 50, 250, 1; Tappert, 315.
46. WA 50, 252, 10; Tappert, 316.
47. Walther von Loewenich, *Duplex iustitia: Luthers Stellung zu einer Unionsformel des 16. Jahrhunderts* (Wiesbaden: 1972).
48. CR 4, 198-201.
49. WA 11, 268, 27; AE 45, 14-15.
50. WA 15, 219; AE 40, 57.
51. WA 26, 137ff.
52. WA 26, 145, 22.
53. WA 26, 154, 22.
54. Paul Althaus has written in detail concerning this in *Die Theologie Martin Luthers* (1962), pp. 303-317; his arguments are not always convincing.
55. WA 27, 32ff.
56. WA 27, 49, 20.
57. WA 30, II, 209.
58. WA 30, II, 212, 35; 30, II, 213, 20.
59. WA 31, I, 183ff.; AE 13, 39-72.
60. WA 31, 198, 12; AE 13, 51.
61. WA 31, 208; AE 13, 63-64.
62. WA 31, 208, 30; AE 13, 64-67.
63. WA 31, 208, 30; AE 13, 65-67.
64. WA 30, III, 510ff.; AE 40, 379-394.
65. CR 4, 737ff.; (there incorrectly dated 1541).
66. CR 4, 740 and WABr 6, 223.
67. CR 3, 195ff.; similarly WA 50, 6ff.
68. WA 50, 10.
69. WA 50, 11, 26.

70. WA 50, 13, 5.
71. WA 50, 14, 4.
72. WA 50, 15.
73. WATR 5, no. 5232b.
74. WA 38, 336ff.; 38, 341ff.; 1535.
75. WA 30, III, 528.
76. WA 39, II, 290, 15; WA 39, II, 337.
77. Ernst Bizer, *Studien zur Geschichte des Abendmahlstreites im 16. Jahrhundert* (Gütersloh: 1940; 2nd ed. 1962); the text of the formula can be found in Bizer on pp. 117-118 and in WABr 12, 200ff.
78. WA 54, 119ff.; AE 38, 279-319.
79. Enders, *Martin Luthers Briefe,* vol. 15, 275; cf. WABr 10, 420ff.; 10, 427ff.; WATR 5, 300, 15.
80. WA 54, 162, 31; AE 38, 313.
81. WA 54, 126ff.
82. WA 54, 158, 28; AE 38, 308.
83. WA 54, 159, 3; AE 38, 308.
84. WA 54, 144, 13; AE 38, 291.
85. WATR 5, no. 6050.
86. Köstlin and Kawerau II, 577 and 603-604.
87. WA 39, I, 342-358.
88. WA 50, 468-477; AE 47, 99-119.
89. WA 39, I; 39, I, 343, 27.
90. WA 39, I, 571-574.
91. WA 39, I, 572, 8.
92. WA 50, 472; AE 47, 111.
93. See Walther von Loewenich, *Duplex iustitia,* pp. 60ff.
94. Reinhold Lewin, *Luthers Stellung zu den Juden* (Berlin: 1911); Wilhelm Maurer, "Kirche und Synagoge," *Handbuch zur Geschichte von Christen und Juden,* eds. K. H. Rengstorf, Siegfried Kortzfleisch, vol. 1 (1968), Chap. 5: "Die Zeit der Reformation," pp. 363-452; Gerhard Müller, "Antisemitismus VI," in *Theologische Realenzyklopädie* (TRE), vol. 3 (1978), pp. 143ff.
95. WA 51, 195.
96. WA 51, 195, 27.
97. WA 4, 486, 38.
98. WA 56, 436, 13; AE 25, 428-429.
99. WA 11, 307; AE 45, 195-229.
100. WA 11, 315, 3; AE 45, 200.
101. WA 11, 325, 25ff.; AE 45, 213-221.
102. WA 11, 336, 14; AE 220-221.
103. WABr 3, 101.
104. WA 53, 461, 28.
105. WABr 8, 89.
106. WA 50, 309; AE 47, 55-98.

107. WA 50, 313; AE 47, 65-66.
108. WA 50, 315, 26; AE 47, 73.
109. Jeremiah 31:31ff.
110. WA 50, 323, 9; AE 47, 87-88.
111. WA 50, 323, 36ff.; AE 47, 88ff.
112. WA 50, 336, 15; AE 47, 96-97.
113. WA 53, 412ff.; AE 47, 121-306.
114. WA 53, 417, 22; AE 47, 137.
115. WA 53, 419, 19; AE 47, 140.
116. WA 53, 419, 22ff.; AE 47, 140ff.
117. WA 53, 421, 37; AE 47, 143.
118. WA 53, 426; AE 47, 148.
119. WA 53, 427, 20; AE 47, 149.
120. WA 53, 439, 32; AE 47, 164.
121. WA 53, 447, 27; AE 47, 174.
122. WA 53, 449-481; AE 47, 177-216.
123. WA 53, 481, 23; AE 47, 216.
124. WA 53, 492-511; AE 47, 229-253.
125. WA 53, 513; AE 47, 256.
126. WA 53, 514; AE 47, 257.
127. WA 53, 519, 19; AE 47, 262.
128. WA 53, 520, 8; AE 47, 264-265.
129. WA 53, 520, 33; AE 47, 265.
130. WA 53, 521, 8; AE 47, 265-266.
131. WA 53, 522, 34; AE 47, 268.
132. WA 53, 522, 38; AE 47, 268.
133. WA 53, 523, 1; AE 47, 268.
134. WA 53, 523, 24; AE 47, 269.
135. WA 53, 523, 30; AE 47, 269.
136. WA 53, 523, 32; AE 47, 269.
137. WA 53, 524, 6; AE 47, 270.
138. WA 53, 524, 18; AE 47, 270.
139. WA 53, 525, 31; AE 47, 272.
140. WA 53, 526, 11; AE 47, 272.
141. WA 53, 527, 14; AE 47, 273-274; WA 53, 541, 25; AE 47, 292.
142. WA 53, 528, 18; AE 47, 274-275.
143. WA 53, 530, 18; AE 47, 277.
144. WA 53, 541, 11; AE 47, 291-292.
145. WA 53, 573ff.
146. WA 53, 610ff.
147. WA 54, 16ff.
148. WA 54, 85ff.
149. WA 54, 100, 20.
150. WATR 6, pp. 589-591.

Chapter 29. Preacher and Pastor, Professor, and "Church Father"

1. Ulrich Nembach, *Predigt und Evangelium: Luther als Prediger, Pädagoge und Rhetor* (1972); Gerhard Ebeling, *Evangelische Evangelienauslegung: Eine Untersuchung zu Luthers Hermeneutik* (Munich: 1942; reprinted Darmstadt: 1962).
2. WA 4, 590ff.; 4, 595ff.; AE 51, 5-13.
3. WA 1, 60-141; AE 51, 5-31.
4. WA 9; WA 4; WA 1; WA 2; WA 7; AE 51, 35-392; AE 52.
5. WA 10, I, 2, 209-441.
6. WA 17, II.
7. WA 21.
8. WA 21 and 22.
9. WA 52.
10. Walther von Loewenich, *Luther als Ausleger der Synoptiker* (Munich: 1954).
11. WA 11, 415, 30; AE 39, 312.
12. WA 5, 537ff.
13. WATR 4, no. 4426.
14. WATR 4, no. 4719.
15. WABr 1, 563.
16. WATR 5, no. 5198.
17. WATR 4, no. 4759.
18. WATR 2, no. 1312.
19. WATR 3, no. 3421.
20. WATR 4, no. 5006.
21. WATR 4, no. 5047; AE 54, 384.
22. WATR 4, no. 5047; AE 54, 382-383.
23. WATR 5, no. 5489; AE 54, 428.
24. WATR 1, no. 868.
25. WATR 2, no. 2408b.
26. WATR 3, no. 3143a.
27. WATR 1, no. 965.
28. WATR 3, no. 2869.
29. WATR 4, no. 3493.
30. WATR 3, no. 3143a.
31. WATR 4, no. 4719.
32. WATR 2, no. 2606a.
33. WATR 2, no. 1590; AE 54, 158.
34. WATR 4, no. 4812.
35. WATR 6, no. 6793.
36. Hermann Steinlein, *Luther als Seelsorger* (Leipzig: 1918).
37. WATR 2, no. 2194b.
38. WATR 1, no. 360; AE 54, 54 (trans. from author, not AE).
39. WA 30, II, 580, 9; AE 46, 253.
40. WABr 9, 168; AE 50, 208-209.
41. WA 23, 323ff.; AE 43, 113-138.

42. WA 23, 375, 28; AE 43, 136-137.
43. WA 53, 202ff.; AE 43, 243-250.
44. WA 53, 207, 17; AE 43, 249.
45. WA 42, 650, 30; AE 3, 143-144.
46. *Opera latina* III/IV, pp. 81-82.
47. WATR 1, no. 518, p. 238, 13; AE 54, 93.
48. WABr 2, 372; AE 48, 282.
49. WABr 5, 374.
50. WABr 5, 518.
51. WABr 5, 547.
52. WABr 7, 104.
53. WA 38, 351; AE 43, 187-211.
54. WABr 1, 106.
55. WA 38, 372, 30; AE 43, 209.
56. Gunnar Wertelius, *Oratio continua: Das Verhältnis zwischen Glaube und Gebet in der Theologie Martin Luthers* (Lund: 1970); Hans Preuss, *Martin Luther: Der Christenmensch* (Gütersloh: 1942), pp. 189-249.
57. WABr 7, 347; AE 50, 123.
58. WA 40, I and II; AE 26 and 27.
59. Karin Bornkamm, *Luthers Auslegungen des Galaterbriefes von 1519 und 1531: Ein Vergleich* (Berlin: 1963).
60. WA 40, I, 285, 3; AE 26, 168.
61. WATR 1, no. 146; AE 54, 20.
62. Lectures on Genesis.
63. WA 42; 43; 44; AE 1; 2; 3; 4; 5; 6; 7; 8.
64. Heinrich Bornkamm, *Luther und das Alte Testament* (Tübingen: 1948); *Luther and the Old Testament*, trans. Eric W. and Ruth C. Gritsch (Philadelphia: Fortress, 1969).
65. See Walther von Loewenich, *Luther und der Neuprotestantismus*, pp. 371-375.
66. WADB 8, 13, 6; AE 35, 236.
67. WADB 8, 11, 19; AE 35, 236; WA 10, I, 1, 626, 2; AE 52, 205.
68. Romans 10:4.
69. WA 16, 378, 11; AE 35, 167.
70. WA 16, 380, 6; AE 35, 168.
71. WA 39, I, 47, 27.
72. WA 16, 377, 18; AE 35, 166-169.
73. WA 16, 391, 7; AE 35, 173.
74. WADB 10, I, 99; AE 35, 253-257.
75. WADB 103, 9; AE 35, 256.
76. WA 39, I and II.
77. WA 50, 488-653; AE 3-178.
78. WA 50, 284; AE 34, 231-267.
79. WA 50, 288, 1; AE 34, 235.
80. Ibid.
81. WA 50, 509-547; AE 41, 14-52.

82. WA 50, 509, 2; AE 41, 9.
83. WA 50, 510; AE 41, 9.
84. WA 50, 512; AE 41, 13.
85. WA 50, 515; AE 41, 14.
86. WA 50, 516; AE 41, 14.
87. WA 50, 517; AE 41, 17.
88. WA 50, 526; AE 41, 27-29.
89. WA 50, 546; AE 41, 51.
90. WA 50, 520; AE 41, 20.
91. WA 50, 522; AE 41, 23-24.
92. WA 50, 547ff.; AE 41, 53-142.
93. WA 50, 543, 6; AE 41, 48.
94. WA 50, 551; AE 41, 55.
95. WA 50, 552; AE 41, 58-59.
96. WA 50, 552, 25; AE 41, 59.
97. WA 50, 575; AE 41, 91.
98. WA 50, 576; AE 41, 91.
99. WA 50, 581; AE 41, 95.
100. WA 50, 583; AE 41, 95.
101. WA 50, 583-591; AE 41, 96-104.
102. WA 50, 591; AE 41, 104.
103. WA 50, 592ff.; AE 41, 106-121.
104. WA 50, 593; AE 41, 106.
105. WA 50, 592, 30; AE 41, 107.
106. WA 50, 604, 11; AE 41, 119.
107. WA 50, 604, 11; AE 41, 120.
108. WA 50, 605, 25; AE 41, 120.
109. WA 50, 607, 7; AE 41, 123.
110. WA 50, 607, 18; AE 41, 123; WA 50, 613, 19; AE 41, 130.
111. WA 50, 609, 14; AE 41, 124-125.
112. WA 50, 618; AE 41, 136.
113. WA 50, 614, 28; AE 41, 131-132.
114. WA 50, 615, 1; AE 41, 132.
115. WA 50, 617, 23; AE 41, 135.
116. WA 50, 616, 2; AE 41, 133.
117. WA 50, 618, 36; AE 41, 136-137.
118. WA 50, 622; AE 41, 137-138.
119. WA 50, 624-625; AE 41, 143-145.
120. WA 50, 624, 19; AE 41, 143.
121. WA 50, 625, 16; AE 41, 44.
122. WA 50, 626; AE 41, 146.
123. WA 50, 627, 34; AE 41, 147.
124. WA 50, 642, 1; AE 41, 164.
125. WA 50, 644, 16; AE 41, 167-168.
126. WA 50, 645; AE 41, 168.
127. WA 50, 645, 25; AE 41, 170-171.
128. WA 50, 647, 6; AE 41, 172-173.

129. WA 50, 652, 18; AE 41, 177.
130. WA 50, 197-198; Tappert, 291-292.
131. WA 50, 262; AE 34, 201-202.
132. WA 50, 263, 6; AE 34, 202.
133. WA 30, III, 552, 12.
134. WA 50, 572, 22; AE 41, 83; WA 50, 573, 3; AE 41, 84.
135. WA 8, 117, 33; AE 32, 243-244.
136. WA 46, 436, 7.
137. WA 39, I, 186, 10.
138. WA 30, II, 687, 31.
139. There is a detailed discussion of this in Walther von Loewenich, *Luther und der Neuprotestantismus,* pp. 398-415.
140. WA 50, 384, 15.
141. WA 50, 384, 29.
142. WA 50, 385, 1.
143. WA 53, 1-182.
144. WA 53, 171, 1.
145. WA 53, 261-396.
146. WABr 10, 160.
147. WA 53, 561ff.
148. WA 51, 634ff.
149. WA 51, 197ff.; AE 13, 143-224.
150. WA 51, 264, 10; AE 13, 224.
151. WA 38, 132.
152. WA 38, 133-134.
153. WABr 8, 99; AE 50, 171-174.
154. WA 50, 654; AE 34, 284-285.
155. WA 50, 659, 4; AE 34, 285.
156. WA 50, 660, 35; AE 34, 288.
157. WA 54, 176; AE 34, 329-338.
158. WA 54, 185, 12; AE 34, 336-338.
159. CR 6, 155ff.
160. WA 50, 615, 1.
161. December 8, 1534; WABr 7, 124.
162. WABr 8, 624.

Chapter 30. Illnesses and Death

1. Paul J. Reiter, *Martin Luthers Umwelt, Charakter und Psychose,* 2 vols. (Copenhagen: 1937, 1941).
2. Ibid., vol. 2, p. 57.
3. Ibid., p. 555.
4. Ibid., p. 98.
5. WABr 1, 209.
6. WABr 4, 341.
7. WABr 4, 160.

8. WA 23, 671.
9. WABr 4, 226.
10. WATR 3, no. 2922b.
11. WABr 4, 228, 5.
12. WABr 4, 319.
13. WABr 4, 227.
14. WABr 4, 294.
15. WABr 5, 53.
16. WABr 8, 48.
17. Genesis 32:31.
18. WABr 8, 50; AE 50, 167.
19. WABr 8, 55.
20. WABr 8, 59; AE 50, 170.
21. WABr 9, 365.
22. 1544; WABr 10, 554; AE 50, 245.
23. WABr 10, 548.
24. WABr 11, 263.
25. WATR 3, no. 3733; AE 54, 266.
26. WATR 5, no. 5378.
27. WATR 5, no. 5368.
28. WATR 4, no. 4784.
29. WABr 8, 51; AE 50, 167-168.
30. WATR 1, no. 266.
31. WA 17, II, 203, 29.
32. WABr 11, 148.
33. WA 50, 348.
34. WATR 4, no. 4032.
35. WABr 11, 264.
36. WATR 4, no. 4429.
37. WABr 10, 335; AE 50, 242.
38. WABr 9, 114.
39. WABr 9, 626.
40. WABr 11, 225; AE 50, 283-284.
41. WATR 6.
42. WABr 11, 269; AE 50, 286-287.
43. WABr 11, 275; AE 50, 290-292.
44. WABr 11, 284; AE 50, 300.
45. WABr 11, 286; AE 50, 301-304.
46. WABr 11, 286, 8; AE 50, 302.
47. WABr 11, 291; AE 50, 305-306.
48. WABr 301; AE 50, 314.
49. WABr 11, 300; AE 50, 311-313.
50. WA 51, 187; AE 51, 381-392.
51. WATR 5, no. 5468; WA 48, 241.
52. Jakob Stieder, "Authentische Berichte über Luthers letzte Lebens-
    stunden," in *Kleine Texte*, ed. H. Lietzmann, no. 99 (Bonn: 1912);
    Christof Schubart, *Die Berichte über Luthers Tod und Begräbnis*

(Weimar: 1917); Gustav Kawerau, *Der Briefwechsel des Justus Jonas,* vol. 2 (1884–1885), p. 177; the reports by Justus Jonas and Michael Cölius are found in WA 54, 478ff.

53. Psalm 31:5.
54. 2 Kings 2:12.
55. CR VII, 59.
56. CR 11, 726.
57. Hans Preuss, *Martin Luther: Der Prophet* (Gütersloh: 1933).
58. WA 7, 313, 15; AE 32, 9-10.
59. WA 30, III, 290, 28; AE 47, 29.
60. WATR 3, no. 3711.
61. WA 46, 717, 21.

Index